BOCCACCIO'S NAKED MUSE:
EROS, CULTURE, AND THE MYTHOPOEIC IMAGINATION

Boccaccio's Naked Muse

Eros, Culture, and the Mythopoeic Imagination

Tobias Foster Gittes

UNIVERSITY OF TORONTO PRESS
Toronto Buffalo London

© University of Toronto Press Incorporated 2008
Toronto Buffalo London
www.utppublishing.com
Printed in Canada

ISBN 978-0-8020-9204-5

Printed on acid-free paper

Library and Archives Canada Cataloguing in Publication

Gittes, Tobias Foster
Boccaccio's naked muse : eros, culture, and the mythopoeic
imagination / Tobias Foster Gittes.

(Toronto Italian studies)
Includes bibliographical references and index.
ISBN 978-0-8020-9204-5

1. Boccaccio, Giovanni, 1313–1373 – Criticism and interpretation.
2. Myth in literature.   I. Title.   II. Series.

PQ4293.L2G58 2007   858'.109   C2007-905683-0

This book has been published with the help of a grant from the Canadian
Federation for the Humanities and Social Sciences, through the Aid to
Scholarly Publications Programme, using funds provided by the Social
Sciences and Humanities Research Council of Canada.

University of Toronto Press acknowledges the financial assistance to its
publishing program of the Canada Council for the Arts and the Ontario
Arts Council.

University of Toronto Press acknowledges the financial support for its
publishing activities of the Government of Canada through the Book
Publishing Industry Development Program (BPIDP).

Contents

Acknowledgments

Like the Fiesole and Florence described in Giovanni Villani's *Cronica*, this book has been partly razed, refurbished, and rebuilt innumerable times. Each draft, like each successive stage of the growth of a city, has been shaped in part by the hands and minds of those generous-spirited readers who have wandered through its pages, filling its margins with exclamations, exhortations, and suggestions for revisions.

Teodolinda Barolini, the first of these readers, and the one to whom I owe the greatest debt, could justly say of my book what Augustus allegedly said of Rome: that she found a city of clay and left one of marble. Who else would have seen in this mud-and-wattle miscellany of material – the spawning of fish, garrulous trees, denuded muses, and bastardies – the basis for a solid book? Every sentence (and there was no lack of these!) was written with Teodolinda, my ideal reader, in mind. Without her generous guidance and numerous incisive interventions, this book might well have been written, but would not, I think, have been worth reading.

Like Martianus's Grammar with her file, Dialectic with her hook, and Rhetoric with her flashing arms, Joan Ferrante stormed through the early drafts of this book marking up the margins with repeated appeals to heed logic, aim for clarity, and prune, prune, prune! Were Wisdom truly wise, she'd find another place to preach and grouse, and let Joanie set her table in the seven-pillared house.

To Kathy Eden I will be forever grateful, and not just for her extensive notes and revisions to my original manuscript. Whereas I gave Kathy mere descriptions of the golden age diet, peaceful reign of Saturn, and the terrestrial paradises of the Tuscan countryside, she gave me the real thing, gold for bronze. Purveyor of Edens – for Montreal is nothing less – Kathy is living proof that *nomina sunt consequentia rerum*.

To Giuseppe Mazzotta, my first teacher of Dante, Marilyn Migiel, my first teacher of Italian, and Barbara Spackman, my first teacher of Boccaccio, I owe a debt that cannot possibly be repaid. It was in their company that I first found my vocation; their teaching is the invisible foundation upon which I have built this book: *per loro studioso fui, per loro italianista.*

While there's no single page of this book that isn't somehow shaped and quickened by Vittore Branca's guiding spirit, his influence is most immediately felt in the third section of chapter 3 – 'The Restoration of Knowledge: The Poet as Pedagogical Pimp' – which has been vastly improved by the numerous corrections and recommendations made by Professor Branca in the course of editing the article, originally published in *Studi sul Boccaccio,* upon which this section is based. Though I would gladly honour him with a handsome marble sepulcher, like Boccaccio's Guido he would simply vault over it, for death has no sway over such active intellects.

I must also thank Pier Massimo Forni, scholar of civility and most civil of scholars, for a fertile exchange of Boccaccio-related articles, conference papers, and emails. Christian Moevs, epitome of *humanitas* and *caritas,* has earned my thanks many times over not only for reading this book in chrysalid form but for his many unsolicited acts of kindness and support. To Michael Papio, I am grateful for so graciously allowing me to use passages from his forthcoming translation and edition of Boccaccio's *Esposizioni sopra la Comedia.* To friends and fellow students from my Columbia years, I'm thankful for companionship, support, and many an engaging *chiacchierata* at conferences and in the corridors, offices, and classrooms of Hamilton Hall: Karina Attar, Martin Eisner, Scott Failla, Elsa Filosa, Manuele Gragnolati, Andrea Malaguti, and Patrizia Palumbo. Particular thanks must go to Kristina Olson, longtime interlocutor on Boccaccio-related matters, a dear friend and a friend in deed. To Madeline Aria, classicist, cabinetmaker, and cat-lover, I shall be forever indebted for her early and unstinting help in wrestling with medieval Latin passages; even the contumacious Nimrod – that 'most stupid of men' – no match for her dry wit and keen linguistic powers, was soon stripped of Latin rhetoric and forced to speak an unfamiliar tongue.

Could I build cities, in lieu of books, I'd gladly raise a seven-walled citadel, a *nobile castello* governed by the late Harvey Shulman, *maestro di color che sanno* (and, no less impressively, *of those who get things done*), for my friends, colleagues, and students at Concordia University's Liberal Arts College. Certainly, they deserve no less. This book has greatly benefited from the meticulous proofreading carried out by three of these exceptional students: Zoe Dickinson, James Phelan, and Jean-Olivier Richard. It was the *laudevoli consolazioni* of my wonderful colleagues at the Liberal Arts College, in particular Ariela Freedman and Katharine Streip, that made it possible for me to continue work on my book over the course of several extremely difficult years.

Books, like cities, have their resident genies, their *penates* and their *lares*. Mine are my grandmother, Cicely Foster, and her brother, Kenelm Foster. Cicely, in her way as skilled a storyteller as Boccaccio, kindled my love of narrative, and Kenelm, though no doubt blissfully unaware of the fact, had an important role in prompting my own, enormously rewarding excursion into Italian studies. It was beneath a certain Cambridge quince tree that I, entranced by Kenelm's austere grace and eloquence, first turned from childish reveries to thoughts of academic life.

Books have their patrons as well, and it has long been clear to me that without the generous support of my parents, Lois Severini and Enrique Foster Gittes, I would have fared no better than Rabelais's Xerxes, reduced to hawking mustard in limbo – a profession easily learned but one with little else to recommend it.

Liane Miller, my friend, companion, and witness to my writing progress *Ab urbe condita* knows better than anyone else the toll it took in sleepless nights, but knows as well the frequent interludes of pleasure and pure joy. *Croce e delizia, delizia al cor.*

Had it not been for the praise of the two anonymous evaluators of the manuscript originally submitted to University of Toronto Press, this book would never have been considered for publication; had it not been for their helpful criticism, it would, though published, have been a far less polished book.

I would like to extend the warmest of thanks to my editor Ron Schoeffel and copy editor Ruth Pincoe of the University of Toronto Press. Without Ron Schoeffel's gracious good-will, generosity, and patient encouragement, this project would have remained a castle in Spain, rather than a beautifully produced book. Without Ruth Pincoe's sensitive and thorough work on the final manuscript, this text would not have answered either of Horace's directives; neither delightful nor useful, it would soon have been sent to join the volumes, 'llenos de viento y de borra,' kicked about by Altisidora's devils in the vestibule of hell. Even a casual glance at the index reveals the scholastic precision – and supernatural patience – of my indexer, Sarah Patterson; her remarkable diligence and reliable good humour will not soon be forgotten. Many thanks must also go to

Barbara Tessman at the University of Toronto Press, who somehow managed to reduce the rough, unordered mass of my manuscript into a form readable to the typesetter.

I dedicate this book with all my love to my children, Venetia and Sebastian.

A Note on the Translations and Editions

The image of the naked Muse that gives this book its title is derived from the *Teseida*, where Boccaccio uses the idea of the 'Muse nude' as a trope for the translation of erudite Latin texts into the Italian vernacular – a variety of knowledge once reserved for a privileged readership has been 'unveiled' for the benefit of the common reader. As Boccaccio's mission to make such forms of privileged knowledge accessible to a wider audience through vernacular translations, commentaries, and public lectures is widely attested in his works, it would have been the height of perversity to thwart this generous ambition by leaving the numerous foreign language passages in this book untranslated. Encouraged by the conviction that even a rough translation is better than none at all, I have done my best to provide translations of all foreign language passages, often benefiting, for the numerous Latin excerpts, from the guidance of classicist friends and the excellent Italian translations of Boccaccio's Latin texts provided in Vittore Branca's Mondadori edition of the complete works. All unattributed translations are my own. Unless a specific edition is referenced, all quotations from Boccaccio's works are taken from *Tutte le opere di Giovanni Boccaccio*, the ten-volume critical edition edited by Vittore Branca.

BOCCACCIO'S NAKED MUSE:
EROS, CULTURE, AND THE MYTHOPOEIC IMAGINATION

Introduction

In a remarkable passage of his *De casibus* animated by the same proud and tameless spirit fated to resurge four centuries later among the Romantic poets, Boccaccio argues that 'by God's gift we contain a soul with a fiery power, celestial origin, and insatiable desire for glory' which, 'when it is noble and not weakened by bodily sloth, can neither be enclosed nor kept in the small prison of the breast; it bounds forth and with its greatness embraces the whole earth and easily transcends the stars, and driven by the flame, burns with sublime desires' (*De casibus* III 13, 2–3).

This rousing optimism concerning our innate dignity and our seemingly unbounded intellectual and artistic potential is easily understood in the case of Boccaccio, who not only witnessed but made vital contributions to the unprecedented revival of poetry and the figurative arts in fourteenth-century Tuscany. His exuberant praise of Dante, Petrarch, and Giotto attests to his conviction that these Tuscan moderns not only rival but surpass their classical forebears. Heir to two mythological traditions – one, biblical the other classical – that tend to locate the state of mortal blessedness (Eden and the Golden Age) in an irrecoverable past and link human striving with transgression (the First Parents, Nimrod, Prometheus, Phaethon, and the like), Boccaccio is forced to recognize that, despite their literary merits, these ancient tales have lost much of their relevance and fall short of their traditional exemplary and didactic functions. Consequently, he sets about scripting a new mythology, a scattered catalogue of innovative myths (understood in the wider sense of a popular or traditional explanation for natural, supernatural, or social phenomena) that more accurately reflect his cultural experience and better address the needs of a new age.

The main concern of this study is to identify, gather, and systematize a selection of these myths strewn throughout Boccaccio's Latin and vernacular works: not just the reworked versions of familiar classical and biblical myths, but the more elusive myths that must be teased out of the strange etiological tales, obscure allegorical excurses, and embedded autobiographies that abound in his works. The mythological 'handbook' that results from this collation of myths reveals a dynamic, revolutionary facet of Boccaccio – the Boccaccio who casts himself as a new Prometheus, the apostle of a new, humanistic, faith that honours God by exalting his creation. Boccaccio's gospel of human dignity is written in myths that boldly contradict the opinion of the Church Fathers by insisting on the innate innocence of humanity; that promote cosmopolitanism and tolerance by granting a new primacy to racial and cultural mixing in the birth of nations; that celebrate the intellectual, artistic, and cultural accomplishment of all people regardless of race or culture; and that locate human beatitude not in a prehistoric past or metaphysical future, but squarely in the present.

Montaigne shrewdly observes that readers habitually conflate authors with their work, modelling their conceptions of an author's character on the evidence of his or her literary production or public reputation. Had he, Montaigne tells us, ever met Erasmus in the flesh, he would have expected his every utterance to take the form of a precept or maxim (*Essais* III, 2, 'Du repentir'). To be conflated to some degree with one's work is, it seems, the inevitable fate of all creative artists. When the fervid talk of kisses mounded upon kisses in Catullus's polished verse moves his friends Furius and Aurelius to suggest that he is less than virile, Catullus famously threatens to prove his virility on their unwilling bodies. Judged a 'doctor of adulteries' for his sometimes scurrilous verse, Ovid protests that a book is not the mirror of an author's mind ('nec liber indicium est animi,' *Tristia* II, 357); it is his muse who is wanton, not he. That the historical Dante should be subsumed by his poetic alter ego, the wanderer through earth's dark cavities and bright celestial reaches, is less surprising; the footsteps Dante left in Hell have proved far more resistant than those he left on the earth. Upon overhearing a woman whisper 'Do you see that man who goes to hell, and returns when he pleases bringing news to us up here of those who are down below?' and her credulous companion, impressed by his crisped-up beard and dark complexion, respond 'Indeed, what you say must be true' ['In verità tu déi dir vero], even Dante, Boccaccio tells us, could not suppress a slight smile (*Vita di*

Dante, chap. XX). That even the most sophisticated readers and critics of the *Divine Comedy* often find themselves, like the credulous woman of Boccaccio's anecdote, responding to Dante's work with a reverential 'In verità tu déi dir vero,' simply confirms the supreme realism of his fiction, one so compelling that reality is, by contrast, a pale shadow. Dante still has good reason to smile.

Boccaccio, however, would find little occasion to smile were he to become acquainted with his current reputation, for it is not the mythographer, nor the philosopher-humanist, nor even the subtle, sympathetic, and delightfully sardonic observer of human sexual desire who has found a foothold in the collective imagination, but a good-natured gadabout, more concerned to plumb the secrets of the wives, widows, and maids who populate his *novelle* than those of Nature or God. The long-standing association of Boccaccio's name with a playful eroticism has so powerfully influenced readers' assumptions about his character that over the centuries a number of excellent critics have confidently asserted that the *Decameron* has much colour but no philosophical depth.

Since the peaking of Boccaccio's reputation as a humanist scholar in the early fifteenth century, his works of erudition have often fared no better. Too hastily judged dreary by admirers of the more vivacious *Decameron* and too easily discounted as a dry, suspiciously medieval sort of encyclopedism by advocates of Petrarch's cleaner brand of classicism, the delightful, vivid prologues of the *Genealogie*, the powerfully dramatic framing device of *De casibus* (an Odysseus-like interview of clamouring shades) and its numerous colourful invectives, diatribes, and novelistic digressions, and the fascinating historical and ethnographic notices in *De montibus* (his geographical dictionary), have received only the scantest critical attention. For many, it is easier to accept that the sublime imagination that shaped the *Iliad* turned to an epic of frogs battling mice, or that the same hand that consigned the lovelorn Dido to the pyre was moved to pen priapic verse or the epic of a flea (the *Culex*), than to credit the author of the *Decameron* with intellectual or philosophical depth in any of his works. It is one thing for authors who inhabit Parnassus to make occasional descents into the hustle-bustle of secular life, quite another for an author whose reputation is forged in the bedroom and marketplace to convince readers that he has had any success – or, indeed, any interest – in spending time with the Muses in Parnassus ('con le Muse in Parnaso' [*Dec.* IV, intro., 7]). Boccaccio's own declaration that he has not strayed as far from Parnassus or the Muses as many people imagine (*Dec.* IV, intro., 36) has been largely ignored.

As recently as 1944 it was possible for as sensitive a critic as Charles S. Singleton to categorically reject the didactic value, use of concealed meanings ('sovrasensi'), or, for that matter, presence of 'ideas' in the *Decameron* by invoking Boccaccio's own words: his affirmations in the Proem, Introduction to Day IV, and the Conclusion of the *Decameron* that his work is directed to 'idle' women, designed to provide consolation, and not suitable reading for those, like students, whose circumstances demand that they make better use of their time. That these statements are probably about as sincere as Rabelais's affirmation that his *Gargantua* and his *Pantagruel* are directed to an audience of dipsomaniacs or Cervantes's suggestion that *Don Quixote* was written for idle readers was not, apparently, taken into consideration.[1] One can only hope that this readiness to take authors at their word falls somewhere short of accepting Rabelais's recommended cure for the toothache (a poultice composed of the *Gargantuan Chronicles* lightly dusted with powdered manure!).

Had critics deliberately set out to compromise Boccaccio's reputation through a carefully orchestrated attack, they could hardly have done more harm to the reception of his works than was wrought by his own habit of self-deprecation and his repeated protestations of poetic mediocrity. It was not cavilling critics but Boccaccio who furnished Singleton – and a small army of like-minded critics – with his most damning evidence. It is far easier to discount the relatively radical views of those such as Coleridge, for whom the *Decameron* is a work of 'gross and disgusting licentiousness [and] daring profaneness,' than to dismantle the more nuanced case that Boccaccio has built against himself.[2] The former can be chalked up to a sort of critical prudishness that ebbs and flows from decade to decade, century to century; the latter, fixed for all time in Boccaccio's own words, is more insidious by far.

In the epilogue of the *Filocolo*, one of his earliest works, Boccaccio addresses his 'little book,' counselling it to cleave to its own middle path, leaving the sublimities of epic, martial, and love poetry to greater intellects. Nor, he adds, should his book aspire to the company of Dante's verses, for these it must follow with great reverence like a humble servant ('tu sì come piccolo servidore molto dei reverente seguire'). In the prologue of his last work, an incomplete commentary on the *Divine Comedy* (the *Esposizioni sopra la Comedia*), Boccaccio notes that if even Plato, a man of divine genius, thought it expedient to invoke the gods' help in the first book of his *Timaeus*, how, then, can he, only too aware that his wit is slow, his memory weak, and his intellect small, presume to reveal the sublimity of the hidden sense of Dante's famously complex text?

Far from being isolated instances, these two dramatic professions of intellectual inadequacy and poetic mediocrity bracket a life-long habit of presenting himself as an intellectual subaltern, a mere follower in the path carved out by greater minds.[3] In an often cited passage of *Genealogie* XV, Boccaccio asserts that his father's repeated attempts to bend his mind – one naturally disposed to poetic composition – towards more lucrative professions for which he had no natural inclination had the disastrous result that he 'turned out neither a business man, nor a canon-lawyer, and missed being a good poet besides' (XV 10, 8; *Boccaccio on Poetry*, trans. Osgood [hereafter cited as Osgood], 132). The temptation to dismiss Boccaccio's self-deprecation as rhetorical blather, a conventional *recusatio*, is natural but best resisted. Like Ovid's protestations that he, not equal to the task of writing epic, is perforce a poet of love, or Montaigne's similar assertion that his chosen genre, the essay, is shaped to his limited abilities, Boccaccio's claims are at once proud and humble, disingenuous and sincere.

Upon hearing of Boccaccio's intention to burn his youthful vernacular works, Petrarch, a close friend and particularly acute judge of Boccaccio's character, writes: 'I fear that this fine humility of yours is pride' (*Letters of Old Age* V, 2). Boccaccio's actions, Petrarch observes, resemble those of the man at a banquet who, denied the seat of highest distinction, seeks out, with the pretext of modesty, the least honorable seat. Insofar, Petrarch continues, as Boccaccio does not claim the first place among poets, he exhibits humility; insofar as he would sooner remove himself from the ranking altogether than be judged second or third, he exhibits pride.

Too often, critics have taken Boccaccio at his word, casting him as a dilettantish scholar (against the Petrarchan model of rigorous scholarship), a dabbler in rhyme (not a 'true' poet like Dante or Petrarch), and a scribbler of frivolous tales. The unfortunate legacy of Boccaccio's habit of self-deprecation has been to depreciate his work, often making it impossible for readers to recognize the merit of his contribution to humanistic studies in his scholarly Latin works and the great originality of his vernacular fiction. This is indeed a pity, for it can be said without exaggeration that no genre passed through Boccaccio's fingers without undergoing some fundamental and enriching transformation. Boccaccio's prose works are marked by a vigorous experimentalism, a generic hybridity and liquidity; neither formless nor yet fully crystallized, they tend to confound critics' attempts at classification. Confronted by such structural and ideological ambiguities, a certain kind of critic will respond by alleging that Boccaccio's works have neither structure nor ideas. Others, more comfortable in this fertile slurry, this disordered order, have come to recognize that these works are the very stuff from which, in later years, such successful genres as the short story, the psychological romance, the roman à clef, the chivalric romance, the 'triumph' (among others, Petrarch's *Trionfi*), and the 'labyrinth of love' will be fashioned.

In the wake of numerous excellent studies of the concealed meanings and ideological agendas in the *Decameron* produced over the last half century, it has become increasingly difficult, not to say impossible, to hold, with Singleton, that the *Decameron* is devoid of 'sovrasensi' and original ideas. Indeed, it has become ever more apparent that all of Boccaccio's works are not merely seeded with new ideas, but bound by subtle reticulations of interconnected ideas: that is, with patterns of meaning – *ideologies*. Readers with the patience to work their way from node to node, tracing out these networks of linked ideas, are rewarded by the discovery of new myths and the glimmerings of a new, revolutionary mythology.

Sometimes the innovative quality and greater philosophical implications of Boccaccio's revised myths are obscured by the narrative drama and sheer delight of the examples furnished to illustrate these new perspectives. Upon reading, in a passage of Boccaccio's commentary on Dante's *Inferno* (*Esposizioni* IV lit., 196), the notice that Caesar's laurel crown was actually an expedient to hide his bald pate (for, Boccaccio informs us, before somebody came up with this inspired solution, Caesar had been constrained to use a 'comb-over'), most readers are more likely to chuckle and turn the page than to meditate on the important philosophical argument – a defence of ornament – in support of which this humorous example has been submitted. Similarly, Boccaccio's theory that wall-eyed individuals were, in their infancy, victims of poorly placed night lights (presumably the prolonged strain of focusing on an inconveniently located light had the effect of dislocating the infant's eyeball) is more likely to remind us of the brilliant deduction of Rabelais's Friar John that nose size is directly proportionate to the softness of a wet nurse's breasts – the softer and more accommodating the breast, the larger the nose – than to impress us with Boccaccio's attempt, unusual for his age, to identify an empiric basis for physical phenomena previously ascribed to supernatural causes.[4] Distracted by the naiveté and charmed by the anecdotal qualities of such observations, many readers fail to recognize in them the germ of the sort of empiricism that would blossom in the seventeenth century.

More often, though, these new ideas have been overlooked because their novelty is masked by an external, formal resemblance to traditional patterns or perspectives. As C.S. Lewis has shrewdly observed, 'What is new usually wins its way by disguising itself as the old.'[5] Like a honeyed sop, this external resemblance to traditional forms has the effect of placating more conservative readers, thus providing a secure passage for even the most revolutionary ideas.

Though Petrarch, like Singleton, is inclined to view the *Decameron novelle* as light reading, a frivolous product of Boccaccio's youth, he does at least recognize a moral utility in both the Introduction (the account of the plague) and *novella* X, 10, the story of Griselda. Indeed the latter, as is well known, so moved him that he honoured Boccaccio by composing a Latin translation of the tale, 'De obedentia ac fide uxoria mythologia' [A Fable of Wifely Obedience and Faith] (preserved in Petrarch's *Letters of Old Age* [*Rerum senilium* XVII, 3]).

Like the Job story to which it has been so often compared, the Griselda story accommodates multiple interpretations. Nestled in the protective frame of an ancient Hebrew parable exemplifying the rewards of piety and patience (the honeyed sop), lies a revolutionary, polemical text calculated, among other things, to force a reevaluation of the traditional doctrine of exact individual retribution. Likewise, the Griselda tale may be read as a moralizing tale designed to sustain normative values or – even more convincingly – as a subversive text designed to force a reevaluation of these same values. Those readers (the vast majority) who feel that the virtuous and long-suffering peasant Griselda has a better claim to her noble title than the cruel Gualtieri, have wittingly or unwittingly endorsed the view that social hierarchies are purely conventional, have no intrinsic merit, and are shaped by historical accident (what Boccaccio regularly refers to as the 'sin of Fortune' ['peccato della Fortuna']), not divine providence. By acknowledging this element of historical contingency, Boccaccio shifts responsibility for moral behaviour from God to his creation. With the divine gift of free will comes the duty to 'show the heavens more just' by using our capacity for compassion and liberality to compensate and correct the 'sins of Fortune.' His *novelle*, Boccaccio announces in the *Decameron* Proem, were written with the specific aim of 'amending,' at least in part, the 'sin of Fortune' ('acciò che in parte per me s'amendi il peccato della fortuna' [*Dec.* Proem, 13]). Indeed, all of Boccaccio's work, in particular his mythopoeic activity, is guided by this same generous concern.

Just as the formal congruity of the Griselda tale with conventional saints' lives and sermons has the effect of distracting the reader from its potentially subversive content, the close correspondence between Boccaccio's youthful opuscule, the so-called *Allegoria mitologica,* and the first two books of Ovid's *Metamorphoses* had, until quite recently, encouraged critics to view the work as purely derivative, devoid of any original ideas. Even its most recent editor makes a point of emphasizing the degree to which Boccaccio's *Allegoria* cleaves to its Ovidian model, characterizing the first part of Boccaccio's opuscule (the part which corresponds to the cosmogony and primitive history of *Metamorphoses* I) as a paraphrase, and the second part (which retells the tale of Phaethon of *Metamorphoses* II) as 'a transcription in which the metric structure is only slightly breached by occasional shifts in the order of words.'[6]

A series of more recent critical studies has done much to crush this damning preconception by drawing attention to some of the important ways Boccaccio's version deviates from its Ovidian source. For all the apparent similarity of these two Phaethons, it is clear that their resemblance is largely formal and superficial. Whereas Ovid's Phaethon is engaged in a self-serving quest to establish his paternity (and to prove his taunting schoolmate Epaphus wrong), Boccaccio's Phaethon is involved, it turns out, in a purely altruistic mission to bring intellectual and spiritual illumination to an ignorant crowd. This motif – that of pedagogue as martyred culture-hero – crops up with such great regularity in Boccaccio's works that it may fairly be described as one of the defining features of Boccaccio's new mythology.

The 'historical' appendix (octaves 436ff) of Boccaccio's delightful pastoral poem, the *Ninfale fiesolano,* has suffered a similar fate at the hand of critics, who have almost universally dismissed it as little more than an awkward pastiche of accounts drawn from the chronicles of Giovanni Villani and the other Tuscan historians. The unfairness of this judgment is immediately evident to even the most casual reader of the *Ninfale* – provided, that is, that he or she does not come to the text predisposed to find evidence of imitation and blinkered to signs of innovation. If the general details of the tales of colonization outlined by the Tuscan chroniclers and Boccaccio coincide, the underlying premise could not be more different. Whereas the chroniclers present the colonized land as an uninhabited territory, a 'world without people' to use Dante's evocative phrase, one of the principal – if not the principal – concerns of Boccaccio's etiology of Fiesole and Florence in the *Ninfale* is to show us that these cities were populated long before Atalante, the great colonizer of the chronicle tradition, set foot on Tuscan turf. Viewed on its own, this peculiar emphasis on indigenous peoples – and on their significant cultural and genetic contribution to the evolution of Fiesole and Florence –

is little more than an eccentric idea. Considered, however, in the context of Boccaccio's other works, it soon becomes apparent that this inclination to not only acknowledge the cultural and genetic contribution of indigenous populations, but to implicitly attribute civic growth and excellence to cultural and racial mixing, is a recurrent and characteristically Boccaccian pattern. Linked together, these isolated ideas – scattered testimonies to the fruitful consequences of genetic and cultural syncretism – form a revolutionary ideology, another lynchpin of Boccaccio's new mythology.

What is true of such youthful works as the *Allegoria mitologica* and *Ninfale fiesolano* is, as noted above, no less true of the great work of Boccaccio's middle age, the *Decameron*. Too ready to take him at his word, many readers have simply assumed that Boccaccio is more imitator than innovator, that his achievement is principally that of having turned the stick figures that populate the fabliaux, exempla and anecdotes of the medieval florilegia into living beings, fleshed them out and quickened them (with a breath of a realism as unprecedented in literature as Giotto's plastic realism had been in the sphere of the visual arts). This may be true, but it overlooks the fact that the transformation is not simply one of degree, but one of quality. Like real people, these fictional surrogates, when quickened by the hand of the truly creative artist, have a way of asserting their freedom, often striking out from whatever path traditional tales or conventional plots have prescribed them.

When the classical figure of Numenius, a philosopher who in Macrobius's *Commentary on the Dream of Scipio* epitomizes the dangers of seeking forbidden knowledge, is resurrected by the anonymous author of the *Novellino*, he is refurbished, given contemporary dress, and placed in a contemporary context; the moral lesson, however, remains the same. By contrast, Boccaccio's Numenius, an exemplary culture-hero in lieu of a counter-exemplum, bears about as great a resemblance to Macrobius's Numenius as Milton's Satan bears to the Satan of Scripture or Shelley's Prometheus to his Aeschylean forbear. Boccaccio does not simply breathe life into the characters whom he resurrects from the exempla, fabliaux, histories, romances, and popular tales: with this new life comes a new purpose.

In the rhetorically brilliant self-defence that introduces the fourth day of the *Decameron*, Boccaccio alleges that the matter narrated in the *Decameron* is not of his own invention but received second-hand from other sources. Whether he is referring to the actions of the *brigata* members that, as he has told us in the Introduction, were related to him after the fact by a 'trustworthy person' ['persona degna di fede'] (Intro., 49), to their words (in particular the narrated tales), or to both, is left unresolved. Consequently it is not clear whether his suggestion that readers offended by the subject or substance of his version of events seek out the original sources upon which these are based (IV, intro., 39) refers to the activities of the narrators or to their narrations. In either case the task is impossible, for both acts and words would have long since passed into the shadowy vaults of memory. Unless one is willing to accept Boccaccio's conceit of the 'historical' *brigata* at face value, it is necessary to shift the terms of this challenge. Insofar as both the acts and the words have been shaped by Boccaccio's fertile imagination, the question is no longer whether Boccaccio faithfully recounts the tales narrated by his fictional *brigata* (a claim made in the Epilogue to defer responsibility for their content), but whether his *novelle* are faithful to their literary sources.

Those who accept the terms of this new challenge soon discover that some of the tales have no traceable source (including such philosophically probing stories as those concerning Cepparello's 'confession' [I, 1], Cimone's 'domestication' [V, 1], Madonna Filippa's successful bid to legalize adultery [VI, 7], Tingoccio's otherworld vision [VII, 10], and the full Calandrino 'cycle' [VIII, 3; 6: IX, 3; 5]); other tales have only a superficial resemblance to one or more possible sources (the majority of the hundred tales fall into this category); and even those *novelle* whose derivation from a particular source can hardly be doubted tend to resemble these sources as a mule resembles a donkey, or a hinny a horse. The 'crossing' of source material with new concerns and philosophical convictions invariably results in the creation of something strange and new: a literary hybrid. No tale passes through the filter of Boccaccio's mythopoeic imagination unchanged; each emerges like Aeson from Medea's pot, with lineaments similar enough to the original sources to render it recognizable, yet infused with a new life and tending to a different end.[7]

Of course Boccaccio was by no means the first medieval author to engage in such a deliberate and programmatic manipulation of source material. In Dante, his 'praeceptor,' Boccaccio had an example of a poet whose repeated reworking of source material is not only self-conscious but performed with the confidence of one who views himself as a shaper not merely of metre and rhyme but of human histories and metaphysical destinies. Emboldened by his Christian faith and intellectual brilliance, his 'altezza d'ingegno,' Dante sets about correcting – with a reverence sometimes real, sometimes affected and with a tone, sometimes patient, sometimes patronizing – the errors of the pagan authorities. The same poet who so movingly owns that the formal quality of his poetry, his 'style,' owes much to Virgil, declares in equally forceful terms his superiority to Virgil and the other pagan poets and philosophers in matters of content. Among the most dramatic examples of Dante's bold correction of a classical authority is that found in the twentieth canto of *Inferno,* where he not only has his fictional Virgil provide an account of the Theban seer Manto that directly contradicts the one supplied by the historical Virgil in the *Aeneid,* but has Virgil's shade advise Dante, pilgrim, that should he hear any account conflicting with this one, he should not permit such a falsehood to compromise the truth![8]

Dante's temerity in matters of this sort is, of course, authorized and made possible by the framing fiction of the transcendent vision. Christian knowledge, however imperfect, is inherently superior to pagan knowledge; and by the same token, revealed truths of the sort which, according to the terms of Dante's fiction, have been made available to him are inherently superior to the speculations of earthbound theologians. Dante's otherworld is characterized by a radical temporal and geographical telescoping. The flame-swathed Ulysses flickers with Guido da Montefeltro, and Hugh Capet cleaves to the hard ground with Statius, while King David and William II exult with the princes that form the eagle's eye in the Heaven of Jupiter; all social, political, and other forms of temporal hierarchy have submitted to a new, exclusively moral ordering principle. Boccaccio, by contrast, still firmly bound by the laws of time and space, of temporal successiveness and geographical distance, is only too keenly aware of the difficulties associated with any attempt to reconstruct the external facts of a historical moment – let alone the more elusive intellectual and private spiritual dramas of the individuals whose actions collectively shape that history.

In *Esposizioni* X, 32–3, for instance, when he addresses the powerful image of the heretic Farinata degli Uberti emerging from his incandescent sepulchre 'from his belt up' ['dalla cintola in su'], he cannot resist noting that the portion of Farinata's body projecting from the tomb is actually not as great as it would be were he a modern Florentine, for men of Farinata's day men wore their belts above the hip and did not, like contemporary Florentines, go about 'belted above the buttocks' ['cinti sopra le natiche']! This apparently fatuous observation – one, moreover that seems to be little more than a pretext for taking his fellow Florentines to task for their fallen morals – indirectly reveals Boccaccio's awareness that our interpretation of texts is inevitably conditioned by our own social experience; Farinata's position with relation to the incandescent sepulcher is not fixed, but a function of each reader's historical circumstances and the capricious winds of fashion. If the scant one hundred years that separate Farinata from the Florentines of Boccaccio's day have the potential to produce misreadings of this sort, how can one hope to fully understand the texts of the ancients? If Dante's intention vis-à-vis Farinata's position relative to his sepulchre rests on as fragile and ever-shifting a foundation as a belt, how can we be sure that his intention with regard to more significant matters is not similarly distorted by the vicissitudes of historical circumstance and social convention – not to mention the personal bias introduced by each individual reader? Boccaccio's sensitivity to the difficulties involved in reconstructing an author's intention from an ancient text is made explicit in the proem of the *Genealogie*: 'Who in our day can penetrate the hearts of the Ancients? Who can bring to light and life again minds long since removed in death? Who can elicit their meaning? A divine task that – not human!' (*Genealogie*, preface; Osgood, 11).

If Dante is able to do precisely this – telling us, for instance, that Statius was a closet Christian, that Pier della Vigna never broke faith with Frederick II, and that a late repentant Buonconte da Montefeltro died with Mary's name on his lips – it is, as noted above, because he has, according to the terms of his fiction, been vouchsafed a vision of metaphysical ends, of indisputable truths in a journey underwritten by God. Though Dante does make a point of showing us that not even the blessed, those who 'see God,' can sound the depths of the divine mind (*Par.* XX, 130–8), his poem nonetheless comforts the reader with the illusion that it is possible, to paraphrase Pope, to look through the bearings, ties, connections, and just gradations of the divine machinery. Boccaccio can offer us no such satisfaction.

Far from handing us an exquisitely symmetrical, crystalline universe neatly tied up in three canticles, Boccaccio constantly reminds us that, with few exceptions, the divine will and mind are closed to human beings. Causes may be speculatively inferred from effects, God's mind from a study of his creation – the book of the universe, to use Dante's evocative metaphor, from its scattered leaves – but such inferences are, like glosses of a difficult passage in Scripture, characterized by their varying degrees of plausibility, not by certainty: 'Let the high Muse chant loves Olympian: / We are but mortals, and must sing of man.'[9]

In the course of an animated dialogue with Fortune in *De casibus* VI 1, 9, Boccaccio acknowledges that he lacks the wings of a bird with which to penetrate the skies, survey its secrets and, having seen them, reveal them to others. Even, he adds, were such a privilege granted him, he would lack the rhetorical skills to record this information for posterity. This is not to say that occasional glimmers of transcendent truths, fragmentary intimations of the divine plan, if not the entire design, are not available to human beings. In his brief digression on dreams in *De casibus* II, 18, Boccaccio argues that something of sublime divinity is hidden in all mortal souls, the influence of which allows us, under certain conditions, when 'sleeping, or with clear or slightly veiled vision, to hear and see a number of matters relating to the future' ('Pauca de somniis,' 4–5). This brief digression ends with a concession that the sleeper's soul does not always exploit this potential; such moments are conceded by divine grace. Given this inherent uncertainty, it is best, Boccaccio advises us, to take a considered approach to dreams, neither rejecting them out of hand, nor accepting them unthinkingly ('Pauca de somniis,' 11). The potential accuracy of prophetic dreams and visions finds support in the *Decameron* tales of Lisabetta and Lorenzo (IV, 5) and of Andreuola and Gabriotto (IV, 6) – which is prefaced by Panfilo's sensible observation (clearly echoing Boccaccio's views in *De casibus* II, 18) that while dreams can reveal the future, they can also mislead, and are, therefore, best judged by the more reliable standard of one's moral intuition.[10]

In the twenty-sixth chapter of his *Life of Dante*, Boccaccio informs us that the last thirteen cantos of *Paradiso* would have been forever lost to posterity had it not been for the timely intervention of Dante's spirit, who, appearing to his son Iacopo in a dream, directed him to a hidden cubby where they had been tucked away. Also in the *Life of Dante* is an account of Dante's mother's prophetic dream, an accurate 'pre-demonstration' ['predimostrazione'] of Dante's future glory (*Vita di Dante*, XXIX). Because, however, these fragments of truth, conveyed through dreams and waking visions, are of necessity cast in a metaphoric language, they are inherently susceptible to misprision or incomplete readings. In concluding his exposition of Dante's mother's dream, Boccaccio acknowledges that there may be others better equipped to analyse certain aspects of this dream. Like the blind Gloucester, dreamers and dream interpreters can 'see,' but only feelingly, tracing the contours of a truth that cannot be related in human discourse.

In some respects what dreams are to the individual myths are to the cultures that produce them. Like dreams, myths have a claim to some element of the transcendent, but, also like dreams, their truths are fragmentary and, like all metaphorical modes of discourse, subject to interpretation. Boccaccio is only too aware that for every inspired interpreter, every Daniel, Joseph, or John of Patmos, there are scores of pretenders to knowledge who 'fetch a deep sigh, then blab away about having consulted God himself, to give an impression that only by the greatest effort of speculative genius were their minds torn from the penetralia of the divine mind' (*Genealogie* XIV, 3; Osgood, 20).

In the wake of Dante's supremely confident and comprehensive vision of metaphysical realities Boccaccio's more cautious, roundabout attempts to understand temporal causes and consequences cannot help but seem somewhat fumbling and tentative. Boccaccio's quest for knowledge does not, like Dante's, take place in the corrugated funnel of hell, the terraced precipice of purgatory, or the rose petal amphitheatre of the Empyrean, but in the monastic and university libraries, merchant exchanges, and marketplaces. Boccaccio's guides are not an apostatic Virgil (for Dante's Virgil has reviled his Pagan gods), beatified Beatrice, or sainted Bernard but a motley crowd of classical authors whose authority, in light of their paganism, is inherently suspect. Surrounded by the scattered wreckage of classical learning (the metaphor used throughout the *Genealogie*), Boccaccio is constrained to compile, examine, and assess the various opinions and authorities without, however, drawing any categorical conclusions. Boccaccio views his mission – not just in the *Genealogie*, but in the *Decameron* and several other works – as a variety of salvage operation. Like a forensic archeologist poking about the wide-strewn wreckage of a crash site, he sets himself the task of gathering up the scattered evidence of a once great culture. In the *Genealogia* the sublime wreck that must be salvaged and reconstructed is classical culture; in the *Decameron* it is the world and way of life that vanished in the plague of 1348. Boccaccio's antiquarian, archeological impulse to resurrect and poetic instinct to reconstitute and breathe new life into these gathered fragments, 'like another Aesculapius restoring Hippolytus' (*Genealogie*, preface; Osgood, 13), is attested throughout his works.

When, for example, Boccaccio broaches the traditional myths in the *Genealogie*, he does not aim at the fixed blank of absolute truth, but the ever-shifting target of relative truths. First-time readers of the *Genealogie* are likely to be somewhat perplexed to discover that there is not just a single Jupiter, but three. Likewise, Mercury, Diana, Apollo, Hercules occur not as individuals but as types. This kaleidoscopic proliferation of individuals is due not to a lack of decisiveness on Boccaccio's part but to the recent availability of an unprecedented wealth of source material and variant traditions coupled with a deep-rooted reluctance to make any absolute judgments on the basis of such partial, contradictory, and fragmentary evidence. While Dante drew his mythological allusions in the *Commedia* from a relatively extensive collection of texts including the poetical works of Virgil, Ovid, Lucan, Statius, mythological notices in the various commentators (for instance Servius's commentary on the *Aeneid*), encyclopedists (Isidore and Brunetto Latini), the Church Fathers, Christian apologists and the like, Boccaccio was able to consult not only these texts, but a number of works whose availability to Dante is uncertain (for instance Livy's Roman history, Valerius Maximus's compilation of notable facts and deeds, Pomponius Mela's geographical survey, Seneca's tragedies, Justin's epitome of Pompeius Trogus's *Philippic History*, Macrobius's *Saturnalia*, Bernardus Silvestris's *Cosmographia*, Fulgentius Planciades's *Mythology*, and Lactantius Placidus's commentary on Statius's *Thebaid*), as well as an important body of mythological material that was certainly not available to Dante: the Homeric poems (in Leontius Pilatus's translation), Apuleius's *Golden Ass* (the source for the tale of Cupid and Psyche recounted in *Genealogie* V, 22), and, perhaps most importantly, the vast store of curious mythological notices that Boccaccio gathered during his formative years in Robert's Neapolitan court from such contemporary authorities as the royal librarian Paul of Perugia (whose *Collections*, a compendium of mythological lore is cited throughout the *Genealogie*), the astronomer Andalò di Negro, the Calabrian erudite Barlaam, and, of course, Leontius Pilatus.[11]

Since the 'true' myth is every bit as elusive as the 'true' religion in Boccaccio's famous *novella* of the three rings (*Dec.* I, 3), identifying the 'true' Jupiter is a task best assigned to staunch dogmatists or eager idealists, chasers after hen's teeth and mares' nests. From the perspective of a scholar-philologist, the suppression or elimination of any but the most extravagant mythological variants would be arrogant and irresponsible in equal measure: 'All these discrepancies,' Boccaccio declares in the preface of his *Genealogie*, he will 'not purpose to reconcile or correct, unless they naturally submit to some order,' restricting himself to writing down what he 'finds,' and leaving 'learned disputation to the philosophers' (*Genealogie*, preface; Osgood, 13). This prefatory claim is reiterated in the last book of the *Genealogie*, where Boccaccio explicitly denies having 'mingled any new myths or stories with the old' and insists that all of his tales are derived from the 'commentaries of the Ancients' (*Genealogie* XV, 5; Osgood, 110). While this is an accurate enough account of the majority of the myths cited in the *Genealogie*, it conveniently overlooks the many cases where Boccaccio has shown little reservation in reconciling or correcting these various mythological traditions (through selective trimming and embroidering) and been quite content to preempt or supplement the learned disputation of philosophers with his own often highly original assumptions and conclusions.

Evidence abounds that Boccaccio does not, as he claims, simply reproduce the myths of the ancients, but reshapes them. One of the more notable examples of this reshaping is found in his discussion of the Hermaphrodite myth (*Genealogie* III, 20–1) which begins with a review of the various interpretations of the myth – ranging from Paul of Perugia's wonderfully progressive, naturalistic account (which rescues hermaphrodites from the traditional association with the supernatural and monstrous), through Ovid's highly influential version of the tale (the marvellous melding together in one body of the passionate nymph Salmacis with Hermaphroditus, her unwilling prey), Andalò del Negro's astrological and Albert the Great's extravagant embryological interpretations to Boccaccio's own interpretation of the tale as a parable of civilization. The tale, Boccaccio proposes, preserves in allegorical form the historical process whereby a Carian font, the Salmacis, contributed to the domestication (not, as other mythical variants would have it, the effeminization) of the barbarous Carians and Lelegians. It provided, with its pure waters, a site ideally suited for the establishment of a tavern where these barbarians, regularly gathering for food and conversation, were gradually reduced to civility. Weighing the relative merits, the pros and cons, of the various models he wishes to emulate, Boccaccio assesses each of these theories in turn, sometimes favouring one or another that is congenial to his own way of seeing things and often fashioning a new tale from this miscellany of old material.

Boccaccio's revision of the Orpheus myth in *Genealogie* V 12, 2–3 (repeated in part in the *Esposizioni*) provides another instructive example of his method of trimming traditional tales into conformity with his own agenda. In the excellent introduction of his translation of books XIV and XV of the *Genealogie*, Charles G. Osgood notes that the Orpheus tale is one of a relatively small group of myths unaccompanied by the usual 'interpretation or comment' and speculates that Boccaccio 'is quite content with mere narration, partly, it may be, to leave room for the reader's poeticizing imagination, partly, perhaps, because the tale justifies itself in the telling.'[12] At least in the case of Boccaccio's Orpheus myth the suggestion that it is 'justified' by the consummate skill of its narration, and hence requires no historical or allegorical gloss, is a bit misleading. Though Boccaccio's version of the Orpheus myth may indeed be notable for its aesthetic attributes – which, according to Osgood, have 'the essential quality of the *Decameron*' – it is less remarkable for these than for the significant ways in which it manipulates and revises its declared source.

In the tenth book of the *Metamorphoses*, Ovid tells us that Orpheus's devastation upon losing Eurydice a second time was such that he was first driven to celibacy and then to pederasty. Indeed, he became an illustrious advocate of pederasty, advising the Thracians that love of young boys 'was the better way' and that they would do well to 'enjoy that springtime, / Take those first flowers!' (*Met.* X, 83–5; trans. Humphries, 236). Reluctant – or so it would seem – to reproduce this etiology of Thracian pederasty, Boccaccio informs us that as Ovid tells us, ('ut ait Ovidius'), Orpheus rejects women and counsels men to embrace celibacy. No trace remains of what is undoubtedly the most striking feature of Ovid's version of the Orpheus myth: Orpheus's transference of his erotic interest to young boys. Whereas the Maenads of Ovid's tale are driven to kill Orpheus not only because they have been rejected, but because they have endured the additional insult of seeing Orpheus seek out the company of boys, Boccaccio finds a new cause for the Maenads' rage – one contemplated by neither Virgil nor Ovid: the Maenads, Boccaccio explains, are menstruating women, whose participation in the Bacchic chorus has been carefully arranged by Orpheus to prevent them from 'contaminating' men! Upon discovering Orpheus's ploy, the Maenads are so enraged that they chase him down, attack him with mattocks and hoes, and cast his butchered body in the river (*Genealogie* V 12, 11; *Esposizioni* IV lit., 325). This unacknowledged suppression of pederasty coupled with the addition of new information about the menstruating Maenads has the effect of entirely shifting the emphases and import of the classical versions of the tale. Whether the revisions of this particular tale should be ascribed to a distaste for pederastic activities, a squeamish aversion to female physiology (similar attitudes to menstruation are represented in numerous passages), or simply represent a bid to distance the figure of Orpheus – long regarded as a sort of epitome of the Poet – from activities likely to sully the reputation of all poets is an open question. No doubt each of these elements has wielded some influence on the final shape of his revised myth. What is clear, however, is that this is not 'mere narration' but a radical revision of the traditional sources, and that while the absence of an accompanying gloss may provide the illusion of a certain freedom for the reader's 'poeticizing imagination,' such freedoms are drastically curtailed by Boccaccio's programmatic suppression and interpolation of details. No longer invited to accompany Orpheus as he chases boys about the Thracian countryside, the reader's imagination has effectively been corralled into an extended contemplation of such dreary matters as the virtues of chastity and the allegedly irrational violence of women.

If Boccaccio's revision of Ovid's Orpheus tale seems, from the perspective of a twenty-first century reader, to be a rather insidious manipulation of mythological material, witness to an unexpected and unflattering bigotry, numerous other passages in Boccaccio's works are no less striking for their pragmatic, progressive view of humanity. Even Boccaccio's most heavy-handed, moralistic works are interlarded with harangues, exhortations, and reasoned arguments testifying to his tolerance, liberality, and sympathy. Such passages often take the form of a reworking of traditional myths with the aim of vindicating the social and sexual desires whose fulfilment Boccaccio – often in defiance of traditional views – takes to be a natural human necessity and therefore an inalienable right.

Revised myths are Boccaccio's weapon of choice in this quiet campaign to console and compensate human beings for this destructive bondage to obsolete myths, a long-standing subjection to self-doubt, guilt, and suspicion. It is not by chance that in his greatest and most influential work Boccaccio attempts to remedy the consequences of the most powerful, and pernicious, myth of the Judeo-Christian tradition: the Fall. Not only does he contrive to extend our stay in the Terrestrial Paradise by giving us ten days ('Decameron') in the paradisal gardens of Tuscany in lieu of the six ('Hexameron') in Eden; he even goes so far as to suggest that our dire sentence to a life of agricultural labour, sweat, and skin coats may be conveniently satisfied through the industrious use of such agricultural implements (the 'dibble with which one plants men' [Dec. IX 10, 18]), and acreage (the 'little field' [Dec. II 10, 32]), as are readily at hand. Who, indeed, can doubt that a vigorous 'shaking of skin coats' ['scuotere il pilliccione' (Dec. X 10, 69)] is bound to produce some sweat on the brow? Boccaccio even finds a way to put a positive spin on God's gloomy revelation that we are made of dust and destined to return to dust. Like the mark of Cain, this quality of the human condition becomes a source of comfort and protection since, as Boccaccio argues in the Introduction to Day IV of the Decameron, he can no more be affected by the harsh winds of critical assaults than the wind-wafted dust, which, land where it will, can never sink lower than the place from which is was originally raised (Dec. IV intro., 40).

Boccaccio's modesty has tended to blind readers to his originality. His affirmation that he simply reports and does not shape myths has, as I

have already insisted, too often been taken at face value. Confronted
with an unwieldy and often discrepant array of myths, Boccaccio's scholarly and critical instinct impelled him to collate, organize, and weigh the
relative merits of these different variants (the objective of the *Genealogie*);
his poetic soul, however, inspired him to fashion new myths from these
fragments. The experience of sifting through such a rich and varied
body of mythological variants and allegorical interpretations would have
quickened the myth-making instinct in the least imaginative archivist, let
alone a reader with Boccaccio's creative spirit. Like Boccaccio, this hypothetical archivist would very soon have made the critical discovery that
myths do not merely reflect or record cultural values and concerns, but
play a no less vital role in prescribing, authorizing, and perpetuating cultural values and concerns. However, it required someone with Boccaccio's combination of scholarly diligence and intellectual insight to fully
understand the implications of this discovery: to understand, that is, that
traditional myths, and myth fragments, are the stuff of which new myths,
and by extension, new mores, are most effectively fashioned. The task of
scripting such innovative myths demands a rare combination of qualities: the diligence of an archivist, the understanding of an intellectual,
and the creative spirit of a poet. It is, in short, a labour for which Boccaccio was ideally suited.

My investigation of Boccaccio's myth-making activity is divided into four
chapters, each of which attempts to chart the evolution through Boccaccio's works of one of four interrelated 'myths.' The first chapter, 'Universal Myths of Origin: Boccaccio and the Golden Age Motif,' begins with a
brief survey of the principal variants of the classical 'Golden Age' motif
that would have been familiar to Boccaccio, before going on to examine
the numerous imitations and innovations of these traditional Golden
Age models in Boccaccio's Latin and vernacular works. Attracted as Boccaccio is by the notion of a prehistoric age of moral innocence (a characteristic feature of Golden Age life), he is clearly put off by the qualities
of intellectual and cultural innocence that appear to be the necessary
corollaries of this moral innocence. He resolves this dilemma by advancing a radically new model of human origins that seamlessly joins elements of these traditional models into a new etiological myth: neither a
Cockaigne-like wonderland of sensual delights nor a rustic paradise of
acorn-eating austerity, but a 'cultural Eden' where intellectual sophistication and moral innocence are united beneath the aegis of reason.

In the second chapter, 'Local Myths of Origin: The Birth of the City

and the Self,' I propose that the same syncretistic method used by Boccaccio to create a new myth of universal origin is applied to the construction of local myths of origin: the idiosyncratic accounts of the birth of
Certaldo, Fiesole, and Florence. A comparison of Boccaccio's etiological
tales with their sources (in poetic mythologies, popular histories, and
chronicles) reveals that his innovations tend to highlight the seminal
role of racial, social, and cultural mixing in the birth and evolution of cities. Observing that the romanticized autobiographies embedded in Boccaccio's youthful works tend to recapitulate, in miniature, these larger,
national patterns of miscegenation and social hybridism, I argue that
Boccaccio would have us believe that what is true of the corporate entity
– the city – is no less true of the individual. Dissatisfied with the classical
myths of national and personal origins (nations born of ants, people
riven from oaks, etc.) or mythical histories of nation founding (the unre-
alistic ethnocentric accounts found in the chronicles), Boccaccio produces a series of new etiological tales which not only acknowledge, but
celebrate the role of genetic mixing and cultural cross-pollination in the
production of individuals and nations.

In the third chapter, 'The Myth of a New Beginning: Boccaccio's Palin-
genetic Paradise,' I argue that a close examination of the language and
literary schemes used to describe the plague of 1348 in the *Decameron*
'Introduction' reveals Boccaccio's intention of situating the plague
within a far larger literary and philosophical discourse on the theme of
universal (or semi-universal) cataclysm and rebirth. Though the accounts
of such catastrophes familiar to Boccaccio from Scripture, classical
poetry, and the philosophical works of Seneca and Macrobius all describe
the survival of a human remnant – the preservation of human life – none
address what was to Boccaccio an equally pressing question: how could
the cultural patrimony of an entire civilization be preserved? Only in
Plato's treatment of cataclysm in the *Timaeus* do we find a similar preoccupation with the continuity of culture. Like the eternal archives of the
Saïtic district described in Plato's *Timaeus* – immune, we are told, to fires
and floods – Boccaccio's *Decameron*, is, I argue, a literary bulwark, a monumental compendium of human knowledge, designed to safeguard the
intellectual legacy of human civilization from the corruptive forces of the
plague (understood not just physically but morally). To the traditional
myths of cataclysm, Boccaccio adds a new, intellectually invigorating
strand: the promise of a cultural continuity.

In the final chapter, 'The Myth of Historical Foresight: Babel and
Beyond,' I argue that although the *Decameron* retains many of the forms

of medieval homiletic – with its characteristic emphasis on spiritual salvation – its focus has quite clearly been shifted to temporal 'salvation.' An avid reader and translator of several decades of Livy's Roman history (*Ab urbe condita libri*), Boccaccio was familiar with the Livian perspective that a thorough knowledge of the past not only allowed one to make informed decisions in the present, but also to anticipate, and thereby avert, future misfortunes. Like Livy's *Ab urbe condita*, the *Decameron* seems to offer its readers a sort of immunity to present strife (plague) and future misfortunes (personal and political) by supplying its readers with a program for social renovation based on self-knowledge. By tempering the spiritual preoccupations of the Christian moralists with the distinctly secular concerns of Livy's history, Boccaccio produces a didactic text aimed at fostering civic virtue in the political sphere: a myth of political self-determination.

chapter 1

Universal Myths of Origin:
Boccaccio and the Golden Age Motif

In his fifth *Eclogue*, 'Silva cadens' [The Falling Forest], Boccaccio invokes the classical motif of a degenerative sequence of ages to describe the political and moral decadence of Naples. Here, we are introduced to Robert, the Angevin king of Naples, under the allegorical mask of Tytirus, a primal lawmaker whose wise and enlightened reign nurtures the flowering of the first of these ages, the Golden Age:

> ... it's Tytirus
> who first sang laws salubrious to the sheep
> and woods; the copious learning of those laws
> was nowhere more illustrious, nor did
> the primal centuries make better ones
> while yet the Golden Age was flourishing ...[1]

With the passing of Robert's reign and the calamitous succession of his granddaughter Giovanna, golden salubrity rapidly yields to a plague of political intrigues of one sort and another, culminating in Giovanna's scandalous flight from Naples in the company of her lover, Louis of Taranto. The once lofty trees come crashing down; the forest, once teeming with life, is abandoned.[2]

Though such an evocation of the Golden Age is by no means unusual in Boccaccio's works – indeed, as we shall see, it is rarely absent – his use of the motif in this particular case cannot simply be dismissed as the usual encomiastic elevation of a political leader on the model of Virgil's fourth *Eclogue*, but is, in all likelihood, charged with a deeper personal significance.[3] Certainly this pattern of a fall from an idyllic, carefree existence to one fraught with cares could just as fittingly be applied to

Boccaccio's own personal history, for the most glorious and carefree years of his life were precisely those youthful years spent in King Robert's Naples, while his return to Florence – one dictated by financial and political woes – marked the beginning of a fall from grace and the reluctant assumption of a yoke of domestic responsibility that would burden him throughout the remainder of his life. Though he was born and nourished in the 'dolce seno' [sweet bosom] of Tuscany, it was his young adulthood in the cultured and elegant society of Naples that shaped his intellect. It was here, in the heart of a classical revival fostered by the learned Angevin monarch that Boccaccio first became acquainted with the literary treasures of the ancient world. It was here too, in the sophisticated milieu of the Angevin court, that Boccaccio first laid eyes on his most enduring muse, the elusive Fiammetta, and produced his first literary works.[4]

The effect on Boccaccio of these vastly divergent experiences is easily traced in his works, where one often finds Florence and Naples recast as the temporal analogues of hell and heaven. This tendency is perhaps most succinctly expressed in the *Elegia di madonna Fiammetta,* where Florence is described as a city of lofty rhetoric but petty acts, ruled not by law but caprice and populated by vainglorious, avaricious, and envious warmongers: a portrait of abject anarchy. Naples, by contrast, is 'lieta, pacifica, abondevole, magnifica e sotto ad uno solo re' (II 6, 21): a portrait of Golden Age felicity, unity, and simplicity under the guidance of a single king.[5] Through the device of locating 'heaven' and 'hell' on a horizontal, temporal plane, Boccaccio effectively historicizes a metaphysical drama; the eternal places of salvation and damnation cede the stage – for the time being – to the terrestrial places of beatitude and pain.[6]

Confronted with the overwhelmingly positive role of King Robert's Naples in Boccaccio's development as poet, scholar, and lover, it seems reasonable to conjecture that his application of the Golden Age pattern to Naples reveals more than a simple penchant for panegyric and a humanistic delight in classical models. His young adulthood in Naples left him with the deep-rooted belief that a certain kind of beatitude could be enjoyed within a temporal frame, the conviction that life is not, as Dante's Beatrice would have it, simply a 'correre a la morte' [running to death] (*Purg.* XXXIII, 54). For Boccaccio the period bracketed by birth and death is a time not merely for redemption but for recreation: the earth is a place not just of passage but of real, if passing, pleasure. So convinced is he of the intrinsically wholesome property of the temporal experience that in the *Genealogie* (in the course of elucidating the allegorical sense of the Ovidian tale of king Phineus), he goes so far as to make the heretical pronouncement that we are all, by divine grace, born good and first 'wedded' to goodness and innocence: 'dico quod divino munere omnes boni nascimur, et sic prima mortalium coniunx bonitas, seu innocentia est' (IV 59, 3). While Boccaccio does go on to say that, upon reaching adulthood, most of us, guided by the 'concupiscent appetite,' are induced to exchange our first 'wife' for a second far less virtuous one, this complaint is nevertheless a far cry from the crippling pessimism of such familiar Patristic authorities as Ambrose, who would have us born in sin ('sub peccato nascimur' [*De poenitentia* I, 2]) and Augustine, who would have us born into a variety of carnal bondage ('carni subditi nascimur' [*De libero arbitrio* XIX, 54]).[7]

Though couched in this colourful wife-swapping metaphor, Boccaccio's statement is by no means frivolous, for it essentially reproduces, in terms that would have had far greater resonance with his contemporary readers, a heretical Pelagian doctrine vigorously condemned by Augustine according to which each newborn child enjoys Adam's original condition of complete innocence – a state of 'Original Righteousness' that Christian orthodoxy assigns exclusively to the prelapsarian period. Boccaccio's readiness to contradict the conclusions of the Church Fathers does not, I believe, reflect a studied theological stance – much less a hankering for polemic – but may be ascribed to his more general tendency to reject determinism in all its guises. Indeed, all of Boccaccio's works attest to his conviction that no circumstances, however dire, can deprive us of our capacity for self-determination. Just as Boccaccio views the state of moral innocence as innate and, therefore, at least potentially recuperable, Eden, the garden where 'the root of mankind was innocent' (*Purg.* XXVIII, 142), is likewise within reach.

The *Decameron*, as I will argue at length in my final chapter, supplies the most compelling proof of this unwritten precept, for it is, paradoxically, the relentless and seemingly inescapable plague of 1348 that paves the way for the successful recuperation, by a small group of virtuous men and women, of an 'edenic' lifestyle in a series of pleasure gardens explicitly associated with Eden. The suffocating pall of necessity that colours the plague account of the introductory pages is gradually dispersed as the *brigata* illustrates – through narrative examples as well as their own actions – the exhilarating freedom of the human will.

Whatever his motivation, it is evident from the unusually high incidence of allusions to the Golden Age in his work that this model of temporal blessedness holds an abiding fascination for Boccaccio. His tendency to flee the rarefied delights of eternity and embrace the more tangible pleasures of the temporal experience is amusingly dramatized in the *Amorosa visione*, which begins with a burlesque reenactment of Dante's famous dilemma in the first canto of *Inferno*. Confronted with the forest of human iniquity on the one side and a perilous, heavily guarded path to virtue on the other, Dante, without deliberation, chooses the latter, whereas Boccaccio, offered a similar choice between two paths – the one, a wide, inviting portal leading to what is effectively a gallery of temporal achievement, and the other, the narrow door of virtue leading to eternal peace – blithely opts for the former, protesting to his guide that there will be time enough for eternity. Importantly, Boccaccio's choice does not prevent, but merely postpones his admittance to the door of eternal peace.

During approximately the same years that Iacopo Passavanti, the ascetic prior of Santa Maria Novella, was striking terror into the hearts of his parishioners, urging them to penitence with deftly painted examples of vice punished, Boccaccio was hard at work shaping his own persuasive arguments that there would be time enough for penitence: youth, as the vivacious Bartolomea of *Decameron* II, 10 and the progressive (if somewhat scurrilous) go-between of V, 10 make quite clear, is better spent on sensual pleasures. Thus it is that Boccaccio can, without gross impiety, refer to a woman's cleavage as the 'graziosa via ... alle case degli iddii' [delightful path ... to the abodes of the Gods] (*Comedia delle ninfe* IX, 26); for Boccaccio, temporal delectation and eternal salvation are not mutually exclusive.[8] Indeed, the former, though transient and intrinsically misleading, has the quality, particularly in its most paradigmatic form – the Golden Age – of adumbrating sacred, eternal truths. Though there are critics who continue to embrace the reductive perspective that the young Boccaccio's devotion to secular pleasures is irreconcilable with any more elevated, spiritual goals (and therefore find it necessary to postulate a dramatic midlife 'conversion'), the truth of the matter is that Boccaccio never entirely loses sight of eternity; he diverges from Dante not in the final objective, paradise, but in the means of achieving that objective.[9]

Boccaccio's dedication of the *Decameron* to women (whom he seeks to supply with an implicitly erotic variety of 'consolation'), taken together with the explicitly sexual content of so many of the *novelle*, has had the cumulative effect of projecting an image of Boccaccio as pander and pornographer so well-entrenched in the collective imagination that his name has long been synonymous with these qualities.[10] Efforts to dispel this common perspective have resulted in an equally simplistic view of

Boccaccio as moralist, one that attempts to discover beneath the erotic text a scathing critique of precisely those qualities that it seems to promote. While both perspectives have the virtue of simplicity, simplicity cannot be counted among Boccaccio's many virtues. Consequently, any approach to his works that clings too closely to either of these extremes is bound to miss the point. Though the *Decameron* is not a moralizing text, it is a supremely moral one, and hence fully compatible with a Christian ethic. As Joan Ferrante has observed: 'the *Decameron* exalts love and related virtues in a well-regulated order, and condemns all excess. This is a morality directed more towards life in the world than towards salvation, but one which fits without violence into the Christian framework.'[11] While the older, and at times quite priggish, Boccaccio is hardly the most trustworthy witness to his own conduct as a youth, it is nevertheless significant that he presents himself as having been relatively immune to the promptings of the libido:

> Sinner that I am, I am not by grace of Christ like young Cherea, in Terrence, who by looking at a picture of Jove falling in a shower of gold from the roof to the lap of Danae, was inflamed to desire of a similar misdeed. Any weak susceptibility of that sort, if it ever existed – *and I am not sure at all that it did* – left me with my youth. (*Genealogie* XV 9, 12; *Boccaccio on Poetry*, trans. Osgood [hereafter cited as Osgood], 127; emphasis mine).

Those inclined to sneer at this declaration and dismiss it as a transparent bid to burnish his reputation (it is, after all, precisely this sort of rhetorical sleight of hand that magically 'restores' Alatiel's virginity after passing through the hands of eight lovers!) would do well to take a closer look at the way Boccaccio portrays sexual attraction and courtship throughout his works. For the most part it is not an unregulated but a remarkably shrewd and calculating Venus who orchestrates the erotic dramas of Boccaccio's fiction. His *novelle* are not peopled by profligates barrelling headlong into the arms of strangers. For every raffish Guccio Imbratta, who, Boccaccio tells us, swoops upon the object of his lust with all the discretion of a vulture feeding on carrion, there are numerous young men and women whose choice of lover is as spiritual as religious faith and as reasoned as a scholastic argument. (Consider the ardour, eloquence, and ingenuity of Ghismonda and Guiscardo, Lisabetta, Madonna Filippa, and Federigo degli Alberighi, among others.) This principle of erotic discrimination is so deeply ingrained in Boccaccio's worldview that its governing influence is evident not only in the sphere of human erotic activity, but in that of irrational creatures as well. In the

Esposizioni, Boccaccio informs us that in fashioning Pasiphae's wooden cow, Daedalus produced no generic heifer but one modelled on the particular cow to which the desired bull had taken a fancy: 'una vacca di legno contrafatta ad una della quale il toro mostrava tra l'altre di dilettarsi molto' [a wooden cow crafted to resemble one which the bull showed signs of preferring to the others] (*Esposizioni* V, lit., 13).[12]

Boccaccio's ideal society is not an orgiastic colony dedicated to serving the senses – that imagined Cockaigne of mounded parmesan bestrewn with capons and steaming sausages that proves so irresistible to the loutish Calandrino – nor is it found on the upper reaches of Mount Asinao where Filippo Balducci preaches his austere creed of abstinence from all worldly pleasures. For Boccaccio, the earthly paradise is in part a place, in part a philosophical attitude, and the recuperation of a personal state of beatitude (Adamic innocence) or of a collective state of beatitude (the Golden Age) is not simply the stuff of vain poetic imaginings but an empirically feasible and morally commendable aspiration.

As we shall see, Boccaccio's attitude towards the traditional Golden Age paradigm of temporal blessedness is marked by tremendous ambivalence and shifts notably throughout his life. However, in order to gauge these shifts more accurately it is useful to first provide a brief overview of those Golden Age accounts that most clearly had a role in informing Boccaccio's own ubiquitous – if widely varying – evocations of the motif.

The Classical Golden Age Traditions

Though the Greek poet Hesiod (eighth century BC) first introduces an etiological scheme of the ages of humanity (described as 'races') ranged sequentially from Gold to Iron, it is the Augustan poet Ovid who, through a fully articulated account in *Metamorphoses* I, is primarily responsible for furnishing the general scheme to the Latin Middle Ages.[13] In addition to Ovid, Virgil (*Aeneid* VI, VIII; *Georgics* I, II, etc.), Horace (*Epodes*, 16; *Satires* I, 3), Seneca (*Epistles* XC and *Phaedra* X, 5, 483–558), Juvenal (*Satires*, VI and XIII), and Boethius (*Consolation of Philosophy* II, V) each make an important contribution to the evolution of this notion of a Golden Age. However, because their models are often at variance both with Hesiod and with each other, the cumulative picture that emerges from these accounts lacks true resolution.[14]

Despite such divergences, these accounts generally concur in beginning with a primal Age of Gold corresponding to Hesiod's Race of Gold under the reign of Kronos (whom the Latin poets identify with Saturn), which cedes to a succession of progressively debased ages culminating in our own, the most degenerate. Whereas the first age is blessed by Earth's spontaneous generation of wholesome fruit and grain, in the ages that follow such bounty can be extracted only through the laborious violation of earth with hoes and ploughshares. Like the unfurrowed earth, time, in this first age, enjoys a sort of unity for it has yet to be parsed into seasons. So perfect is the concord of this age that judges and soldiers are as yet unheard of. In the second age, that of Silver, this primal unity is splintered as time is carved into seasons, and earth into cultivated plots. In the ages that follow the original picture is further muddied by the advent of aggression and war together with a more wide-ranging desecration of Earth as humans spread horizontally over her surface to colonize new lands and penetrate vertically into her very vitals to extract precious metals: that execrable dyad of gold and iron – the former a motive for, and the latter a means of engaging in war.

The preceding summary, though useful for conveying a general sense of the myth, represents a gross simplification of the ambiguities and contradictions inherent in even the first such account. Indeed, the common tendency to evaluate Hesiod's conception of the human condition on the basis of the stark scheme of five 'races' alone is akin to reducing Genesis, the Hebrew Bible's account of origins, to the single chapter, Genesis 3, that chronicles humanity's fleeting passage from a state of primal blessedness to one of exile and travail; in both cases, the mythical story of a radical loss serves as a prelude and foil for the complementary, and no less important, drama of restoration.

A close examination of Hesiod's text reveals that in addition to delineating a formal pattern of movement from a state of primal blessedness to one of corruption (the five 'races'), Hesiod proposes a less rigidly defined series of intermediate forms of blessedness, each of which preserves some aspect or quality of the original, Kronian ideal. By including Hesiod's allusions to such belated and partial restorations in my analysis, I have actually found that while the 'historic' Golden Age may itself be indivisible, the idea of the Golden Age is susceptible to parsing into at least four distinct types:

1 Etiological: the idealized, mythical reign of a god, Kronos (later identified by Latin poets with Saturn), over the first humans. This model provides the basis for future idealizations of human origins. Here, blessedness is not contingent on the ethical status of the individual, but is simply the universal state of existence.

2 Eschatological: the subsequent reign of a 'retired' Saturn over the souls of heroes on the Isles of the Blessed in what is effectively an eternal Golden Age. This, together with Homer's Elysian fields, is the prototype for the idea of a place of eternal blessedness where the virtuous are rewarded for their temporal conduct.

3 Political: the proposition that any era ruled by fair judges is a type of Golden Age. This is the prototype of later political golden ages (eras of unity and peace under the wise rule of a virtuous leader).

4 Ethical: the notion that the virtue and hard work of an individual (in particular, agricultural labour) will redound in profit to that individual by restoring a measure of Golden Age fruitfulness to the Earth. This is the prototype of later pastoral or rustic Golden Ages.

It should be noted that the first two Golden Age models, the 'etiological' and the 'eschatological,' seem to provide the basis for later idealistic, and the second two, the 'political' and the 'ethical,' the basis for later rationalistic models of human blessedness. Although a strongly elegiac mood attends the falling away from primitive perfection, a hopeful counterpoint is struck by the frequently invoked motif of a partial restoration. Importantly, though the Hesiodic scheme begins with the Race of Gold, a period characterized by similitude with divinity – 'both gods and men began the same' – and ends with the Race of Iron, a period of radical dissimilitude, even this last age, the most benighted, harbours a glimmer of hope, for we are told that under the guidance of fair judges, a town may recuperate aspects of the primal Golden Age: peace, prosperity, and the opportunity to reap the earth's bounty through the practice of agriculture in what is effectively a political Golden Age (*Works and Days*, 225ff).[15] After Hesiod, these two characteristics of the Golden Age motif – an indeterminacy, or flexibility, with regard to time and place, together with an underlying intimation of a possible renewal or restoration – are rarely absent.

While Boccaccio himself did not have direct access to Hesiod's account, the ambivalence introduced by Hesiod pervades all subsequent accounts and will, as we shall see, become a fundamental characteristic of Boccaccio's own richly nuanced conception of the temporal paradise.[16] Of the later accounts, those by Virgil and Ovid exercise the greatest influence on medieval attitudes towards primitivism, one easily discerned in all of Boccaccio's frequent evocations of the Golden Age motif.

In Book VIII of the *Aeneid*, Virgil presents the Golden Age as the historically remote, terrestrial reign of a deposed Saturn; having been chased from Olympus by Jupiter, Saturn seeks refuge in Latium, where he establishes Saturnia, the terrestrial correlate of his lost Olympian kingdom. Here, we are far removed from the Cockaigne-like pleasures of Hesiod's (or Ovid's) first age, for the uncultivated mountain that serves as the site of Saturnia presents a challenging rusticity, one that nurtures not an easeful indolence but a studied austerity; one in which virtue is the fruit not of childlike innocence but of mature deliberation: a profoundly moral Golden Age. Whereas Hesiod's emphasis on universal contentment and cherished peace in his description of the Golden Age implies the absence of law, Virgil, by contrast, casts Latium's Saturn as a primal lawgiver and city founder (*Aeneid* VIII). By the device of having King Evander, the founder of Pallantium (a city built on the site of the future Rome), identify Saturn's reign in Latium as 'the Golden Age so often spoken of' (VIII, 324), Virgil deftly confers upon this revised Golden Age model (a conflation of the etiological and political Golden Ages delineated by Hesiod) the canonical status previously reserved for Hesiod's Golden Age. It is not by chance that the Golden Age that Virgil presents in Book VIII of the *Aeneid* is not only posterior to law but actually contingent on law – a political, not a pastoral, paradise.[17] Significantly, this engrafting of a political (and, at least potentially, real) shoot onto a mythical (and ideal) root results in the creation of a new model in which a divine ruler assumes the political governance of a temporal state (a conception that seems to anticipate, and in any case, does much to facilitate, the later euhemeristic perspective so dear to Boccaccio according to which the classical gods are none other than deified political leaders and culture-heroes).[18] Though this mytho-political Golden Age of *Aeneid* VIII is particularly influential, Virgil is the source of several other seminal models of the Golden Age.

In the first book of the *Georgics* (125ff) Virgil seems unresolved concerning the qualities of the Golden Age – here viewed as a Hesiodic variety of idyllic indolence. If, Virgil remarks, the passing of this period of natural bounty is to be lamented, it is equally certain that the development of human arts necessitated by this loss is hardly to be despised. Agriculture is here viewed as both a precursor to and prerequisite for all loftier forms of culture, and a direct correlation is established between human contentment and the various amenities made available through technology. In the second book of the *Georgics* (458ff), Virgil associates the Golden Age with a pastoral present (it is among husbandmen, Virgil maintains, that a fugitive Justice left her last traces). In *Aeneid* VI (791ff) the Golden Age is identified with the reign of Augustus; and finally, in his messianic fourth *Eclogue*, Virgil prophesies the imminent restoration of the Golden Age under the political leadership of a reborn 'Saturn' whose auspicious reign will witness the long-awaited restoration of justice.[19]

Through such widely varying applications of the motif Virgil does much to strengthen the Hesiodic notion of the Golden Age as the dynamic embodiment of a political and moral ideal that is not bound in the mythical realm of prehistory, but faithfully accompanies humanity throughout the vicissitudes of history. However, Virgil goes further than Hesiod in his campaign to reclaim the Golden Age, for by assimilating the mythical and ideal model to a historical and real one – the synthesis exemplified by the divine kingship of Saturn in Saturnia – Virgil introduces the possibility of a complete restoration within a temporal framework, an idea whose importance to Boccaccio cannot be overstated.

Additionally, though Virgil's use of the Golden Age motif represents a kind of amalgamation of the Hesiodic applications, there is such an emphasis placed on an imminent restoration that the elegiac note so pervasive in Hesiod's model is, though ever present, at times quite hard to make out. Even the nostalgic contemplation of Saturnia's ruins in *Aeneid* VIII is counterbalanced by the certainty of renewal; it is Virgil's own voice that interrupts Evander's discourse to remind us that the Capitol, once overgrown with thickets, is now golden, 'aurea nunc' (348).

Virgil's most conspicuous contribution to the evolution of the idea of the Golden Age is that of historicizing a distant epoch that had previously been the exclusive property of myth – an 'empiric' status corroborated by the architectural ruins of Saturnia (*Aeneid* VIII, 356–8). The same pattern of the demise and rebirth of an ideal polity that serves Virgil's political agenda so well (by casting the Augustan Age as a renewal of the first Golden Age) is later exploited with little restraint by an endless succession of political ideologues and court panegyrists for whom every prince is a Saturn and every city a Saturnia.[20] Even though political realities rarely – or never – coincide with such inflated rhetoric, the Virgilian historicizing model is, finally, most influential in its implication that the achievement of some semblance of temporal beatitude is within the realm of human possibility.

Whereas Virgil never elaborates a formal scheme of ages, Ovid, in the first book of the *Metamorphoses*, furnishes the Latin-speaking world with its most rigorous epochal systematization of universal history. If Ovid's description of the ages of humanity seems initially to be little more than a replication of the Hesiodic model, a closer look reveals at least two divergences so basic as to render Ovid's scheme almost entirely new. On the one hand, Hesiod's five-part scheme is contracted to four (the Hesiodic Race of Heroes is eliminated); on the other, it is effectively pro-tracted through the incorporation of this abbreviated, four age scheme into a broader, more emphatically moralistic pattern of cyclical annihila-tion and regeneration. These critical innovations have the effect of strengthening the causal relations among the individual ages (which had been nebulous, at best, in the Hesiodic model) while simultaneously foregrounding the role of morality in this process of passage from one age to another. Whereas Hesiod's racial model of historical change (the metallic races) implicitly assigns the responsibility for degeneration to intrinsic, 'biological' factors (a sort of built-in obsolescence), Ovid is clearly proposing that historical change be viewed as causally linked to moral conduct; racial and genetic determinism cedes to a model of his-torical change based on moral and spiritual agency.[21]

However, Ovid goes further, embedding this streamlined scheme into the larger context of an emphatically moral history. In the first book of the *Metamorphoses*, the present age is no longer associated, as it is in Hesiod, with the last of the ages, that of Iron, but rather corresponds to a period of postdiluvial regeneration. Here, the Iron Age is followed by the moral dramas of the giants' foiled coup d'état and Lycaon's nefari-ous attempt to test Jupiter's divinity by feeding him human flesh and, as though this were insufficient evidence of his depravity, conspiring to kill him in his sleep! Here, too, is the exquisite description of the torrential flood, unleashed by Jupiter to purge Earth of her impious brood, and of the two lone survivors, the virtuous Deucalion and Pyrrha, first parents of a new generation born of stone.

After Ovid, the Iron Age must be viewed not only as the terminus of a sequence but, more compellingly, as the threshold of a new age. Addi-tionally, Ovid's application of a cyclical pattern to describe moral flux – the apex of the cycle, the Golden Age, is characterized by primal virtue, an innocence to sin, the nadir, Lycaon's act, by radical moral depravity – implies that postdiluvial generation is simultaneously a moral restora-tion, a gradual recuperation of Golden Age qualities.[22]

While Virgil's Golden Age allusions certainly reveal an ethical con-cern, morality is always considered in the context of polity. For Virgil, moral rectitude is both the basis for and the effect of good government; as we have seen, in *Aeneid* VIII the initiation of the Golden Age is predi-cated on Saturn's dispensation of law. In Ovid, by contrast, law is intro-duced belatedly to curb a long-entrenched moral degeneration; the primal state of humanity is one of natural, voluntary virtue, unconstrained by legal edicts. Whereas the elimination of the Age of Heroes clears the way for a moralization of the Hesiodic scheme, Ovid's introduction of the story of Lycaon's transgression and the punitive flood has the effect of further defining the character of this morality as one concerned with the relation of humans to gods.[23] By reinforcing the role of divine justice in this moral scheme through the familiar pattern of blasphemous transgression, divine punishment, and divine restoration, Ovid provides a model tremendously congenial to the Judeo-Christian tradition and irresistible to Christian scholars such as Boccaccio whose profound reverence for the literary works of antiquity and whose desire to somehow 'redeem' them, had predisposed them to recognize even the subtlest glimmers of Christian truths in pagan fictions.

Indeed, long before Boccaccio tried his hand at harmonizing the concealed truths of pagan poetic intuition with the revealed truths of Christian doctrine, the Church Fathers and Christian apologists had already devoted much ingenuity to achieving the same end. The relative congruity between certain superficial elements of this myth of the ages of humanity and the Old Testament account of an Edenic 'Golden Age' followed by a precipitous fall, resulted, naturally enough, in a tendency to make a typological assimilation of the classical Golden Age to its Christian counterpart.[24] In his *Divine Institutes* (V, 5) the fourth-century Christian apologist Lactantius goes so far as to present the Golden Age as a time of monotheistic piety for he discerns the 'true,' Judeo-Christian, god under the guise of Saturn.[25] Though Christian/pagan syncretism of this sort is ubiquitous in Boccaccio's works, what is striking about certain passages in the *Filocolo* is precisely the implication that the more virtuous pagans are in a sense monotheistic (see, for example, II 67, 3, where Jupiter is cast as a Christian God-Creator). In the *Genealogie* we find a particularly revealing passage in which Boccaccio declares that 'as sensible men we must easily admit that the learned [including some of the pagan poets] have been most devoted investigators of the truth, and have gone as far as the human mind can explore; thus they know beyond any shadow of doubt that there is but one God' (XIV, 13; Osgood, 65). For Boccaccio monotheistic belief is not predicated on divine inspiration or religious faith but may be arrived at through a process of logical deduction.

In his *Epitome* (59) Lactantius presents the advent of Christianity as a restoration of the Saturnian quality of justice. As we have seen, the introduction of a restorative event or period immediately following the culmination of the downward cycling is a conspicuous feature of Ovid's account; that early Christians should assign Christ the role previously reserved for Astrea, the incarnation of Justice whose apotheosis is prophesied in Virgil's fourth *Eclogue*, is, therefore, all but inevitable.[26]

In addition to drawing informal analogies between the classical scheme of ages and Scripture, an effort was made to effect a wholesale replacement of the classical paradigm with a Christian model – one naturally that would include a period of spiritual restoration corresponding to the Incarnation and reintroduce the Hesiodic notion of an eschatological Golden Age: the Heavenly Jerusalem or Christian Paradise.

Though a tripartite, periodic model of universal history based on human existence under Nature (before Law), under Law (that is, Mosaic Law), and after Law (an era of grace in Christ) is already implicit in Paul's epistles, Augustine, no doubt influenced by the classical, Hesiodic, tradition, proposes a refinement of this scheme which further parses history by introducing an additional three (or sometimes four) ages.[27] In the *De diversis quaestionibus* (LVIII, 2), he furnishes a scheme of six ages of the world – the first from Adam to Noah; the second from Noah to Abraham; the third from Abraham to David; the fourth from David to the Babylonian exile; the fifth from the Babylonian exile to the advent of Christ; the sixth from the advent of Christ to the End-Time – in which these ages are correlated with the six 'ages' of an individual – *infantia, pueritia, adolescentia, juventus, gravitas, senectus*. In *De genesi contra manichaeos* (I, 23), Augustine extends this parallelism to include the six days of creation, an addition that leads him to postulate a seventh age corresponding to the seventh day, that during which God rested, one which brings with it the promise of Christ's Second Coming together with a well-merited rest in Christ for those who have engaged in good works. Just as the 'old man,' Adam, is restored by the 'new man,' Christ, this End-Time will usher in a period of general rejuvenation for the aged 'body' of humanity.[28] In the *City of God* XXII, 30, he makes an important distinction between the first five, 'historical,' ages and the sixth, which, bracketed by Christ's initial advent and projected return, is viewed as a sort of bridge between time and eternity.

Elements of these ingenious, if somewhat arid, symmetries of Augustine's grand concordance of divine (the six days of creation), human (the six ages of an individual life), and historical (the six ages of the world) ages are replicated with little innovation in numerous theological texts of the Middle Ages. However, an unusual application of these ideas, and one that invests them with new vitality, is found in Philippe of Harveng's inspired application of the scheme to the famous colossus of metals described in the Book of Daniel (II, 31–45). Daniel himself furnishes an

allegorical interpretation of the imposing statue according to which the
four metals – gold, silver, bronze, and iron – of which the colossus is composed represent the diachronic succession of four progressively debased
kingdoms (Babylonian, Median, Persian, and Greek respectively), all of
which are destined to be crushed by a stone (cut without hands from a
mountain) representing a fifth and everlasting kingdom: the Kingdom
of God. Philippe, inspired by the then current strategy of interpreting
the Old Testament in the revelatory light of Christian 'truth,' could not
help but see in this marvellous colossus of metals a symbol not simply of
local and secular, but of universal and sacred history: an Old Testament
prefiguration of, and hence, confirmation of, the Augustinian model.
Accordingly, in Philippe's exegesis, the gold head once identified with
Nebuchadrezzar's kingdom is made to correspond to the first Augustinian age (that bracketed by Adam and Noah), the silver chest and arms to
the second Augustinian age, and so forth. The effacement prophesied by
Daniel is complete; the colossus of the Book of Daniel, that poignant literary testament to the vanity of temporal kingship, has been charged
with a new task, that of charting the more complex course of Judeo-
Christian sacred history.[29]

Since the use of a series of metals to chart a historical process of decline
cannot help but recall the Hesiodic ages of metal, it seems likely that the
conspicuous absence of any traces of the classical model in Philippe's exegesis does not reflect an ignorance of the classical paradigm so much as
a deliberate effort to avoid contaminating Christian 'history' with pagan
mythology. Dante, it would appear, has no such apprehensions, for in his
own famously enigmatic evocation of the colossus of metals, the imposing
'Veglio di Creta' of *Inferno* XIV, he makes the association explicit. Indeed,
in what is one of his most significant departures from his primary source
in Daniel, he locates the statue in Crete, which he further identifies as the
historical site of the Saturnian Golden Age:[30]

'In mezzo mar siede un paese guasto,'
diss'elli allora, 'che s'appella Creta,
sotto'l cui rege fu già'l mondo casto ...
(*Inf.* XIV, 94–6)

'A devastated land lies in midsea,
a land that is called Crete,' he answered me.
'Under its king the world once lived chastely ...
(*The Divine Comedy*, trans. Mandelbaum [hereafter cited as Mandelbaum])

The natural inclination to view this passage as a sort of encomium to the classical Golden Age must be tempered by the observation that Dante's poetic consolidation of classical and Christian culture is one that, like the Veglio itself, leans more heavily on one foot. In the *Commedia* classical civilization is never granted a full historical autonomy but is viewed, rather, as constituting a necessary part of universal, Christian history – one fully integrated into God's providential plan (a unitary conception of history familiar to Dante from Paul Orosius's early fifth century *Seven Books of History against the Pagans*). Thus it is that in the *Commedia* the ancillary gods of the Olympian pantheon are revealed to be foreshadowings of, a functionaries in, a Christian cosmos, while beneath the mask of Jupiter, the supreme pagan deity, are concealed the lineaments of the Judeo-Christian God. Similarly, in the classical myth of the Golden Age, Dante sees a distorted image of Eden, a confused reminiscence of that ancient period of monotheism that preceded the blight of polytheism. This interpretation is confirmed in canto XXVIII of *Purgatorio*, where Dante has Matelda, the virgin-custodian of the terrestrial paradise, suggest that the classical authors of Golden Age accounts are unwittingly 'dreaming' of Eden: 'Quelli ch'anticamente poetaro / l'età dell'oro e suo stato felice, / forse in Parnaso esto loco sognaro' ['Those ancients who in poetry presented / the golden age, who sang its happy state, / perhaps, in their Parnassus, dreamt this place'] (*Purg.* 28, 139–41; Mandelbaum).[31] Golden Age Crete, the pagan backdrop in Dante's allegory of the Colossus, is enlisted exclusively to represent Christian history and is not, as might appear to be the case to those unfamiliar with Dante's method, in any sense a eulogy of the classical Golden Age.[32]

In the *Commedia*, where Dante adheres to a Christian eschatology, he locates the Golden Age at the beginning of time, Eden, or at the end of time, the celestial paradise. The temporal expanse bracketed by these two coordinates is – within the otherworld frame of the *Commedia* – devoted to a pilgrimage; it is viewed as a means, not as an end. In other works, in particular *De monarchia*, Dante, like Virgil and Hesiod before him, advances the notion of a political 'Golden Age,' one defined as any period – past, present, or future – enjoying political unity under the aegis of a virtuous emperor.[33] However, whereas pagan culture had practically institutionalized the deification of its political leaders – a cultural habit reinforced by the widespread custom among Roman patricians of tracing their ancestry to the gods (and given a mytho-historical imprimatur by Virgil's story of Saturnus in *Aeneid* VIII) – Christianity grants this privilege to Christ alone.

Moreover, since Christian doctrine assigns Christ both a temporal and an eternal reign (corresponding respectively to the Incarnation and the Second Coming), and both are associated with the advent of a new Golden Age (one temporal, the other eternal), Christian authors could select as their corollary to the classical Golden Age whichever of the three canonical periods of blessedness best suited their needs: the tenure of the First Parents in Eden, the state of Grace ushered in by the Incarnation, or, finally, the End-Time, with its promise of celestial beatitude. Furthermore, the Pauline notion of Adam (the 'old man') as a prefiguration of Christ (the 'new man') has the effect of cementing Christ's identification with the Edenic 'Golden Age,' thereby creating a symmetrically pleasing pattern of three Christs and three Golden Ages.

Boccaccio's Elegiac Primitivism

The foregoing survey represents a sampling of some of the Golden Age models that prevailed in the Middle Ages with which Boccaccio was thoroughly conversant. That Boccaccio was grappling with these varied models even in his earliest period is evident in his so-called *Allegoria mitologica*, a short work written, according to Manlio Pastore Stocchi, its most recent editor, during his Neopolitan period, probably in or around 1339.[34] Vittore Branca speaks for most critics when he describes the *Allegoria* as little more than an 'artificioso centone dei due primi libri delle *Metamorfosi* in una confusa contaminazione di allegoria mitologia e storia, di paganesimo e cristianesimo' ['an adroit cento drawn from the first two books of the *Metamorphoses* in a confused mingling of mythical allegory and history, of paganism and Christianity'] (*Giovanni Boccaccio*, 41; *Boccaccio: The Man and His Works*, trans. Monges [hereafter cited as Monges], 42).[35] However, to dismiss Boccaccio's *Allegoria* as a derivative, confused pastiche of Ovidian and Christian themes is to overlook the underlying rigour of his conception. The *Allegoria* is not, I would argue, simply a 'confused mingling' of pagan and Christian themes, but represents a systematic effort to harmonize the Ovidian and 'Augustinian' schemes of periodization. That Boccaccio should attempt such a demanding task is not only evidence of an early humanist's keen desire to 'redeem' classical culture, but also a testament to the congeniality of Ovid's model to the Christian pattern of trespass and redemption.

Though book I of Ovid's *Metamorphoses* is the predominant model for his delineation of the ages in the *Allegoria*, Boccaccio, like Augustine, relates the initiation of the Golden Age to the earthly advent of a divinity – in this case, 'Prometheus,' who has left Elysium in order to inaugurate a terrestrial Age of Gold. This 'Prometheus,' both a God incarnate and a figure for Adam, reigns over an innocent people who enjoy the dubious pleasures of an acorn and water diet until Lycaon's depravity prompts Jupiter to unleash the cleansing flood.[36]

Already, we cannot help noting a significant deviation from the Ovidian scheme; whereas, in *Metamorphoses* I, Lycaon's transgression functions as a watershed between the four 'metallic' ages and the universal deluge that follows, Boccaccio places the transgression – and universal purgation – at the end of the first, Golden, age.[37] Clearly, this decision is not arbitrary but reflects Boccaccio's desire to accommodate the classical, epochal scheme of the terrestrial ages to the Augustinian pattern, in which the universal Deluge punctuates the end of the first age, that which runs from Adam to Noah. As a result, the remaining three ages – Silver, Bronze, and Iron – are all postdiluvial, and represent the period of moral degeneration that calls for a renewal in the person of Christ. Accordingly, Boccaccio associates the Silver Age with Deucalion and Pyrrha's restoration of humans from stone, and the Bronze Age with the historical period of Moses's leadership (here, represented by the mythical reign of the Argive king Phoroneus) and introduction of Mosaic law – a necessary though insufficient effort to staunch the moral corruption. However, the flagrant immorality and impiety of the fourth age, that of Iron, is such as to demand a more drastic solution. Thus, Boccaccio tells us, it comes to pass that at the close of the Iron Age, through the compassion and grace of God – the same who modelled the first man ('Prometheus') – we have been offered a new means of salvation in Christ (whose name, however, is not mentioned); the Saturnian reign has been reestablished, and power has finally been restored to the Virgin Astrea's sword:

> through the ineffable favour of the compassion of he who with his own hands had shaped Prometheus was provided to all a road to salvation. Indeed, by opening his delights to us he granted us a more precious treasure [thesaurum cariorem] and by restoring the reign of Saturn returned strength to the sword of the Virgin Astrea. (*Allegoria*, 9)[38]

Using the familiar terms of Virgil's fourth *Eclogue* (one that in the Middle Ages was commonly viewed as a prophesy of Christ's birth) Boccaccio here commemorates the restoration of deity (the Incarnation) and law (the New Testament) to a people destitute of both. (Indeed, the use of a comparative form, 'cariorem,' to describe the 'treasure' subtly insists on the superiority of this period of restoration to the original state of blessedness.)[39] In place of the devastating deluge that follows the Iron Age in Ovid's scheme and ushers in a new generation sprung from stone, Boccaccio supplies a purgative shower – 'sacris ymbribus dealbatum' (*Allegoria*, 11). The punishing flood has effectively been replaced by the sacrament of baptism in this Christianized scheme.

Even this brief synopsis of the first part of the *Allegoria* confirms both Boccaccio's profound interest in the Golden Age motif and his syncretistic methodology. Just as Ovid encapsulates and integrates the Greek, Hesiodic, sequence of ages into his broader, Latin, scheme, Boccaccio absorbs Ovid's pagan pattern into a Christian, moral scheme, thereby, fittingly enough, 'restoring' the Golden Age paradigm itself.

That Boccaccio had this idea of the six ages of sacred history in mind when writing the *Allegoria* is suggested not only by the internal evidence presented above, but by the existence of a fully fleshed-out exposition on the six 'Augustinian' ages of the world written in approximately the same years. This account, found in the *Filocolo* (V, 53–4), provides a thorough description of the events corresponding to each of the six ages, and, tellingly, describes the first age in terms that unambiguously recall the features of the classical Golden Age. This merging of the Christian with the classical model is particularly evident in the beginning of the description where the spectre of the Golden Age acorn diet is invoked: 'Piacqueli ancora di dire quanto il principio della prima età fosse dalle seguenti variato, mostrando come i loro digiuni le ghiande solveano, e gli alti pini davano piacevoli ombre, e i correnti fiumi davano graziosi beveraggi agli assetati' ['It also pleased him to say how much the beginning of the first age was different from those that followed, indicating how they broke their fasts on acorns, and how the tall pine trees gave them pleasant shade, and the running rivers gave welcome drink to them when thirsty'] (*Filocolo* V, 53; trans. Cheney, Bergin, 426).[40]

Like so many abstract, artificial schemes, the classical pattern of epochal degeneration proves an ideological scaffolding amenable to a wide variety of agendas. This flexibility is particularly evident in the *Esposizioni sopra la Comedia*, Boccaccio's uncompleted commentary on Dante's *Inferno*, where each of the evocations of the Golden Age has a very distinct emphasis. The cumulative effect of this technique of viewing a single motif through a constantly shifting optic is to provide us with a fairly complete anatomy of the motif itself – that is, as interpreted by Boccaccio.

Naturally enough, these shifts in emphasis are to a great degree determined by the surrounding context. So it is that in commenting on Dante's obscure, seemingly messianic prophecy of the 'veltro' [greyhound] (*Inf.* I, 101) whose advent is associated with a period of restoration, Boccaccio advances the opinion held by some that the 'veltro' represents a future political leader destined to flush avarice from the world: a reprise of the Virgilian notion of a Golden Age under a just monarch. Advocates of this view, notes Boccaccio:

> a roborare questa loro oppinione inducono questi cotali tempi già stati, cioè quegli ne' quali regnò Saturno, li quali per li poeti si truovano essere stati d'oro, cioè pieni di buona e di pura simplicità, e ne' quali questi beni temporali dicon che eran tutti comuni; e per conseguente, *se questo fu, anche dover poter essere che questi sotto il governo d'alcuno altro uomo sarebbono.* (*Esposizioni*, I, alleg., 171, emphasis mine)

> to shore up their opinion, invoke ancient times, those in which Saturn reigned and which the poets describe as having been golden, that is, filled with good and plain simplicity, of which times it is affirmed that temporal goods were held in common; *and therefore, if this was true, it follows that these* [the ancient times of Saturn] *could be possible under the rule of some other man.*

The last line of this citation is arguably the most important, for in it, beneath the familiar Golden Age rhetoric, we note a peculiarly Boccaccian emphasis on the historical indeterminacy of this restoration. The Golden Age here proposed is like a moveable feast, a phenomenon that can, in theory, be reproduced under the governorship of any virtuous leader – a politically, not historically, determined phenomenon (Hesiod's 'political' Golden Age). A conception that had been little more than fodder for political panegyrists is here elevated to the level of political theory; this passage represents no insincere apologia for some petty tyrant, but a sincere profession of hope for, as we shall see later, this element of reproducibility is at the very heart of Boccaccio's conception of temporal blessedness in the *Decameron*.

In his allegorical interpretation of *Inferno* VI, the canto of the gluttons, Boccaccio provides a lengthy account of the traditional degenerative sequence of ages in which the cultural decadence is both initiated and perpetuated by acts of gluttony. In pursuing this particular agenda, Boccaccio naturally finds it most expedient to gather together only those specific elements from both the Christian and classical schemes most congenial to his argument.[41] As a result, it is a highly tendentious account of the transgression of the First Parents in Eden that initiates the scheme; in this gloss the eating of the apple is understood to have been exclusively a sin of gluttony. Curiously enough, the classical Golden Age is here assigned to the postdiluvial period (*Esp.* VI, alleg., 4), one of acorn-eating austerity, wedded chastity, and virtuous simplicity:

> Non si sapeva che invidia fosse, non avarizia, non malizia o falsità alcuna, ma santa e imaculata semplicità ne' petti di tutti abitava: per che merita-mente, secondo che i poeti questa età discrivono, 'aurea' si potea chiamare. (*Esposizioni* VI, alleg., 8)

> It was not known what envy was, nor avarice, nor malice or falseness of any sort, but saintly and immaculate simplicity dwelt in every bosom: for which with good reason, according to what poets describe of this age, it could be called 'golden.'

The 'diabolical' influence of ambition coupled with the arrival of Ceres (goddess of grain) and Bacchus (god of wine) more or less cements both the culinary fate of acorns, which are henceforth held in disdain, and the moral destiny of humanity, which is progressively corrupted by the canker of Asiatic decadence which has reached, sad to say, its culmination in Tuscany (*Esp.* VI, alleg., 19).

In his commentary on *Inferno* VII, the canto of the avaricious and prodigal, the demise of the Golden Age is attributed, fittingly enough, not to gluttony but to avarice (45–51). Here, Boccaccio cites lines 27–30 of the well-known Golden Age description in the *Consolation of Philosophy* (II, meter V), where Boethius inveighs against that anonymous individual who first plundered the earth for gold and gems, treasures better kept hidden (51).[42]

Common to all these evocations of the Golden Age motif is a tendency to idealize this age by identifying it historically as an age of peace, prosperity, and good government, or morally as a time of unsurpassed virtue. However, this idealistic perspective is by no means the only one reproduced in Boccaccio's works. As Boccaccio slyly observes in the Epilogue to the *Decameron*, though he may appear heavy, those who have actually 'weighed' him have found him so light that he floats; beneath the leaden mask of the moralist lies the quicksilver tongue of the satirist.

Boccaccio's Rationalistic Reevaluation of the Golden Age

De casibus VI, 13, begins with an eloquent tongue-lashing of those prating fools who attack rhetoric, perversely enlisting in their futile campaign the instruments of the very art – rhetoric – that they are maligning. Such detractors, observes Boccaccio, argue that as all intellectual concepts can be adequately described in simple language, the complexities of rhetoric are not necessary but result from a calculated desire to deceive. In response to such charges Boccaccio notes that whereas other animals express themselves in a cacophony of bleats, whistles, and so forth, humans alone have been granted the gift of meaningful discourse: the same that is used to communicate knowledge, cement friendships, praise virtue, and condemn vice.[43] However, Boccaccio continues, there are two sorts of language, the one a mother tongue – natural, rough, and common – the other a product of artifice: a polished, florid, and highly rational language spoken by a handful of experts. Who, asks Boccaccio, would be so foolish as to deny that this charming tongue is to be preferred to the other: 'quis ergo erit tam dementis sententie qui facile non assentiat lepidam comptamque minus lepide preferendam?' (6). After praising such refined language for its various socially constructive qualities, Boccaccio concludes that even if necessity does not demand its use, we should be drawn to it for the sake of convenience; though thatch and reeds would suffice to shield us from winter rain and summer sun, we not only hire expert architects, masons, and carpenters to construct our homes from squared stones and hewn timbers, but further embellish them with ivory, gold, and paintings. The same holds true of our bodies, which we do not clothe in simple skin coats, though these would give us ample protection, but in beautiful garments.[44] Similarly, Boccaccio continues, we ennoble the food and drink offered us by nature with artful preparation and elegant presentation. Given all this, how can we neglect eloquence so long as we can find those who would teach us: 'Quomodo ergo eloquium negligemus, si preceptores invenerimus?' (15).

Let us not forget that in the *Esposizioni* it is precisely the subtle transition from 'mestiere' [trade] to 'arte' [art] that signals the far-reaching shift from an era of cultural sobriety to one of decadence. Wealth and the infiltration of Asiatic customs transform cooking from a 'mestiere' to an 'arte' (VI, alleg., 15), with the disastrous result that it is not only such rustic foods as 'ghiandi, e' salvatichi pomi e l'erbe' [acorns, crab apples, and greens] that are disdained, but even the usual, less rustic fare is cast aside in favour of exotic ingredients and novel preparations. Despite the moralizing tenor of *De casibus* we have in this defence of artifice an almost point-by-point rebuttal of the glowing portrait of the primitive state of humanity painted by Seneca in his *Epistle* XC, where Seneca distinguishes between the gifts of philosophy, represented by Diogenes, and those of ingenuity, represented by Daedalus; wisdom, 'sapientia,' teaches moral conduct, ingenuity, 'sagacitas,' teaches practical, mechanical skills. The former is satisfied with the bare necessities and supports unity; the latter, encumbered with excess, breeds avarice, luxury, and division. Nature, writes Seneca, tells us 'that we can live without the marble cutter and the engineer, that we can clothe ourselves without traffic in silk fabrics' (XC, 15). Thatched roofs suffice to give us shelter, skin coats to keep us warm. Even eloquence comes under scrutiny in this glib panegyric to the primitive life, for, Seneca cautions us, 'the charm of eloquence wins even great men away from the truth' (XC, 20).[45]

Faced with such obvious discrepancies it is almost inevitable that one should ask oneself what could possibly have inspired Boccaccio, the righteous upbraider of Apicius and eloquent advocate of the acorn diet, to advance this doctrine of decoration, an attack of ascetic sobriety and defence of aesthetic excess? (Could it be that his prolonged immersion in the human tragedies of *De casibus* granted Boccaccio the insight so movingly expressed by Lear: 'Allow not nature more than nature needs, / Man's life is cheap as beast's'? [II, iv, 261–2]) Although no fully satisfactory answer can be offered to this question, it should, at least, be observed that Boccaccio is by no means unique in assuming two such conflicting positions. Indeed, parodic reevaluations of the primitive life enjoy a literary pedigree no less distinguished than that of the traditional, moralizing motif.

While poets given to moral pronouncements are pleased enough to reproduce the well-worn paeans to rustic simplicity and lament its passing, others, taking a more rationalistic approach, display a notable ambivalence with regard both to the feasibility and desirability of such rustic perfection. Among other things, these sceptics find it difficult to reconcile either easeful indolence or austere rusticity with sexual chastity; in their view, both the surfeit of natural amenities (one that promotes passive sensualism), and their scarcity (accompanied by rude rusticity) are more convincingly associated with sexual promiscuity than prudery. No less an authority than Ovid had pronounced 'otium' [leisure] the root and sustenance of erotic desire and recommended that those wishing to free themselves from Cupid's mastery (to 'break his bow') begin by eliminating *otium*: 'Otia si tollas, periere Cupidinis arcus'

(*Remedia amoris*, 139). Certainly, the combination of leisure with material communism implies (particularly for those inclined to view women as chattel) that such primitive communities had both the time and the means to engage in an orgiastic free-for-all. Nor do these sceptics express any qualms concerning the demise of what (to the cosmopolitan sensibility) can be viewed as little more than an assault on the palate: the ubiquitous acorn diet – a food whose culinary possibilities are, in Dante's time, explored by pigs alone. In his twelfth *Eclogue*, 'Saphos,' Boccaccio is quite clear on this subject: 'Don't you know, stupid dolt, / acorns are served to pigs, and laurel wreaths / to poets ...' (*Giovanni Boccaccio: Eclogues*, trans. Smarr [hereafter cited as Smarr], 129).[46]

The earliest Latin text to present this more realistic perspective, Lucretius's Epicurean *De rerum natura*, is also one of the most influential. In the fifth book of *De rerum natura*, Lucretius proposes an evolutionistic theory according to which the history of humanity describes a continuous progress from an intellectual and cultural 'infancy' to an intellectual and cultural 'maturity.' Far from being despised as a strictly corrupting influence, human technology is here viewed as instrumental to the highly desirable process of civilization (although, it is acknowledged, one frequently attended by evil consequences). It is only, Lucretius affirms, after the introduction of the technological innovations of shelter and fire that monogamy and social communities become practicable (V, 1011ff). Before then humans are entirely promiscuous, given not only to indiscriminate couplings but to rape and the retailing of sexual favours for acorns!

Lucretius's vivid account of human origins in book V of *De rerum natura*, though familiar to Carolingian scholars, was apparently not directly available to Boccaccio. Certainly, in the *Genealogie*, where one would expect to see many allusions to Lucretius's work, the only references to Lucretius are drawn from passages in Servius's commentary on the *Aeneid* and Priscian's work on grammar.[47] Though Boccaccio may not have had direct access to the *De rerum natura*, the more optimistic elements of Lucretius's views on technological innovation are amply reproduced in Vitruvius's *De architectura* II, 1. Happily, Boccaccio's familiarity with this particular passage is not a matter of conjecture; he actually cites it at length in his profile of Vulcan in the *Genealogie* (XII 70, 9) with the objective, or so it would seem, of garnering support for his own unusually forthright acclamation of human technology.[48]

In response to the peculiarities of a corrupt medieval version of the story of Vulcan (which Boccaccio attributes to Theodontius), according to which Vulcan, cast from Olympus, lands on Lemnos where he is raised

by apes – 'symiis' in lieu of Sintians – Boccaccio devises an ingenious allegorical interpretation; by 'apes' is intended mankind, and by Vulcan,
fire. This bizarre story of Vulcan's cohabitation with apes is thus revealed
to be a veiled evolutionistic account of the birth of technology; with the
conquest of fire comes the mastery of a hostile environment and the
advent of a communal lifestyle.[49]

Boccaccio, it should be noted, was by no means constrained to accept
Theodontius's improbable, if colourful, tale of Vulcan's infancy among
the apes, for he was doubtless familiar with the Homeric account of Hep-
haestus's fall and the role of the Sintian people in succouring him from
Leonzio Pilato's Latin translation of the *Iliad* (one cited with great regularity in the *Genealogie*) where Vulcan acknowledges the help received
from Sintians – not simians! – upon landing in Lemnos with the following unambiguous words: 'Ubi me sinties homines statim acceperunt lap-
sum ...' (I, 594).[50] Boccaccio's unaccountable, even perverse, adherence
to the 'symiis' of Theodontius's patently corrupt text in lieu of the 'sinties homines' of Homer's authoritative text testifies to his great fondness
for this evolutionistic model whereby 'apes' are humanized through the
mediation of technology.

It is directly after proposing this allegorical reading of Vulcan's benefaction of apes that Boccaccio reproduces the lengthy passage from Vitruvius's *De architectura* II, 1 to support his interpretation. Boccaccio's
pietistic observation at the end of this citation to the effect that Vitruvius
would have read a very different account in the Pentateuch only confirms, in its obvious insincerity, his clear preference for Vitruvius's comparatively rational account of origins.

Vitruvius, however, was not alone in conveying the Lucretian (Epicurean) view of primitive humanity to the Middle Ages. In his *Satires*, a work
well known to Boccaccio, Horace presents a similarly naturalistic, unvar-
nished view of early humans:

> When living creatures crawled forth upon primeval earth, dumb, shapeless
> beasts, they fought for their acorns and lairs with nails and fists, then with
> clubs, and so on step by step with the weapons which need had later forged,
> until they found words and names wherewith to give meaning to their cries
> and feelings. Thenceforth they began to cease from war, to build towns, and
> to frame laws that none should thieve or rob or commit adultery. (I 3, 99–
> 106)[51]

Acorns, the ubiquitous emblem of Golden Age bounty in the idealized
accounts, here become a source of contention, and cultural progress

goes hand in hand with technological progress. Whereas the poets of the idealized Golden Age accounts describe populations that are either sexually continent or sexually communist – thereby conveniently eliminating the threat of sexual conflict – Horace, in a trenchant line that seems to deliberately mock this naïve perspective, proclaims that long before Helen's day, lust (to put the matter delicately) was the most heinous cause of war: 'nam fuit ante Helenam cunnus taeterrima belli causa' (*Satires* I 3, 107–8).

No less eager to debunk the notion of primitive virtue was Boccaccio's beloved Ovid, whose derisive allusions to the crudity of primeval times are reinforced by glowing references to the urbanity of Augustan Rome. In the *Metamorphoses*, where Ovid deserts his wanton elegiac muse for the more temperate muse of epic, the first Golden Age account (*Met* I) corresponds, in the main, to the traditional model of blissful indolence, whereas in the second (*Met.* XV), a Virgilian variety of virtuous austerity predominates.[52] However, in his *Art of Love*, where he is concerned less with celestial machinery than with social machinations, the Golden Age is not the exclusive patrimony of prehistory, but the rightful heritage of the historical present, and true wealth lies not in sufficiency but in surfeit. In the third book of his *Art of Love*, Ovid celebrates the new Golden Age (one which is quite literally golden), casts a scornful glance at the rustic Arcadias of yore, and snidely observes that the ancient matrons' failure to cultivate their bodies did not reflect a commendable austerity so much as a lack of sophisticated lovers! These flippant observations are capped by what is effectively an epitaph to the traditional Golden Age: 'Let ancient times delight other folk: I congratulate myself that I was not born until now; this age fits my nature well ... because culture is with us, and rusticity, which survived until our grandsires, has not lasted to our days' (*Art of Love* III, 121–8; trans. Mozley, 127).[53]

That Ovid, the same poet whose *Metamorphoses* had conferred the most influential version of the Hesiodic scheme to the Middle Ages, was among the most outspoken exponents of a conflicting, rationalistic assessment of the Golden Age was not a fact likely to have escaped Boccaccio's notice and would, no doubt, have alone prompted Boccaccio to reevaluate the traditional model of degenerative ages. Nor would Boccaccio have been unaware of the similar ambivalence that tempers Seneca's enthusiastic excursus on the virtues of the primitive lifestyle and the pitfalls of technology in his ninetieth *Epistle* – one which ends with the sobering observation that primitive man's excellence did not derive from wisdom, but from ignorance, for men were good by default rather than design: 'It was by reason of their ignorance of things that the men of those days were innocent; and it makes a great deal of difference whether one wills not to sin or has not the knowledge to sin' (Seneca, *Epistle* XC, 46; trans. Gummere, 429).[54]

Such sceptical reevaluations of the idealized Golden Age are not, however, found in the works of classical authors alone. The Latin Christian poet Prudentius, in his *Against the Address of Symmachus* II, derides those fanatical custodians of established custom who unthinkingly advocate the return to a barbarous life of acorns, impiety, and infanticide (a rationalistic interpretation of the myth of Saturn's cannibalism of his own infants): to wit, the so-called Golden Age. He discards the traditional, Hesiodic, scheme of progressive degeneration in favour of one in which the life of the species, patterned on that of the individual, waxes before it wanes:

> ever by slow advances does human life grow and develop, improving by long experience. Such is the changing succession of ages in man, such, one after another, the variations of his nature. Infancy creeps; the child's step, like its purpose, is weak and unsteady; vigorous youth burns with hot blood; then comes the steadfast age of ripe strength; and last of all old age, better in counsel but feeble in energy, declines in body though its mind is cleared. By just such stages has the race of men led its changeful life through differing periods of time. (*Against the Address of Symmachus* II, 315–25)

However, in attempting to replace the artificial, Hesiodic pattern of a gradual falling away from an ideal state with the more organic, Aristotelian model of the life-arc, Prudentius inevitably draws attention to the troubling paradox (one already noted by Seneca) destined to bedevil all such schemes; infancy, though vigorous, presumes a condition of intellectual ignorance, and old age, though blessed with intellectual clarity, is beset by physical frailty. It is in middle age alone, at the apex of this life-arc, that the individual enjoys a perfect balance of knowledge with physical vigor.[55] Since, however, both the Hesiodic and Christian conceptions of temporality tend to stress a linear, end-driven process, the life-arc is a model congenial to neither.

Not surprisingly, Boccaccio's own views concerning the Golden Age represent an uneasy synthesis of many of these elements. His constantly shifting attitudes regarding the relative merits of the ascetic and the Cockaigne-like Golden Age paradigms reveal his own peculiar circumstance: his philosophical sympathies are drawn to the Virgilian model of austerity whereas his sensualistic nature, like Ovid's, cannot help but rejoice in the many cultural amenities of his day.[56] The already challenging task of selecting from among these conflicting strands of primitivism is made far worse by the need to harmonize these selected etiological myths with the Judeo-Christian scheme of universal history. Matters are further complicated by the lack of any true consensus among Christians with regard to primitivism; for every hair shirt ascetic preaching a gospel of cultural austerity, a return to the sober pleasures of the acorn diet, there is an equally commanding theologian or writer who sees certain products of culture – in particular literary and philosophical texts – not as stumbling blocks, but stepping stones on the path to salvation.

The representative of this radical asceticism who immediately comes to mind when considering Boccaccio is, of course, the maniacal Beato Pietro Petroni, that great enemy of culture best remembered for his initially successful campaign to have Boccaccio forswear his 'vain' literary pursuits and turn instead to the cultivation of his soul in preparation for his 'imminent' death. In a letter written to console Boccaccio while he was still reeling from Petroni's dreadful premonitions, the marvellously clear-headed Petrarch observes that he knows 'of many who have attained the highest saintliness without literature' but of 'no one excluded from it by literature' and adds the theologically dubious boast that for every unlettered saint he can name a greater learned one (*Rerum senilium libri* I, 5).[57]

Both of these perspectives are amply represented in Boccaccio's work. In the *Decameron* (IV, Intro.), it is, perhaps, Filippo Balducci who best exemplifies the shortcomings of asceticism when his elaborate scheme to shelter his son from temporal – in particular erotic – attachments backfires; his imposition of an anchoritic lifestyle on his son does not extinguish, but inflames his son's sexual desire. Similar concerns are expressed with an almost polemical vehemence in a passage towards the end of the biographical vignette of Rhea Ylia in *De mulieribus* (c. 1361) where Boccaccio delivers a scathing indictment of those miserly hypocrites who, under cloak of piety, contrive to spare themselves the cost of a dowry by consigning their young daughters to the convent, apparently oblivious to the fact that such constrained abstinence is the surest recipe for making prostitutes of decent women. 'Shameless,' he says, 'are those parents and near relations and anyone else at all who think that others can endure what they themselves flee from as intolerable!' (*De mulieribus* XLV, 7; *Famous Women*, trans. Brown [hereafter cited as Brown]).[58]

Clearly, erotic and cultural ignorance should not be mistaken for moral innocence; a lack of acquaintance with the forms of vice is not the same as saintliness. Nor, as we learn in the story of the scholar and the widow of *Decameron* VIII, 7, should the cultural knowledge inculcated by a rigorous academic education be assumed to have a civilizing effect; the scholar's training does not prompt him to respond to the widow's abuses with a philosophical equanimity, but instead provides a sophisticated means of exacting a supremely cruel revenge.

It is no wonder that Boccaccio never resolves this ambivalence towards culture; though it may, from a moral standpoint, be laudable to follow Filippo Balducci's example by retiring to a little cell on the slopes of one's own 'Monte Asinaio' and subsisting on a meagre diet of prayer and alms, from an intellectual and physiological standpoint, it is natural to crave something more. Moreover, when Boccaccio ventures outside of the austere 'cell' of classical and Christian moral precept, he does not find confirmation of the conventional, pessimistic views of cultural and technological progress, but instead finds himself, like Filippo Balducci's son, casting his eyes with wonder at the cultural marvels of his time. For Boccaccio culture-heroes are not merely glorious shades exhumed from the archives of Greco-Roman myth, nor are extraordinary cultural accomplishments the stuff of legend alone; culture-heroes are real, living individuals, and the dynamic transformations of the intellectual and physical landscape of fourteenth-century Tuscany bear witness to the boldness of their enterprise and magnificence of their vision.[59]

Whereas in his *Commedia* Dante recognizes the cultural supremacy of such men as Giotto, he does so in a context – the 'Terrace of Pride' of *Purgatorio* (cantos X–XII) – expressly designed to illustrate the moral lesson that what to mortal minds appears insuperable and permanent, is, like all temporal things, subject to a seasonal flux and reflux: 'la vostra nominanza è color d'erba, / che viene e va' [your fame is like the colour of grass that comes and goes] (*Purg.* XI, 115–16). The shade of Oderisi advises Dante that just as Giotto has recently supplanted Cimabue, so too is Guido [Cavalcanti] destined to surpass Guido [Guinizelli]. If Giotto's claim to preeminence in the figurative arts remains, for the time being at least, uncontested, the same cannot be said of Cavalcanti's literary fortune, for we are told that a third, unnamed, poet – who, one must assume, is Dante himself – is destined to surpass both Guidos.

The same Giotto who serves Dante as an exemplum of the fleeting nature of temporal fame in *Purgatorio* XI is granted an equally central place in *Decameron* VI, 5, where Boccaccio sings his praises for having almost single-handedly restored to light that long-neglected mimetic art, designed to nourish the intellect of the wise rather than delight the eyes of the ignorant. Indeed, in *Genealogie* XIV 6, 7 we are told that Giotto is not merely a new Apelles (a classical model of mimetic skill), but has actually surpassed him.[60] Similarly, Boccaccio sees in Dante that person who has not only revived the poetry of the ancients, but has restored to it its original sacred function by emulating the method of the greatest poet of all, the Holy Spirit, whose poem, Scripture, is a compilation of the most sacred hidden truths: 'Dico che la teologia e la poesia quasi una cosa si possono dire, dove uno medesimo sia il suggetto; anzi dico più, che la teologia niuna altra cosa è che una poesia di Dio' [I say that theology and poetry may almost be considered one and the same thing where their subjects are the same; indeed, I would go further and declare that theology is nothing less than a poem by God] (*Trattatello in laude di Dante* [prima redazione], 154).[61]

For Oderisi's fugitive *color d'erba* Boccaccio substitutes an entirely different, though no less evocative, hue: the enduring refulgence of gold. The idea that such culture-heroes as Giotto and Dante are heralds of a new Golden Age – one implicit in all these allusions to a resurgence of classical skills and values – is made explicit in Boccaccio's *Life of Petrarch* (*De vita et moribus Domini Francisci Petracchi de Florentia*). Here, Petrarch is described as a reincarnated Virgil (9), the first postclassical poet to be honoured by a laurel crown, and one whose excellence seems to confirm the restoration of the Saturnian reign: 'I truly believe that it seemed to all that the happy time and the reign of Saturn, vanished for so long, had been restored' (16–17).[62] In short, Boccaccio sees Florence as the birthplace – natural or intellectual – of a new pantheon of culture-heroes: Giotto, Dante, and Petrarch. (Though born in Arezzo, Petrarch, according to Boccaccio, was 'nourished at the breast of the Muses ... in Florence' [*De vita Francisci Petracchi*, 1].)

In Dante's *Commedia* the figure who best epitomizes this spirit of constant striving, of going beyond the preconceived limits of our mortal condition, is without question Ulysses. It is Dante's Ulysses who rallies his shipmates with the call to seek experience of the unknown, the unpeopled world beyond the sun, asserting that they were not made to live like brutes, but to follow the path of virtue and knowledge:

a questa tanto picciola vigilia
    d'i nostri sensi ch'è del rimanente
non vogliate negar l'esperïenza,
    di retro al sol, del mondo sanza gente.

Considerate la vostra semenza:
fatti non foste a viver come bruti,
ma per seguir virtute e canoscenza
(*Inf.* XXVI, 114–20).

to this brief waking-time that still is left
    unto your senses, you must not deny
experience of that which lies beyond
the sun, and of the world that is unpeopled.
    Consider well the seed that gave you birth:
you were not made to live your lives as brutes,
but to be followers of worth and knowledge.
(Mandelbaum)

Despite his obvious partiality for Ulysses's magnanimous character, Dante finally characterizes Ulysses's voyage as a reckless flight, a 'folle volo' (XXVI, 125), and ironically fulfills Ulysses's desire to experience a 'mondo sanza gente' [world without people] by consigning him to a world of flame-swathed larvae; not men, but incandescent shades. It is particularly significant, therefore, that in his ardent defence of Alcibiades in *De casibus*, Boccaccio makes a point of redeeming Ulysses by asserting that his example is worthy of emulation; to do otherwise, Boccaccio maintains, is to succumb to the blandishments of a decadent inertia:

Far more famous was Ulysses, battered across the seas, than Aegisthus immersed in sensual pleasures beneath the sky of his native country; we condemn the licentious inertia of the latter whereas we praise and admire the wanderings of the former. (*De casibus* III 13, 9)[63]

It is in this defence of Alcibiades in *De casibus* that we find Boccaccio's most impassioned expression of this proto-Romantic notion that the state of striving is a praiseworthy, even pious, effort to realize the potential intimated by that spark of divinity contained by each of us:

Seldom do I find a person content with his lot, and it is no wonder: by God's gift we contain a soul with a fiery power, celestial origin, and insatiable desire for glory. This spirit, when it is noble and not weakened by bodily sloth, can neither be enclosed nor kept in the small prison of the breast; it bounds forth and with its greatness embraces the whole earth and easily

transcends the stars, and driven by the flame, burns with sublime desires ...
(*De casibus* III 13, 2–3)[64]

What is to be condemned is not this Ulyssean seeking after greater things but rather the failure to chart one's course in accordance with the precepts dictated by reason. Indeed, in the next sentence Boccaccio informs us that it is the vice of the magnanimous to seek a route to higher things other than that sanctioned by reason: 'Vitium igitur ingentium spirituum est altera via quam permictat ratio velle celsiora conscendere' (*De casibus* III 13, 4). By the same token, the desire to know everything is praiseworthy provided that the quest for knowledge is mapped in accordance with morality: 'Ogni cosa del mondo a sapere / non è peccato, ma la iniquitate / si dee lasciare e quel ch'è ben tenere' [To know all worldly things is not a sin, but iniquity must be abandoned and good embraced] (*Amorosa visione* III, 31–3). It is consistent with this philosophy that in the *Filocolo* Boccaccio has the resolutely moral Florio deliver a version of Ulysses's 'picciola orazione' (*Inf.* XXVI, 112ff.) in which, however, the declared objective is not so much the acquisition of knowledge in the abstract as it is a concrete bid for eternal fame:[65]

> ho io fatti chiamare voi, sì come a me più cari, per caramente pregarvi che della vostra compagnia mi sovegnate, e meco insieme essilio prendiate [...] E in verità questo, di che io e te e gli altri priego, il mio partire di qui, credo che degl'iddii sia piacere, acciò che i miei giovani anni non si perdano in accidiose dimoranze: con ciò sia cosa che noi non ci nascessimo per vivere come bruti, ma per seguire virtù, la quale ha potenza di fare volante fama le memorie degli uomini etterne, così come le nostre anime sono. (*Filocolo* III 67, 12)

> I have called for you, since you are the ones most dear to me, to beg you earnestly to aid me with your company, and accept voluntary exile along with me ... And in truth I believe that what I am asking of you and the others, namely my departure from here, is the will of the gods, so that my youthful years may not be wasted in slothful delay. Furthermore, we were not born to live like beasts, but to follow virtue, which has the power by means of fleeting fame to make the memories of men eternal, just as our souls are. (Cheney, Bergin, 218)

Readers familiar with the *Commedia* will, perhaps, have distinguished in this passage not only the unmistakeable voice of Dante's Ulysses – the exhortation to shun bestiality and seek virtue ('non ci nascessimo per vivere come bruti, ma per seguire virtù') calqued on Ulysses's oration in *Inf.* XXVI – but the more muffled voices of Dante's Virgil and Brunetto. 'Accidiose dimoranze,' a condemnation of slothful delay, recalls Virgil's appeal to a bone-weary Dante to cast off his sloth and resume his journey, for fame, Virgil reminds him, eludes those who spend their days lazing about on feather beds (*Inf.* XXIV, 43ff), and the phrase 'fare volante fama le memorie degli uomini etterne' [to make the memories of men eternal] brings to mind Brunetto's lesson concerning how it is that man makes himself eternal: 'come l'uom s'etterna' (*Inf.* XV, 85). This other-world chorus of the damned seems to have been assembled by Boccaccio for the exclusive end of validating temporal fame and vindicating those great-spirited men such as Ulysses, Alcibiades, and their ilk ready to desert hearth and home – in short, all that is familiar – and leap into the abyss of the unknown, of eternity, for the sake of temporal fame.

Any suspicion that this bold advocacy of Ulysses is nothing more than a symptom of youthful brio is quickly dispelled by a glance at *De casibus* VIII, 1, Boccaccio's most elaborate defence of temporal fame. 'Fame,' Boccaccio declares in this passage, 'should not be neglected nor trodden upon by idleness, nor detested as an empty and superfluous thing. Rather, it should be sought with all of one's strength *for God's sake*' (*De casibus* VIII 1, 18, emphasis mine).[66] In short, the Ulyssean journey of the sort contemplated by Florio (the same that had been condemned by Dante) is redeemed by Boccaccio, for whom it represents not only a way of combating the natural inclination to idleness, but a means of serving God. Importantly, Florio's restless spirit does far more than triumph over sloth; it goads him to undertake a great pilgrimage that culminates in his conversion to Christianity. Boccaccio clearly views this desire to cast out in search of greater things as evidence of the divine spark that God has granted each of us; a fiery spirit of celestial origin whose nature is to rise ever upwards in search of glory.[67]

The revolutionary quality of Boccaccio's bold advocacy of the proto-navigator Ulysses is best appreciated against the backdrop of the deeply ambivalent and often resolutely negative portraits of navigation found in the traditional Golden Age accounts, where nautical technology is usually linked with mercantile activity and viewed as a source and symptom of cultural decadence.

If Boccaccio is inclined to lionize Giotto for restoring the figurative arts and Dante for redeeming literature (and the vernacular), it is the Italian merchant of the fourteenth century, a sworn enemy of idleness, who is implicitly credited with the burgeoning of a vital middle class and the restoration to civic life of a measure of cultural sophistication and intellectual vitality last seen in classical times. Indeed, the merchant is granted the role of protagonist in the resuscitation of civil life itself; the restless striving of this latter-day Ulysses does not result in the catastrophic death of his shipmates but guarantees their spiritual and social salvation.[68] Through this identification with a redeemed Ulysses, the merchant-explorer is effectively promoted to the rank of culture-hero.

Boccaccio's involvement in the mercantile world, both as a young intern for the Neapolitan branch of the Bardi bank and as the son and grandson of merchants, contributes, no doubt, to this notable tendency to celebrate merchants and the mercantile experience.[69] However, if the merchant is a culture-hero for Boccaccio, he is a hero only in the sense that he is a protagonist in the dramatic transformation of fourteenth-century society; his role in this process is not so much romanticized as recognized. For Boccaccio, a merchant is, like Ulysses, magnanimous in the sense that his great spirit seeks to 'embrace the whole earth.' The merchant's trajectory is not the fixed course of the Christian pilgrim but a wild foray into the very thick of life, both its vice and its virtue (to paraphrase Dante's Ulysses).[70] So much, at least, is apparent from the nuanced and highly variegated portrait of merchants presented in the *Decameron*.

According to the view expressed in the traditional Golden Age model, Boccaccio, insofar as he engaged in mercantile activities, would be affiliated with that very activity, navigation, that had come to epitomize the application of human ingenuity (nautical technology) to immoral ends. In his *Odes*, Horace writes:

> Vain was the purpose of the god in severing the lands by the estranging main, if in spite of him our impious ships dash across the depths he meant should not be touched. Bold to endure all things, mankind rushes even to forbidden wrong. Iapetus' daring son [Prometheus] by impious craft brought fire to the tribes of men. (*Odes* I 3, 21–8)[71]

Boethius echoes these sentiments in his elegiac recollection of an age before navigation:

> Not yet did they cut deep waters with their ships,
> Nor seeking trade abroad
> Stand strangers on an unknown shore.
> (*Consolation*, II, metrum V, 13–15)[72]

For all their eloquence and affecting rhetoric, these denunciations of navigation and mercantile activity are in complete and obvious contradiction to Boccaccio's reality, his lived experience. The moral lessons preserved by literary convention are entirely out of joint with the evidence supplied by historical observation; merchants, far from serving, like Charon's earthly protégés, to ferry us into the bowels of a cultural hell, actually fulfill the civilizing function of conveying culturally useful knowledge from shore to shore.[73]

It is not by chance that the nautical metaphor undergirding the whole of the *Genealogie* is one that casts Boccaccio, the mythographer, as an intrepid sailor, even, as we shall see, a new 'Prometheus,' braving the perils of an unfamiliar sea in search of the scattered flotsam of classical antiquity. According to this model, the acquisition of knowledge is best pursued not in the protective seclusion of one's study but through a dynamic and potentially dangerous immersion in the vital realm of experience. In Boccaccio's time the recovery of the lost literary treasures of classical culture often involved arduous excursions to those rare places such as Monte Cassino where ancient parchments had miraculously weathered successive centuries of barbarian invasions and cultural neglect.

In commenting on his sources for the *Genealogie*, Boccaccio notes that the information supplied by his former teacher of astronomy, Andalò di Negro, is particularly trustworthy because, 'he not only knew the motions of the stars according to the laws discovered by the Ancients – which is our way of learning them – but he had traveled nearly all over the world, visiting every clime and horizon, and had used his experience [experientia] and observation to inform himself first hand of what we learn by mere hearsay [auditu]' (XV 6, 4; Osgood, 112). In his famous description of the ascent of Mount Ventoux in *Familiares* IV, 1, Petrarch expresses his frustration that the Thessalian Mount Hemo is not as conveniently accessible as Mount Ventoux, for he would like to establish, once and for all, the truth or falsity of the contradictory claims made by Livy and Pomponius Mela concerning Philip of Macedonia's success in seeing two seas, the Adriatic and the Black, from its summit. The erudition of the ancients, mere 'hearsay,' must submit to the test of experience, and the armchair philologist must cede to the humanist-explorer.[74]

Interestingly, even Seneca, that paragon of stoic morality – the author, as we have seen, of an important declamation against cultural progress – implicitly advocates cultural advancement through nautical exploration in what is ostensibly an encomium of a natural phenomenon, the wind:

He [God] gave us the winds so that we might get to know distant lands. For man would have been an untaught animal and without experience of affairs if he had been circumscribed by the limits of the land where he was born. He gave us winds in order that the advantages of each region might become known to all; but not in order to carry legions and cavalry or to transport weapons to destroy mankind. (*Naturales quaestiones* V 18, 14)[75]

A similarly bittersweet evaluation of navigation is to be found in Seneca's *Medea*:[76]

Too bold was he who first in fragile ship broke through the treacherous seas, and looking behind him at his lands trusted his life to the fickle blasts, and cutting the water with uncertain course put his faith in thin wood – too slim a boundary laid down between the ways of life and death [...]

Our fathers knew an age of honesty, far removed from deceit. Each man sluggishly clung to his own shores and grew old on his paternal fields, rich with little, unknowing other wealth than what the native soil produced. The Thessalian pine drew together into one the communities of a well divided world [...]

Now the sea has yielded and is subject to all men's bidding. No famous Argo made by the hand of Pallas and bearing the oars of kings is sought for; any ship may now wander over the deep. Every boundary has been moved, and cities have placed their walls in new lands: the globe, accessible in every part, has left nothing in the place where it was. The Indian drinks from the frozen Araxes, the Persians imbibe the Elbe and the Rhine. An age will come in future years when Ocean shall loosen the chains of things and the huge earth lie open and Tethys shall uncover new worlds, nor will Thule then be the uppermost part of the world. (Act 2, ll. 301–79)[77]

Seneca seems unresolved whether to condemn the first men who dared to brave the treacherous seas for their reckless courage or congratulate them for taming the sea. Nor is it clear whether we are to lament the loss of insular communities or celebrate the creation of what is effectively a global community. The gloomy prophecy that concludes this passage – the apocalyptic vision of a chaotic reshuffling of land and water – would, however, seem to blot out whatever benefits the sea may have conferred on humanity by facilitating this panculturalism.[78]

A far more optimistic assessment of the advantages that accrue to humanity through nautical exploration and the resulting intermingling of far-flung cultures was almost certainly familiar to Boccaccio from

Ambrose's *Hexameron*:

> The good sea ... by which distant people are connected [quo distantes pop-
> uli copulantur], by which the dangers of wars are removed, by which the
> rage of barbarians is contained, provider of assistance in time of need, ref-
> uge in danger, pleasure for the senses, soundness of health, union of the
> separate, shortening of routes, respite for the weary, source of revenues, sus-
> tenance in times of scarcity. (*Hexameron* III, v, 22; *PL* 14, col. 165)[79]

However, even Ambrose's optimistic inventory of the advantages granted
us by the sea seems restrained when compared with Boccaccio's exuberant praise of navigation in the Proem of *Genealogie* X:

> The most ancient men believed that the Mediterranean, hemmed in by the
> coasts of Africa, Asia, and Europe, and noted for a thousand isles, was intro-
> duced by Hercules's labour ... between Abila and Calpe, the western prom-
> ontories that Pomponius Mela calls the columns of Hercules, into our lands
> from the Ocean. By which means, God generously seeking our good, great
> advantages were bestowed upon mortals. Indeed, what are we to think of
> boats, designed by human ingenuity with the aid of divine illumination and
> built with human artifice, now cutting through the waves with oars, now
> propelled by wind-filled sails, in which all manner of heavy cargo is trans-
> ported? What are we to think of the courage of those who first entrusted
> themselves to the unknown waves and untested winds? It is truly awesome to
> consider. Nevertheless, in most cases, though not always, there was courage
> enough or good fortune in those daring ones who transported in great jour-
> neys across the sea not, I must add, on their chartered course alone, but car-
> ried by a rapid flight, gold, and the other metals of the East, purple-dyed
> clothing and perfumes, precious stones and ivories from the West, exotic
> birds and balsams, woods foreign to our forests, gums and other distillations
> from trees, and roots not native to all lands, from which are compounded
> innumerable medicines and balms for both sick and healthy; and, what is
> hardly a negligible contribution to humanity, such sea journeying has made
> it possible for the Cimbri and the Celta [both Celtic peoples] to have knowl-
> edge from the opposite side of the world of the Arabs, the Red Sea and the
> distillations of the Sabian woods. That the Hyrcanian [from a province of
> ancient Persia] and the inhabitant of Tanays are thus acquainted with the
> Hesperides of the Atlantic and taste its golden fruits. That the gelid Hyper-
> borean and Sarmatian [a northern, nomadic tribe related to the Scythians]
> can thus look upon the fervid Ethiopians and the Nile and the plagues of

Libya. Likewise, that the Spaniard and the Moor can, visited, themselves visit the Persians, Indians, and Caucasians. And that the distant Thulians [from Thule, an island in the North Sea] tread on the Taprobane shore [Sri Lanka] and, while exchanging their goods, not only observe each others' customs, laws, and ways of life, but, what is more, when he observes the other and notes the ways in which his world is distinct and that he is not sur-rounded by the same ocean as the other, he mixes rites, establishes the exchange of merchandise, forms friendships, and, as they teach their language, they learn the foreign language, and thus it is that those, the distance of whose lands had rendered strangers, are united and joined in concord by navigation. (1–3)[80]

The striking novelty of this portrait of cosmopolitanism is seen most distinctly against the foil of Boethius's *Consolation of Philosophy* where Philosophy belittles those who pant after temporal glory, observing that the world is but a point in comparison with the heavens, and that only a negligible fraction of this tiny point is actually inhabited. Moreover, Philosophy continues, even this exiguous area lacks true unity, for it is subject to internal divisions due to geographic distances, and linguistic and cultural differences:

in this little habitable enclosure there live many nations, different in language and customs and in their whole ways of life; because of the difficulties of travel, and differences of language, and the rarity of trading contacts, the fame not merely of individual men but even of cities cannot reach them all. (*Consolation* II, prose 7)[81]

A standard topos deriving from Cicero's 'Dream of Scipio' (a passage from the last book of *De republica*), this meditation on the cosmic insignificance of the earth and the vanity of fame was available to the Middle Ages through Macrobius's commentary (II, 5–9), and is evoked in Dante's acerbic appraisal of the earth as the 'aiuola che ci fa tanto feroci' ['the little threshing floor / that so incites our savagery'] (*Par.* XXII, 151; Mandelbaum). Boethius alone stresses the rarity of human intercourse and discourse as a source of further alienation; not only is the earth a negligible point in space, but it is characterized, despite its smallness, by geographic, cultural, and linguistic disunity. It is this nightmarish vision of radical segregation that Boccaccio seeks to replace with his own, admittedly earth-bound, model of universal solidarity.[82]

In his consolatory letter to his friend Pino de' Rossi, whose political views had resulted in his forced exile, Boccaccio (whose affiliation with Pino had prompted him to undertake a voluntary exile in Certaldo) dwells at length on the topic of cosmopolitanism:

> Vogliono ragionevolmente gli antichi filosofi il mondo generalmente a chiunque ci nasce essere una città; perché, in qualunque parte di quello si truova il discreto, nella sua città si ritruova; né altra variazione è dal partirsi o essere cacciato da una terra e andare a stare in un'altra, se non quella ch'è, in quelle medesime città che noi, da sciocca oppinione tratti, nostre diciamo, d'una casa o d'una contrada partirsi e andare ad abitare in un'altra. E come i popoli hanno nelle loro particulari città al bene essere di quelle singulari leggi date, così la natura a tutto il mondo l'ha date universali. In qualunque parte noi andremo, troveremo l'anno distinto in quattro parti; il sole la mattina levarsi e occultarsi la sera; le stelle igualmente lucere in ogni luogo; e in quella maniera gli uomini e gli altri animali generarsi e nascere in oriente, che nel ponente si generano e nascono; né alcuna parte è ove il fuoco sia freddo e l'acqua di secca complessione, o l'aere grave e la terra leggiera; e quelle medesime forze hanno in India l'arti e gl'ingegni che in Ispagna; e in quello medesimo pregio sono i laudevoli costumi in Austro che in Aquilone. (*Consolatoria a Pino de' Rossi*, 12–16)

With reason the ancient philosophers hold that for everyone born here, the whole world is one city, for a thoughtful person will, no matter what part of the world he should find himself in, consider himself to be in his own city. Nor is the change brought about by leaving or being chased from one country and going to stay in another any greater than that caused by moving from one home or neighbourhood among those same cities that we, swayed by foolish opinion, call our own, to live in another. And just as different peoples have given specific laws to their own particular cities to ensure the cities' wellbeing, in like fashion, Nature has assigned universal laws to all the world. Voyage where we may, we will find the year divided into four parts; the sun rise in the morning and hide itself in the evening; the stars shine equally in all parts; and men and the other animals generated and born in the same manner in the orient as in the occident. Nor is there any place where the fire is cold or water of a dry nature, or the air heavy and earth, light. And the arts and intellects are as vigorous in India as in Spain, and laudable practices are esteemed as much in the austral as in the arctic region.

Since, Boccaccio concludes, it is clear that conventional ethnographic and geographic distinctions are more apparent than real, the circumstance of moving, or being forcibly moved, from one land to another is more accurately termed a 'permutazione' [change of place] than an 'esilio' [exile] (16). Though this brief excursus on the world-citizen was most probably inspired by Socrates's declaration (as reported in Cicero's *Tusculan Disputations* V 37, 108) that he considered himself to be a native and citizen of the whole world, Boccaccio's curious elaboration of this motif – in particular his observation that human intelligence and technical accomplishments are qualities of the species as a whole and not the exclusive property of any given population – reveals, I would argue, a genuine commitment to this notion of pan-human unity and equality.[83] It is an attitude clearly expressed in the life of Nicostrata in *De mulieribus*, where Boccaccio acknowledges Italy's privileged place with respect to cultural and intellectual accomplishments, but notes that 'great splendour' has been achieved under other skies as well:

> With its many blessings Italy was the most flourishing of any region of the world and glittered with almost divine light. But such great splendour was not gained only under her skies. From Asia came opulence and royal furnishings. Noble blood originated with the Trojans, although the Greeks made a substantial contribution. The Egyptians contributed the arts of arithmetic and geometry. From the Greeks, too, came philosophy, eloquence, and almost all of the mechanical arts. Saturn while in exile instituted agriculture, which at that time was known only to a few. The unfortunate worship of the gods came from the Etruscans and from Numa Pompilius. Public laws first emanated from Athens and were then enacted by the senators and the emperors. Simon Peter brought from Jerusalem the papacy and true religion. Military training, however, was discovered by the ancient Romans who used this as well as their strength of spirit and body and their devotion to the public to acquire for themselves dominion over the whole world. (*De mulieribus* XXVII, 9–11; Brown, 109)[84]

Thus, Boccaccio becomes a dynamic point of confluence for two conflicting views of primitivism: the idealized image of Golden Age primitivism espoused by some of his most beloved authors on the one hand, and the 'anti-primitivistic' celebration of human cultural and technological advances on the other. However, even in this radical ambivalence, Boccaccio is following a long-established tradition.

Like Boccaccio, Virgil too had both witnessed and personally benefited from the profound transformations wrought by an extended period of political and cultural renaissance: the Augustan Golden Age. It is not surprising, therefore, that his work betrays a similar ambivalence towards culture. This is most evident in the *Georgics* I, when he considers the innovations wrought by Jupiter:

> The great Father himself has willed that the path of husbandry should not be smooth, and he first made art awake the fields, sharpening men's wits by care, not letting his realm slumber in heavy lethargy. Before Jove's day no tillers subdued the land. Even to mark the field or divide it with bounds was unlawful. Men made gain for the common store, and Earth yielded all, of herself, more freely, when none begged for her gifts. 'Twas he that in black serpents put their deadly venom, bade the wolves plunder and the ocean swell; shook honey from the leaves, hid fire from view, and stopped the wine that ran everywhere in streams, so that practice, by taking thought, might little by little hammer out divers arts. (121–33)[85]

Here, the introduction of a work ethic by a divine taskmaster is viewed as a necessary evil, the only effective antidote to lethargy. If the loss seems incalculable, the gain, the invention of 'divers arts,' is not easily dismissed. That Virgil should invoke the myth of an age of spontaneously generated natural bounty in a didactic poem concerned with agriculture and animal husbandry is not unexpected; the juxtaposing of these ideas is at least as old as Hesiod's *Works and Days*. What is most distinctive in Virgil's use of the motif is his assertion that the demise of this Golden Age was neither punitive nor inevitable but was instigated, rather, by Jupiter, if not for our physical pleasure, at least for our intellectual profit – to 'sharpen our wits by care.'[86]

The ambivalence inherent in this influential passage from the *Georgics* is reflected in the number of conflicting interpretations that it inspired. Notable among these, and of particular importance because they occur in works well-known to Boccaccio, are those presented by the fourth-century poet Claudian in his *De raptu Proserpinae* and the thirteenth-century poet Jean de Meun in his continuation of Guillaume de Lorris's *Roman de la Rose*.

Claudian has Jupiter deliver a scathing indictment of the Golden Age in which he characterizes it as an age of indolence and sloth; since 'extravagance is a dissuasion from a virtuous life and abundance muddies the minds of human beings,' Jupiter 'acted so that poverty, becoming ingenious, should challenge men's sluggish spirits and gradually investigate the hidden ways of nature, and so that cleverness should give birth to skills and practice nourish them' (*De raptu*, Bk. III, 28–32).[87]

Though little more than a paraphrase of *Georgics* I, 125ff, this passage is notable for its neat resolution of the Virgilian ambivalence in favour of the arts and other cultural institutions. Claudian pointedly presents all technological innovation in a strictly positive light.

Jean de Meun, in a passage that draws from both Virgil's and Ovid's Golden Age accounts, takes the opposite position. Dwelling almost exclusively on the negative consequences of Jupiter's coup d'état (20,100ff), he depicts Jupiter as an astute but unprincipled schemer whose introduction of agricultural labour is just the sort of benefit one might expect from a god who thinks nothing of castrating his own father.

The task of defining Boccaccio's own attitude towards Jupiter is complicated somewhat by the occurrence of no less than three Jupiters in his *Genealogie.* His euhemeristic account of the first of these Jupiters, the king of Athens (II, 2), suggests a literary kinship with Claudian, for this Jupiter, a primal lawgiver responsible for domesticating the rustic Athenians through the introduction of marriage and religion, is rewarded with kingship (and with the honorific title 'Jupiter' – his given name is Lisanias). It is significant that in attempting to convey the abject depravity of the age preceding that of Jupiter, Boccaccio grants particular importance to sexual promiscuity, for, he maintains, before the institution of marriage women were considered common property, a perspective consistent with that expressed by Vitruvius.[88] Here, the age that preceded Jupiter's reign is condemned on the grounds that dissolute sexuality admits the formation of neither genealogical distinctions (blood lines) nor territorial distinctions (property lines) and is, therefore, basically antagonistic to the development of social and political institutions.[89]

The second Jupiter (V, 1), an Arcadian king, is likewise noteworthy for his benefaction of humanity. Boccaccio cites Theodontius's belief – apparently a rationalization of Ovid's account in *Metamorphoses* I – that this Jupiter, opposed to 'King' Lycaon's habit of feasting on human limbs, conquers the latter and is thereafter called 'Jupiter' in recognition of this successful strike against savagery.

The third Jupiter (XI, 1), a son of Saturn, is credited with, among other things, having suppressed the revolt of the Giants – another episode from Ovid's account in *Metamorphoses* I. After he has chased his dissolute father from the realm and married his sister, he shrewdly devises a campaign of self-promotion. Once he has sown both his wild oats and his cult, he devotes himself to the betterment of his species. If Jupiter's decision to marry his sister casts doubt on his suitability to govern (the notorious endogamy of Homer's Olympians is better suited to the heavens than to the earth), his successful campaign to abolish cannibalism – a custom that had been widespread during his father's reign (535) – tends to confirm the moral character of his mission.

For all their superficial variation, these three faces of Jupiter collectively furnish the portrait of that archetypal culture-hero whose primary benefaction to humanity consists in the introduction of social laws and agricultural technologies – an innovation which results in the elimination of both sexual promiscuity and cannibalism, thereby redeeming Silver Age industry while simultaneously tarnishing the Golden Age lustre.[90]

The notion that indolence breeds sexual prurience is ubiquitous in ancient and medieval literature. Even the author of Genesis finds it necessary to temper the easeful qualities of a life surrounded by natural, spontaneously generated bounty with the seemingly superfluous addition of agricultural labour; Adam is placed in the garden of Eden not, as one might have thought, to pursue a life of ease but rather to 'till it and keep it' (2.15).[91] It is the charming Oiseuse, a personified Idleness, who opens the garden of erotic delectation to the Lover in the *Roman de la Rose*. The state of idleness is one of susceptibility to erotic impulse; among the idle Cupid's tyranny is assured. When Fiammetta's husband, solicitous of her health, proposes a curative jaunt to a seaside resort, he unwittingly contributes to her further deterioration, for the same amenities so effective in curing physical ailments are detrimental to the spiritual health of those afflicted by Cupid's arrows:[92]

> Quivi la maggiore parte del tempo ozioso trapassa, e qualora più è messo in essercizio, si è in amorosi ragionamenti, o le donne per sé, o mescolate co' giovani; quivi non s'usano vivande se non dilicate, e vini per antichità nobilissimi, possenti non che a eccitare la dormente Venere, ma a risuscitare la morta in ciascuno uomo. (Boccaccio, *Elegia di madonna Fiammetta* V 17, 4)

> There, for the most part, time is spent in idleness, and when it is spent more actively, women, either alone or in the company of young men, speak of love; there people consume nothing but delicacies, and the finest old vintage wines strong enough not only to excite the sleeping Venus but also, if she were dead, to bring her back to life inside every man ... (*Elegy of Lady Fiammetta*, trans. Causa-Steindler and Mauch [hereafter cited as Causa-Steindler and Mauch], 73)[93]

That Golden Age indolence should have resulted in a virtuous, wholesome lifestyle is, of course, entirely at odds with this common perspective.[94]

This starkly ambivalent attitude towards the advent of culture is perhaps most vividly illustrated in Boccaccio's profile of Ceres in *De mulieribus*, his book in praise of famous (though, as Boccaccio himself notes in
the Proem, not necessarily virtuous) women. Here (*De mulieribus* V) Boccaccio presents a euhemeristic account of the birth of agriculture that
rapidly gives way to a highly personal and unresolved assessment of culture. He does not know, he says, whether to condemn or to praise Ceres
for her contribution of agriculture: that a population of bestial cave
dwellers has been transformed into city dwellers, thoughtless ciphers
into contemplative thinkers, acorn-eaters into well-nourished consumers
of grain – who could possibly condemn such a change? Then again, he
continues, who can praise Ceres for ending an era of rustic simplicity,
subject to nature's law alone, unfamiliar with the refined foods that ini-
tiate the gradual down-spiraling towards vice, unacquainted with private
property, hard labour, poverty, slavery, hatred, war, and, worst of all, fam-
ine? Although Boccaccio concludes with the affirmation that, all things
considered, the wholesome rusticity of the Golden Age is much to be
preferred to the corrupt sophistication of the present age, such statements can hardly make us forget the equally cogent arguments offered
in favour of culture.

A similar ambivalence can be discerned in the *Allegoria mitologica*. The
programmatic insertion of the great culture-hero Prometheus at two critical junctures – first as God/Adam, then as Christ – reveals Boccaccio's
true objective: that of proposing an agonistic model of history in which
the progressive forces of culture grapple with the degenerative tendencies of an aging nature.[95] The apparent awkwardness of this identification
of Christ with Prometheus is resolved by the consideration that Boccaccio
generally adopts an allegorized interpretation of Prometheus's gift of fire
in which fire is understood to be a gift of divine and spiritual, not secular and technological, knowledge. (The introduction to humanity of
technology is attributed, rather, to that other fire god, Vulcan.)[96] From
this proposition that Christ's benefaction of humanity is somehow
'Promethean,' that is, pedagogic and intellectual in nature, can be inferred the precept that salvation is itself somehow predicated on knowledge (a perspective that no doubt provided a great measure of comfort to
a young man intending to forsake a life of mercantile activity for one of
scholarship).

If it is to Ovid's *Metamorphoses* that Boccaccio is most indebted for the
structure and imagery of the *Allegoria*, the ideological content has an
unmistakably Christian cast. Though Ovid's text develops the notion of a

postcataclysmic renewal, the restoration is conceived in almost strictly biological terms as a replenishment of the human species. For Boccaccio, the physical restoration of the species is far less important than its ethical, intellectual, and spiritual restoration through law and education. In the *Allegoria* the legal element takes the form of Mosaic (Old Testament) Law and Christian (New Testament) Law. These laws find a sanctuary in a marvellous garden – a metaphor, as Manlio Pastore Stocchi has argued, for the Church – where they are carefully cultivated by Pallas Tritonia (a figure for divine wisdom), who prunes, weeds, and irrigates the garden with such skill that the young shoots grow strong and the trees soon flower and bear fruit (10). Through the application of Christian doctrine, the garden of the Church has succeeded in restoring a Golden Age bounty. Though a personified Wisdom is entrusted with the upkeep of this garden, it is clear that the actual work must be carried out by her ministers, the 'wise' clerics and scholars charged with nurturing and disseminating the fruits of Scripture.[97]

Beneath this 'new Prometheus' it is hard not to see the figure of the medieval compiler, whose work of restoration consists in the philological task of reassembling a lost intellectual tradition. Indeed, in the *Allegoria*, the 'new Prometheus,' Christ, does not create new laws ex nihilo, but gathers together long dispersed, chaste laws: 'castaque leges, in sui robore duraturas, vagantes in loco debito recollegit' (9). This interpretation is confirmed by Boccaccio's similar use of the figure of Prometheus in the *Genealogie*. Here, Boccaccio explicitly likens his task of gathering the scattered fragments of the 'shipwreck' of classical culture to that of reconstituting a body (I, 7), a task, he avers, that would be better suited to a new Prometheus:[98]

> And yet I shudder to embark on so huge a task; why, if another Prometheus should appear, or the very one who, as poets tell, upon a time made men from clay, I hardly think they would be equal to the task, let alone me. (*Genealogie* I, Proem; Osgood, 11)

In addition to being identified with the author-compiler, the figure of Prometheus is later granted a more universal function as a symbolic representation of the learned educator, who transforms the untutored clay of bestial ignorance into a cultured and virtuous human being. This Prometheus, like that of the *Allegoria*, is associated with Athena (here under her Roman name Minerva), who represents divine Wisdom.

In sum, the task of cultural restoration is entrusted to pedagogical culture-heroes: those, like Boccaccio himself, committed to the gargantuan task of reconstituting the *membra disjecta* of classical learning and of harmonizing the members of this newly resurrected body with Christian doctrine. That this ambitious pursuit should occasionally spawn Horatian monsters is not at all surprising.

As one of the outstanding writers and scholars of his time, Boccaccio is clearly to be identified with the budding pantheon of culture-heroes that includes Giotto, Dante, and Petrarch. As a banker's son and member of the flourishing middle class, Boccaccio is additionally associated with that colourful hero of popular culture: the Ulyssean figure of the merchant. As a result, the sententious, moralizing Boccaccio inclined to idealize the primitive simplicity of yore is constantly at loggerheads with that other Boccaccio, a progressive advocate of cultural and technological innovation. It is no wonder that Boccaccio vacillates between models of temporal blessedness.

In the *Allegoria* this intersection of cultural decadence with cultural renaissance is mediated by a culture-hero, Prometheus, identified with Christ and with the dissemination of Christian doctrine. Prometheus's traditional role as technological benefactor of humanity through the gift of fire here cedes, as we have seen, to a Christian allegory of divine illumination. There is, however, another extensive description of the ages of the world in which the role of human technology is addressed.

In his literal commentary on *Inferno* XIV, the canto in which the enigmatic figure of the Old Man of Crete [Veglio di Creta] is introduced, Boccaccio, having first appealed to the authority of Euhemerus to discard the popular notion that a divine Saturn was the temporal king of Crete, goes on to laud Golden Age chastity, citing the first lines of Juvenal's famous encomium of Golden Age modesty in his sixth Satire: 'Credo pudicitiam, Saturno rege, moratam in terris' [chastity, I believe, still lingered on earth during the reign of Saturn] (*Esposizioni* XIV, lit., 61).

In his allegorical commentary on the same canto Boccaccio proposes that the golden head represents the Edenic, prelapsarian state of the human race: one of complete innocence. In Dante's account of the imposing colossus the variation of metals does little more than provide the means for a superficial distinction among the otherwise undifferentiated stages of an abstract, quite literally iconic, process of moral decrepitude. Such generic distinctions do not disrupt but rather confirm the pattern of an incremental, temporal decline. In a move so subtle that it has not, to my knowledge, received any critical attention, Boccaccio subverts this traditional function by mining the symbolic potential of each individual metal in such a way as to endow each stage with a distinct personality. This method results in a dramatic revision of the conventional model; instead of making a facile correlation of the various metals of the colossus with the usual degenerative sequence, Boccaccio, beneath the screen of a traditional moralization, has surreptitiously advanced what in any other context would be immediately recognized as an encomium to human physical and cultural advances.

Here the colossus's golden head represents the beginning of time, the state of human innocence and purity. The silver arms and chest are, remarkably enough, described as having a higher lustre than the gold head, 'quanto l'ariento è più lucido metallo che l'oro' [for silver is a shinier metal than gold] (27). Likewise, human beings of this second period are brighter and more beautiful than the First Parents. In an argument reminiscent of that used in the *Decameron* by Michele Scalza (VI, 6) to prove that the Baronci were among God's first creations (to wit, the proverbial ugliness of the Baronci reflects the fact that they were created before God had perfected his technique!), Boccaccio maintains that the process of human reproduction – an exclusively postlapsarian phenomenon – has the effect, over many generations, of refining the species as a whole. In other words, Boccaccio is espousing an evolutionistic theory whereby humanity is, at least aesthetically, improved by sexual reproduction.

This perspective stands in stark contrast to the usual Platonizing view, one expressed by Dante in *Paradiso* XIII (73–8), where Nature is likened to an artist working with a trembling hand, capable only of imperfect reproductions of the divine idea; direct divine creation, of the sort that occurred in the case of both Adam and Christ, is the only means of achieving a perfect impression of the divine seal.[99]

Boccaccio's apparently blasphemous assertion that biological creation achieves, over time, a perfection superior to direct, divine creation, is tempered somewhat by his observation that though more beautiful than God's first creation, the *umana generazione* of this silver period is less valuable, just as silver is less valuable than gold (28). If the age of silver gives the lie to original beauty, the intellectual accomplishments of the age of bronze – the introduction of speculative science and of the liberal and mechanical arts – have the equally unflattering effect of recasting Edenic innocence as ancient ignorance. This allegation is somewhat less controversial, since no less an authority than Dante had argued that whereas Adam and Christ were endowed with insuperable wisdom, knowledge could be garnered through experience alone (a topic discussed at length in *Paradiso* XIII).[100] In this passage, it is patently knowledge and not wisdom that accrues to *l'umana generazione* over time. Admiration for the celestial bodies fosters the birth of speculative knowledge which, in turn, is organized into the sciences and the liberal and mechanical arts: 'dalla ammirazione de' corpi superiori e ancora dagli ordinati effetti della natura nelle cose inferiori cominciarono a speculare e dalla speculazione a formare le scienze, l'arti liberali e ancora le meccaniche' (*Esp.* XIV, alleg., 29). Whereas the men and women of the silver age have a silvery gleam, those of the bronze age resonate, like the sonorous metal that gives their age its name, with the fame of intellectual accomplishment: 'sì come il rame è più sonoro metallo che alcuno de' predetti, divennero gli uomini infra se medesimi più famosi e di maggior rinomea che quegli davanti stati non erano' (*Esp.* XIV, alleg., 29). However, and here we are reminded of the sadistic refinements of the scholar in *Decameron* VIII, 7, the cultural boons of intellectual knowledge are very soon offset by the perverse application of knowledge. With the increase in knowledge comes a proportional increase in wicked acts as people begin to adopt the recently acquired knowledge for vicious, rather than virtuous, ends: 'adoperando le discipline acquistate più tosto in cose viziose che in laudevoli' (*Esp.* XIV, alleg., 30).

Edenic innocence no longer eludes scrutiny but is conflated with ignorance, and primacy, once synonymous with physical perfection, comes to describe the fumbling crudity of a neophyte – albeit divine – artist. Boccaccio's intellectualistic disdain for innocent ignorance echoes Seneca's belief that there is no merit in being innocent through ignorance and finds further support in Petrarch's contention (expressed in his consolatory letter to Boccaccio in the wake of the Pietro Petroni melodrama) that 'the road to virtue through ignorance is level perhaps, but too easy,' and that 'uncouthness, however devout, is not comparable to literary devotion' (*Rerum senilium libri* I, 5; *Letters on Family Matters*, trans. Bernardo et al., 25).[101]

Though this rationalistic approach cannot help but weaken the ideological scaffolding of the Edenic and Golden Age traditions, Boccaccio's aim is not to dash our cherished reminiscence of the temporal paradise but to create a new, accessible paradise thereby substituting the tangible pleasures of the real, for the insubstantial allurements of the ideal.

The Escape to Paradise

When he sermonizes from the pulpit of a moralist, Boccaccio, as we have seen, tends to idealize the natural state and deplore the corrupting influence of culture. When he speaks as a poet, and an advocate of poetry, he becomes a great champion of high culture, painting an idealized portrait of Florence as a birthplace of poets and the site of a new Saturnian reign. When he speaks as a scholar, one inclined to adopt a rationalistic approach in confronting the numerous discrepant mythological variants, he reveals that beneath the image of an earthly deity, a 'Saturn' or 'Jupiter,' lies an idealized historical leader and that the dream of a Golden Age reflects an analogous tendency to romanticize a past – whether realistic (Arcadia and its avatars) or fantastic (the Cockaignes, Elysiums, and Avalons) – perceived as having offered a simpler, freer, and more fulfilling life.

The problem, of course, is that more often than not these discordant voices are intermingled in Boccaccio's texts. Hence, though one certainly finds arguments in which a moralistic, poetic, or rationalistic approach predominates, such arguments are usually tempered by traces of contrasting perspectives. Boccaccio, moralist, demands a return to the wholesome rusticity and 'chaste laws' of an earlier 'natural' age uncorrupted by culture; Boccaccio, poet and writer of *novelle*, revels in the technological and social dividends of culture, eagerly endorsing the Ulyssean desire to embrace all aspects of the world – including, it would seem, one's neighbour's husband or wife!; Boccaccio, scholar, sees knowledge as a route to blessedness and, a pragmatist, demands that this paradise be empirically feasible – with respect to both geographical location and sociopolitical organization. Where, then, can one find a place that satisfies such diverse and self-contradictory demands?

Simply put, the *Decameron* describes just such a paradise. Here, the *brigata* escapes to the outskirts of Florence: a place where nature strikes a balance with culture, labour with recreation, chastity with erotic play, and so forth. However, since the *Decameron* represents the culmination of this 'synthetic' paradise, and will be treated at length in a chapter of its own, the remainder of this chapter will be devoted to an examination of two descriptions of the Golden Age – one in the *Elegia di madonna Fiammetta* and the other in the *Comedia delle ninfe fiorentine* – that seem, in many respects, to serve as 'shadowy prefaces' to the models of temporal beatitude (moral and physical) presented in the *Decameron*.

Like the paradisal pleasure gardens of the *Decameron* frame narrative, these earthly paradises materialize not on the mythical margins of the world – the remote west of the Hesperides or distant east of Eden – but in the periphery of cities, seeming to sprout almost spontaneously from the interstices of nature and culture. It is neither in the dark wood nor in the populous city that golden equilibrium reigns, but in that liminal region where dissolute nature is domesticated by culture, and decadent culture is infused with the restorative sap of nature. The result of this reciprocal arrangement is to produce a magical precinct – the villas and gardens of the city periphery – replete with both natural and cultural amenities: diminutive Edens, scaled down Saturnias. The very marginality of these paradisal places lends them a fragility; like the iridescent spheres of soap bubbles, their beauty is perfect, but fleeting, for the opposed forces that they briefly compass place too great a strain on their fabric. Nevertheless, though such perfection may be ephemeral, it is, in pointed contrast to Eden, fully accessible – that is, to those rare individuals willing to undertake the pilgrimage.

While it seems unlikely that Boccaccio was acquainted with Horace's sixteenth *Epode*, the escapist variety of Golden Age portrayed in this poem bears an uncanny resemblance to Boccaccio's own model in the *Decameron*, for it anticipates Boccaccio's notion of a Golden Age that can be recuperated by fleeing the corruption of the city for the relative peace of the country.[102] Horace, responding to the self-inflicted devastation of Rome's civil wars, proposes that the only course left open to the virtuous few who remain is to flee the city and seek out the Blessed Fields and Blessed Isles, places where the land spontaneously gives up its bounty, the honey flows from trees, and so forth. He ends his *Epode* with the resonant proclamation:

> Jupiter set apart these shores for a righteous folk, ever since with bronze he dimmed the lustre of the Golden Age. With bronze and then with iron did he harden the ages, from which a happy escape is offered to the righteous, if my prophecy be heeded. (*Epode* XVI, 63–6)[103]

In Seneca's *Phaedra*, Hippolytus reprises this notion that it is possible to escape to a terrestrial paradise, but in lieu of casting the escape as a heroic, collective exodus to some geographically remote location – the Blessed Fields or Isles – he argues that the escape to paradise is achieved simply by fleeing the city for the forest: 'There is no life so free and innocent, none which better cherishes the ancient ways, than that which, forsaking cities, loves the woods' (Act II, 483–5).[104]

Boccaccio was not just passingly familiar with this passage but apparently found it so affecting that he chose to reproduce large portions of it almost verbatim in his *Elegia di madonna Fiammetta*.[105] Buffeted by erotic anxiety, Fiammetta is moved to sing – in words drawn from Hippolytus's

excursus on the uncorrupted joys of nature – the praises of the forest
and the Golden Age. However, while Hippolytus envisions a life free of
subjection to kings (there is no serving of monarchs or desire for monarchy [490]), laws (for there is no crime [494]), or religion (no oxen are
slaughtered on bloodied altars [500]), Fiammetta actually introduces
kingship (the Saturnian reign), legislation ('pure laws'), and, it is
implied, religion ('primitive rites'):

> Oimè, niuna è più libera, né sanza vizio, o migliore che questa, la quale gli
> primi usarono, e che colui ancora oggi usa il quale, abbandonate le città,
> abita nelle selve. O felice il mondo, se Giove mai non avesse cacciato
> Saturno, e ancora l'età aurea durasse sotto caste leggi! però che tutti alli
> primi simili viveremmo, Oimè! che chiunque è colui li primi riti servante,
> non è nella mente infiammato dal cieco furore della non sana Venere,
> come io sono; né è colui, che sé dispose ad abitare ne' colli de' monti, subi-
> etto ad alcuno regno: non al vento del popolo, non allo infido vulgo, non
> alla pistolenziosa invidia, né ancora al favore fragile di Fortuna, al quale io
> troppo fidandomi, in mezzo l'acque per troppa sete perisco. (*Elegia* V 30,
> 15–17)

> Oh, no other life is without vices or more free or better than the life lived by
> primitive people or by the person who still today abandons the city to live in
> the forest. How happy the world would be if Jupiter had never chased Sat-
> urn away and the golden age still lived on under pure laws! We would all
> then be living like these early people. Alas whoever follows the rites of the
> ancients does not burn as I do, with the blind fury of the corrupt Venus, nor
> is the man who chooses to live in some neck of the mountainous woods a
> subject of any kingdom; he is not subject to whims of the populace, nor to
> the untrustworthy mob, nor to pestilential envy, and not even to the fragile
> favour of Fortune, for now I, from having trusted it too greatly, perish from
> too much thirst while in the midst of water. (Causa-Steinler and Mauch, 91)

While Hippolytus does speculate that this sort of country life would
reproduce the freedoms enjoyed by those who lived in the primal age
(526) and follows this conjecture with a traditional 'Golden Age' description (527–64), it is significant that no mention is made of an ideal
kingship, pure laws, or primitive rites. Though Boccaccio's use of the
Senecan text is most often cast in terms of a slavish reproduction, these
subtle, but significant, discrepancies indicate that Boccaccio has altered
his Senecan model to better correspond to his own idiosyncratic view of

temporal blessedness. Boccaccio certainly shares Hippolytus's view that temporal monarchies tend to breed despots; religious practices, corruption; and communal living, crime. However, he is far too pragmatic to dispense with these social and political institutions altogether.[106] Like his own character Pampinea, he is acutely aware that 'le cose che sono senza modo non possono lungamente durare' ['nothing will last for very long unless it possesses a definite form'] (*Dec.* Intro. 95; trans. McWilliam, 20); the complete elimination of such organizing structures – the usual trappings of culture – is less likely to result in the peaceable kingdom envisioned by Hippolytus, than in the brutal free-for-all described by Horace in the *Satires*: a lawless world peopled by shapeless creatures ready to cudgel and claw each other over every unclaimed acorn (*Satires* I 3, 99). Well aware of the pitfalls of temporal kingships, positive law, and organized religion, but equally leery of Hippolytus's anarchic utopianism, Boccaccio opts for a divine monarch (rule without despotism), 'pure' laws (laws without constraint), and 'primitive' rites (a religion free of petty doctrinal disputes, hierarchies, and other sources of contention). Boccaccio's subtle modifications to Hippoloytus's somewhat naive picture of an untrammeled, vice-free ('libera et vitio carens' [483]) life in the forest result in a synthesis that seems to anticipate the escapist paradises of the *Decameron*, where the implementation of moderate laws (based on 'natural reason') and a revolving – hence 'democratic' – system of kingship are integral components of the *brigata*'s sociopolitical experiment.

Significantly, though Fiammetta's words may seem at first little more than the traditional elegy to a paradise lost, closer scrutiny reveals that she believes that such a loss is by no means irreparable. Even as she writhes beneath the yoke of a 'dissolute' love, she applauds those others who have succeeded in returning to a Golden Age of sorts: one whose coordinates are not mythical but historical, not metaphysical but moral. The Golden Age, Fiammetta proposes, can be recovered by those select few who have the moral resolve to leave the pestilential city and establish themselves in the wholesome country: 'e che colui *ancora oggi* usa il quale, abbandonate le città, abita nelle selve' ['or by that person *who still today* abandons the city to live in the forest'] (*Elegia* V 30, 15; Causa-Steinler and Mauch, 91; emphasis mine).[107]

It would seem that in this passage Boccaccio not only provides a blueprint for the hybridous variety of *locus amoenus* that he later constructs in the *Decameron*, but also anticipates the basic exodic pattern that undergirds the whole of the *Decameron* frame narrative. Here Fiammetta tells us that the virtuous are able to gain immunity from the plagues of envy, impiety, even of fortune itself, by taking refuge in the country and assuming a temperate lifestyle of the sort enjoyed in the Golden Age. That the plague is unbridled passion of one sort or another is confirmed by Boccaccio's consistent use of the word 'pestis' to describe immoderate desire. For example, in the profile of Thisbe in *De mulieribus*, Boccaccio describes youthful passion as a plague: 'Passionate desire is ungovernable; it is the plague [pestis] and the disgrace of youth' (XIII, 14).[108] A similar view is expressed in *De casibus* where concupiscence is called an 'infanda pestis' [unspeakable plague], and a 'laberintum' [labyrinth] (IV, 19; 7, 11). In *De casibus* we find gluttony, too, described as a plague, one contrasted with Golden Age sobriety (VII); and in the *Esposizioni*, the introduction of the possessive pronouns 'mine' and 'yours' is likened to a 'veleno pestifero' [pestilential venom] that spells the end of Golden Age equality (VII, 49ff). In short, all forms of sensual incontinence contribute to a metaphorical plague – with historical repercussions even more devastating than those of the bubonic plague.[109]

Another invocation of the Golden Age that anticipates the sociopolitical experiment of the *Decameron* is found in the twenty-sixth book of the *Comedia delle ninfe fiorentine*.[110] Here, the traditional perspective of the Golden Age as a historically remote period of moral virtue is invoked as a pointed contrast to the present age of dissolute love. Pomena, the goddess of fruits, treats us to an encomium of an idealized variety of Golden Age, praising the 'chaste laws' and the abundance of foods, in particular acorns, bestowed on a faithful people by the earth. Indeed, Pomena affirms that the temperate spirit of those times was such that human libido, like that of other animals, was restricted to acts of procreation. Soon after, however, a virginal Earth, perversely eager to seek her own damage, welcomed the reign of Jupiter and was rapidly carved up by the tools of agriculture. In short measure humanity was reduced to its present lamentable condition of corruption and perversity. Pomena, solicitous of these dissolute times ('alle età dissolute') has dedicated herself to the cultivation of a meticulously organized specimen garden which, it is implied, somehow serves as a prophylactic to further deterioration. Certainly, the allegory of an organized garden as a means of counteracting the breakdown of social order is one of the guiding themes of the *Decameron*.[111]

Clearly, Boccaccio's ambivalence regarding the traditional Golden Age paradigm by no means implies that he believes human beings cannot partake in an idyllic existence. Here, the specimen garden – a symbol of the fruitful union of human artifice and nature – becomes the model for a new Eden; restoration does not demand a return to crude primitivism so much as a productive marriage of nature and culture, natural liberties tempered by 'chaste' laws. Indeed, the *Decameron* proposes what is effectively a blueprint for such an existence, one in which the true Golden Age is implicitly associated with a golden mean. Both Golden Age indolence and the decadent culture of the present age nourish a sexually dissolute lifestyle. In the *Decameron*, Boccaccio proposes to create a middle ground, an earthly sanctuary sheltered from both these extremes: a place where muses are women, and women, muses.

chapter 2

Local Myths of Origin:
The Birth of the City and the Self

Physical Restoration: The Fertile Loam of Tuscany

That the parables of physical or cultural rebirth prominent in so many of Boccaccio's youthful works unfold against the exquisite natural scenery of the Fiesolan mountains is no coincidence. Indeed, this area, though peripheral with respect to fourteenth-century Florence, is one that had by long-standing tradition been identified as the geographic womb of Florence itself, instrumental not only in contributing to its physical population but also in shaping its cultural, intellectual, and genetic identity.[1]

According to Giovanni Villani's authoritative account in the *Cronica*, Fiesole's primacy is not defined in relation to Florence alone; it is the first city in all of Europe. In the wake of the Great Deluge, the world, Villani tells us, is divided into three parts, Africa, Asia, and Europe, assigned, respectively, to the descendants of each of Noah's three sons: Shem, Ham, and Japheth. When Attalante, Japheth's descendant, voyages to Europe to claim his patrimony he is advised by his astrologers to set out for the uninhabited region of Tuscany, where he settles on a Fiesolan mountain. It is, then, in this, the most salubrious land in Tuscany, famed for its healthful winds, curative waters, and propitious stars, that Attalante builds the great city of Fiesole: the same ancient citadel whose crumbling foundations, Villani claims, are yet visible (*Cronica* I, 7). The historical primacy suggested by such 'archeological' evidence draws additional confirmation from a (false) etymology of the name Fiesole itself: 'fu nominata Fia sola, cioè prima sanza altra città abitata nella detta parte' [it was named *Fia sola*, that is, the first, with no other inhabited city in that region] (*Cronica* I, 7).[2]

If the initial chapters of Villani's chronicle are remarkable for their transparently nationalistic agenda (and for the striking nonchalance with which Scriptural references are marshaled to provide a 'historical' basis for this biased account), at least one popular chronicle of Boccaccio's time, the *Libro fiesolano*, is even more unabashedly propagandistic. In the second chapter of this delightfully ethnocentric history, we are informed that the hills of Fiesole were not merely the cradle of European civilization, but of all postdiluvian civilization:

> Fue uno primo signore, lo quale ebbe nome Atalam Egipter: e sua moglie fue una bella donna, la quale ebbe nome Eletta: con li quali era Appollonio, grande maestro di strolomia: i quali per suo consiglio tutti i loro fatti ordinavano. Ellino con esso lui elessono sopra a tutti i detti confini, per lo più sovrano luogo, quello dov'è Fiesole, *la quale fu la prima città fatta nel mondo, poi che fue il diluvio dell'arca Noè*: e questo fue eletto per Appollonio, lo più sano aire e per lo migliore pianeto e di maggiore vigore che si trovasse.
> E per che fue la prima città fatta si fue in tutto chiamata Fiesole.[3]

> There was a great lord whose name was Atalam Egipter: and his wife was a beautiful woman whose name was Eletta. With them was Appollonio, a great master of astronomy: they arranged all their actions according to his advice. They and he together chose before all these aforementioned territories, as the most excellent place, that where Fiesole is found, *which was the first city to be built in the world after the deluge of Noah's ark*. And this [site] was chosen by Appollonio, as having the most wholesome air and most auspicious and vigorous astrological influence.
> And as it was the first city to be founded it was, for this reason, named Fiesole.

So outrageous is this claim of universal primacy that Villani's assertion that Fiesole was the first European city seems conservative by contrast. That Boccaccio, at least in his youth, was taken by this notion of Fiesolan primacy is suggested by a remarkable passage in the *Filocolo* in which he not only asserts that a hill in central Tuscany was preserved from the ravages of the deluge, but goes so far as to offer an 'empiric' basis for this opinion:

> Nella fruttifera Italia siede una picciola parte di quella la quale gli antichi, e non immerito, chiamarono Tuscia, nel mezzo della quale, quasi fra bellissimi piani, si leva un picciolo colle, il quale l'acque, vendicatrici della giusta

ira di Giove, quando i peccati di Licaon meritarono di fare allagare il mondo, vi lasciò, secondo l'oppinione di molti, la quale reputo vera, però che ad evidenzia di tale verità si mostra il picciolo poggio pieno di marine conchiglie. (*Filocolo* V 8, 1)

There is a little part of fruitful Italy that the ancients called (not inappropriately) Tuscia, in the middle of which, between lovely plains, there rises a little hill, which was left there by the flood which avenged the righteous anger of Jove when Lycaon's sins justified the flooding of the world. This is the opinion of many, and I think it right, since as evidence of its truth can be seen the little knoll full of sea shells. (trans. Cheney, Bergin, 379)

Here, a central hill of Tuscany (and most of these early histories agree in assigning Fiesole a place of centrality with respect not only to Tuscany but to the whole of Europe) is granted a historical role analogous to that generally reserved – in the classical tradition – for the Phocian Parnassus; it represents a terrestrial place miraculously preserved from the universal devastation of a great deluge.[4] Moreover, that the deluge referred to in this passage is not just a local inundation but identical with the Universal Deluge of Genesis 7 can, I would argue, be confidently inferred from Boccaccio's allusion to hill-borne 'marine conchiglie' [seashells], a topos ubiquitous in patristic and scholastic excurses on the Noachic Deluge and clearly invoked in Boccaccio's entry for 'Elsa' in *De montibus* where he observes that though the Elsa passes through many places, 'of all the sea-things that it scours with its current, it uncovers only some empty shells, white with age, the greater part of which are broken or half-consumed.' These shells, Boccaccio believes, were 'left in that region by the great deluge by which the human race was nearly destroyed [diluvium illud ingens quo genus humanum fere deletum est] when the sea bottom was churned up by the great agitation of the waters' (*De montibus*, [*de fluminibus*], 368).[5]

The literary motif of hill-borne shells seems to have been first introduced by pagan authors, who submit this strange phenomenon as a graphic illustration of the universal principle of change (evidence that the mountains were once a seabed and vice versa). Ovid uses the motif to illustrate the principle of change in *Metamorphoses* XV, 264ff. as does – strangely enough – the second-century Christian apologist Tertullian in *De pallio* (II). In the *Esposizioni* Boccaccio paraphrases a passage from Pomponius Mela's *Cosmographia* (first century) that describes the discovery of shells, anchors, and other evidence of a vanished sea in the sands of the Numidian desert: 'le quali cose assai ben paiono testimoniare quivi altra volta essere stato mare' [which things testify quite clearly that the sea had once been there] (XIV, lit., 19).

Whereas in the *Esposizioni* faith surrenders to reason and the presence of 'conche marine' is submitted in support of a principle of change, in the *Filocolo* it is apparent that Boccaccio is guided by Christian moralizations of the motif. Indeed, for Christian authors of sacred history, compelled by their faith to see the hand of divine providence in all temporal phenomena, such hill-borne seashells bear witness not to the vicissitudes of geology but to the radical upheaval caused by the waters of the Universal Deluge.[6]

Such Christian moralizations of the classical motif of hill-borne shells would have been readily available to Boccaccio in Isidore of Seville's seventh-century *Etymologies* (XIII, 22: *On Floods*) or Rabanus Maurus's ninth-century *De universo* – works frequently cited by Boccaccio in his scholarly compendia.[7] In the *Etymologies* Isidore identifies three historically distinct deluges: the first, a universal flood in the time of Noah; the second, an Achaean flood in the age of the patriarch Jacob and Ogygus (the first ruler of Thebes); and the third, 'Deucalion's flood,' a Thessalian flood in the age of Moses and Amphictyon (king of Athens). It is, notably, to the first and most devastating of these floods, the Universal Deluge of Genesis 7, that Isidore attributes the presence of mountain-borne shells:

> The first flood occurred at the time of Noah, when the Almighty was offended by the sins of humans. The entire world was covered, everything was destroyed, there was a united expanse of sky and sea. To this day we observe evidence of this in the stones we are accustomed to see on remote mountains, stones that have hardened with shellfish and oysters in them, and often stones that have been hollowed out by the waters.[8]

That Boccaccio should elect to dress this episode of sacred history in pagan myth – Deucalion's Flood – in *Filocolo* V, 8 is hardly exceptional; the application of an identical methodology in his treatment of the Universal Deluge in the *Allegoria mitologica* has already been noted. Evidence that this particular typological association was current in the fourteenth century may be found in Iacopo della Lana's commentary on Dante's *Commedia* where we read that poets prefer casting sacred truths in the form of mythological fictions, 'sichè volendo parlare del diluvio, del quale per Dio fatto assapere a Noè e alla moglie, sicome è scritto nel Genesis, fingeno e diceno a Deucalion ed a sua moglie' [so that wishing to speak of the Deluge, of which Noah and his wife were apprised by

God, as is written in Genesis, they spin a fiction and speak of Deucalion and his wife].[9] Boccaccio's penchant for typological allegory of this sort is noted by Attilio Hortis, who observes that this variety of 'bizzarro travestimento' [bizarre costuming] so dear to Boccaccio occurs only rarely in Petrarch's works.

Although the numerous correspondences between the Ovidian account of Deucalion's flood and the Biblical account of the universal flood made a symbolic association between the two all but inevitable, there is a critical difference; in the former the deluge is not truly 'universal,' for the peaks of Parnassus continue to project from the water. It is here that Deucalion and Pyrrha land their small skiff, for the sea has covered all else: 'nam cetera texerat aequor' (*Met.* I, 318).

Inconsequential as this detail may seem, it actually represents the infinite difference between an absolute and a relative, a universal deluge as opposed to a partial (if admittedly vast) inundation. This distinction is not lost on Lucan, who thinks it worthwhile to further accentuate this aspect of Ovid's account by allowing that only one of the twin peaks of Parnasssus projects from the ravening waters:

> When the Flood covered the earth, this height [Parnassus] alone rose above the level and was all that separated sea from sky; and even Parnassus, parted in two by the flood, only just displayed a rocky summit, and one of its peaks was submerged. (*The Civil War* [*Pharsalia*] V, 71–8)[10]

A single peak may seem insignificant in the scope of things, but it represents nothing less than the difference between the survival or extinction of the human race, the only anchorage in an otherwise unbroken expanse of water. In the Genesis account no such terrestrial havens from the swelling waters remain:

> The waters swelled so mightily on the earth that all the high mountains under the whole heaven were covered; the waters swelled above the mountains, covering them fifteen cubits deep. (7.19–20)

The difficulty, therefore, that arises from Boccaccio's decision to represent the Tuscan hill of *Filocolo* V, 8 as a place somehow immune to the Noachic Deluge is that this particular deluge is defined by its universality, the absolute and total absence of such terrestrial sanctuaries; God's grace alone supplies a means of escape – the salvific ark. Since, however, the evidence – the presence of seashells – advanced to prove that this Tuscan hill was preserved from the universal deluge ('il quale l'acque ...

vi lasciò' [which hill the waters ... left there]) would seem to indicate that it was nonetheless covered by the waters of the deluge – and how could it be otherwise?, for it is no towering Parnassus, but a *picciolo colle* (little hill) – it seems likely that Boccaccio's principal objective is to draw attention to the extraordinary privilege of this Tuscan hill which has been spared the sorry fate of the countless other mountains torn up and reduced to a slurry by the rushing waters of the deluge.[11]

Almost three hundred years after Boccaccio's death Milton, a poet no less sensitive to the dramatic potential of this powerful image of mountains wrenched up from the seabed, has the archangel Michael prophesy that the mount of paradise, the highest of all hills, will 'by might of waves be mov'd / Out of this place, push'd by the horned flood' (*Paradise Lost* XI, 830–1). As sanctity, in Milton's view, is never an inherent quality of terrestrial places, but the endowment of the 'Men who there frequent, or therein dwell' (XI, 838), even Eden does not enjoy the special privilege that Boccaccio grants the Tuscan hill of *Filocolo* V, 8.

Considered on their own, cut off, that is, from the theological context that produced them, these strange accounts of mountains, fugitive or fixed, are easily dismissed as the unconnected and idiosyncratic fantasies of two historically and culturally distant poets. However, both Boccaccio and Milton (the one as thoroughly conversant with the patristic and scholastic literature as the other) are actually responding to a single, rather eccentric belief sanctioned by some of the most prominent theologians of the Middle Ages. Despite the clarity of Scripture with regard to the universal quality of the deluge – which, we are told, covered even the highest mountain peaks by a depth of fifteen cubits – a handful of medieval Christian theologians and exegetes were moved to make an exception to this rule: the terrestrial paradise.

In the ninth century, long before Dante decided to perch Eden on the crest of his purgatorial mountain, Rabanus Maurus (influenced, perhaps, by the Venerable Bede) speculated that the terrestrial paradise was located in a part of the east so far removed from the places of human habitation that even the welling waters of the Deluge could not reach it. Several centuries later, the authors of the *Glossa ordinaria* refined this thesis by situating the terrestrial paradise in the ocean's centre on an 'altum situm' [high place] where the waters of the deluge hardly touched it ('unde aquae diluvii illuc minime pervenerunt' [*Glossa ordinaria Patrologia Latina* (*PL*) 113, Col. 0086A]): it was not distance alone, but elevation that accounted for the relative immunity of Eden.[12] In his twelfth-century *Hexameron*, Abelard, dispensing with the qualifier 'hardly,' simply states that the diluvial waters could not reach the terrestrial paradise ('Unde nec aquae diluvii, quae totam nostri orbis superficiem altissime cooperuerunt, ad eum pervenire potuerunt' [*PL* 178, Col. 0775D]).

Milton, profoundly antagonistic to the notion that any material place might enjoy a sanctity independent of the spiritual condition of its occupants, enlists the authority of the archangel Michael to quash these patristic and scholastic theories of Edenic immunity once and for all. Boccaccio, less concerned with the theological implications of these theories than with their poetic and symbolic potential, readily exploits this motif of immunity to invest his beloved Tuscany with a suggestive semblance of Eden. Though neither Parnassus nor the terrestrial paradise, Boccaccio's Tuscan peak seems to have been expressly designed to encompass important characteristics of both.

Another passage identifying a Fiesolan hill as a place of immunity (or relative immunity) from the deluge is found in the curious etiology of Florence presented in the *Comedia delle ninfe* XXXVIII. Here, we read of an antediluvian oak ('piantata anzi che Giove allagasse il mondo' [planted before Jove flooded the world (24)]) located on the future site of Florence – indeed, on precisely the spot that would later be occupied by the temple of Mars (the future baptistery of St Giovanni). Boccaccio's insistence here on a biological (albeit exclusively botanical) continuum bridging the pre- and postdiluvial epochs attests once again to his desire that Tuscany be associated with a sacred antiquity, immunity, and a potential for regeneration.[13]

A more sober, historical basis for the association of mountain tops with the preservation and regeneration of the human species is furnished by Boccaccio's beloved Seneca, who presents an unusually realistic account of diluvial calamity in the *Naturales quaestiones*. Particularly striking is Seneca's description of the scattered survivors, forced to seek an uncertain sanctuary in the highest mountain peaks:

> Only on the highest ranges of mountains are there shallows. To these heights men have fled with children and wives, driving their cattle before them. Communication and exchange has been cut off among the miserable survivors, since the water has filled the ground that lies lower. The remnants of the human race clung to whatever peaks are highest. (*Naturales quaestiones* III, 11–12)[14]

A 'Senecan' prejudice in favour of rationalistic interpretations of mythical accounts of generation and regeneration is particularly evident in Boccaccio's discussion of Deucalion in *Genealogie* IV, 47. Here, Boccaccio informs us that Barlaam, an erudite Calabrian monk familiar to Boccaccio from his youthful years in Naples, claimed to have read in some ancient Greek chronicle that once the diluvial waters had subsided, the men and women who had taken refuge in mountain caves were approached by Deucalion and Pyrrha, who, comforting them, led them back to their homes. Boccaccio follows Barlaam's relatively strait-laced account with the mythographer Theodontius's more extravagant opinion. Deucalion and Pyrrha, claims Theodontius, having summoned this same handful of mountain-bound survivors from their caves, discovered that the number of women far outstripped that of men since the women, more fearful of the advancing waters than the men, had taken refuge sooner. Under the circumstances, it was considered expedient that the women, having first veiled their heads so that anonymity might serve as an antidote to modesty, 'mix' indiscriminately with the few remaining men so that their numbers might be more rapidly replenished![15]

That Boccaccio should choose to report Theodontius's picturesque thesis of postdiluvial repopulation attests not only to his fondness for mingling erotic and etiological themes but also, and perhaps more importantly, to his keen desire to furnish a rational underpinning for the widespread association of mountain sanctuaries with human generation and regeneration. In Boccaccio's hands the same Parnassian promontory that had witnessed the chaste birth of men and women from stones becomes the site of an orgiastic free-for-all, one, moreover, that enjoys a certain immunity to moral censure for it is implicitly officiated by *Venus genetrix* and underwritten by God's injunction to multiply.[16]

Although a cursory glance at such passages may convey the impression that Boccaccio, inspired, perhaps, by the venerable models of *translatio imperii* and *translatio studii* has taken the liberty of fashioning a third species of *translatio* – the translation of the site of biological regeneration from Phocis and Armenia to Tuscany – such a conclusion is probably unwarranted. Though by no means free of patriotic sentiment, Boccaccio characteristically exhibits a refreshingly open-minded, cosmopolitan perspective; Tuscany is not alone in furnishing the world with cultural benefactors. In the *Genealogie*, for example, he observes that it is hardly remarkable that so many different people dwelling in far-flung parts of the earth have been credited with the discovery of such boons as medicine and honey, for thoughtful, ingenious people are to be found everywhere: 'quod pluribus hactenus attributum est, nec propterea admirandum; possibile enim est talium multos variis in locis repertores fuisse, cum ubique ingenia meditationesque valeant' (VII, 65). At the end of the Arachne vignette of *De mulieribus*, Boccaccio dryly notes that only a dunderhead ('stolide mentis') would imagine that artistic – or other – skills were the exclusive property of any single individual.[17]

It seems entirely feasible that this notion of a pluralistic, simultaneous origin of cultural amenities may be taken to apply to human origins as well. Certainly, Augustine clears the way for such a model of multiple biological origins in his treatment of the postdiluvial distribution of fauna in the *City of God* XVI, 7. How is it, Augustine asks, that such animals as wolves, propagated not by spontaneous generation but sexual reproduction, are to be found in even the remotest islands? If, he reasons, all but two wolves were annihilated in the course of the deluge (the two preserved in the ark), it follows that the presence of wolves in such improbable places must have been achieved either by swimming (an impossible feat) or through human conveyance (improbable – and manifestly self-destructive). Though Augustine allows that this conundrum may be solved by the usual strategy of invoking divine (more specifically angelic) intervention, he proposes a less far-fetched solution. It is possible, he argues, that such creatures were produced by the earth itself in a sort of replication of the first creation ('And God said, "Let the earth bring forth living creatures of every kind"' [Genesis 1.24]). Augustine's pietistic theory of a belated reactivation of Earth's productive spark is surprisingly close to Ovid's account of the spontaneously generative earth of the golden age (*Met.* I, 101–2), and is consistent in many respects with the Epicurean views expressed by Gaius Velleius in Cicero's *De natura deorum* (I 20, 53; II 10, 27), who credits the earth both with the nurturing of seeds received in her 'womb' and with the spontaneous generation of plants. These broad theological, poetic, and philosophical testaments to earth's generative capacity are supplemented by the more specific, 'scientific' observations made by Pomponius Mela to the effect that the Nile's fecund silt produces spontaneous births (*De chorographia* I, 49) and that the eroded funeral mound of Antaeus is paradoxically restored by rain (*De chorographia* III, 98). Other well-known instances of spontaneous generation or regeneration would naturally have included Virgil's golden bough (*Aeneid* VI, 143–4), Ovid's Myrmidons who, generated from ants, serve to replenish the population of a plague-ravaged Aegina (*Met.* VII, 517–660), and Dante's adaptation of the Virgilian golden bough motif in the guise of the self-renewing reeds that skirt the shores of the purgatorial isle (*Purg.* I, 134–6).[18]

A particularly evocative instance of this theme of spontaneous generation is found in *Teseida* XI, 20, where Boccaccio speaks of a virgin forest whose ancient, self-renewing trees shelter countless generations of nymphs and fawns: 'e' fauni e le lor greggi permutati / fosser da lei, che continuamente / di sterpi nuovamente procreati / si ristorava, in etterno durando' ['it was thought that it had seen the nymphs and fauns and their flocks often come and go, while it continually renewed itself with freshly created stock, as it stretched into eternity'] (McCoy, 292–3).[19] Though based on Statius's *Thebaid* VI, 94 (where the theme of regeneration is never made explicit), this passage, as David Anderson has shown, was almost certainly mediated by the 'In principio' commentary on the *Thebaid*, which informs the reader that new nymphs are generated to replace those who have died. However, not content to merely repeat this passing reference to regenerated nymphs, Boccaccio, Anderson notes, has 'elaborated on the wood-nymphs' regeneration through most of the stanza ... and then developed the topic further in a *chiosa* [gloss]' (48).[20] Boccaccio's insistence on this particular characteristic of the wood nymphs and their ancient wood clearly reveals the firm grip that this idea has on his imagination. For Boccaccio, this belief that certain precincts of the earth have somehow retained the generative spark of the primal age is not simply a suggestive poetic trope, but has an empiric basis. Like the ancient forest of the *Teseida*, the antediluvian woods, rivers, and rocks of the Tuscan landscape continue to burgeon with new life.

Fiesole's identification as one of the ancient precincts which has retained this procreative potential is dramatically illustrated in Boccaccio's entry for 'Fiesole' in his geographical dictionary, *De montibus*, where the Fiesolan rocks are credited with a truly supernatural trait; like Antaeus's barrow, they are able to continuously regenerate whatever mass they lose to erosion:

> Fiesole is a mountain with two peaks in Tuscan Florence, most illustrious of cities, filled with olive trees, the lead-like rocks of which are, upon falling, quickly restored – a well-authenticated fact – with new growth [ex quo si lapides qui plumbei sunt excidantur brevi tempore spatio novis incrementis restaurari compertissimum est]. On the peak of this mountain once stood an ancient city of the same name, as the half-eroded ruins attest. (*De montibus*, 234)[21]

In his gloss to the lines of Dante's *Inferno* concerning the hard, intransigent character of the Fiesolan people – 'tiene ancor del monte e del macigno' ['still keeping something of the rock and mountain'] (*Inf.* XV, 63; *Divine Comedy,* trans. Mandelbaum [hereafter cited as Mandelbaum]) – the fourteenth-century commentarist Benvenuto da Imola invokes this passage from *De montibus*:

> The modern poet Boccaccio of Certaldo, writes of the stones of Fiesole that they are leaden, and he tells this marvel about them – that if they are broken, they quickly regenerate with new growth; if this is true, it is well-attested by the nature of the Florentines themselves, whose race continuously sprouts from the root.[22]

Benvenuto's conjecture that this spontaneous regeneration of Fiesolan stone – 'si verum est' [if it is true] – is reflected in the almost supernatural resilience of the Florentine people does much to reinforce this image of Fiesole as a place of origin. Like the earth-born men of the familiar Jason and Cadmus narratives, or the humans regenerated by Deucalion and Pyrrha on Parnassus through the casting of stones (*Met.* I, 381ff; *Genealogie* IV 47, 2), the Fiesolans are here regarded as autochthons who, in a sort of travesty of golden age bounty, issue continuously from their ancient leaden root, whose hoary, sterile exterior – like that of the inorganic *lapides plumbei* – belies the vital, regenerative sap that continues to course within.

Indeed, this etiological account of human hardness is most probably inspired by the Ovidian passage where we read: 'Hence [from our origin in stone] we derive / The hardness that we have, and our endurance / Gives proof of what we have come from' (*Met.* I, 414–15).[23] The self-replenishing characteristic of the leaden stone no doubt reflects too the popular histories of Fiesole according to which Fiesole, though continually sacked and razed, is in every case rebuilt – a testament to the flinty tenacity and resilience of its inhabitants.

The same entry in *De montibus* that describes Fiesole's regenerative stone further supports this symbolic affiliation of Fiesole with Parnassus by insisting on the geological peculiarity of twin peaks: 'Fiesole is a mountain with two peaks in Tuscan Florence.' The widespread popularity of this view of Fiesole as a Tuscan Parnassus is suggested by a passage in Filippo Villani's *De origine civitatis Florentie et de eiusdem famosis civibus* [On the Origin of the City of Florence and Its Famous Citizens] where, in speaking of Fiesole, he notes that like Parnassus, it has two peaks: 'Fuit siquidem fabulosi Parnasi similitudine montium duorum iugata verticibus' (251).[24]

Parnassus is not only the place of human, biological regeneration, it is also among the most venerable sources of poetic, intellectual creation:

an oft-sung seat of the Muses, from whose foothills flow the Castalian springs, 'a font very well known to the poets, as it is sacred to the Muses' (*De montibus [de fontibus]* 'Castalius'). For Boccaccio, if the limpid Castalian Springs and other rural hideaways far removed from the commotion of the city are sacred to the Muses, it is primarily because they represent places of contemplation which favour lucid thoughts and inspire poetic composition:

> To the Muses is consecrate the Castalian and many other springs because the limpid spring has the property not only of delighting the eyes which see it, but also, by a certain hidden virtue, of leading one's mind into meditation and prompting one with the desire to compose. It is for this reason that the woods are sacred to them, that we might understand solitude, of which poets must make use, whose task it is to meditate poems, an act which cannot well take place in the midst of the city's clamour, nor among country crossroads. (*Genealogie* XI 2, 14)[25]

Finally, both its topographic similarity to the twin peaks of Evander's Latium and its symbolic function in Boccaccio's vernacular works convey the overwhelming impression that Fiesole is not only a site of biological preservation and regeneration but also a matrix of political and cultural creation. Boccaccio's nostalgic evocation in *De montibus* of Fiesole as an ancient place of origin left to ruin – 'le mezze consunte rovine' [the half-consumed ruins] – is, I suspect, deliberately reminiscent of Evander's description of Latium in *Aeneid* VIII (415ff), both the site of the past glory of Saturn's kingdom and the site of the Golden Age destined to be restored by Aeneas's descendants. Here, too, the site of a past and future glory bears the familiar trait of the twin peaks, Janiculum and Saturnia, named after Janus and Saturn respectively.[26] Indeed, it is upon these two peaks that Boccaccio, following Virgil, situates the Golden Age described in *Genealogie* VIII: 'They say, moreover, that while Saturn reigned in concord with Janus and the cities constructed by a common labour, that is, Saturnia and Janiculum, lay close by, it was an age of gold' (*Genealogie* VIII 1, 15–20).[27]

In sum, this widespread – and often contradictory and confusing – contamination of pagan, Biblical, and popular myths of origin and rebirth contributes to the overwhelming sense that the area on the outskirts of Florence, be it Fiesole or Certaldo, fulfills a liminal function as the site of an ancient biological and cultural birth, one which, like the self-replenishing rocks of Fiesole, somehow preserves a regenerative property. Given the preponderance of the traditions relating Fiesole to Parnassus, it is no wonder that Boccaccio selects the villas and gardens of the Fiesolan countryside as the setting for the telling of such glorious *novelle* and the site of a symbolic rebirth.

In the preceding arguments, I have tried to illustrate the way in which ethnocentric histories (those granting a historical – at least postdiluvial – primacy to Tuscany), a semantic slippage facilitated by formal, geographic analogies (the twin peaks of Parnassus merge with the twin peaks of Golden Age Rome and Fiesole), and a misconstrued empiric record (the presence of fossilized shells on Tuscan mountain peaks), coalesce in Boccaccio's poetic imagination to conjure up a convincing picture of the outskirts of Florence as a place of ethnic, political, and poetic origin. However, in addition to tantalizing us with these relatively subtle intimations that Tuscany is a matrix of both people and poetry, Boccaccio seeds his works with a complementary series of complex, highly original histories concerned with a belated, and corporate, variety of creation: the birth of nations.

These fictional histories are of particular interest since each one represents an attempt on Boccaccio's part to reconstruct the social and political events involved in reducing a chaotic assemblage of peoples into a formidable nation: the process whereby the joining together of warring groups of indigenous and colonizing peoples results in the creation of a society far superior to that enjoyed by either singly. In these accounts where Boccaccio, poet, works in concert with Boccaccio, scholar, the traditional poetic accounts of physiological origins (nymphs riven from gnarled trees, men sprouted from sown dragon's teeth, and so forth) or ideal polities (Golden Age government) are not rejected but rationalized. The same scepticism prompted by Ovid's whimsical notion of stone transformed to flesh that led Boccaccio to offer Theodontius's distinctly worldly opinion on the matter is even more readily provoked by poetic tales concerned with the birth of whole nations.[28] Individuals, Boccaccio insists, are not created through the casting of stones, nor do whole nations sprout like the Spartoi from the earth; both are produced through a process of sexual coupling and genetic mixing.

Political Restoration and Miscegenation: *Ex Pluribus Unum*

That Fiesole is associated with both birth and rebirth is amply illustrated by the previous examples. However, Boccaccio is concerned not merely with the idea of a physical birth or rebirth of rustic individuals or societies but with the subsequent debarbarization of such creations: the 'birth' of a civilization.

Naturally, the two closely related themes of natural and cultural origin tend to arise in the same texts. In many of those episodes where Boccaccio touches on origins, both physical and social, his tendency is to portray the first inhabitants of a given place as autochthons – sprung, as it were, from the natural environment (issuing from oaks, rivers, earth, etc.) – or aborigines (in the etymological sense – *ab origine* – of having been in a given place since the beginning) and to attribute the advent of an increasingly sophisticated culture to a process of miscegenation entailing the intermarriage of autochthonic, aboriginal, and colonist populations (in various combinations).

Though this model of the birth of culture is far from novel – indeed, it seems to be among the ideologies that has best served advocates of imperialism at least since the day that Romulus devised the rape of the Sabine women in a desperate bid to produce much-needed offspring for a dwindling population of Romans[29] – Boccaccio devotes particular industry and creativity to fashioning a series of mythological histories designed to confirm a process whereby miscegeny is at the root of social and cultural 'advancement.' However, Boccaccio is careful to recognize both the great sacrifice exacted by this process of civilization in its early stages and the moral dissolution that invariably accompanies the more sophisticated varieties of culture: one that can only be offset by a continuous introduction of new blood, 'gente nuova.'

Another pattern prominent in these fictive histories is that of a colony of refugees who must confront the daunting task of undertaking a complete social restoration in an alien, often inhospitable territory. In reading these histories it soon becomes apparent that Boccaccio regards the nostalgic attempt to recover lost empires as a fruitless endeavour, destined to fail. Like Virgil, who portrays Helenus's reconstructed Troy, the 'parvam Troiam' [little Troy] of Chaonia in *Aeneid* III, 349, as a sterile simulacrum whose familiar forms – poor replicas of the Xanthus, the Scaean Gate, and so forth – commemorate a loss, not the promise of a thriving metropolis in days to come. Boccaccio understands that empires are living, organic entities and a fallen empire can no sooner be restored to life than a corpse. The cultural and genetic future of a population of refugees is best secured through the introduction of new blood, the reinvigoration of their genetic and cultural heritage through the integration of racially and culturally diverse peoples. Cultural and genetic syncretism alone can supply the dynamism necessary for the creation of new empires.

This powerful idea is dramatized in the historical fictions of the *Aeneid*, where we learn that the seemingly monolithic unity known as the Roman Empire is actually an ethnic and cultural composite forged through a series of political pacts and bloody clashes between colonizing Asiatic (Trojan) and indigenous Italic peoples. When Juno, famously antagonistic to the Teucrians ever since Paris insulted her vanity, finally agrees to a peaceful resolution of the Trojan–Latin hostilities on the condition that the peoples thus united retain the name and customs of the Latins, Jupiter readily capitulates:

> I grant your wish. I yield, I am won over
> Willingly. Ausonian folk will keep
> Their fathers' language and their way of life,
> And, that being so, their name. The Teucrians
> Will mingle and be submerged, incorporated.
> Rituals and observances of theirs
> I'll add, but make them Latin, one in speech.
> The race to come, mixed with Ausonian blood,
> Will outdo men and gods in its devotion ...
> (Virgil, *Aeneid* XII, 1130–8; Latin XII, 833–9)[30]

In his *History of Rome from Its Foundation*, a work so admired by Boccaccio that he actually translated several 'decades' into the vernacular, Livy departs somewhat from the Virgilian account by crediting Aeneas with this decision to apply the name 'Latin' to the new political alliance.[31] By dispensing with the implausible interference of meddling gods, Livy's history does much to enhance the historical verisimilitude of Virgil's basic model (that concerned with the rewards of racial mixing). Aeneas's shrewd gesture succeeds in securing the allegiance of the Latins, and soon the two originally separate peoples, emboldened by their new unity, strike out against the Etruscans: 'Trojans and Latins were rapidly becoming one people, and this gave Aeneas confidence to make an active move against the Etruscans, in spite of their great strength.'[32]

Lucius Annaeus Florus, the author of the *Epitomae de Tito Livio bellorum*, an epitome of Livy's Roman history drawn upon on various occasions by Boccaccio, underscores this theme even more forcefully. His Romulus, something of a political visionary, conceives of Rome long before he has the population necessary to sustain a civic infrastructure on such a grand scale. Determined not to let this shortage of future Romans interfere with his farsighted scheme, Romulus sets about gathering into a single body a diverse group made up of Latin and Tuscan shepherds (who have sought asylum in a nearby grove), Aeneas's Phrygians, and Evander's Arcadians: 'ita ex variis quasi elementis congregavit corpus unum, populumque Romanum ipse fecit rex' (I, 1, 9–10).[33] Like Boccaccio, Florus is fond of drawing analogies between the biological and the social entity: the individual and the state. He likens the life of the Roman people to that of an individual, one susceptible to parsing into four stages: birth, growth, maturation, and old age, each corresponding to a historical period (I. Intro., 4). Though Livy does not, like Florus, make this biological analogy explicit, it may nonetheless be inferred from a passage in his *History of Rome* where he has one of Romulus's envoys – dispatched on a mission to find a viable people with whom to intermarry – remark that cities, like all other things, are born 'ex infimo' [from the lowest beginnings] and must gradually acquire stature through their own merit (I 9, 3). Like humans, cities are born, and also like humans, they must undergo a process of physical and moral growth if they are to become worthy of praise.

The account of Dido's colonization of Africa preserved in Justin's *Epitome of the Philippic History of Pompeius Trogus* suggests an amusing travesty of the Virgilian pattern of racial mixing:

> Their first landfall [that of Dido and her fellow fugitives] was the island of Cyprus [...] It was a custom in Cyprus to send young girls down to the seashore on specific days before their marriage to earn money for their dowry by prostitution, and to offer Venus libations for the preservation of their virtue in the future. Elissa had some eighty of these girls abducted and taken aboard so that her young men might have wives and her city a posterity. (18, 1–5)[34]

Whereas the political and social alliance of the Phrygians with the indigenous peoples of Hesperia – the robust, vigorous Latins and Arcadians – implicitly virilizes the Asiatic stock, the introduction to the Tyrian stock of this peculiarly Venusian, sybaritic strain through intermarriage with Cypriot prostitutes – sexual profiteers – clearly heralds a process of cultural decadence (or, at the very least, a heightened susceptibility to sensual things).

Though Trogus's decision to grant Cypriot prostitutes such a prominent place in the genetic constitution of early Carthage certainly invites scrutiny, it is, nevertheless, not Virgil's but Trogus's account of Carthaginian history that Boccaccio chooses to reproduce not only in the *Esposizioni* (V, lit., 77), *De casibus* (II 10, 15), and *De mulieribus* (XLII, 6) but also in the *Genealogie* (II 49, 2; 53, 4–5), a work dedicated to Hugh, King of Cyprus! It is not at all clear how Boccaccio, who, after all, sought Hugh's patronage, thought that such allusions to the Cypriot habit of pimping their daughters to plump their dowries was going to expedite his cause.[35] Boccaccio's ready acceptance of Trogus's tendentious, even libelous, assertion that intermarriage with Cypriot prostitutes was somehow necessary for the creation of the Carthaginian nation is due, perhaps, to the clear replication in Trogus's history of the pattern of miscegenation that dominates the early history of the Roman nation as described by Virgil and Livy. Indeed, Boccaccio's mythic histories all bear witness to this notion that nations, like children, are born through labour, and that cultural preeminence is not the product of genetic and social homogeneity, but of a fruitful variety of ethnic and cultural 'cross-pollination.'

In a sense then, Boccaccio's histories supplement Virgil's fictionalized history and Livy's historicized fiction by tracing the continuation, in the area of Tuscany, of this phenomenon whereby nations are spawned from the merging of nations in a process that mimics biological reproduction: if Fiesole is the Tuscan Parnassus, Florence is, in a sense, the Tuscan Rome. (Indeed, according to G. Villani Florence was founded by Julius Caesar and briefly called 'piccola Roma.') Given Boccaccio's appropriation of such a 'biological' model, one in which nations are the progeny of cultural intercourse, it should come as no surprise that his nations, like individuals, almost invariably betray their ethnic roots in their cultural habits.

Insofar as the following 'histories' are shaped less by popular traditions than by the vagaries of Boccaccio's imagination, they are a particularly valuable source of information concerning Boccaccio's personal views regarding the origin and ultimate destiny of complex social organizations. All three of the etiologies that follow are concerned with the foundation of Tuscan cities; however, these very original accounts diverge not only from such traditional foundation myths as are recorded in Giovanni and Filippo Villani's chronicles, but are also incompatible with one another. It is, as we shall see, precisely in such discrepancies that Boccaccio most clearly reveals himself.

The first of the etiologies that follows is not, properly speaking, concerned with the foundation of a city but of a town: Boccaccio's beloved

Certaldo. In this particular etiology the pattern of a conflict between indigene and colonizer (the former, as we shall see, represented by Fiesolan refugees and the latter by Florentine refugees), though implicit, is masked somewhat by the historical distance that separates the foundation of Certaldo from that of Florence; with the passing of time, the distinction between colonizer and aborigine has become somewhat hazy. This history of Certaldan origins is so patently artificial in its flawless symmetries and contrived drama that it can hardly be doubted that Boccaccio's intention is to portray not a real but an ideal history.

The second and third of these etiologies – those concerned with the origin of Florence – support the usual view that both Florence's political strength and its susceptibility to internecine conflict can be traced to its origins in the reconciliation and intermarriage of Roman (imperialist) and Fiesolan (indigenous) stock. However, Boccaccio's interest lies not so much in perpetuating this etiology of Florentine divisiveness as it does in illuminating the paradox that this conflictive process is always at the root of cultural progress; the birth of nations, like that of individuals, proceeds haltingly, through a sort of political peristalsis.

The Birth of Certaldo

Though the vast mosaic of episodes that constitute the *Filocolo* do, as a general rule, resolve themselves into something resembling a unified narrative, there are a number of episodes so clearly independent of the surrounding text that it is tempting to view them as interpolations. Famous among these is the episode of the so called 'questions of love' of Book IV (heavily influenced by Capellanus's *De Amore*). Less noted – because it is of less obvious interest – is the sequence of eleven chapters (V, 38–49) that provides a mytho-historical account of the foundation of Certaldo through the reconciliation of two bitterly warring factions, the Caloni and the Cireti, brought about through the mediation of a foreign prince, Florio.

Both factions are made up of 'gente rustica nel sembiante' [people of a rustic appearance] (V 38, 2) who dwell in primitive twig huts on either side of a river and wage war with wooden clubs, rudimentary bows, a few dull, misshapen swords, and ancient shields, black with tarnish – these last two, no doubt, evocative relics of a more heroic past. The Caloni consist of Fiesolan fugitives forced out of Fiesole after Cataline's failed coup d'état, whereas the Cireti are composed of Florentine refugees driven from Florence by Attila. Their rivalry, then, represents an adaptation of

the traditional pattern of Fiesolan/Florentine enmity, and a recapitula-
tion of the tensions partially resolved by the foundation of a city, Florence, in which the two peoples were mixed.[36] Here, the pathetic
physical circumstances, a travesty of wholesome Golden Age rusticity,
serve to dramatize the moral debasement inherent in all civil conflict.
Both factions proudly bear red and white pennants that epitomize the
paradox, and perversity, of civil conflict, for each is the mirror image of
the other: an absolute difference that is simultaneously a perfect identity
(and a graphic reminder that the Florentines and the Fiesolans are
descended from the brothers Dardanus and Italus).

Florio, urging the estranged peoples to follow the example of Saturn
(by practicing agriculture or adopting a Golden Age ethos) rather than
Mars (V, 41), soon succeeds not only in reconciling the two factions but
in establishing, 'in restaurazione de' loro danni' [in compensation for
their losses] (V 40, 5), a new land to be crowned by a city, 'Calocepe,' situated 'quasi in mezzo tra l'una abitazione e l'altra de' due popoli tornati
uno' [almost in between the one dwelling place and the other of these
two peoples become one] (V, 42). The location of this city on a fertile
elevation approximately equidistant from Fiesole and Florence and traversed by the river Elsa (V 42, 3) permits us to identify Calocepe with
Certaldo, Boccaccio's adopted *borgo*, the seat of his ancestors and, perhaps, the place of his birth.

Though Boccaccio sculpts this allegory of origins on the all-too-famil-
iar political armature of Fiesolan/Florentine civil strife, the story that
unfolds along the central axis of the Elsa represents a striking departure
from the usual history of perennial conflict, for it is one in which 'due
popoli piccoli e cattivi' [two small and wicked nations] are rendered
'uno buono e grande' [one good and great] (V 41, 5) through political
unification under a single strong leader – first Florio, and later Caleon,
his hand-picked successor. Interestingly, this new city is unified not only
politically but socially, for it enjoys an unprecedented cultural egalitarianism. Though social distinctions do exist – Caleon builds himself a
royal residence on an elevation overlooking the entire city – it is noteworthy that the liberal and mechanical arts are treated as complementary halves of a single unity: 'egli similmente a diversi studii delle liberali
arti ne dispose alcuni, e altri alle meccaniche' [he likewise assigned some
to various studies of the liberal arts and others to the mechanical arts]
(49). Boccaccio's willingness to merge these traditionally opposed
branches of the *Artes* into a single whole not only suggests a cultural mirroring of the process of political unification, but implies, however indis-

tinctly, a type of social equality: fishermen and philosophers are deemed equally important to the smooth functioning of this ideal city.[37]

Since this story of the foundation of an ideal government not only lacks a historical basis but projects an unmistakably mythic symmetry, it is difficult not to view it as Boccaccio's bid to falsify a 'historical' precedent for postclassical Italian unity under a just prince, Caleon (who happens to be a figure for Boccaccio himself!). That the pseudo-Greek confabulation 'Calocepe' corresponds to the Italian 'bel giardino' [beautiful garden] is not irrelevant, for this *locus amoenus* is the site not only of a creation but of a cultural and political re-creation, a restoration of the *bel giardino* of empire, and the terrestrial analogue of the 'bel giardino / che sotto i raggi di Cristo s'infiora' ['that / fair garden blossoming beneath Christ's rays'] (*Par.* XXIII, 71; Mandelbaum).[38] Dante's dream of Empire is fulfilled, if only textually (and in microcosmic fashion), through Boccaccio's poetic utopia, Calocepe, an anticipation, one need hardly point out, of the similar literary utopia imagined in the *Decameron*.

In the fourth chapter of *Boccaccio: L'invenzione della letteratura mezzana*, Francesco Bruni briefly considers the various etiologies of Florence found in Boccaccio's pre-*Decameron* works in relation to the historical chronicles of his day. Though Bruni acknowledges the originality of Boccaccio's story of the Caloni and Cireti, he tends to view the episode as little more than a replication, on Certaldan soil, of the familiar Florentine pattern of a double ethnicity destined to engender civil strife.[39] Furthermore, he discounts the likely Virgilian influence in this pattern arguing: 'Non mi pare probabile che abbia potuto influire il modello piú illustre e antico dell' *Eneide,* con la fusione di Troiani e Italici (che doveva condurre a un popolo omogeneo, non tormentato dalle divisioni)' [It seems unlikely to me that this could have been influenced by the more famous and ancient model of the *Aeneid,* with its fusion of Trojans and Italic peoples (which was to lead to a homogeneous people, not one tormented by divisions)] (285).

In my opinion, the story of the Caloni and Cireti represents Boccaccio's ingenious attempt to accommodate the traditional motif of a problematic Florentine/Fiesolan fusion to the Virgilian model of a productive cultural and genetic fusion – the intermarriage of Trojans and Latins. In both accounts war serves as a tragic but necessary prelude to peace and to the subsequent construction of a politically exemplary, culturally, and racially integrated nation. Bruni's reluctance to accept the influence of Virgil's model seems to be based on the assumption that a 'fusione' [fusion] does not take place at Calocepe (as it did between the racially and culturally integrated Trojans and Latins) and that the political utopia of early Certaldo so clearly delineated by Boccaccio is consequently destined to succumb to civil war. It is worth noting, therefore, that we are given every reason to believe that the Fiesolan and Florentine factions that constitute Calocepe's population do 'fuse' both socially and genetically (they intermarry) and that Calocepe is free from any internal divisions. Indeed, Boccaccio's primary objective in tracing such clear parallels between the foundation myths of Certaldo and Florence is, it seems to me, to highlight a fundamental difference: Florence represents the 'unweeded' garden, a seedbed of political strife whereas Certaldo (Calocepe), Florence's virtual 'twin,' represents a 'bel giardino.' Indeed, we are told that the well-governed Certaldans persevere in their enviable lives for many centuries until they are conquered by a new prince (V 49, 8) – an allusion, states Quaglio in his notes to the Mondadori edition, to the conquest of Certaldo by the Florentines in the thirteenth century (and therefore a political collapse unrelated to internecine conflict). Given all this, it is not clear to me why Bruni is so ready to dismiss the possible Virgilian pedigree of the pattern reproduced by Boccaccio in *Filocolo* V, 38–49.

Though Boccaccio does not supply sufficient information to resolve the question of whether his birthplace is Certaldo or Florence, he does consistently present Certaldo as the site of his ancestral origin.[40] In the *Decameron* he glorifies Certaldo's past by identifying it as a place once inhabited by noble and wealthy families: 'Certaldo, come voi forse avete potuto udire, è un castel di Valdelsa posto nel nostro contado, il quale, quantunque piccol sia, già di nobili uomini e d'agiati fu abitato ...' ['Certaldo, as you may possibly have heard, is a fortified town situated in the Val d'Elsa, in Florentine territory, and although it is small, the people living there were at one time prosperous and well-to-do'] (*Dec.* VI 10, 5; trans. McWilliam, 469). In *De montibus [de fluminibus]* the entry for the river 'Elsa' includes a passage that indicates Boccaccio's underlying agenda in painting this flattering portrait of early Certaldo; apparently these noble Certaldans are none other than Boccaccio's ancestors:

> to the right, on a mound of middling height, it bathes the ancient citadel of Certaldo, whose memory I gladly celebrate. This was in truth the dwelling place and native land of my ancestors before Florence received them as citizens. (*De montibus [de fluminibus]*, 368).[41]

Both this celebration of Certaldo and Boccaccio's foundation history in the *Filocolo* must be viewed as elements in a larger campaign to redeem the reputation of a *borgo* famously spurned in the *Commedia*, where Dante unhesitatingly lumps Certaldo together with various other *borghi* whose inhabitants' descent into Florence resulted in the bastardization of the 'pure' Roman bloodline (*Par.* XVI 50ff). By presenting Certaldo as having been initially constituted of Fiesolan and Florentine stock, Boccaccio substantially weakens this thesis, for the migration of Certaldans (among them, Boccaccio's ancestors) into Florence represents not the introduction of new blood, but rather the reunion of an alienated people with their genetic forbears.[42] The success of Boccaccio's campaign to redeem Certaldo is confirmed by Benvenuto da Imola, who observes that the sweetness of Boccaccio's wisdom and eloquence have restored Certaldo's reputation: 'qui sua suavitate sapientiae et eloquentiae reddidit ipsum locum celebrem et famosum.'[43]

Although this embedded etiology of Certaldo may initially strike the reader as extraneous to the larger tale of Florio and Biancifiore, it actually functions in many respects as a mirror, or distillation, of the latter. In a broad sense, the traditional tale of Floire and Blancheflor is a political allegory concerned with the union of the pagan prince of Spain, Floire, with a Roman Christian noblewoman, Blancheflor, which results in the foundation of the glorious Spanish Christian monarchy. Though Boccaccio by no means neglects these religious and political elements of the ancient tale in his *Filocolo*, he grants an unprecedented degree of importance to the racial component – a characteristic of the *Filocolo* noted long ago by the French Boccaccio scholar Henri Hauvette, who remarks: 'A la différence de religion, nettement marquée dans les rédactions antérieures, Boccace a substitué la distinction de race: Lelio et Giulia sont de vieille souche romaine, tandis que les païens descendent de rois africains' [For the difference of religion, clearly marked in the early versions, Boccaccio has substituted the difference of race: Lelio and Giulia are of the old Roman stock, whereas the pagans are descended from African kings].[44] Barely visible beneath the rich embroidery of the *Filocolo's* notoriously Byzantine plot lies hidden a familiar ideology: cultural, religious, and racial mixing, though a perennial source of tears and travail, is simultaneously the most effective recipe for political unity and strength.

As we shall see in the following two fictive histories of Florence, Boccaccio goes even further in his advocacy of miscegeny, by proposing, in the *Comedia delle ninfe fiorentine*, that Florence's original population was a synthesis of Greek and Roman stock, and, in the *Ninfale fiesolano*, a synthesis of indigenes, nymphs (autochthons), and colonizers, thereby for-

cing us to reassess the racial purity – 'Romanity' – of even the earliest Florentine population.

The Greek Invasion of Fiesole: A Cultural Etiology of Florence

The second of these fictional histories, one found in the thirty-eighth chapter of the *Comedia delle ninfe fiorentine*, which traces the origins of Florence itself, is the most idiosyncratic and fantastical of the three. Whereas Giovanni Villani tells us that Florence (a well-garrisoned Roman outpost charged with keeping the feisty Fiesolans in line [*Cronica* I, 38]) was built by Caesar in the wake of his victory over the Fiesolans, Boccaccio seems to blithely contradict this long-established tradition by granting Ulysses's long-suffering shipmate Achaemenides – a character first encountered in the third book of Virgil's *Aeneid* (lines 614–91) – full credit for the foundation of Florence.

Boccaccio's selection of Achaemenides for this particular function may well strike most readers as peculiar if not completely unfathomable. If anybody truly deserves a place of honour in the annals of the ill-augured, that person is certainly Achaemenides. His fame – or, rather, notoriety – derives, after all, from Virgil's account of his inadvertent desertion among the enraged Cyclopes by the impious Ulysses, 'devisor of crime' (*Aeneid* II, 164), and his thoughtless shipmates as they make their precipitous flight from Sicily: a colourful, but distinctly unflattering, episode. Achaemenides's restoration to human society is, moreover, not achieved by dint of his own industry or ingenuity but results from the fortuitous – or rather providential – intervention of Aeneas, who, mooring in the great harbour beneath Aetna's lowering heights, encounters the unkempt Achaemenides and, swayed by the harrowing account of his desertion and days spent dodging bloodthirsty Cyclopes, agrees to take him aboard. Of Achaemenides's subsequent activities in Italy, Virgil tells us nothing.

Indeed, Virgil seems to have conjured the figure of Achaemenides from thin air with the purely jingoistic aim of contrasting Trojan piety with Greek impiety, Trojan civility with Greek savagery. What better, more convincing confirmation of Greek depravity could be offered than the damning testimony of another Greek – one, furthermore, who cannot easily be accused of disloyalty for he has not deserted his compatriots but has, quite literally, been deserted by them. Having fulfilled his dramatic function by supplying this vivid object lesson in Greek treachery and Trojan piety, Achaemenides silently disappears from the pages of the *Aeneid*.

In the years bracketed by Virgil's account of Achaemenides and Boccaccio's extended treatment in the *Comedia delle ninfe*, Ovid alone appears to have been sensitive to the narrative power and poetic possibilities of the Achaemenides interlude.[45] In the 'little *Aeneid*' of *Metamorphoses* XIV, he devotes about sixty lines (159–222) to Achaemenides's first-person account of his travails on the island of the Cyclopses after being deserted by the thoughtless scaramouch Ulysses and his joy at being restored to safety and human society by Aeneas. Achaemenides, though Greek, has clearly – and understandably – shifted his allegiance to the Trojans: 'May I,' Ovid's Achaemenides declares, 'look on Polyphemus yet again, and those wide jaws of his dripping with human gore, if I prefer my home and Ithaca to this ship, if I revere Aeneas less than my own father' (*Met.* XIV, 167–71).[46] Under the circumstances, it is difficult to fault him; if ever there was a Greek whose defection to the Trojan side was fully justified, that Greek is Achaemenides.[47] Whereas Virgil stresses Aeneas's statesman-like magnanimity, Ovid is more concerned to relate Achaemenides's psychological state: the terrifying thoughts that assail him as he watches the Cyclops gorge on his companions, seeing his own cruel destiny reflected in theirs, and the exhilarating sense of relief and gratitude experienced upon being rescued by Aeneas – an emotion so deeply felt that it results in the forging of a new allegiance every bit as strong as the natural bond between a father and son, capable, even, of transcending the deep-rooted rancour between Greek and Phrygian.

Whereas Virgil used the Achaemenides interlude for political ends, setting the Roman qualities of civic-mindedness, generosity, and tolerance off against the antisocial 'sauve qui peut' ethos of the Greeks, Ovid – and this is characteristic – appears to have been more concerned to probe the inner workings of the human psyche, the hidden mechanism whereby fear is turned into desire, wrath into gratitude, and enmity into friendship.

Boccaccio, whose objective is altogether different from Virgil's (for his aim is not to discredit but to redeem Greek culture) and from Ovid's (for he is more interested in Achaemenides's actions than his emotions) does not simply resuscitate the figure of Achaemenides, but reinvents him: an intriguing feature of the *Comedia delle ninfe* that has received almost no critical attention.[48] No longer a political pawn, a personified object lesson in Greek perfidy or Roman largesse, this new Achaemenides assumes the more dynamic, self-determining guise of a real, if somewhat idealized, person: a conqueror, city founder, and educator.

It is one of the more pronounced features of epic poetry that personal identity is inextricably enmeshed with national and family identity. Even the grisly spectacle of violent death does not deter, nor the din of clashing bronze drown out, the Homeric hero's meticulous recitation of his genealogy. Given the considerable importance granted such richly elaborated genealogies in the epic tradition (and more particularly the seemingly endless genealogy provided the refugee Theoclymenus, Achaemenides's Homeric forbear), it can hardly escape notice that Virgil provides Achaemenides with the most paltry, perfunctory genealogy possible. We are told only that he is from Ithaca, a companion of Ulysses, and the son of Adamastus (a name, moreover, that does more to suggest nonentity than identity, for it appears in none of the usual mythological sources). Though this scant genealogical information is more than adequate in serving Virgil's objective of illustrating the gross impiety of Ulysses – whose deserted companion, it turns out, was not just any Greek, but a fellow Ithacan – it is evidently found lacking by Boccaccio, who takes the liberty of discarding it in favour of a family dynasty memorialized (though most often in blood and ashes) by such poets as Statius and Seneca: the House of Thebes.[49]

So it is that Achaemenides, a bit player in the drama of the *Aeneid*, unexpectedly finds new life. Once the son of the unremarkable Adamastus, he is here recast as the issue of Laius's sister Ionia and the noble Theban Orcamo (both, it should be noted, conjured up for this express purpose by Boccaccio), assigned a central role in the foundation myth of Florence, and conscripted in Boccaccio's campaign to refurbish and redeem the cultural legacy of Greece.[50]

Given this objective, one might reasonably ask why Boccaccio has chosen to endow Achaemenides with this famously sordid legacy of sexual trespass and civil strife. Might not the anonymity of Adamastus have been preferable to the notoriety of Oedipus and his kin? Certainly, this particular affiliation seems less than ideal for a representative of the foreign stock whose melding with the local population is destined to serve as the genetic foundation of the Florentine future. That Boccaccio is aware of this problem is indicated by his decision to trace Achaemenides's ancestry to Laius's sister, Ionia, rather than to Laius himself. This free-handed tinkering with the Theban genealogical table – the introduction to Labdacus's line of a Theban royal, Ionia, undreamt of by Seneca or Statius (Boccaccio's principal sources for the Theban material) – allows Boccaccio to conveniently sidestep the line of Oedipus with its sordid history of incest and parricide, and focus instead on the commanding figure of the founding father of the House of Thebes, Achae-menides's great ancestor, Cadmus.[51]

Though most accomplishments of the Cadmean dynasty are eclipsed by what seem to be an endless succession of sex scandals (Oedipus and Jocasta), civil conflicts (Polynices and Eteocles, the feuding sons of Oedi-pus), and blasphemy (Pentheus and Dionysus), none has fully obscured the extraordinary achievements of Cadmus himself, who is traditionally credited not only with the foundation of Boeotian Thebes but with the introduction to Greece of the Phoenician alphabet (a notice available to Boccaccio in Pliny's *Natural History* VII 56, 192).

That this association with the great city founder and culture-hero Cad-mus is what inspired Boccaccio to select the Theban dynasty is suggested by Boccaccio's decision to begin his tale of the foundation of Florence in the thirty-eighth chapter of the *Comedia delle ninfe* with a brief recapitula-tion of the myth of Cadmus's foundation of Thebes, and is later con-firmed by Mars, whose disembodied voice (perhaps, Boccaccio tells us, the very same once heard by Cadmus) assigns Achaemenides the duty of renewing the fallen Thebes on the hallowed ground, the *Campi di Marte* (fields of Mars), where Dardanus had once built his altars to Mars. Just as Aeneas was charged with the task of founding a new 'Troy' (Rome), Achaemenides is given the duty of founding the new 'Thebes' (Florence).

The problem that presented itself to Boccaccio was that of finding a credible way of transposing the prototypical Cadmean city-founding myth from a mythologized Boeotia to a historicized Italy. Achaemenides, though not the obvious choice, is revealed, upon closer scrutiny, to be in many respects the ideal choice. In Achaemenides, Boccaccio has found a character whose 'historical' existence is underwritten by Virgil, but about whose other qualities Virgil – for the reasons outlined above – says nothing. What better candidate for creative poetic elaboration? Cer-tainly, the little information that Virgil does provide is ideally suited to Boccaccio's own agenda; Achaemenides is a 'good' Greek who ends up in Italy. Moreover, Ovid's reprisal of the episode in *Metamorphoses* XIV only reinforces this impression of Achaemenides's conscientious, civic-minded character, for here we read that even as Achaemenides watches his comrades flee, leaving him stranded among enemies, his concern is not for his own safety, but for theirs: 'I feared lest the waves or the wind should sink the ship, forgetting that I was not in her' (XIV, 185–6).[52] The composite narrative rendered by Boccaccio's synthesis of the Virgilian/ Ovidian Achaemenides with the (largely Ovidian) figure of Cadmus is that of a civic-minded Greek who ends up in Italy where he founds a city and introduces the arts of culture. However this is not all, for Boccaccio further enhances Achaemenides's stature by implicitly affiliating him with the great Persian conqueror Cyrus.

Enveloped, Boccaccio tells us, in a post-coital languor, Achaemenides's mother, Ionia, drifts to sleep and dreams that she is giving birth to a towering cloud of unbounded circumference that extends from the earth to the heavens. This cloud, a symbol of Florence, is subjected to a number of assaults and restorations which signify, proleptically, the famously tortuous course of Florentine history. Boccaccio likens this dream to that attributed to the Median King Astyages (familiar to Boccaccio from the account in Valerius Maximus), in which Astyages's daughter, Mandane, gives birth to a vine that covers all of Asia – a premonition of the birth of Cyrus, the child destined to usurp his throne and conquer all of Asia.[53]

Like Virgil's Achaemenides, Boccaccio's reconceived Achaemenides has the qualities of a civic leader. Like Cadmus, he is a founder of cities and champion of culture, and like Cyrus, he is a conqueror whose influence is destined to be felt not just locally, but universally. If Boccaccio's choice of Achaemenides seems, at first glance, fanciful or even awkward, this brief exploration of Boccaccio's underlying method and motivation suggests that there is nothing remotely arbitrary about his choice. What individual could better represent the spiritual legacy of Florence, a city that has inspired as many invectives for its long history of civil strife and sexual decadence as encomia for its long-acknowledged role as the epicentre of the most celebrated cultural restoration the western world has known? A close examination of the more specific circumstances of this city founding as described in the *Comedia delle ninfe* tends to confirm these conjectures.

During a ritual honouring Mars celebrated in a sacred precinct shaded by an antediluvian oak (24) a wandering Achaemenides happens upon the celebrating Coritans (Fiesolans) only to be violently carried in front of the altars by his horse, who proceeds to tear at the sacred turf with its hoofs 'quale Pegaseo fece negli alti monti' [just as Pegasus did on the high mountains] (37). Outraged by this desecration, the Coritans are at first inclined to kill him on the spot. Achaemenides, whose control of language is notably better than his control of his horse, manages to allay their anger by first treating them to a moving account of his sufferings among the Cyclopses (the same strategy that had proven so useful in winning Aeneas's trust), and then asserting that his colonization of the site of the Coritan celebrations has been foreordained by Mars, a claim almost immediately confirmed by a succession of auspicious portents. Their wrath transformed to wonder, the Coritans invite Achaemenides and his men to join them at their sacred feast. Upon hearing that a noble stranger has arrived on their shores, Sarnia, a noble nymph of Coritan descent (56), hastens to the feast, welcomes Achaemenides into her home and promptly marries him; an act that would seem precipitous were it not, in some sense, predestined. Her name, 'Sarnia' – one evidently derived from the name of the river, 'Sarno' [Arno] (56), adjacent to her estate – is also the name used to identify a Coritan city, 'Sarnia city' (presumably one situated in the Valdarno, near the future site of Florence), thereby suggesting that in addition to having the finest Fiesolan pedigree, she somehow embodies the preeminent political (Sarnia city) and natural (Sarnia/Sarno) aspects of the Coritan nation as well.

According to the traditional etiology of Fiesole that provides the mytho-historical armature for Boccaccio's imaginative revision, the population of Fiesole derives from the very same stock that gave rise to Dardanus, the mythical progenitor of the Trojans. Consequently, the union of the Greek Achaemenides (a descendant of Cadmus) with a Fiesolan woman (a descendant of Corythus, Dardanus's father)[54] implies a genetic synthesis of the whole of the classical world, both the Latin and the Greek, in a new civilization destined to supersede both. The construction of the 'new Thebes,' Florence, on a site consecrated to Mars by Dardanus and Siculus establishes a political and spiritual continuity between Rome and Florence.[55] Whereas the destruction of Troy, the literary epitome of civilized refinement, resulted from Greek and Trojan enmity, the construction of Florence, the new paragon of cosmopolitan sophistication, is here based on a reparation of this, the most notorious of ancient rifts, 'the mortal hatred among the Phrygians and Argives for the kidnapped Helen' (*L'Ameto*, trans. Serafini-Sauli, 118).[56]

Boccaccio appears to have deliberately shaped Achaemenides to serve as the Theban counterpart to Virgil's Aeneas. Both are descended from great city founders (Cadmus and Laomedon respectively); both are destined to replicate, on foreign soil, their famous ancestors' city-founding activity; each proves indispensable to the other in facilitating this task of city founding (just as Aeneas rescues Achaemenides from the Cyclopses, Achaemenides rallies to Aeneas's cause in Italy, contributing to his military victories); both engage in a nostalgic, counterproductive effort to recreate the venerable cities – Troy and Thebes – responsible for shaping the cultural and political identity of their respective nations; each forges, through marriage, a genetic union with a local woman of ancient and noble pedigree whose political, symbolic function is underscored by the application of her name to a settlement or city (Lavinia/Lavinium; Sarnia/Sarnian City); both establish a hereditary kingship based on the ethnically mixed issue of their unions with these noblewomen; and finally, the long-term success of both of their cities is contingent on skillful governance, racial integration, and religious tolerance. By securing these striking correspondences between Achaemenides and Aeneas through the construction of what is essentially a parallel history, Boccaccio not only implies that Florence and Rome, the cities founded by each, are themselves somehow equivalent, but suggests that they are also, in some sense, interdependent. From the moment Aeneas takes the suppliant Achaemenides aboard, the histories of these two great cities are destined to be interlinked (a view already given much currency by the chroniclers).

Any lingering doubts that Boccaccio would have us view Achaemenides as a 'new' Cadmus are dispelled by Boccaccio's characterization of the city built on the *Campi di Marte* (field of Mars) in the wake of this marriage of Greek interloper and Coritan indigene as a 'nuova Tebe' [new Thebes] (58). The reigns of Achaemenides and his son Iolao are marked by universal peace and contentment; their successors are less fortunate. Peeved by Fortune's obvious – and from their perspective, excessive – partiality to their neighbours, the spiteful Fiesolans set about inciting a series of battles that prove detrimental to both peoples. Unaccustomed to setbacks of any sort, the New Thebans turn to prayer and sacrifice in a futile bid to arrest this spate of bad fortune. Finally, the citizens of New Thebes are forced to conclude that their misfortunes are due, at least in part, to the 'sfortunato nome' [inauspicious name] (65) of the city; presumably the Gods have forgotten neither Oedipus's moral outrage nor the civil strife wreaked by his sons (65).

The remainder of this history of Florence is, accordingly, concerned with the proceedings of a divine naming committee. Mars wins the honour of naming the city, but shrewdly elects to share it with Venus; thus it is that the white, Venusian lily is set off against the Martian field of red in the Florentine coat of arms.[57] This fruitful confluence of Trojan and Achaian blood – in a mytho-historical context shaped by the Homeric account of the Trojan war – the most radical example of miscegenation possible, is symbolically mirrored by an equally extreme union of opposites: that of Venus and Mars.

Though the previous parallels between Achaemenides's foundation of Florence and Cadmus's foundation of Thebes are inescapable, there is

an equally significant similarity that is less immediately obvious. The etiology of Florence in *Comedia delle ninfe* XXXVIII begins, as noted above,
with a brief summary of the Cadmus myth. In the wake of Europa's
abduction by Jupiter, Cadmus, her brother, is instructed by their father
to retrieve her or endure a permanent exile. Despairing, after a long and
fruitless search, of ever finding his sister, and at the same time spurred by
the noble ambition to found a city for his travel-weary companions, Cadmus appeals to Apollo, who advises him to follow an untamed heifer
through the Aonian mountains, and to found a city for himself and the
'sons of the serpentine teeth' on the site where the heifer, lowing, com-
pletes her course (*Comedia delle ninfe* XXXVIII, 4).

If the part of the Cadmus legend concerning the spontaneous generation of armed warriors (the Spartoi – 'sown men') who immediately set
about killing one another is not further elaborated in the *Comedia delle
ninfe,* it is probably because Boccaccio deemed it unnecessary as the
details of the tale were widely known from Ovid's masterful telling in
Metamorphoses III, 102ff. Those familiar with the tale will perhaps recall
that of these men generated from the sown dragon's teeth, all but five
are killed in the internecine brawl that follows so hard upon their birth.
What is most significant about this small remnant of the autochthonic
population is that its members later collaborate with Cadmus in the construction of Thebes (*Met.* III, 130). Beneath the supernatural drama of
this vivid tale it is possible to make out an allegory of miscegenation
involving an initial conflict between a population of colonists and aborigines which, resolved through the political and social integration of the
two peoples, results, finally, in the founding of a great city-state.

Whatever the merits or faults of such an interpretation it is, at least,
significant that this is how Boccaccio chooses to understand the tale.
That this is the case is confirmed by Boccaccio's idiosyncratic explication
of the Cadmus myth in *Genealogie* II, 63. To a précis of Ovid's account in
the *Metamorphoses*, Boccaccio adds the somewhat bizarre information
(derived from the fourth-century BC Greek mythographer Palaephatus
by way of the Jerome-Eusebius *Chronicon*)[58] that Cadmus was originally
married to the Sphinx. The Sphinx, we read, possessed by a jealous rage
upon discovering that her beloved Cadmus has fixed a lecherous eye on
the lovely Harmonia, resolves to desert her fickle husband and declare
war on the Cadmeians. Boccaccio then goes on to elucidate the meaning
of various other aspects of the story. The serpent's teeth, he tells us, signify the discord among those indigenes who, instigated by the Sphinx,
take up arms against Cadmus. The five survivors represent the indigene

elect, whose task it is to work out an accord with Cadmus that results in the merging of the foreigners (Cadmeians) and the indigenes (the Sphinx's followers) into a single people: 'cum Cadmo in concordiam devenere et ex incolis atque forensibus unum fecere populum' (II, 63): a recapitulation, in miniature, of the Latin/Phrygian alliance described in Livy.[59]

That Boccaccio should see in the autochthons of the Ovidian narrative an indigenous population engaged in civil conflict and in the friendship struck between the five remaining Spartoi and Cadmus a mythical record of an intermarrying of races is eloquent testimony to his belief in the productive consequences of racial mixing.

The analogy used by Boccaccio to describe the manner in which Achaemenides's horse tears at the sod of the *Campi di Marte* – 'quale Pegaseo fece negli alti monti' [just as Pegasus did in the high mountains] (37) – is a clear allusion to Pegasus's creation of the Hippocrene spring, sacred to the Muses (Ovid's *Met.* V, 254–67).[60] That this Pegasus-like tearing at the turf is also, perhaps, a way of suggesting that the foundation of the 'New Thebes' by Achaemenides is patterned on the foundation of the original Thebes by Cadmus is supported by the following entry for 'Ippocrene' in *De montibus [De fontibus]*:

The Hippocrene is a Boeotian font. Some believe that this font was born of the blow dealt by the horse Pegasus and draws its name from this. The source of this fabrication is easily uncovered if one examines a version of the tale subscribed to by some. These maintain that it was near this fountain that Cadmus, mounted on his horse, first stopped while seeking a dwelling place for himself and his companions; and as he was the inventor of the Greek letters, the conception of which perhaps came to him in this very place [quarum forsan meditacionem ibidem sumpsit], this font is held sacred to the Muses. (*De fontibus*, 71)[61]

Here, Boccaccio offers two variant stories aimed at accounting for the prominence granted 'hippo' [horse] in the name of such an important spring. According to the first variant, this name simply commemorates the traditional belief that it was the sharp kick of a horse, Pegasus, that unleashed the subterranean spring. The second account – one that I have found only in Boccaccio – traces this unusual name to the moment when an equestrian Cadmus, having briefly interrupted his quest for a new homeland to gaze at the spring's waters, is inspired to invent the letters of the Greek alphabet. In *De casibus* we read that Cadmus not only invented the letters of the alphabet as he gazed upon a fountain (here, no longer the Hippocrene but the 'Libetridem' spring – named after the Thracian town of Libethrum, putative home of Orpheus),[62] but undertook the intellectual education of an ignorant and rustic people: 'doctrinam rudibus indoctisque populis dederat' (I 6, 3). Boccaccio's partiality for this variant of the Cadmus myth in which the mesmerizing waters of a font induce meditation and spark invention is suggested by its presence not only in *De montibus* and *De casibus* but in the *Esposizioni* (II, lit., 33–4) and the *Genealogie*: 'others hold that while sitting, lost in thought, in front of the Hippocrene fountain, he invented the signs of the sixteen letters which were later used throughout Greece' (II 63, 4).[63]

Examples of this association of geological springs with poetic inspiration are found throughout Boccaccio's works.[64] Nor is this simply a poetic contrivance, for, as Boccaccio frequently reminds us, Petrarch, the greatest poet of his age, had sought refuge in 'a secluded valley, in an exceptionally lonely part of France, where the Sorga, the greatest of springs, takes its rise' (*Genealogie* XIV, 19; Osgood, 89). This same theme is taken up with even greater enthusiasm in Boccaccio's description of the Sorgue in *De montibus [de fluminibus]*. Here the Sorgue's fertile waters are said to nourish the growth of such appetizing sod that cows, greedily plunging their heads beneath the water's edge to nibble the tasty greens, are often at risk of drowning. The same miraculous waters that spark this bovine felicity were, Boccaccio goes on to say, no less inspiring to the great Petrarch, for it was precisely in the Sorgue valley that he wrote, among other things, his *Africa* and *Eclogues* (though, it should be added, in composing the former, Petrarch seems to have fared little better than the cows, for like them, he is so completely immersed in the copious waters – the font of classical erudition – that he often comes close to drowning both himself and his readers).

Boccaccio's integration of precisely those elements of both the Cadmus and the Pegasus myth that evoke the complementary themes of poetic composition and literacy invites us to view Achaemenides's colonization of Fiesole as a synthesis that is not merely racial and political, but cultural.[65]

Certainly, the emphasis on Cadmus as inventor of the Greek alphabet is highly suggestive, for it is likely that Boccaccio intends that we see in the 'new' Cadmus, Achaemenides, the founder of the 'New [Italic] Thebes,' the figure of a culture-hero responsible for introducing the Greek alphabet (taken, synecdochally, for the whole of Greek literary culture) to Italy and, in this sense, a worthy precursor of Boccaccio himself.[66]

Indeed, this mythological drama of cultural synthesis and reconciliation mirrors, and provides a 'historical' precedent for, the cultural synthesis spearheaded by Boccaccio, perhaps the greatest advocate of Greek
literary culture among the early humanists, for whom this tale of the
rediscovery and reinstatement of Achaemenides may well serve as an
allegory of the 'repatriation' of Greek learning – a body of knowledge
that had been 'marooned' on the margin of culture for much of the
Middle Ages – to the classical tradition. It is no wonder that the guiding
metaphor of the *Genealogie* is that of a perilous sea voyage ventured with
the aim of salvaging, and reassembling into a single body, the wide-
strewn members of the corpus of classical learning. Whether or not this
is the function of Boccaccio's tale of Achaemenides, the desire to effect
a synergistic union of Latin and Greek learning – and to somehow legit-
imize the latter – is apparent in both Boccaccio's fiction and his scholarly compendia.

In the vignette of Nicostrata in *De mulieribus claris*, Boccaccio credits
the Greeks with having introduced philosophy, eloquence, the mechanical arts, and legislation to Italian soil. Boccaccio's enthusiasm for Greek
letters is equally apparent in his biography of Proba (*De mulieribus*
XCVII), whom he praises not only for her mastery of Latin, apparent in
her famous Virgilian cento, a virtuosic (if tedious) sacred history composed of a 'patchwork' of verses drawn from Virgil's poetry, but for her
no less consummate mastery of Greek – one presupposed by the tradition that she had composed a Homeric cento as well (8). This philhel-
lenic attitude comes through with particular clarity in the following
much-cited passage from *Genealogie* XV:[67]

> Since nobody knows Greek, the old custom must perforce be obsolete, I am
> sorry, then, for Latin learning, if it has so completely rejected the study of
> Greek that we do not even recognize the characters. Though Latin litera-
> ture be sufficient unto itself, and enjoys the exclusive attention of the whole
> western world, yet without question it would gain much light through an
> alliance with Greek. Besides the ancient Latin writers have not by any means
> appropriated all that is Greek. Much yet remains unrevealed to us, and
> much by knowledge of which we might profit greatly. (*Genealogie* XV 7, 4;
> *Boccaccio on Poetry*, trans. Osgood [hereafter cited as Osgood], 119)

The lines that follow this manifesto-like statement are no less remarkable, for in them we read Boccaccio's declaration, punctuated with the
imperious anaphora 'Ipse fui,' that it was *he* who first cultivated Greek

poetry among the Tuscans, *he* who detained the Byzantine Greek Leontius Pilatus in Tuscany to elucidate the works of Homer for the Florentines, and thus, finally, *he* who must ultimately be credited with the restoration to Tuscany of the long-neglected works of Homer and the other Greek authors: 'Ipse insuper fui, qui primus meis sumptibus Homeri libros et alios quosdam Grecos in Etruriam revocavi' (XV 7, 5).

Readers disposed to view these claims with some suspicion as being, perhaps, a bit too self-congratulatory and rhetorically overblown should consider that Petrarch, in his letter to Homer (*Familiares* XXIV, 12), identifies Boccaccio (though not by name) as one of a select group of writers able to appreciate Homer's contribution; Filippo Villani (fourteenth century) notes the remarkable diligence with which Boccaccio, aided by Leonzio Pilato, pursued his study of Greek; Giannozzo Manetti (early fifteenth century) remarks that Boccaccio made greater progress in the study of Greek than Petrarch and was the first to import Greek literature to Italy;[68] Ugo Foscolo, the great Romantic poet and literary critic, observes in his 1825 *Discorso storico sul testo del Decamerone* that Petrarch 'knew nothing of Greek' and that 'whatever acquaintance, in Tuscany or Italy, they had with the writers of that language, they owed entirely to Boccaccio';[69] Attilio Hortis (late nineteenth century), far more measured in his evaluation of Boccaccio's practical knowledge of Greek, nonetheless concedes that Boccaccio 'made a great step forward' in Greek studies.[70] While Boccaccio's pivotal role in inaugurating the new ascendancy of Greek studies in general, and of Homer in particular, during the second half of the fourteenth century has certainly not been neglected by Boccaccio scholars of more recent years, it is too little acknowledged by scholars in the wider sphere of medieval and Renaissance studies, for many of whom Boccaccio (notwithstanding the tremendous influence of such erudite Latin works as *De casibus*, *De mulieribus*, and the *Genealogie*) will always be associated with that Silenus-like, facetious *buontempone*, whom countless generations of readers have conjured up from the pages of the *Decameron* (or had foisted upon them by wide-circulating popular misconceptions): an all too resilient caricature that does not square well with the far more sober and nuanced picture of the dedicated scholar whose tireless efforts restored the Homeric poems to the Latin West.[71]

The third, and last of these cultural models of miscegeny to be discussed in this chapter does not represent a curious 'historical' parenthesis within a larger fiction, but is itself the presiding theme of the text, the

Ninfale fiesolano, in which it is found. In this short work describing the Fiesolan origins of Florence we are presented with a fairly complete anatomy of the process of acculturation; sylvan, nomadic nymphs (implicitly autochthonic) are sexually preyed upon by members of a more settled community of local shepherds (whether indigenes or primitive settlers it is impossible to say) who, in turn, are eventually integrated into a culturally sophisticated community of colonizers governed by Atalante. Though the early stages of this process are fraught with sexual violence and cruel metamorphoses, there is much beauty and genuine ardour in this bucolic setting and it is, therefore, by no means certain whether Atalantes's cultural innovations should, finally, be viewed in a positive or a negative light. However one may view such matters, what cannot be disputed is the critical place granted miscegenation throughout this imaginative history of Fiesolan and Florentine origins.

The Ninfale fiesolano: *Boccaccio's Erogenous Eden and the Fall into Culture*

The *Ninfale fiesolano*, a poetic account of the origins of both Fiesole and Florence, unfolds in a technologically primitive, pre-agricultural era when bread is made from chestnut flour, and 'wine' from boiled herbs sweetened with honey. The local population is limited to a handful of settlers who have made their home in the foothills of the Fiesolan mountains since ancient times and a wandering population of nymphs who inhabit the mountain forests. The homes of the valley-dwelling settlers are every bit as crude as their diet; there are no palaces or residential complexes, but only dry-laid stone or mud-and-wattle hovels. All of the action of the *Ninfale* takes place within a loosely scribed trapezoid skirted by mountains and rivers: hemmed in to the north by the system of mountains upon which Fiesole is constructed, to the south by the Arno, to the east by the Mensola river, and to the west by the Mugnone river.[72]

If the absence of grain and wine recalls the classical Golden Age, the presence of fire (their meat, though uncondimented, is cooked) and of the rudiments of architecture suggests elements of the Epicurean, evolutionistic, strand of primitivism familiar to Boccaccio through such texts as Vitruvius's *De architectura* (II, 1) and Horace's *Sermonum* (I, 3, 96ff).

Against this background of rustic simplicity unfolds the story of a young man, Africo, who is smitten with love for Mensola, a mountain nymph of Diana's party. Though both Africo and Mensola come to tragic ends, their son, Pruneo, is destined to become an important figure in Fiesole's political hegemony: a seneschal to Atalante (the mythical founder of the city of Fiesole), governor of the Fiesolan people, and father of the future leaders and governors of Fiesole.

Girafone, Africo's father, repeatedly warns Africo that their family has been selected out for punishment by Diana due to the rape of Cialla, one of Diana's virgins, by Africo's grandfather Mugnone, and that he, Africo, must therefore scrupulously avoid any contact with the mountain nymphs. Such warnings, however, are destined to fall on deaf ears, for the nymphs are presented as sylvan beauties clad in diaphanous linen gowns (which they are perpetually hiking up to their waists to unfetter their feet in flight).[73] Africo, endowed with a no less angelic sort of beauty, and to whom few, if any, local women are available (none are mentioned), can hardly be faulted for directing his sight upwards towards Diana's flock; indeed, such a decision seems all but inevitable.

In the first of several scenes coloured by an Actaeon-like strain of illicit – and, at least initially, inadvertent – voyeurism, Africo, himself unseen, catches a glimpse of a beautiful nymph, Mensola. Having unwittingly stumbled into the toils of love, the accidental predator becomes the accidental prey (in Boccaccio's revised version of Ovid's Actaeon motif the raw physical horror of Actaeon's muted tongue and cruelly mutilated body cedes to a subtler, though no less acute, psychological variety of torment). From this point on, the mytho-historical etiology of Fiesole and Florence is inextricably bound up with the eternal warring between Diana and Venus: a supernatural contest which plays out in the natural sphere in the ongoing antagonism between the chaste wards of Diana (implicitly identified with a conventual community of nuns) and the followers of Venus (a secular community of Amor's devotees).[74]

It is fully consistent with this dynamic that when Africo appeals to Venus to help him seduce Mensola (one of Diana's wards), she readily supplies him with a number of wily stratagems, including persuasive rhetoric and cross-dressing, aimed at giving him the opportunity to get close enough to Mensola to rape her (octave 203). Nor is Africo the sort to balk at such a suggestion; indeed, upon first seeing Mensola, he soliloquizes to the effect that were it not for his fear of Diana, he would have taken her by force ('i' l'arei per forza presa' [octave 27]). Though awkward pleas (modelled on Polyphemus's bumbling entreaties to Galatea in the *Metamorphoses*) garner him a glimpse of Mensola's face (octave 104), and transvestitism secures his safe conduct into the closed society of nymphs, it is, finally, force alone that allows him to achieve his final object; he ends up raping Mensola:

Per la contesa che facean si desta
tal che prima dormia malinconoso,
e, con superbia rizzando la cresta,
cominciò a picchiar l'uscio furioso;
e tanto dentro vi diè della testa,
ch'egli entrò dentro, non già con riposo,
ma con battaglia grande ed urlamento
e forse che di sangue spargimento.
(octave 244)

And as they struggled thus, something awoke that, till that time, had slept dejectedly. Lifting its haughty crest, it commenced wildly to knock against the gate and thrust its head so far within that it gained entry, though not without great struggle and loud shrieks and not without perhaps some loss of blood. (*Nymph of Fiesole*, trans. Donno [hereafter cited as Donno], 70)[75]

Whatever else might be said of this elaborate metaphor, a sexualized storming of the castle gate coloured by a worldly, ribald humour that seems grotesquely out of place in the pastoral *Ninfale*, it is clear enough that Boccaccio has gone to great lengths to draw attention to the coercive violence of Africo's act, to the fact that Mensola's virginity was taken against her will ('tolta / la sua virginità contro a sua voglia' [246]). Consequently, it is particularly important to note that Boccaccio does not attribute Mensola's pregnancy to this initial rape but to the consensual lovemaking that takes place later that same evening. In fact, the procreative potential of their sexual union seems to have been deliberately avoided in the context of the rape, for the very first allusion to pregnancy occurs in the octave (306) directly preceding this scene of consensual lovemaking where we are told that Mensola's innocence is such that she does not know how humans are conceived and born ('per qual degnitade / l'uom si creasse, e poi come nascesse'), and therefore does not suspect that sexual coupling has any consequences at all – let alone a relation to conception or to birth. The octaves (307 to 310) in which the actual lovemaking is described are characterized by a crescendo-like movement from a condition of violent disparity to one of unity (their two bodies merge into a single body), ecstatic communion (a flurried exchange of kisses, bites, and caresses), and orgasmic resolution (the scene is punctuated by the onomatopoeic anaphora, 'omè, omè, omè'). In the octave (311) immediately following this lovemaking scene, we are told that Mensola has become pregnant with a baby boy: 'd'Africo Mensola s'ingravidava / d'un fantin maschio.' This artful insertion of the lovemaking interlude between an allusion to the physiological mechanics of human conception on one side and an affirmation that such a conception has taken place on the other, leaves no doubt that Boccaccio would have us associate Pruneo's conception with a fully consensual and loving act.

This element of volition on Mensola's part is important, for in addition to suggesting that Boccaccio adheres to the notion, widespread in the Middle Ages, that a child could be conceived only if the woman experienced pleasure (it was postulated that a female 'semen' released, like that of the male, upon climax, was necessary for the formation of the fetus)[76] it imbues the *schiatta africana* [Africo's lineage] with a somewhat more benevolent air; physiological 'law' demands that the actual conception be traced not to the initial, violent, but to the subsequent, amorous, union. Although one can hardly dismiss the brutality of the rape, it is, finally, an act of reciprocal love that produces Pruneo, the first in a series of great civic leaders born of the African lineage.

Though in the moments immediately following this consensual coupling Mensola offers Africo many assurances of her desire to see him again, all his subsequent efforts to find her prove fruitless, for Mensola, racked by guilt and fearful of Diana's wrath, has forsworn the company of nymphs and sequestered herself in a cave where she anxiously awaits the birth of her child. Consumed by desire and despairing of ever seeing Mensola again, Africo is gradually reduced to a state of such profound depression that he decides to take his own life: 'pervenuto all'acqua del vallone, / ove Mensola sua sforzata avea' ['arriving in that stream in the valley where he had seized Mensola and forced her to his will'] (octave 356; Donno, 101), he plunges a sharp spear into his chest and falls into the stream, staining its waters with his blood. His cremated body is buried on the bank of that portion of the river that still runs red with his blood: 'acciò che'l nome suo non si spegnesse, / ma sempre mai quel fiume il ritenesse' ['so that his name should never perish, but that the river should retain it as its own'] (octave 371; Donno, 107).[77]

The watery site of Africo's suicide is described as having been the same as that in which he raped Mensola. Consequently, Africo chooses to end his life and spill his blood in the same water where he brought about Mensola's symbolic death, water very possibly infused with Mensola's blood shed at the loss of her virginity ('e forse di sangue spargimento' [and perhaps a shedding of blood, octave 244]).[78] The carefully orchestrated symmetry of these two moments – the rape and the suicide – not only encourages the reader to view the rape as a variety of 'suicide' (a principle already dramatized in Girafone's tale of Mugnone), and the suicide a type of 'rape' (a notion most memorably dramatized in Dido's suicide in the *Aeneid*), but encourages the reader to consider the important structuring role that other, related conjunctions of opposites play in the narrative: colonizer/indigene, consensual/coercive, suicide/'murder,' death/birth, and so forth. The morbid mixing of blood – more, it is true, conceptual than real – implied by Africo's shedding of his own blood in the same place where he once shed Mensola's blood, is reminiscent of the similarly macabre mixing of blood recorded by Boccaccio in his retelling of Ovid's tale of Pyramus and Thisbe in *De mulieribus* XIII. Though Pyramus and Thisbe die virgins, the union, Boccaccio tells us, that cruel Fortune prevented in life is fulfilled by the mixing of their blood in death: 'envious Fortune could not prevent the mingling of the unhappy blood [sanguinem misceri prohibuisse non potuit] of those whom she had prevented from joining in a gentle embrace' (*De mulieribus* XIII, 11; *Famous Women,* trans. Brown [hereafter cited as Brown], 59) – hardly a satisfactory solution, but confirmation that Boccaccio saw such an extra-corporeal mixing of blood as having a potentially sexual connotation.[79]

The procreative resonance that this mixing of blood would have had to Boccaccio's contemporaries is easy to overlook in an age when much that was once inscrutable in the human reproductive process has entered the realm of the banal. It is useful, therefore, to recall Statius's account of human embryology in the *Commedia,* according to which sperm is a form of purified blood that mixes with the woman's blood in her 'natural vasello' [natural vessel] (*Purg.* XXV, 43–5). This travesty of biological conception, the posthumous mixing of Mensola's and Africo's blood in the very same place where Pruneo was conceived, is a poignant reminder of the extraordinary sacrifice demanded for the foundation of the *schiatta Africana.*

With the advent of the empire-building Atalante, the curtains are finally drawn on the nymphaen idyll. Not long after his arrival, he embarks on the foundation of Fiesole while his men set about flushing the free-roaming nymphs from their forest haunts and marrying them off against their will – a distinctly Romulan solution that recalls Livy's account of the violent assimilation of the Sabines to the Latins: 'e così fûr le ninfe allor cacciate, / e quelle che fûr prese, maritate' [and thus were the nymphs chased down, and those who were captured, married off] (octave 437).

The disturbing notion that civic and cultural institutions arise from the violent domestication of recalcitrant women is found in many of Boccaccio's works. The *Teseida* begins with an account of Theseus's battle with the Amazons, who, though valiant warriors, are eventually forced not only to surrender, but to submit to wedlock with the Athenians. In the *Teseida*, the allegory of civilization is marred by few ambiguities; Theseus is cast as a humane champion of civility whereas the Amazons are portrayed as a band of man-hating extremists. Boccaccio's description of their premeditated, barbaric slaughter of their own husbands does little to ingratiate them to the reader.[80] This is certainly not the case in the *Ninfale*, where the process of debarbarization is fully nuanced.

Though the polluting of a virgin cult is viewed as a prerequisite for the creation of an exalted genealogical line, the violence involved in this process is not forgotten, but amply commemorated through the device of toponyms. Indeed, the various rivers that constitute the majority of the geographical boundaries of the future cities of Fiesole and Florence preserve the names – Africo, Mensola, Mugnone – of the earliest victims in this process of domestication. However, it is not the names alone that are preserved, for in every case the victim's physical body has itself, through a process of metamorphosis, coalesced with the surrounding waters. It is the death of the mythical progenitor and subsequent transformation into a geographic boundary of some sort that establishes a tenable basis for the demarcation of private property. If the territorial claim of the autochthons derives from their original union with the natural environment, that of the colonists is based on a posthumous, belated melding with the natural environment; the former are united by birth, the latter by death.

It is for this reason that Atalante, in determining the property that will be Pruneo's wedding gift, selects the land that lies between the Mugnone and the Mensola. That, Africo, in his river avatar, is located in between the Mugnone and the Mensola is entirely fitting, for in so many respects he is a transitional figure representing the process of debarbarization that enables the *schiatta africana* to legitimately extend its territorial claim from the hovel in the foothills of Mount Cèceri to that fertile tract of the Arno valley destined to become Florence.

Whereas Mugnone seems to have been driven by an antisocial desire for sexual satiation alone, his grandson, Africo, expresses from the first a socially constructive interest in marriage: 'Qual saria / di me più grazioso e più felice, / se tal fanciulla io avessi per mia / isposa?' [Who would be happier or more fortunate than I, if I could have that maiden for my bride?] (octave 27). Though Africo's erotic obsession so drains him that he is driven to suicide, his belief in the social convention of marriage is rewarded, or so it seems, by the gift of a child – his spitting image – who is destined to continue his genetic, though not his erotic, legacy. Perhaps because Atalante's campaign to marry off the woodland nymphs effectively prevents him from pursuing his father's bittersweet destiny, or possibly because his parents' tragic fortunes are so deeply impressed on his mind, Pruneo accepts a purely political marriage arranged by Atalante, who gives him Tironea, the daughter of a nobleman, as a bride and the sweeping tract of land between the banks of the Mugnone and the Mensola as a wedding gift (octave 448).

Released, it would seem, from both financial and erotic concerns, Pruneo is free to focus on more civic-minded pursuits and duties. In fact, in the octave immediately following his marriage, we are presented with a picture of Pruneo as a variety of culture-hero, the builder of a 'nobil casamento' [grand residence] – to be contrasted with the mud-and-wattle hut which had been his father's abode – on a promontory overlooking the unruly and savage landscape that he, as seneschal, is destined to tame: 'e quel paese, ch'era molto strano, / tosto dimesticò, sì com'io sento' [and that country, that was so wild, he quickly tamed, as I've been told].[81] A child of love, his social and political agenda is guided by a wholesome, patriotic love: 'e questo fece sol per grande amore / ch'al paese portava di buon core' [and this he did only out of the great and sincere love he bore for that country] (octave 449). Because Boccaccio's authorship of the *Ninfale fiesolano* has been questioned by at least one recent critic, it should be remarked that offsetting the linguistic and other discrepancies that have been submitted to cast doubt on his authorship is an underlying ideological consistency where this notion of fruitful miscegeny is concerned.[82]

Though the synopsis of the traditional history of Fiesole and Florence which constitutes a somewhat awkward appendix to the *Ninfale* (octaves 436ff) may seem like little more than a slipshod bid to accredit the story of Africo and Mensola by integrating it into the authoritative historical tradition of the chronicles (as critics have long noted, it replicates numerous aspects of the *Chronica de origine civitatis* and Giovanni Villani's *Cronica* among others), it actually – and this has been generally overlooked – attests to the truly innovative quality of Boccaccio's historical vision.[83] Francesco Bruni – the only critic, to my knowledge, who has explored the originality of Boccaccio's etiology of Fiesole and Florence in the *Ninfale* – focuses his discussion on Boccaccio's decision to integrate his completely original acount of Florentine/Fiesolan prehistory with the traditional 'histories' of Fiesole and Florence preserved in the chronicles. He argues that Boccaccio's interlinking of his invented prehistory with these conventional histories has the effect not only of validating the invented history (*Boccaccio*, 234), but of highlighting the theme of historical, cultural, and biological continuity between two distinct 'systems': the old, natural, order of the autochthons and the new, political, order instituted by Atalante. The historical, cultural, and biological continuity of the old order is achieved through its incorporation – albeit in a revised form – into the new order (227–34). Bruni also discerns a political agenda in Boccaccio's interlinked histories: that of creating a population of Fiesolans – the descendants of Pruneo – who, in stark contrast to the conventional perspective, are well disposed to Florence (283–84).[84]

Bruni's important insights cast much light on the *Ninfale's* strange etiological 'appendix.' However, the further implications of Boccaccio's decision to conjure up an indigenous, autochthonous population (octave 5) – in complete contradiction of Villani's authoritative history where Attalante encounters a Tuscany 'tutto disabitato di gente umana' [completely uninhabited by humans] (*Cronica* I, VII) – have not been adequately explored. Like the 'mondo sanza gente' [world without people] (*Inf.* XXVI, 117) sought by Dante's Ulysses, Villani's untenanted Tuscany is virgin turf, the ideal site for a new beginning. In a sense, the *Ninfale* represents an attempt to supply a rational underpinning for an otherwise dubious history; the mythical founder Attalante is not eliminated so much as historicized. In place of Villani's implausible 'mondo sanza gente,' with its collateral emphasis on racial purity (there are no natives with whom to mix), Boccaccio substitutes a refreshingly egalitarian paradigm, one which not only acknowledges but celebrates the genetic and cultural contribution of indigenous peoples. This same revision of conventional Florentine historiography can be inferred from a description of Fiesole in the *Comedia delle ninfe fiorentine*:

In Italia, delle mondane parti chiarezza speciale, siede Etruria [Tuscany], di quella, sì com'io credo, principal membro e singular bellezza; nella quale [...] quasi nel suo mezzo e più felice parte del santo seno, inver le stelle dalle sue pianure si leva un fruttuoso monte, *già dagli antichi Corito* [Fiesole] *nominato, avanti che Atalante, primo di quello abitatore, su vi salisse.* (III, 1, emphasis mine)

In Italy, illustrious splendour among earthly places, there lies Etruria, which is, I believe, the principal site and singular beauty of this region. In this place [...] – and almost in the center and most prosperous part of its blessed bosom – a fertile mount rises toward the stars, *called Corythus* [Fiesole] *by the ancients before Atlas, its first inhabitant, ascended there.* (*L'Ameto*, trans. Serafini-Sauli [hereafter cited as Serafini-Sauli, 5, emphasis mine)[85]

Here too, Boccaccio stresses the presence of a pre-Atlantean, indigenous culture, for though Atalante may lay claim to priority where the coloniz-ing of Fiesole itself is concerned, he neither discovered nor named it. Moreover, this characteristic pattern of a productive mixing of ethnicities is repeated during the period of Florence's construction and coloniza-tion by the Romans. Not only are we informed that Africo's descendents intermarry with these Roman colonizers ('si furo insieme tutti imparen-tati, / e fatti cittadin con grande amore' ['the new families were joined in marriage to the old ones. They were made citizens and were invited to share all honors,' octave 457; Donno, 130]), but it is further implied that this ethnic mixing makes a vital contribution to the city's thriving popu-lation, prosperity, and peace: 'Così multiplicando la cittade / di Firenze in persone e'n gran ricchezza, / gran tempo resse con tranquillitade' ['Thus Florence increased in wealth and population and enjoyed peace for many years'] (octave 458; Donno, 130). By foregrounding the central role of the aboriginal population of Tuscany in both its political and genetic future, Boccaccio reminds us once again that cities do not spring from the earth like the Spartoi, fully formed, but evolve gradually through a martial shedding and venereal mixing of blood. Miscegena-tion is the biological wellspring of nations.

The radical quality of Boccaccio's undisguised advocacy of miscegena-tion in the previous etiologies is most effectively measured against the more conventional view epitomized by Dante's Cacciaguida.

Shortly after entering the heaven of Mars in the fifteenth canto of *Paradiso*, Dante comes face to face with his great-great-grandfather Cacciaguida, a martyred crusader and upstanding member of the an-cient Florentine aristocracy, who proceeds to paint for him an idealized portrait of an earlier Florence: one whose simple walls bound a peaceful, sober, and chaste city, not yet corrupted by the infiltration of new people – 'gente nuova' [newcomers to the city] – with their taste for luxury and thirst for quick fortunes – 'sùbiti guadagni' [quick gains] (*Inf.* XVI, 73);

a profoundly wholesome Florence, in which it was not unusual to find one woman babbling sweet nothings to her infant while another, distaff in hand, entertained her rapt audience with ancient tales of Troy, Fiesole, and Rome.

The reader's curiosity concerning what forces could possibly have transformed this idyllic Florence of doting mothers and pious men into a nest of iniquity is soon satisfied, for in the very next canto Cacciaguida declares that it is the promiscuous mixing of peoples that has led, and continues to lead, to the corruption of cities in much the same way, he adds with disgust, that the indiscriminate mixing of foods wreaks havoc on one's body: 'Sempre la confusion delle persone / principio fu del mal della cittade, / come del vostro il cibo che s'appone' ['The mingling of the populations led / to evil in the city, even as / food piled on food destroys the body's health'] (*Par.* XVI, 67–9; Mandelbaum).[86] Oh how much better, he observes in this same elegiac vein, it would have been, had the noble, Roman population of early Florence never been contaminated by the hoards of rustic men and women descending from the outlying villages of Campi, Certaldo, and Fegghine!

One can only imagine how Boccaccio must have bridled at this contemptuous assessment of the immigrant populations of Florence, for his own ancestors were among these early adventurers who had emigrated from Certaldo to Florence in search of better fortunes: men and women whose industry and ingenuity had done so much to revitalize Florence's economy and spark its cultural renaissance. The ancient tales of 'Troy, Fiesole, and Rome' to which Cacciaguida refers with such nostalgia – incredible myths so deeply ingrained in the national psyche that, as we have seen, they found a place even in Giovanni Villani's otherwise levelheaded chronicle of Florence – only fuelled this pernicious myth of racial purity by insisting on the supposed Roman origins of the first Florentines.

Fortunately, in matters of history, Boccaccio was obliged to accept neither the poetic confabulations of the distaff-wielding matrons of old Florence nor the dubious, ethnocentric histories of the Florentine chroniclers; his intimate knowledge of Virgil's poetic and Livy's secular histories of Rome – together with his lived experience of a burgeoning Florence – had taught him an indelible lesson that loudly contradicted Cacciaguida's doctrine of racial purity. Far from vitiating the body politic, the synthesis of racially and culturally diverse peoples alone supplies the dynamism necessary for the creation of true empires: an unwritten precept dramatized in the poetic fictions of the *Aeneid* and confirmed by Livy's Roman history.

It can hardly be a coincidence that when Boccaccio sets about writing his own foundation histories of such Tuscan cities as Certaldo, Florence, and Fiesole, these tales no longer serve to perpetuate a Cacciaguida-like agenda of racial chauvinism, but instead bear witness to this notion that cultural and political preeminence is the product of a fruitful variety of ethnic and cultural 'cross-pollination'; Boccaccio systematically subverts the traditional, nationalistic function of these ancient tales in order to deliver a radically new and thoroughly egalitarian gospel of racial, social, and intellectual inclusivity. Though he certainly acknowledges the negative effects springing from a 'confusion delle persone,' he also recognizes the fruitful consequences of racial mixing; while such mixing may be the origin of the evil that afflicts cities, the 'principio ... del mal,' it is, no less importantly, the fountainhead, 'principio,' of cities themselves.

As I have attempted to illustrate in the first section of this chapter, the outskirts of Florence – in particular Fiesole and Certaldo – are, for a wide variety of reasons, viewed as places of origin, both physical and cultural. In the second section I examined several fictional accounts of city founding in these same peripheral areas in order to better understand Boccaccio's views regarding the mechanics of nation founding and the process whereby a rustic community is transformed into a cosmopolis. In the third and last section of this chapter I will concentrate on the way in which the figure of the poet reproduces, in microcosmic fashion, this larger pattern of genetic mixing. This is accomplished, in large part, by Boccaccio's frequent portrayal of the figure of the poet – usually a projection of himself – as a variety of social hybrid: the product of a socially heterogeneous coupling (most often, that of a sophisticated noblewoman with an unschooled shepherd or merchant).[87]

Boccaccio's Fruitful Bastardy

Long before Edmund, the charismatic bastard of Shakespeare's *Lear,* saw fit to turn conventional assumptions on their ear by arguing that the stale and tired marriage bed produces a tribe of fops whereas bastards, conceived in the throes of passion, are made of fiercer stuff, Boccaccio issued a similar, if far more subtle, vindication of bastardy. Whereas Edmund traces the vitality of illegitimate children to the heat of passion in which they were engendered, Boccaccio, himself a bastard – the natural son of the Certaldan Merchant Boccaccino di Chelino and a mother about whom much is speculated but nothing known[88] – does not argue that the particular circumstances of conception confer advantages on bastards; rather, for Boccaccio, as I will argue in the pages that follow, it is ethnic and social mixing – a phenomenon more often associated with illicit than with socially sanctioned unions – that seems to account for the particular vitality of bastards.

It has long been acknowledged that Boccaccio's early works are seeded with what appear to be autobiographical vignettes. The wholesale mining of these so-called autobiographies by eighteenth- and nineteenth-century critics eager to reconstruct the undocumented chapters of Boccaccio's life – the identity of his mother, the place of his birth, and the course of his youthful dalliances – reaches a sort of climax in Vincenzo Crescini's monograph of 1887, *Contributo agli studi sul Boccaccio*, a monument to the perils of uniting wishful thinking with vast erudition.[89] His often ingenious, sometimes far-fetched, and always tendentious arguments are punctuated with patronizing gibes at the work of the more conservative professor Koerting ('Vani sforzi, prof. Koerting!' [Futile efforts, prof. Koerting!]) and clinched by the truly remarkable discovery of a series of anagrammatic names in one of these embedded autobiographies that appear, at first blush, to correspond to historical characters known, or suspected, to have been involved in Boccaccio's life.

By the time Francesco Torraca published his *Per la biografia di Giovanni Boccaccio* in 1912, the compelling reconstructions of Crescini and his Romantic and Positivist precursors had taken on a life of their own; a sort of tautological method was firmly in place whereby Boccaccio's fictional characters were themselves conscripted to prove their historical reality (a phenomenon first evidenced in Filippo Villani's revised version of his profile of Boccaccio in the *De origine civitatis florentie*).[90] Though Torraca accepts many of Crescini's basic premises, a more temperate critic, he sets about correcting Crescini's monomaniacal inclination to see Boccaccio and his alleged love interest Maria 'dovunque appariscano insieme un uomo e una donna' [wherever a man and a woman appear together].[91] Had Boccaccio, Torraca wryly observes, truly intended to burden his reader with such an abundance of alter egos, Maria (the book's dedicatee), wearied by this masquerade of incessant mirrorings, might well have been driven to cast his 'piacevole libretto' [pleasant little book] into a corner! An outright rejection of Crescini's thesis finally took place in the mid 1940s when the seminal studies of two more clear-headed critics, Vittore Branca and Giuseppe Billanovich, finally succeeded in chasing the wandering phantoms of Boccaccio's idealized autobiography back to the pages of his vernacular fiction.

Branca's central argument, and the one most destructive to Crescini's cherished illusions, was that the thematic unity among these allegedly autobiographical interludes long peddled as certain proof of their authenticity did not result from their common basis in a historical event, but rather from Boccaccio's regular use of conventional literary schemes of a sort widely attested in classical texts, popular legends, romances, the lyric tradition, and love treatises. No one – least of all Branca – would maintain that these embedded 'autobiographies' are purely generic, entirely divorced from Boccaccio's real experiences. However, the puzzle remains. How does one go about the seemingly hopeless task of winnowing character from convention, man from motif?[92] Branca's optimistic resolution to this conundrum is that a true portrait of Boccaccio will be incrementally revealed as such fictionalized autobiographies are reassessed in the light of newly discovered archival data. My own perspective is one that casts a somewhat leery eye on both authorial projections – the idealized portraits of such fanciful autobiographies – and the allegedly 'hard' data extracted from institutional archives. Clearly, poetic fictions based on traditional patterns should not be summarily discounted as an empty show of erudition or evidence of plagiarism, for beneath the veil of fiction lie concealed historical, moral, and spiritual truths. Conversely, documented 'truths' should not be uncritically embraced, for they are often poor indicators of psychological, spiritual truths: there are many children with two parents who are nevertheless 'orphans,' many married couples who are spiritually, if not legally, divorced, and so forth.[93] It is only, I would suggest, by piercing both the idealizing veil of literary fictions and the deadening pall of 'empiric' fact that any progress can be made in grasping something of the 'real' Boccaccio. Only when we have been released from the two-pronged tyranny of abstract generalities and concrete particularities will we finally be free to roam that vast intermediate space inhabited by Boccaccio. This is an approach authorized by Boccaccio himself, who actually provides his readers with a key for understanding his technique of intermingling the 'ideal' – or imagined – events of his narratives with the real events of his life.

In his dedication to Giovanna at the beginning of the *Filostrato*, Boccaccio describes the torments to which he has been subjected ever since her departure, claiming that the necessity of keeping his erotic anguish to himself has resulted in a morbid condition so severe that he would surely have died had it not been for his fortuitous – or providential ('quasi da nascosa divinità spirato' [as though inspired by a hidden deity] (I, 26)]) – discovery of a method ('modo' [I, 26]) to relieve himself of this repressed grief. This inspired method simply consists in using the ancient tale as a narrative surrogate, or 'scudo,' as he puts it, for his private erotic drama: a roman-à-clef. In adapting a tale whose general outlines correspond to the circumstances of his own erotic 'history,' Boccaccio has hit upon a sophisticated means of safely venting his secret passion. Since, however, the literary scheme – the tale of the ancient lovers – does not tally perfectly with Boccaccio's and Giovanna's lived experience, there are, Boccaccio acknowledges, certain inevitable discrepancies between the two. However, and this is critical, Boccaccio indicates that it is precisely in these incongruities that Giovanna may find a key both for understanding his hidden desires and for determining whether or not he deserves her 'pietà' [pity] (I, 35).

This same method of conscripting fictional surrogates to enact lived experience is described again in the dedication of the *Teseida*. Once again, Boccaccio selects a narrative 'mask' – in this case the 'antichissima istoria' [very ancient tale] of the noble Theban youths Palemone and Arcita, and Emilia, the beautiful Amazon who is the object of their mutual desire – to record the no less stormy intrigues of his own relationship with 'Fiammetta.' Once again Boccaccio observes that there are inconsistencies between the ancient tale and the personal history that it encodes. These, he claims, are due to modesty on the one hand, and the need to follow the traditional storyline on the other.

Like the ancient tale, the conventional literary scheme serves Boccaccio as a variety of screen, 'scudo.' Consequently, the reader intent on discovering the true Boccaccio is best advised to look for evidence of subtle fractures: the places where Boccaccio's fiction breaks from the literary scheme, where conventional patterns appear to take on a more personal profile, or where (and this information lies forever buried with Boccaccio and his historical paramours) the events of the private history fall short of the idealized actions portrayed in the poetic fiction.

The rest of this section will be devoted to the examination of Boccaccio's application of, and significant deviations from, one such conventional scheme: the romantic fiction that pervades the Boccaccian 'autobiographies' concerning the ardent love felt by a young man of the middle class for a noblewoman. In this often repeated 'bella storia d'amore,' Branca sees a sort of dramatization of a motif common in lyric poetry, one, moreover, that constitutes a central tenet of Capellanus's influential *De amore*; to wit, men should seek erotic trysts with women whose social station is superior to their own:

La bella storia d'amore ubbidisce nella sua impostazione stessa al precetto
più insistente in tutto il trattato: che cioè si deve scegliere per oggetto del
proprio amore una donna di condizione superiore alla propria, più nobile
che sia possibile.[94]

The beautiful love story adheres, in its essential plan, to the most insistent
precept in the whole treatise: that is, that one should select as the object of
one's love a woman of social standing superior to one's own, as noble as possible.

Given Boccaccio's obvious delight, and consummate skill, in subversive applications of conventional forms, what grounds have we for assuming that the use of conventional literary schemes in his pre-*Decameron*
works is itself conventional? As noted above, Boccaccio's appropriation
of a traditional form does not presuppose a traditional content – a lesson
that Calandrino learns with little pleasure upon ingesting an ordinary
looking treat confected from 'dog ginger' (*Dec.* VIII, 6). Though the
'bella storia d'amore' is indeed common, in what follows, I intend to
show that it is nevertheless particular with Boccaccio.

While Branca only examines Boccaccio's use of this motif in those passages concerned with the amorous trysts of his various literary alter egos,
Ameto, Caleone, Ibrida, Idalogos, and so forth, it is important to note
that the same motif has a no less prominent place in the erotic affairs of
this fictional Boccaccio's philandering father. Had Boccaccio limited
himself to a fictionalized description of his own enactment of this pattern, we would have some justification for viewing these accounts as
purely conventional, bereft of any more personal meaning. However, I
would argue that the faithful replication of this pattern across generations (together with its consistently tragic dénouement) suggests that
these episodes are, at best, bitter parodies of the love manual precept
and perhaps have more bearing on the historical circumstances of Boccaccio than Branca is inclined to admit.

Considering that Capellanus deems it praiseworthy for a middle-class
man to pursue a noblewoman, it may initially seem strange that the two
figures designed to represent Boccaccio's father – Eucomos in the *Filocolo* and the anonymous Certaldan farmer of the *Comedia delle ninfe* – are
not commended for their desire to marry above their station.[95] To the
contrary, both of these father figures are portrayed as sexual and social
predators: ambitious upstarts who wheedle their way into society by winning the confidence, and love, of women whom they subsequently desert

with little ceremony and less regret. It is, no doubt, this element of fraud that accounts for the lack of praise. Capellanus makes no allowance for deceit; it is precisely the authenticity of his ardour that ennobles the lover and legitimates his suit. In applying the external form of the 'bella storia d'amore' to the father figures, Boccaccio is not blindly following the paths set by poetic fictions but is examining the consequences that ensue from a radical discrepancy between precept and practice, letter and spirit.

As true nobility, with its complete innocence to guile, is inherently susceptible to treachery, the mother figure is destined to succumb to the false promises of her scheming suitor. Whereas the socially mismatched lovers of Capellanus's dialogues are unified by a common nobility – one that is not conventional but natural (a nobility of spirit) – the unions machinated by the father figure are purely conventional, emphatically unnatural. As the father figure is not truly 'improved' by his noble consort, and remains, despite appearances, a slave to his baser instincts, it is simply a matter of time before he takes off with another woman. Importantly, the tragic tale does not end with this betrayal, for the noblewomen are left with a bastard son – the 'Boccaccio' figure – destined to repeat the pattern. However, an actual repetition is no longer possible, for whereas the original seduction is perpetrated by a true commoner, a shepherd or a farmer, Boccaccio's literary alter ego, a product of this intermarriage of castes, represents a social hybrid, a half-caste.[96]

It is, therefore, significant that while his own fictionalized romances with the various well-heeled Fiammettas, Emilias, and Marias suggest a repetition of the pattern initiated by his father, none of his literary alter egos actually succeeds in achieving the object of his desires but is somehow thwarted: jilted, betrayed, or proven impotent in the decisive moment. The social, cultural, and spiritual hybridism that informs these literary reflections of 'Boccaccio' appears to have relegated them to a variety of no-man's-land. Though the erotic impulse is every bit as vehement in these 'Boccaccios' as it was in their fictional fathers, their great integrity – the genetic legacy of their noble mothers – prevents them from engaging in the sort of conniving that guaranteed their fathers' success. Neither full-blooded aristocrats nor unscrupulous parvenus, they are destined to be forever stymied in their erotic endeavours. However, all is not lost – indeed, far from it – for, as we shall see in the following 'autobiographies,' the particular variety of tension that derives from this uneasy union of social, ethnic, and spiritual extremes bears fruit in the form of a sublimation of erotic impulse into text: the birth of poetry.

Idalogos: The Anatomy of a Talking Tree

Filocolo V, 6 begins with a dramatic hunting scene in which Filocolo (the pseudonym assumed by Florio, the son of the king of Spain travelling incognito) casts his spear at a stag but misses and instead grazes the trunk of a tall pine. From this fresh lesion issue words and blood together as the pine loudly laments this, the latest in a series of unmerited afflictions (here, Boccaccio makes explicit mention of Virgil's Polydorus). When Filocolo and his awestricken companions beg the forgiveness of what they take to be a sylvan deity, the tree reveals that far from being a deity, it enfolds the embittered soul of a young man whose noble mother had 'given' him Eucomos, a simple shepherd, as a father. Though, the tree continues, he spent his early years following in the footsteps of his rustic father, the noble intelligence with which nature had blessed him eventually prompted him to change course and seek out the more difficult path to loftier things; here, however, he failed to exercise sufficient caution and soon found himself hopelessly entangled in Cupid's toils. Driven to despair by Cupid's cruelty, he was on the verge of committing suicide when the compassionate gods intervened by transforming him into a tree (this theme of suicide inevitably recalls the figure of Dante's Pier della Vigna [*Inf.* XIII]). Intrigued by this story of erotic bondage and metamorphosis, Filocolo asks to hear more concerning Idalogos's origin, identity, and the sequence of events culminating in his metamorphosis.[97]

Since both the details and the larger patterns contained in Idalogos's biographical sketch correspond in many details both to the other embedded 'autobiographies' and to what little documentary evidence we have concerning Boccaccio's life, its status as one of the more authoritative of these 'autobiographies' has long been taken for granted. Without actually advocating a return to the dubious methods of positivist criticism, it seems to me that we should not be so quick to discount the authority of talking trees; we simply cannot dismiss the possibility (indeed, the likelihood) that Idalogos's story preserves something of Boccaccio, if not on the literal level, at least in a spiritual sense.[98]

Idalogos's story begins in Tuscany, where his father, a shepherd named Eucomos leads a peaceful life pasturing his sheep and playing a bagpipe that he has fashioned with his own hands (V 8, 5). Needless to say, such an idyllic existence can only serve as a prelude to a fall of some sort and consequently, when we hear that the lovely daughters of the king Franconarcos have blithely set out to a temple of Minerva adjacent to Eucomos's pastures, we rightly see beyond this sacred drama to the distinctly secular drama of an erotic tryst. Nor are we disappointed, for one of the maidens, Gannai, seduced by Eucomos's melodious piping, deserts Minerva for Cupid. In short order, desire renders Gannai a musical connoisseur even as it prompts Eucomos to hone his musical technique (V 8, 7). Before long, Cupid himself is induced to leave Parnassus to fortify Eucomos's already fervent desire with a poisonous draught of hope. Under Cupid's tutelage, Eucomos's piping becomes refined to the point that Gannai, captivated by the beauty of his music and persuaded by his rhetorical skills, cannot help but grant his every desire. Idalogos is one of two children born from this illicit union before his flighty father, Eucomos, deserts his noble mother to start chasing after another nymph, Garemirta.

Positivist critics can hardly be faulted for discerning in this pastoral allegory a distorted reflection of Boccaccio's youthful years. Eucomos, a man naturally endowed with both *ingegno* and *industria* is taken to be a figure for Boccaccio's merchant father, whereas Gannai (an anagram, as Crescini notes, for Gianna), the daughter of a French King, represents Boccaccio's aristocratic mother, and Garemirta (a near anagram for Margherita), represents Boccaccio's stepmother, Margherita dei Mardoli. Idalogos, the eloquent offshoot of this unlikely pairing, initially follows in his father's steps – 'le pedate dello 'ngannatore padre seguendo' (V 8, 15) – but, repudiated by his father, soon finds himself in the company of a wise friend, Calmeta, under whose expert instruction he comes to master the arcane subtleties of astrology.[99] His intellect awakened, Idalogos turns from animal husbandry (interpreted by many critics as the allegorical correlate for commerce) to the arts of Pallas (in this case, poetry): 'gìa abandonata la pastorale via, del tutto a seguitar Pallade mi disposi' [having already abandonded the pastoral path, I resolved to follow Pallas completely] (V 8, 27). However, his nobility of heart, 'tratta non dal pastore padre, ma dalla reale madre,' [derived not from the shepherd father, but from the royal mother] renders him particularly susceptible to the dangers of love. Though he cannot help but fall in love, he lacks his father's callous detachment – and resilience – so that upon being deserted by his beloved, he sees no means of ending his suffering short of suicide. At this point, moved by pity, the gods intervene by transforming him into a towering pine tree.

Just as the story of Idalogos in its entirety is presented as a *roman à clef* concealing the real or romanticized history of Boccaccio's amorous escapades, the iconic figuration of the towering pine is revealed to be an allegorical portrait of Idalogos, 'Boccaccio' himself, for its essential qualities reflect his own: 'né variò la condizione d'esso dalla mia natura, se ben si riguarda' (V 8, 43). That the heavenward reach of the tree's limbs surpasses that of surrounding trees reflects, we are told, Idalogos's own striving for exalted things, while the roots continue to nourish an unfulfilled hope; the tough shells of the fruit (presumably pine nuts) borne by the tree reflect his initial strength in withstanding Love's siege whereas the tender, and flavorful, kernel nestled within symbolizes the susceptibility of his fragile heart to Love's arrows: 'l'agute saette, passata la dura e rozza forma di me povero pastore, trovarono il cuore abile alle loro punte' [the keen-tipped arrows, having pierced my rustic, tough poor shepherd's form, found my heart receptive to their points] (V 8, 43).[100] Though the analogies continue, it suffices to note that the whole conception is a complex hybrid composed of a series of polarities: roots/branches, hard/soft, rustic/noble, immunity/susceptibility, and so forth. These polarities are simply a reflection of the social and spiritual disparity of the union at the root of Idalogos's conception; a tough exterior, the genetic legacy of his plebian father, is in a state of constant dialectic with the sensitive interior bequeathed upon him by his patrician mother.

Like 'Panfilo,' 'Filostrato,' 'Filomena,' 'Pampinea,' and the other names of the *Decameron brigata* calqued on false Greek etymologies, the name 'Idalogos' has been chosen 'non senza cagion' [not without a reason] (*Dec.*, Int, 51); it is not arbitrary, but somehow reflects the character of its bearer. Having said that, the etymological roots of this name have by no means been satisfactorily established. Crescini, working with 'Idalagos,' a widely diffused variant spelling, proposes that as 'lagos' is Greek for 'hare,' Idalagos 'sarebbe quanto dire lepre [...] dell'Ida' [would be the same as saying a hare ... from Ida];[101] a seemingly bizarre notion that Crescini attempts to rationalize by observing that 'Ida' is often used metonymically to denote any wooded place, and consequently Idalagos would mean 'hare from the woods.' Aware that this still seems well off the mark – what, after all, does a woodland rabbit have to do with a talking tree? – Crescini attempts to shore up his interpretation by invoking a passage from Boccaccio's famous letter to fra Martino da Signa (*Epistola XXIII*) in which people who inhabit the woods are referred to by various animal names. The anticlimactic upshot of all this tireless sleuthing is that 'Idalagos' simply means 'abitatore del bosco' [a forest dweller] – a laboured, and not particularly illuminating etymology.

Antonio Enzo Quaglio, basing his interpretation on the Idalogos variant, advances the far more sensible theory that Idalogos represents a linking of the ideas of 'wood' (Ida) and 'word' (logos); hence, the idea of a talking tree is encoded in the name itself.[102] Conclusive as this may seem, I would nevertheless argue for a third interpretation better suited, I think, to a character who is not merely loquacious, but eloquent, a character, moreover, who has actually declared his passion for poetry: perhaps 'Ida' denotes not 'wood' but 'beauty.'

Indeed, in the *Genealogie*, Boccaccio claims that the word 'Ida' is synonymous with temporal beauty: 'Ida in fact, signifies beauty, and by this he [Dante] wishes to denote the beauty of temporal things' (III V, 6) [Yda enim idem sonat quod formositas, per quam sentire vult formositatem temporalium rerum]. This same definition is reproduced in the *Esposizioni*: 'Ida vuol tanto dire quanto "cosa formosa e bella"' (XIV, lit., 62).[103] If this meaning for 'Ida' were accepted, the name 'Idalogos' would, of course, signify 'beautiful words,' a truly apt description of poetry. Supporting this theory is Boccaccio's false etymology of the word 'poetry' in the *Genealogie*: 'the word poetry has not the origin that many carelessly suppose, namely *poio, pois*, which is but Latin *fingo, fingis*; rather it is derived from a very ancient Greek word *poetes*, which in Latin means exquisite discourse [exquisita locutio]' (XIV 7, 4; Osgood, 40).[104] The close resemblance of the compound word 'Idalogos' to the expression *exquisita locutio* – both are constructed from a conjunction of the ideas of beauty (*Ida/exquisita*) and language (*logos/locutio*) – suggests that Idalogos is indeed a synonym for *poetes*, and therefore an ideal description of Boccaccio himself, a man, after all, who defined both his origins and ends in terms of his poetic mission. In the *Genealogie* he famously declares that his vocation, 'as experience from [his] mother's womb has shown is clearly the study of poetry' (XV 10, 6). In the epitaph he composed for his own tomb, he writes 'genitor Boccaccius illi, patria Certaldum, studium fuit alma poesis' [Boccaccio was his father, Certaldo his fatherland, his passion, nourishing poetry].[105]

Whether or not the figures of Eucomos and Gannai can be taken as faithful portraits of Boccaccio's historical parents is really a moot point; it is enough to recognize that Boccaccio intends that the allegory of Idalogos be understood as a variety of self-portrait. By carefully navigating between the poles of positivist conviction and Branca-like scepticism we discover what is perhaps the single most significant detail of this mythicized portrait. Social and ethnic hybridism – here, in a deliberately radical form – creates poets. The internal conflict that inevitably afflicts the children of such mixed marriages may indeed cause alienation and grief but is simultaneously a source of poetry.

The story is by no means completed with Gannai's seduction and subsequent betrayal by her treacherous lover. Indeed, if the birth of Idalogos were simply a moralizing appendix to this tale of illicit love, there would be no need to explore the psychological and social repercussions of such a mingling of blood on Idalogos himself. However, these tales are less concerned with documenting a social phenomenon or illustrating a precept drawn from the erotic handbook tradition than they are with tracing the factors that contribute to the making of a poet. It is the hybrid fruit born of such heterogeneous unions – Idalogos/Boccaccio – that is revealed to be the true protagonist. How, Boccaccio seems to be asking, is it that Nature comes to hide her treasures beneath the rough bark of a rustic, uncultured individual? These stories of pastoral seductions and rapes supply the rational, 'scientific,' answer: the uneasy coexistence of such incongruous traits in a single individual derives from the profound racial and social differences of that individual's parents.

Thus far, only Idalogos's eloquence and his traditional identification with Boccaccio (and, perhaps, the pine nut as a particularly apt symbol for poetry, which likewise has a 'shell' that must be cracked to access the sweet kernel within) have been submitted as evidence that the lofty pine is to be understood as a symbol of poetry. Though the description of Idalogos's transformation into a tree appears to be modelled on Daphne's metamorphosis in Ovid's well-known tale of Apollo and Daphne (*Met.* I, 452ff), Idalogos assumes the form not of a laurel, but of a pine. While it is certain that Boccaccio's choice of a pine tree is significant, it is not clear to me what we are to make of this choice.

The pine is most often encountered in references to the trees, sacred to Cybele, felled on Ida by Aeneas and his fellow refugees to fashion boats for their journey to Italy (*Aeneid* IX, 80; *Met.* XIV, 535). Perhaps Boccaccio's use of a pine tree is meant to suggest this dynamic, innovative quality; the launching out in search of a new 'poetic' territory – together with the theme of the marvelous transformation of the simple pine ships into sea nymphs, with its implicit suggestion that deity lurks in the most unlikely places. In the *Culex*, a mock epic traditionally ascribed to Virgil, the pine tree is associated with the Argo in a description that recalls Idalogos's reach for the stars: 'Here the great glory of the Argoan ship, the lofty pine, shaggy in her stately limbs, adorns the woods, and on the skyey mountains is fain to reach the stars' (137–9).[106] Perhaps this choice of a pine tree is simply a characteristic expression of Boccaccio's modesty. Loath to compare himself with the laureate likes of his beloved praeceptor Petrarch or his esteemed Virgil, Boccaccio

elects to fashion his own garland from a lesser (albeit far more imposing) evergreen.

Bolstering this identification of a florid tree with poetry is a passage in
Donatus's *Life of Virgil* where we read that when pregnant with him, Virgil's mother 'dreamed that she gave birth to a laurel branch, which, as
soon as it touched the ground, took root and grew immediately into the
form of a mature tree that bore various fruits and flowers.'[107] Though
this passage does nothing to resolve the pine/laurel stumbling block – a
pine, finally, is not a laurel – it is significant that the child is in each case
conflated with a tree, and the tree, moreover, is in both cases an evergreen: a symbol of the permanence of poetic fame.[108]

Ibrida: The Horatian Hybrid Incarnate

Though the theme of genetic hybridism punctuates many of these
embedded 'autobiographies' it achieves its most iconic expression in the
figure of Ibrida, of Boccaccio's fictional alter egos, the one who stands
out as being most realistic: in Billanovich's words, 'più loquace, più minu-
tamente e, in apparenza, più realisticamente determinata' [the most
loquacious, most meticulously and, with regard to appearance, realisti-
cally drawn] of his autobiographical representations.[109]

As Crescini observed – though he did not explore its further implications – Ibrida's very name, 'hybrid,' declares his condition as a child
born 'da parenti di diverso paese e di diversa condizione' [from parents
of different countries and different social conditions]:[110] an ethnic and
social hybrid. This, indeed, is the traditional Latin meaning of the word
ibrida (hybrida/hibrida). Isidore's 'biological' definition of hybrid – the
result, he says, of interbreeding 'apris et porcis' [wild boars and domestic
sows] (*Etymologiae, PL* 82, col. 433) – emphasizes the element of miscegeny, whereas Petrus Comestor's 'social' definition corresponds perfectly,
as we shall see, to Ibrida's predicament: 'spurius et hybrida dicitur igno-
bilis ex patre, sicut manzer, et nothus ex matre' (*Historia scholastica, PL*
198, col. 1311).[111] An actual use of the name 'Ibrida' to convey this quality of ambiguity in a social context might have been familiar to Boccaccio
from Valerius Maximus's *Memorable Doings and Sayings* where we read of a
certain Q. Varius 'surnamed Hybrida because of doubts about his citizen
status' (VIII 6, 4).[112]

Ibrida is actually just one of several Boccaccian alter egos who figure in
the *Comedia delle ninfe fiorentine*, the other two characters who most clearly
fit the autobiographical mould are Ameto, a shepherd, and the resource-

rongly suggest that Boccaccio would have us view her as a per-
on of Pride. Antonio Enzo Quaglio has argued that her
and iconography support a more precise identification with
ess Minerva. No doubt this fiery, armour-clad young woman is
e one nor the other, but a combination of both: a volatile syn-
Minerva-like wisdom and Capaneus-like blasphemous pride, the
r appears to exemplify the dangers of ceding to intellectual
– in particular, to the foolish conviction that reason alone suf-
enetrate the secrets of heaven.

ghly artificial parsing of a single person, Ibrida, into the fiercely
legorical' charioteer of Emilia's vision on the one hand and the
, presumably 'historical' casualty of an aeronautic accident on
is reinforced by the suddenness of the reversal and simulta-
roduction of an implied spirit/flesh antithesis; it is a 'spirito
' [most handsome spirit] (XXI, 19) who careens in Minerva's
carriage whereas the fallen youth tended by Emilia is not simply
'pure' flesh, devoid of spirit, for his soul, we are told, is still
g about the blind alleys of Hell (XXIII, 16).

mpassion aroused by Venus's words, Emilia volunteers to
e the resuscitation of the youth whose senseless body, quick-
her warm caresses, first quivers and then comes back to life.
bleary eyes and disconcerted air of a man more accustomed,
o tells us, to Stygian shadow than to light, Ibrida turns to Venus
ely (for he has yet to recover his voice) begs her forgiveness.
ants his wish on the condition that he forever honour, love, and
ilia. Curious to know something of this man to whom she has
uddenly bound by divine decree, Emilia asks him to tell her his
s country of origin, and something of his life. Ibrida, his body
d voice now fully recovered, is only too pleased to oblige.

other, he tells Emilia, was a Parisian noblewoman of Trojan
whose first husband, a knight, died shortly after their marriage,
er a young, disconsolate widow. His father, the noblewoman's
usband, was the son of a Certaldan farmer and a rustic nymph
ing his coarse nature beneath a cloak of feigned sophistication,
a life of material wealth. When business took him to Paris, he
d his relative anonymity to pass himself off as the son of wealthy
ts. Though enchanted by his father's handsome form – so dif-
om his boorish soul (XXIII, 29) – his aristocratic mother val-
sisted his attempts to seduce her until that fatal day when,
by false oaths, she finally capitulated:

ful and dogged Caleone (Fiammetta's lov
that Boccaccio does nothing but mu
portrait through this confusing prolifera
single work, it should be noted that thes
collectively imply both redundancies a
dividually succeed in clearly delineating p
personality.

If Ameto is less convincingly a historical
ification of the *stilnovista* precept that eroti
of sublimation into intellectual and spiritua
Heaven, Caleon, more person than person
path, moving from an abstract, spiritualized
ies, dreams, and prophetic visions to the
beloved's bedchamber; indeed, he is so be
metta that he resorts to the extravagant plo
in Boccaccio's works) of breaking into her l

In contrast to Ameto and Caleone, Ibrida,
neither an abstract personification nor a f
somewhat unwieldy combination of the tw
theme of a mixed parentage that dominates
Ibrida inevitably draws attention to his biolog
glimpse of Ibrida is overwhelmingly allegoric
in a phantasmagoric vision by the nymph Em
wards is treated to the jarring spectacle of a
conducting a blazing chariot drawn by drago
thither as it strives to force its way into the he
side of this imperious woman, bathed in her
youth (whose identification with Ibrida is co
follow). As they thrust at the heavens, the two
pound their blasphemous deeds with taunti
failed attempts on the Olympian stronghold (
the song [tercets], its general tenor, and signi
[Phlegyas] – a word that occurs only once in t
– is clearly designed to link this episode with th
low blasphemers in the fourteenth canto of
this vision, Emilia turns her eyes back towards
Venus gazing sorrowfully at the recumbent for
man: Ibrida. Though once, Venus informs Em
sook her to become a protégé of her archrival,
oteer. While this young woman is not positively

ful and dogged Caleone (Fiammetta's lover). While it could be argued that Boccaccio does nothing but muddy any truly cogent self-portrait through this confusing proliferation of literary alter egos in a single work, it should be noted that these same vignettes which taken collectively imply both redundancies and contradictions, taken individually succeed in clearly delineating particular facets of Boccaccio's personality.

If Ameto is less convincingly a historical person than a literary personification of the *stilnovista* precept that erotic love can, through a process of sublimation into intellectual and spiritual love, serve as the gateway to Heaven, Caleon, more person than personification, traces the opposite path, moving from an abstract, spiritualized love marked by erotic reveries, dreams, and prophetic visions to the more sensual delights of his beloved's bedchamber; indeed, he is so besotted with the lovely Fiammetta that he resorts to the extravagant ploy (one remarkably common in Boccaccio's works) of breaking into her bedchamber at night.[113]

In contrast to Ameto and Caleone, Ibrida, as his name itself suggests, is neither an abstract personification nor a flesh and blood lover, but a somewhat unwieldy combination of the two. Though the genealogical theme of a mixed parentage that dominates the section concerned with Ibrida inevitably draws attention to his biological, carnal status, our initial glimpse of Ibrida is overwhelmingly allegorical in nature. He is first seen in a phantasmagoric vision by the nymph Emilia, who lifting her eyes skywards is treated to the jarring spectacle of a fiery, armour-clad woman conducting a blazing chariot drawn by dragons which wheels hither and thither as it strives to force its way into the heavens (XXI). Sitting by the side of this imperious woman, bathed in her fiery glow, is an unnamed youth (whose identification with Ibrida is confirmed by the events that follow). As they thrust at the heavens, the two frenzied charioteers compound their blasphemous deeds with taunting words deriding earlier, failed attempts on the Olympian stronghold ([XXII] the metric form of the song [tercets], its general tenor, and significant reference to 'Flegia' [Phlegyas] – a word that occurs only once in the *Commedia* [*Inf.* XIV, 58] – is clearly designed to link this episode with that of Capaneus and his fellow blasphemers in the fourteenth canto of *Inferno*). Overwhelmed by this vision, Emilia turns her eyes back towards the earth, where she finds Venus gazing sorrowfully at the recumbent form of a young, armour-clad man: Ibrida. Though once, Venus informs Emilia, her ward, Ibrida forsook her to become a protégé of her archrival, the haughty young charioteer. While this young woman is not positively identified in the text, her actions strongly suggest that Boccaccio would have us view her as a personification of Pride. Antonio Enzo Quaglio has argued that her attributes and iconography support a more precise identification with the goddess Minerva. No doubt this fiery, armour-clad young woman is neither the one nor the other, but a combination of both: a volatile synthesis of Minerva-like wisdom and Capaneus-like blasphemous pride, the charioteer appears to exemplify the dangers of ceding to intellectual arrogance – in particular, to the foolish conviction that reason alone suffices to penetrate the secrets of heaven.

This highly artificial parsing of a single person, Ibrida, into the fiercely proud 'allegorical' charioteer of Emilia's vision on the one hand and the humbled, presumably 'historical' casualty of an aeronautic accident on the other is reinforced by the suddenness of the reversal and simultaneous introduction of an implied spirit/flesh antithesis; it is a 'spirito bellissimo' [most handsome spirit] (XXI, 19) who careens in Minerva's airborne carriage whereas the fallen youth tended by Emilia is not simply flesh, but 'pure' flesh, devoid of spirit, for his soul, we are told, is still wandering about the blind alleys of Hell (XXIII, 16).

Her compassion aroused by Venus's words, Emilia volunteers to undertake the resuscitation of the youth whose senseless body, quickened by her warm caresses, first quivers and then comes back to life. With the bleary eyes and disconcerted air of a man more accustomed, Boccaccio tells us, to Stygian shadow than to light, Ibrida turns to Venus and mutely (for he has yet to recover his voice) begs her forgiveness. Venus grants his wish on the condition that he forever honour, love, and serve Emilia. Curious to know something of this man to whom she has been so suddenly bound by divine decree, Emilia asks him to tell her his name, his country of origin, and something of his life. Ibrida, his body warm and voice now fully recovered, is only too pleased to oblige.

His mother, he tells Emilia, was a Parisian noblewoman of Trojan descent whose first husband, a knight, died shortly after their marriage, leaving her a young, disconsolate widow. His father, the noblewoman's second husband, was the son of a Certaldan farmer and a rustic nymph who, hiding his coarse nature beneath a cloak of feigned sophistication, pursued a life of material wealth. When business took him to Paris, he exploited his relative anonymity to pass himself off as the son of wealthy merchants. Though enchanted by his father's handsome form – so different from his boorish soul (XXIII, 29) – his aristocratic mother valiantly resisted his attempts to seduce her until that fatal day when, beguiled by false oaths, she finally capitulated:

Giuno fu presente e diede segni d'avere intese le loro preghiere e, dimo-
rando quivi, diede effetto agli amorosi congiugnimenti, de' quali io, a
miglior padre serbato se'l troppo affrettato colpo d'Antropòs non fosse,
nacqui; e da loro Ibrida fui nomato e così ancor mi chiamo. (*Comedia delle
ninfe* XXIII, 34)

Juno was present and gave signs of having heard their prayers; and remaining there she gave effect to their loving union, from which I, who would
have been reserved for a better father had the too hurried blow of the Fate
Atropos not occurred, was born. And they called me Ibrida, and thus am I
still called. (Serafini-Sauli, 58)

Shortly afterwards, Ibrida's father took up with another woman and
his mother, embittered by life, closed her eyes and died. His father fared
no better for the gods, weary of his impiety, afflicted him, his new wife,
and his new family with a plague of misfortunes. Moved to pity by his
mother's genuine piety, Venus took charge of the orphaned Ibrida who,
with her guidance, made great strides in the 'palestre palladie' [Palla-
dian gymnasia] (XXIII, 39) and was soon reputed an 'agrissimo pugna-
tore' [doughty fighter] (XXIII, 39), accomplished in the disciplines of
the medieval curriculum or, as Quaglio maintains, poetry (which, given
the natural inclinations of his patron, would most logically be love
poetry).[114]

Indeed, it is Ibrida's extraordinary success in the 'palestre palladie'
that has gone to his head, prompting him to desert Venus for insolent
Pride:

Questa cosa, avendo partorito graziosissimo fiore, riuscì a pessimo frutto e
non pensato, però che, per questi effetti forse non meno d'Ercule reputan-
domi degno, oltre al piacere dell'iddii, con la mente levato in alto cercava i
cieli, come voi vedeste, ne' focosi carri tirati da' fieri draghi. (XXIII, 40)

This art had given birth to a lovely flower but it ended in foul and unexpected fruit; for reputing myself perhaps no less worthy than Hercules of
these achievements, I sought the sky with a mind raised high beyond the
will of the gods – as you saw in the fiery carriages drawn by the haughty dragons. (Serafini-Sauli, 59)

This, in broad strokes, is the story of Ibrida. Allegorically, he represents the sort of hybridism that characterizes our species as a whole: the

uneasy – and fleeting – marriage of an immortal soul and a mortal body. Historically, he represents the predicament of Boccaccio and all other offspring of similarly mismatched unions: the social alienation of the half-caste. Morally, he epitomizes the warring of Pride and Humility in an ongoing psychomachia.

Finally, Ibrida exemplifies the traditional theme of artistic pride and impotence.[115] In the end, neither their bragging words nor their brash actions provide Ibrida and his allegorical charioteer with the means of penetrating the ramparts of Olympus. As we have seen, the presumptuous youth and his warlike companion are expelled from the heavens, their own attempt on Olympus no more successful than those that they had so contemptuously mocked in their battle song. However, before being cast out of the sky, the two challengers, heady with youthful arrogance, declare themselves able to force an entrance into any stronghold, no matter how well garrisoned:

> La vigorosa e bella giovanezza
> che possegian ne fa vie più sicuri,
> e d'animo e di cuor ne dà fermezza.
>   Qua' torri eccelse o qua' merlati muri
> ci negherien l'entrare in ogni loco
> ove piacesse a noi, per esser duri?
> (XXII, 31–6)

The vigorous and beautiful youthfulness that we possess makes us still more confident, and it gives us firmness of spirit and of heart. What high towers or embattled walls, no matter how stubborn, will deny entrance to us in whatever place might please us? (Serafini-Sauli, 54)

The 'hardness' ['per esser duri'] conferred upon them by vigorous youth, will, they are confident, grant them complete freedom to enter whatever place ('ogni loco') they want.[116] Predictably, the same young man whom Emilia first saw in the company of the proud charioteer sporting a high-crested helmet and a shield, discovers just how 'soft' he truly is upon being cast to the ground. Perhaps this allegory encodes Boccaccio's veiled acknowledgment that the *Teseida*, his recent proud effort at epic (Minerva), has failed and that he should never have deserted love poetry (Venus). Perhaps Boccaccio, like Ovid in the *Amores*, is dramatizing his sense that he, no more a Dante than Ovid was a Virgil, is temperamentally and perhaps intellectually ill-equipped to shoulder the weighty task of writing epic. It is the elegiac, not the epic, Muse who shapes his art; women, not muses, who spark his poetic genius. Or perhaps it simply illustrates the moral that any pursuit of knowledge (Minerva) that is divorced from love (Venus) is destined to fall short of divine wisdom. Boccaccio's intention that we read this passage as an allegory of human impotence is clear enough; his reason for highlighting the sexual dimension of this failed storming of the heavens is less apparent.

The haughty charioteer's 'alta cresta' [high crest] cannot help but recall Dante's use of the *hapax legomenon* 'cresta' to identify the place where Satan's three faces converge at the top of his head (*Inf.* XXXIV, 42). Dante's Satan is an embodiment of pride, the Christian incarnation of Typheus, Briareus, and the various other megalomaniacs of pagan mythology famed for having challenged the very seat of the gods. However, unlike his classical counterparts, Satan successfully violates the immaculate heavens by embroiling a number of like-minded angels in his mutiny. This depredation of the heavenly host is described by Dante as the 'proud rape' of heaven, the 'superbo strupo' (*Inf.* VII, 12).[117] In Dante's figuration of a 'crested' Satan, blasphemous pride, rape, and infernal impotence are united. By using this powerful sexual metaphor – rape – to describe Satan's rebellion, Dante draws attention to the extraordinary violence of Satan's act, granting a visceral, concrete quality to what would otherwise be a purely conceptual, and not particularly affecting, notion.

The sexual character of Boccaccio's application of the word 'cresta' is not only suggested by this Dantean, supernatural precedent but finds additional support in the strongly naturalistic setting of the *Ninfale fiesolano*, where the word *cresta* – once again associated with pride – is used as a sexual metaphor for 'penis' in the passage describing Africo's rape of Mensola: 'con superbia rizzando la cresta, / cominciò a picchiar l'uscio furioso' [proudly raising his crest, he began to pound furiously on the entryway] (244).[118]

In the Ibrida interlude Boccaccio, with an economy worthy of the Metaphysical Poets, has succeeded in yoking together two entirely antithetical varieties of impotence; a metaphysical impotence associated with the failure to acquire transcendent knowledge, and a physical impotence conveyed by the image of Ibrida's flaccid body and muted tongue (for, as readers of the *Decameron* know all too well, tongues and 'tails,' discourse and intercourse, are tightly linked in Boccaccio's metaphoric economy).

It is, then, a doubly crestfallen Ibrida who, sprawled senseless on the earth, requires the dexterous ministrations of the lovely Emilia. Whereas Venus, powerless to contravene the will of another god, can only look upon her former subject with frustration and sorrow, Emilia, through the application of her 'umana mano' [human hand] (XXIII, 10), succeeds in restoring the sap of life to Ibrida's body: a sexual resuscitation or, to use a phrase Boccaccio borrows from Apuleius, a 'resurrection of the flesh' (perhaps under the auspices of the venerable 'Santo Cresci-in-man'! [*Dec.* II 7, 37]). Like the impotent lover of *Amores* III, Ibrida lies, dead as 'a tree-trunk, a mere spectacle, a useless weight,' whether a 'body or ghost,' is is impossible to say (III vii, 15–16).[119] Like Ibrida, the impotent lover of *Amores* III receives assistance from his companion, who readily applies her hand and gently coaxes his flaccid member ('molliter admota sollicitare manu,' III vii, 74). Here, however, the similarities end, for Emilia succeeds where the resourceful 'puella' of Ovid's poem fails.

This motif of a sexual 'awakening' or quickening is frequently found together with the previously mentioned 'nocturnal ambush' scene. In the *Filocolo* IV 67, 7ff (reproduced in somewhat altered form in *Dec.* X, 4), *Filostrato* IV, 118ff., and octave 252 of the *Ninfale fiesolano* we are treated to the morbid, suggestively necrophilic spectacle of a man who undeterred – or more likely goaded – by the corpse-like condition of his beloved, commences to probe, caress, and lavish kisses on her cold and senseless body. The unexpected result of all this physical stimulation is, in every case, that the young woman miraculously comes back to life (in a manner reminiscent of Ovid's ivory maiden, Galatea, whose rigid body softens like warm wax beneath Pygmalion's expert touch). Since Boccaccio uses the erotic night sortie and the necrophilic interlude to foreground a specifically female vulnerability – a sexual accessibility facilitated by the bondage of sleep or by a death-like insentience – the Ibrida interlude represents something of an anomaly; it is the only example that I know of in Boccaccio's works where it is a man, rather than a woman, who is found in this state of somnolence or suspended animation.[120] The effect of this role reversal is, it seems to me, to implicitly feminize Ibrida, thus underscoring his condition of metaphysical impotence (his failure to penetrate the heavens), physical susceptibility (to Emilia's unsolicited caresses), and erotic receptivity (his restoration to life – and virility – by the touch of Emilia's 'umana mano').

These various aspects of impotence – physical, intellectual, and spiritual – that are so rigorously developed in the Ibrida interlude are a regular feature of Boccaccio's embedded 'autobiographies,' where his failure in love is often traced to to his genetic legacy (a half-breed), his intellectual shortcomings to a childhood education squandered on accounting and law, and his spiritual failings to a variety of myopia – a lack of the piercing vision granted such poet-theologians as Dante. Whereas Dante was lifted through the heavens, sustained and nourished by Beatrice's passing blush or glance, Boccaccio recognizes that he, composed of coarser stuff, would soon perish on a diet of such subtle fare. Like a Phaethon or an Icarus, with chariot blasted or wings unbound, he would come tumbling to the ground. For Boccaccio, restoration lies in an Emilia's 'human hand,' not Beatrice's heavenly eyes.

A keen sensitivity to these perceived shortcomings is already evident in the *Filocolo*. 'O piccolo mio libretto' [Oh little book of mine] begins the *congedo* of Boccaccio's *Filocolo* as he instructs his book to cleave to its own, middle path, leaving Virgil's great verses to robust minds, Lucan's and Statius's tales of war to martial spirits, and Ovid's elegies to virile lovers. Dante's measured verses, he advises his book, must be followed with reverence (echoing Statius's well-known explicit in the *Thebaid* which conveys a similar attitude of indebtedness to Virgil). Indeed, all these works must be left to lofty intellects, for his book must fly lower, seeking a middle course: 'A te bisogna di volare abasso, però che la bassezza t'è mezzana via' (*Filocolo* V 97, 7). The reader's natural curiosity concerning the terminus of this 'mezzana via' [middle course] is soon satisfied, for several lines further down Boccaccio concludes that the ideal place for his book to conclude its journey would be his lady's lap, her 'grembo.' It is all too easy to allow the sheer virtuosity of this conceit whereby an author's book-mediator takes the 'mezzana via' to the 'middle' of his lady's favours make us forget for a moment that the author himself enjoys no such good fortune.

This motif of poetic mediocrity, of an impotence which is both physical and metaphysical, cannot simply be discounted as a natural reflection of Boccaccio's youthful insecurity, for it continues to crop up in his late, Latin, works as well.[121] In the colourful introduction to *De casibus* VI, the reader is made privy to a dialogue between Boccaccio and Fortune in which the latter dismisses Boccaccio's attempts to describe her dominion over temporal affairs as superficial and, given the vastness of the subject, futile. Boccaccio responds that he has undertaken the work in an effort to ensure that his name will not perish with his body, and, though well aware that he might have selected a number of more worthy subjects, has chosen to write a survey of moral exempla rather than a work on theology or natural philosophy because he is only too conscious of his limitations:

> I recognize, certainly, that I do not have the wings of a bird with which to penetrate the heavens and survey its secrets, and, having seen them relate them to other men (*De casibus* VI 1, 9)[122]

Moreover, he lacks the poetic skill and authority [verborum maiestas/ sententiarum gravitas] needed to relay such knowledge to others. Boccaccio clearly believes that transcendental, metaphysical flights are reserved for poets with the skills of a Dante. Let Dante disclose the secrets of the otherworld; he must set his sights substantially lower – on the more familiar, but no less textured, landscape of this world.

What Boccaccio learns in the course of perusing this middle realm – and relays to us with an eloquence and understanding that has rarely been equaled – is that the temporal sphere has a hell, purgatory, and paradise of its own. As we are reminded by the resourceful Frate Alberto of Pampinea's tale (*Dec.* IV, 2), humans are chimerical entities, part angel, part wild man; variously clothed in divine plumage, or tarred and feathered.[123] Though Boccaccio is not, like Dante, a poet of the metaphysical, he devotedly constructs his own, terrestrial, 'metaphysics.' Closed off from the prospect of soaring beyond the sphere of experience, beyond sensation to pure intellection, Boccaccio, like his literary double Ibrida, draws sustenance and meaning from the earth (and its Emilias), the fertile *grembo* of life. And it is precisely this aspect of the physical world, its seeming endless capacity to generate and regenerate, that captures Boccaccio's attention. To Dante's vivid portrait of eternal consequences in the *Commedia*, Boccaccio attaches a no less compelling study of temporal causes: of creations and re-creations.

chapter 3

The Myth of a New Beginning:
Boccaccio's Palingenetic Paradise

Tabula Rasa and Saïtic Seed: The Effacement and Replacement of Knowledge

That the notion of re-creation is central to Boccaccio's plan is evident from the title of his work, *Decameron*, one, as critics have long noted, that appears to parody 'hexameron,' the title traditionally used by patristic authors for treatises concerned with the six days of God's creation of the cosmos.[1] If 'hexameron' alludes to the original creation *ex nihilo*, '*Decameron*' quite clearly refers to a re-creation necessitated, within the historical frame of the work, by a plague so virulent and widespread that it cannot help but recall the classical and biblical episodes of a punitive purging of all but a small remnant of the created order.

As all creation, aside from a hypothetical creation *ex nihilo*, is predicated on the destruction (or deconstruction) of a previous creation, it follows that any narrative concerned with creation within a temporal frame – re-creation – most logically begins with an account of disintegration. Viewed from this perspective, the *Decameron* does not disappoint, for as we have seen, its frame drama, one of social, spiritual, and intellectual renewal, is unambiguously premised on a social cataclysm: the great plague of 1348.

In a seeming apology to his readers, Boccaccio protests that the harrowing description of the plague that initiates his work is a necessary evil, one exacted by the internal logic of the narrative (I, intro, 7). He was constrained, it is suggested, to furnish the plague account because the departure of an unchaperoned group of young men and women from Florence to the hills of Fiesole would otherwise seem implausible and morally indefensible.

Boccaccio also offers the argument (one implicit in the opening paragraphs of the Introduction) that a tragic beginning is demanded by the genre, comedy, to which the *Decameron* belongs. Since, as Boccaccio reminds us towards the beginning of his commentary on Dante's *Commedia*, the comedic genre is distinguished by its overarching pattern of a movement from adversity to prosperity (*Esposizioni*, Accessus, 26), it follows that the description of the plague – or of some analogous calamity – is a generic necessity. In both of these arguments Boccaccio is making use of a conventional strategy of authorial self-absolution: the authors' disingenuous protestation that their subject or genre has effectively forced their hand. While efforts of this sort to deflect responsibility for lewd, anticlerical, or other potentially provocative content are common enough, rarely have they been so pressing. It is, after all, no generic comedy to which Boccaccio is affiliating his work, nor is it a generic transgression that prompts this rhetorical bid for self-absolution. Indeed, the comedy that his work most closely emulates is the 'comedy' of a divinely sanctioned regeneration in the wake of a universal cataclysm – a true 'divine comedy' (that is, within a temporal, not an eschatological, frame) – and Boccaccio's transgression consists not in some venial breach of etiquette, but rather in his presumptuous decision to appoint himself architect of this New Age.

The notion that the *Decameron* is a text concerned with palingenesis, with regeneration in the wake of a universal catastrophe, has been eloquently explored by Giorgio Barberi Squarotti in an insightful essay, 'La "cornice" del "Decameron" o il mito di Robinson' [The *Decameron* Frame, or the Myth of Robinson]. Barberi Squarotti observes that the extraordinary privilege of the *brigata* resembles that of Ovid's Deucalion and Pyrrha, entrusted with the task of repopulating an emptied world, or of Dafoe's Robinson, who must construct a new society from the ground up. This privilege is nothing less than that of renewing the world and establishing new ethical standards: 'il privilegio è quello che segna chi è destinato a un'opera decisiva nell'ambito di un rinnovamento del mondo, o alla costituzione di un modello assoluto di comportamento.'[2]

Whereas Barberi Squarotti's fundamental insight relates to the way the *brigata*'s circumstances reproduce an abstract, universal myth of new beginnings in a 'mondo sanza gente' [a world without people] – like the tales of Deucalion and Pyrrha or Robinson Crusoe – in the pages that follow I propose to show that Boccaccio's narrative of cataclysm and rebirth in the *Decameron* does not simply reproduce a generic *topos*. In a characteristic manoeuvre, Boccaccio deftly constructs an entirely new paradigm of cataclysm and rebirth out of elements selected from a handful of established literary models, classical and biblical.

In the two episodes of universal annihilation that tend to dominate the imagination of the Medieval West, the classical episode of Deucalion's Flood in *Metamorphoses* I and the Judeo-Christian account of Noah's Flood in Genesis 7, those virtuous individuals marked for preservation (Deucalion and Pyrrha or Noah and his family) are granted a special immunity from the ravages of the holocaust with the expectation that they will construct a new, ethical society on the *tabula rasa* of a repristinated world. As the Byzantine monk Ilario explains to Filocolo, the moral trespasses of Noah's generation provoked:

> l'ira del sommo fattore, per la quale il mondo allagò, riserbato solamente da Dio un padre con tre figliuoli e con le loro spose, però che erano giusti, nella salutifera arca, con l'altre cose necessarie alla mondana restaurazione. (*Filocolo* V 53, 5–6)

> the wrath of the supreme creator, as a result of which the world was flooded, and there were saved by God only one father and his three sons and their wives, since they were righteous, in the ark that bore them to safety, along with the other things necessary for the restoration of the world. (trans. Cheney, Bergin, 426)

An alternate model, one of periodic annihilations succeeded by epochs of re-creation – both physical and social – was also known to the Medieval West, primarily through Plato's *Timaeus*, the most venerable, and certainly the most elaborate of these creation narratives. Itself a literary 'remnant' of the all-but-vanished Greek intellectual tradition, the *Timaeus* exerted a profound influence on medieval thought by way of Calcidius's widely read Latin translation and commentary.[3] In contrast to the historically anomalous, and thoroughly moralized, cataclysms of the biblical and Ovidian tales, the model postulated by Plato in the *Timaeus* is one of historically recurrent disasters ascribed to periodic variations in the movement of the celestial bodies. In the pages that follow, I shall attempt to show that these three established paradigms of 'universal' cataclysm (together with several other less prominent literary models) collectively exert as great an influence in determining the form and function of Boccaccio's plague motif in the *Decameron* as the actual, historical plague of 1348.

Insofar as history, from a medieval Christian perspective, represented
a temporal unfolding of the eternal, providential pattern, it was inevitable that historical phenomena should be scrutinized for an underlying
symbolic scheme; all history, pagan and Christian, secular and sacred,
could potentially reveal glimpses of the divine plan. It is not surprising,
therefore, that even the most conspicuously 'historical' elements of Boccaccio's account seem to replicate the details and larger patterns of earlier, authoritative plague descriptions by such authors as Lucretius, Ovid,
Cicero, Paul the Deacon, and, though most likely through intermediate
sources, Thucydides. Indeed, as Vittore Branca has shown, Boccaccio
goes so far as to compromise the historical accuracy of his account in
order to secure a better correspondence to such traditional models. In
the course of arguing that Boccaccio's primary source for the plague
description is Paul the Deacon's *History of the Lombards,* Branca notes that
certain phenomena presented by Boccaccio as characteristic of the
plague of 1348 are mentioned in none of the other contemporary
accounts but appear to have been cribbed from Paul's *History*:

> E non v'è pure in essi [the other accounts] il ricordo di quei fenomeni, di
> quegli episodi che dal Boccaccio furono fermati come caratteristici della
> peste del '48, evidentemente perché erano stati rilevati nella sua fantasia
> dalle rapide note dello storico dei Longobardi, scelto dal Boccaccio come
> suo modello ideale nelle pagine più impegnative letterariamente e più ris-
> chiose nell'architettura generale del suo capolavoro. (*Boccaccio medievale,*
> 386–7)

> Nor is there in these [other accounts] so much as a reminiscence of those
> phenomena, those events that had been identified by Boccaccio as charac-
> teristic of the plague of '48, apparently because they had been replaced in
> his imagination by the hurried notes of the historian of the Lombards, cho-
> sen by Boccaccio as his ideal model for these pages that were the most
> demanding, from a literary perspective, and daring, in the general architec-
> ture of his masterpiece.

That Boccaccio, an eyewitness to the plague and an acknowledged master of realism, should choose to clothe his description in conventional
dress must be viewed with some consideration. Aware that any truly personal account of the plague would, by virtue of its novelty and intrinsic
historical interest, have distracted the reader from its larger symbolic
function, Boccaccio has gone out of his way to strike a careful balance
between realistic detail and conventional scheme. The impossibly com-

plex, elusive course of historical change acquires an intelligible shape and a universal significance through this artful alliance with more abstract, mythic patterns.

In the first lines of the plague description of the *Decameron* Introduction Boccaccio reminds us of the universal qualities of the plague, one that has profoundly touched even those whom it has left physically unscathed, a 'pestifera mortalità' [pestilential mortality] the mere recollection of which is painful 'universalmente a ciascuno che quella vide o altramenti conobbe' [universally to all who witnessed or otherwise had experience of it] (I, intro., 2). Recognizing that his description of the plague cannot help but elicit painful memories, he asks that it be viewed in the same way that a walker views a steep and rugged mountain which must be scaled before entering a delightful and restful plain.[4] From the universal, abstract pattern of passion and redemption suggested by the iconic image of the forbidding mountain (one, as has often been noted, strongly reminiscent of the 'colle' [hill] of *Inferno* I), Boccaccio passes to the more concrete patterns traced by the 'historical' responses to the plague (corresponding to four basic attitudes which range from anchoritic isolation to orgiastic immersion in sensual pleasures) before restricting his focus to the studiously atypical response of a group of ten young men and women, the so-called '*brigata*,' whose actions determine the pattern of the *Decameron* frame.

The Introduction ends with an account of the entirely implausible (unless providential) congregation of this select group of virtuous survivors in the church of Santa Maria Novella, and of their subsequent resolution to flee Florence for Fiesole to establish a new social order with its own, revolutionary, systems of governance and legislation. Any concerns provoked by the doubtful morality of this proposed excursion are quickly dispelled by Pampinea, who declares that they are deserting nobody – it is they, rather, who have been deserted: 'noi non abbandoniam persona, anzi ne possiamo con verità dire molto più tosto abbandonate' [we are not abandoning anybody; indeed, we can justly say that it is we, rather, who have been abandoned] (I, intro., 69). Though not a remnant in the universal sense, each woman is a 'remnant' with respect to her own family, the other members of which have perished (while we are not told as much, it seems likely that the same may be said of the men of the *brigata*). In short, all indications suggest that Boccaccio is deliberately reproducing the traditional pattern of a 'universal' cataclysm survived by a virtuous remnant whose principal task is that of ensuring a biological, social, and moral renovation.

According to a common typological scheme, the same salvific role assigned the Ark in Genesis is assumed, after the Incarnation, by the vessel of the Church. In his *On the Ages of the World and of Man*, Fulgentius uses this trope in a way that seems to anticipate many features of Boccaccio's text:[5]

> This nucleus of the world to be [that is, Noah's family and the various animals], destined to come into existence in the age to come, outlived the remnants of the previous population, and the death-dealing waters soared on all sides round this safe contrivance as together with the first destruction of the world they strove to destroy its future seed; but even as the world was destroyed the safety of the righteous could not be imperiled by any upheaval.

In the present age, he continues, Christ's redemption has granted us the possibility of being purged of our sin through the sacrament of baptism:

> then man escaped from the world [ex mundo] into the ark in order to flee [fugiat] the holocaust, now he flees [confugit] from filth [ex immundo] to the ark of the church in order by receiving baptism to evade [effugiat] the fiend.[6]

As we shall see, Boccaccio shares with Fulgentius this tendency to look beyond the chaotic maelstrom to the ordered 'new world' that lies somewhere on the horizon, and to the evocative notion of a remnant of survivors who represent a 'future seed' – an idea that can be traced to the Vulgate translation of Genesis 7.3 where we read that the paired animals (clean and unclean) are gathered in the ark 'ut salvetur semen super faciem universae terrae'[7] [to keep their seed alive on the face of all the earth].

Although Boccaccio never explicitly connects the plague of 1348 with the deluge of Genesis 7, Petrarch does:

> Why is it, then, oh most blessed judge, why is it that the violence of your vengeance lies so extraordinary upon our times? Why is it then when guilt is not absent, examples of just punishment are lacking? We have sinned as much as anyone, but we are alone in being punished. Alone, I say; for I dare assert that if the punishments of all the centuries subsequent to that most famous ark that bore the remains of mortals over unformed seas, were compared to present ones, they would resemble delightful activities, games, and moments of ease. (*Rerum familiarium libri* VIII, 7; trans. Bernardo, 417)[8]

Petrarch assumes the familiar stance of the 'innocent' sufferer. Like Job, he is consumed with a sense of moral outrage that induces him to launch a series of accusations – disguised as questions – addressing the apparently arbitrary actions of a God whose wrath does not distinguish degrees of sinfulness but afflicts everybody with equal vehemence. Petrarch's argument, however, does not consist in protestations of innocence but rather in the bitter observation that though sinful activity pervades all epochs of human history, it is the present age alone that bears the brunt of divine vengeance. The cumulative punishments of all the past centuries would, he sardonically notes, seem as pleasant pastimes were they compared to the afflictions visited upon the present generation. By constructing this rational proportion, Petrarch foregrounds a profoundly irrational disproportion; though our guilt is no greater than that of past generations our penalty is immeasurably greater. The rational basis of God's justice is cast in doubt.

Though Petrarch's complaint is implicitly irreverent (as Dante's Virgil reminds us, 'chi è più scellerato che colui / che al giudicio divin passion comporta?' [who is more wicked than he, who expressing pity, judges God's justice?] *Inf.* XX, 29–30), he nevertheless does show some pious restraint by making a point of excluding the Noachic deluge from his proportion: 'post arcam illam famosissimam reliquias mortalium informi pelago circumferentem' [subsequent to that most famous ark that bore the remains of mortals over unformed seas].[9] This is significant, for it will be recalled that in the wake of the Great Deluge, God made a covenant with Noah (Genesis 9.8) to the effect that he would never again cause a flood to destroy the earth and its inhabitants. Although God does not say as much, it is a reasonable assumption that this covenant is intended to apply to all varieties of universal annihilation (unless, that is, one prefers to view God as a petty sadist who delights in offering such assurances even as he deviously plots alternative methods of exterminating the human race). To have equated the plague of 1348 with the Great Deluge would have been the same as accusing God of having broken his covenant – a charge that Petrarch, at least, is careful to avoid.

A contemporary of Boccaccio's, the Florentine historian Matteo Villani (brother of the great chronicler Giovanni Villani), apparently has no such misgivings, for he not only compares the two events, but maintains that the plague is by far the more devastating of the two. After providing a description of the biblical deluge followed by a catalogue of similar catastrophes visited upon humanity for its sins, Matteo concludes:

Ma per quello che trovare si possa per le scritture, dal generale diluvio in qua, non fu universale giudicio di mortalità che tanto comprendesse l'universo, come quella che ne' nostri dì avenne. Nella quale mortalità, considerando la moltitudine che allora vivea, in comperazione di coloro ch'erano in vita al tempo del generale diluvio, assai più ne morirono in questa che in quello, secondo la estimazione di molti discreti. (I, 25–30) [10]

But according to that which can be found in Scripture, from the Great Deluge to the present day, never was there a universal sentence of death that so encompassed the whole world as that which took place in our time. In which mortality, considering the number of people then alive in comparison to those alive at the time of the Great Deluge, a considerably greater number died in this [mortality] than in that one, in the opinion of many judicious men.

By taking into consideration the vast explosion of the human population since Noah's age, Matteo is able to calculate that, in absolute terms at least, the plague of 1348 has exacted a far greater toll in human life than the Great Deluge. Since Matteo is so ready to affiliate these two 'universal' catastrophes, it should come as no surprise that he views his chronicle as somehow inaugurating an era of renewal, 'uno rinovellamento di tempo e secolo' (I, 40). [11]

In the *Decameron* Introduction we learn that the plague – a 'mortifera pestilenza' [mortal pestilence] – takes place one thousand, three hundred and forty-eight years after the incarnation of Christ, the 'fruttifera Incarnazione' [fruitful incarnation] (I, Intro., 8). The juxtaposition, in the space of a single sentence, of the similar sounding antonyms – 'fruttifera' in describing the Incarnation and 'mortifera' in describing the plague – draws attention to a radical difference. If Christ's Incarnation represents the dawn of a new age, that of Grace, the premature sloughing off of flesh brought about by the plague represents the twilight of that age – and consequently implies the birth of a new age. [12] Like Matteo's history, Boccaccio's novella is the chosen vessel for a universal 'rinovellamento' [renewal]. The very title of Boccaccio's masterpiece declares this intention while implicitly acknowledging the transgressive nature of his project; whereas God's creation is celebrated by such Church authorities as Basil and Ambrose in their respective *hexamera*, Boccaccio's recreation is recorded in the *Decameron*, a palpably secular celebration of human creation. [13]

Though the physical terrain upon which the action of the *Decameron* is situated pullulates, as has been shown, with a generative and regenerative quality, the *Decameron* is not primarily concerned with the biological repopulation of the world by a morally superior stock – the central concern of the Biblical and Ovidian deluge stories – but with an intellectual, spiritual, and cultural re-creation in the wake of the great plague. Concerned though he may be with the unprecedented death toll from the plague, Boccaccio is even more worried by the long-term intellectual and cultural implications of this wide-ranging annihilation. It is, after all, not just a handful of rural hamlets and backwaters that succumb to the ravages of the plague, but the thickly populated cities, with their monastic and university libraries, local chronicles, and urban myths, each one a densely packed and many-chambered storehouse of precious information accumulated over the course of many centuries. Hard as it is to confront the immediate suffering and devastation of his compatriots, it is harder still – particularly for a man as passionately devoted to literary culture as Boccaccio – to contemplate the universal return to an unlettered rusticity that would ensue were the most sophisticated, educated segment of the population to be obliterated by the plague. This concern for the future of literary culture is particularly evident in the preface to the *Genealogie* where Boccaccio laments the wholesale destruction of pagan literary texts by over-zealous Christians, avaricious men disdainful of learning, and princes who 'conspired against books as against their enemies':[14] 'The number [of books] which perished thus, not merely on mythology, but on various arts, could not be easily computed' (Proemio, 30; *Boccaccio on Poetry*, trans. Osgood [hereafter cited as Osgood], 9). Boccaccio goes on to acknowledge that our cultural heritage is not threatened by human antagonists alone, but by the 'adamantine tooth' of time:

> But if all these enemies had relented, they would never have escaped the silent and adamantine tooth of fleeting time, which slowly eats away not books alone, but hardest rocks, and even steel. It has, alas, reduced much of Greek and Latin literature to dust. (Osgood, 9)

Attilio Hortis observes that although Boccaccio's is not the first anguished description of such a persecution of books, his is 'uno de' primi lamenti per la perdita degli antichi libri,' [one of the first laments for the loss of ancient books] and that he and Petrarch 'si nominano con buon dritto tra' primi bibliofili' [are rightfully named among the first bibliophiles].[15] A similar preoccupation with intellectual and cultural continuity, one, as has been noted, entirely absent in the Noachic and Ovidian deluge stories, dominates Plato's *Timaeus*, a text that records the destruction (in a single day) of two culturally unparalleled ante-diluvial (that is, pre-existing the deluge survived by Deucalion and Pyrrha) warring cities, pre-Classical Athens and Atlantis, together with details of their political and social organization that have been preserved in the archives of the Saïtic district of Egypt – the only place, according to Plato's account, geographically immune to devastation by both water and fire. Critias, one of four interlocutors in the *Timaeus*, begins the dialogue by reporting a conversation that allegedly took place between the great Athenian legislator Solon and an aged Egyptian priest of the Saïtic district. The latter, marveling at Solon's near complete ignorance of antiquity informs him: 'There have been and will be many different calamities to destroy mankind, the greatest of them by fire and water, lesser ones by countless other means' (35).[16] This, explains the priest, is why the Greeks have no knowledge of the remote past. He goes on to note that when the earth is scorched by fire, it is the valley dwellers who survive and when, conversely, a deluge inundates the earth, it is the mountain-dwellers who are preserved. Moreover, such individuals as do survive these periodic scourges are invariably the most primitive, unsophisticated representatives of their respective cultures and consequently the nascent civilization must progress stumblingly, like a child, from primitivism to sophistication:

> with you and others, writing and the other necessities of civilization have only just been developed when the periodic scourge of the deluge descends, and spares none but the unlettered and uncultured, so that you have to begin again like children, in complete ignorance of what happened in our part of the world or in yours in early times. (36)

Since the geological peculiarities of the Saïtic district have ensured that of all the earth's regions, it alone enjoys immunity from such periodic devastations, the Saïtic district has come to assume the function of a universal archive for all cultural and intellectual achievement, ancient and modern.[17]

A contrasting, strongly pessimistic perspective on the cultural consequences of such large-scale devastation was available to Boccaccio through the following passage in Cicero's 'Dream of Scipio' (from *De republica*), preserved for the Middle Ages in Macrobius's popular *Commentary on the Dream of Scipio*:

> Not even if the children of future generations should wish to hand down to posterity the exploits of each of us as they heard them from their fathers,

would it be possible for us to achieve fame for a long time, not to mention permanent fame, owing to the floods and conflagrations that inevitably overwhelm the world at definite intervals. (VII, 1)[18]

Macrobius, commenting on this passage, touches not only on the theme of destruction, but on the complementary theme of renewal (though one that is exclusively biological), describing those areas that have weathered the cataclysm as 'seedbeds' for the perpetuation of the human species:

> Certain portions of the earth, escaping utter destruction, become the seed-beds for replenishing the human race, and so it happens that on a world that is not young there are young populations having no culture, whose traditions were swept away in a debacle. (X, 15)

Though the human species has eluded extinction, its cultural accomplishments and traditions have been forever lost, 'swept away in the debacle.'

Seneca, a classical authority upon whom Boccaccio draws extensively for matters related to natural philosophy, writes that water and fire are the dominant components of terrestrial things, bringing both life and death in accordance with divine will: 'when it seems best to god for the old things to be ended and better things to begin' (*Naturales quaestiones* III 28, 7).[19] Although Seneca maintains that all natural forces will collaborate in producing such an extinction, he grants particular importance to the role of water:

> Therefore, whenever the end comes for human affairs, when parts of the world must pass away and be abolished utterly so that all may be generated from the beginning again, new and innocent, and no tutor of vice survives, there will be more water than there ever was. (*Naturales quaestiones* III 29, 5)

This accolade of innocence, of a regenerated world where 'no tutor of vice survives,' can hardly dispel the somewhat less heartening thought that in this new world there will be no tutors of virtue either; all knowledge, good and bad, will presumably have evaporated together with the receding waters.

In discussing the inevitability of periodic floods, Seneca likens the world to semen, for into the fabric of the world is 'incorporated ... from its beginning to its end everything it must do or undergo.' Likewise, the sperm contains 'the entire record of the man to be, and the not-yet-born infant has the laws governing a beard and grey hair' (*Naturales quaestiones* III 29, 3). Indeed, the universe itself is subject to this same law; human ontogeny, cosmogony, and the fate of the earth are all regulated by this sperm-like prescription.

Long before Seneca presented this dreary model of intrinsic biological obsolescence in his *Naturales quaestiones*, Plato, in the *Timaeus*, had conceived a far more optimistic model of cultural renascence secured through extrinsic, artificial means: Egypt's Saïtic district. Plato creates for us a terrestrial sanctuary, a place of immunity from inundation and conflagration, one which ensures the perpetuation not of the species alone, but of the intellectual traditions, ethical teachings, and historical record of the species: the ultimate cultural *remedium*. Though Plato's model is, like Seneca's, a variety of 'sperm,' the seed preserved in the Saïtic district is not one that encodes extinction, but restoration, for it contains nothing less than the blueprint for an ideal society. Whereas Noah is supplied with only a representative sampling of divine (natural) creation, and Deucalion and Pyrrha are constrained to conjure life from scattered stones, Plato's survivors are furnished – at least potentially – with a full archive of human (artificial) creation: the Saïtic 'seed.' This conceit of a preserved ancient ideal both authorizes and lends credibility to what is effectively Plato's own blueprint for an ideal society. The Saïtic 'seed' represents the possibility of dispensing with the toilsome process of submitting to a gradual cultural evolution – together with its attendant flaws and inherent uncertainty. What emerges from such a seed is a full-formed, ideal society rooted in the marriage of biological youth to the intellectual sophistication of untold ages.

Although Cicero, Macrobius, and Seneca all address the topic of a periodic scourge, Cicero is concerned primarily with illustrating the futility of seeking enduring fame; Macrobius seems more interested in using the theme to suggest that humanity is destined to repeat a pattern of growth and decline against a canvas, the world, that remains largely unchanged; and Seneca aims to describe, in a markedly objective tone, the natural principles – the equilibrium and disequilibrium of the components of matter – that determine, in accordance with divine will, periodic catastrophes. It is significant that, presented with these various models, Boccaccio follows Plato's lead by introducing the theme of a devastating scourge as a counterpoint for the complementary theme of a social renovation; one that is founded on the careful and methodical recollection (through the collation of the one hundred *novelle*) of the myriad elements of a culture that have been forcibly dispersed and threatened with extinction by the plague. However, whereas in the *Timaeus* the theme of an ideal civilization is explored as an intellectual exercise among philosophers (albeit one with possible social applications), in the *Decameron*, the same theme assumes a fully dynamic quality, for the members of the *brigata*, themselves survivors, are concerned not with the hypothetical effacement or replacement of a mythic ideal culture, but with the immediately pressing need to orchestrate a true social reconstruction in the wake of a real disaster. It is no wonder, given this basic difference, that the form of discourse chosen by the *brigata* is not the Socratic dialogue but the *novella*, a genre that is neither the language of the stoa nor that of the marketplace, but somewhere in between.

Unlike the scraggly and ignorant survivors who populate these real or imagined accounts of natural catastrophe, Boccaccio's remnant – and this is a critical innovation – is composed of an educated and socially privileged segment of Florentine society. In complete contradiction to the opinion pronounced by Plato's Egyptian priest that such periodic scourges spare 'none but the unlettered and uncultured,' Boccaccio pointedly 'spares' only the best educated and most cultured representatives of his society: a living 'Saïtic' seed designed to ensure both a biological and a cultural posterity. It is not by chance that the young women who gather in Santa Maria Novella are 'savia ciascuna e di sangue nobile e bella di forma e ornata di costumi e di leggiadra onestà' (I, Intro., 49); wise, noble, beautiful, well-mannered, and virtuous, these young women represent the ideal architects and first citizens of a new culture founded on knowledge and virtue. Similarly, the young men who join them are remarkable not only for their virtue in a general sense, but for having preserved in particular their capacity for love, one which 'né perversità di tempo né perdita d'amici o di parenti né paura di se medesimi avea potuto ... non che spegnere ma raffreddare' [neither the depravity of the times, nor the loss of friends or relatives nor the fear for their own safety could lessen, let alone extinguish] (I, Intro., 78). To the compound of knowledge and virtue is added the quickening agent of love: a sure recipe for social, intellectual, and spiritual renovation. Whereas the deluge survivors Deucalion, Pyrrha, Baucis, Philemon (*Met.* VIII, 619ff), and Noah epitomize such conservative qualities as piety, obedience, and innocence, Boccaccio's *brigata* embodies a new, progressive order of values. For blind faith, Boccaccio substitutes a discerning love; for passive obedience, an active virtue; and for untutored innocence, knowledge. The newly generated humans of Seneca's bleak account, unschooled in virtue or vice, have yet to develop an ethical awareness, and the survivors in Macrobius's account have been stripped of all cultural knowledge. Boccaccio's remnant alone is equipped with the moral, intellectual, and cultural sophistication necessary to fruitfully exploit the extraordinary licence introduced by the breakdown of conventional institutions. It is for this reason that only in Boccaccio's model do we encounter the actual implementation of a rationally planned re-creation in the wake of a cultural purgation – the scrupulously designed microsociety of the *brigata*.[20]

In the *Genealogie*, Boccaccio observes that the loss of so many authoritative texts through the accidents of time or negligence of scribes has left a wide space for the wanderings of mendacity, allowing writers to write as they please about the ancients: 'amplissimus vagandi locus mendacio relictus est, cum scribat de antiquis unusquisque quid libet' (V 16, 3). What he does not mention is that he is among those who have most greatly benefited from the licence provided by this vacuum of knowledge; if the destruction of authority – of old models – creates a space for specious histories, it also creates a space for Boccaccio's new ideologies. While the widespread destruction of civilization by the plague imposes upon Boccaccio the task of preserving the distilled essence of culture in prose, it simultaneously provides him with the opportunity to advance a blueprint for social and cultural reconstruction. The embedded *novelle* serve to commemorate and preserve the myriad facets of a lost world whereas the 'frame' – the microsociety of the *brigata* – constitutes the projection of an ideal society onto the ruins of Fiesole, an idealized place of origin. Within the world of the *Decameron*, it is the *brigata*, of course, that assumes responsibility for the task of establishing the new social norms (the rigorous schedule of activities, code of conduct, etc.) and of disseminating and preserving knowledge (the *novelle*). Outside the frame of this compelling fiction, however, stands Boccaccio, and it is he alone whom one must finally credit with both the creation of the *brigata* and with the collation of that vast assortment of stories that constitute a 'Saïtic' archive of human experience.

In his fourteenth-century commentary to the *Commedia*, Guido da Pisa draws a structural analogy between the three-canticle division of Dante's poem and the three-chamber division of Noah's Ark: 'Ista re vera Comedia figurari potest etiam in archa Noe, que fuit tricamerata.'[21] In this section I have attempted to show that like the three chambers of Noah's Ark and the three canticles of Dante's poetic 'ark,' the ten days of Boccaccio's *Decameron* serve a salvific, ark-like function. In the section that follows, I will endeavour to show that it is not the ark alone that Boccaccio has in common with Noah, but the role of ferryman, or 'galeotto.'

The Restoration of Knowledge: The Poet as Pedagogical Pimp

In the proem of the *Genealogie* Boccaccio claims that it is at the request of King Hugh, the monarch to whom the whole of the *Genealogie* is dedicated, that he, a novice sailor in a frail bark, has left the sterile, shell-encrusted hills of Certaldo ('Certaldi cocleis et sterili' – an image, as I have argued, drawn from Patristic treatments of the Great Flood) on a quest to gather together into a single genealogical body ('in unum genealogie corpus'), like the scattered fragments of a great wreck ('ingentis naufragii fragmenta'), the relics of the gentile gods strewn throughout myriad damaged tomes.[22] Were a second Prometheus, or even the same who first shaped men from clay, to appear, neither of these, he thinks – let alone himself – would be equal to such a task.

Boccaccio's disingenuous protestation that he is hardly Prometheus's equal (a strategy reminiscent of Dante's 'Io non Enëa, io non Paulo sono' [*Inf.* II, 32]) only reinforces this strong identification with the figure of Prometheus.[23] Like the original Prometheus, Boccaccio is not motivated by self-interest; a stalwart galeotto (in the sense both of sailor and *mezzano* [go-between]), he knowingly puts his safety at risk so that he might bring enlightenment to the King – and, of course, his other readers.

The further elaboration of the myth of Prometheus in *Genealogie* IV, 44 confirms and casts more light on Boccaccio's identification with Prometheus. Having surveyed some of the obscure and contradictory traditions associated with the figure of Prometheus, Boccaccio concludes that the name Prometheus may be taken to refer variously to God the creator and to the 'historical' Prometheus, the eldest son of the Titan Iapetus, who, according to the mythographer Theodontius, freely relinquished his hereditary rights and his children to his brother Epimetheus so that he would be free to pursue a life of scholarship.[24]

Just as Prometheus is a binary conception, so too is Prometheus's creation, man, who may be parsed into two distinct halves, 'homo naturalis' [natural man] and 'homo civilis' [civilized man]. The first Prometheus, God, creates natural man, upon whom he generously bestows a body, soul, and reason. However, insofar as humans are corporeal entities, they are subject to a gradual corruption and therefore require the intervention of a second Prometheus, a 'doctus homo' [learned man], who arises in the midst of the crude, ignorant progeny of nature and 're-forms' them through education, thereby making 'of natural, civilized men':

> gathering them as though they were stone to be newly created, teaches and instructs them and with demonstrations makes of natural, civilized men, of such remarkable customs, knowledge, and virtue that it becomes fully apparent that some have been formed by nature and others re-formed by education. (*Genealogie* IV 44, 12)[25]

Boccaccio goes on to elucidate the traditional story concerning Prometheus's theft of divine fire. As might be expected, he interprets this fire allegorically as knowledge, with the consequence that Prometheus's furtive act is taken to symbolize the acquisition of the light of truth by the diligent scholar, while the stolen flame itself represents the clarity of education that the wise man encloses in the chest of the ignorant (thereby effecting a variety of intellectual redemption).

The Prometheus of classical mythology is most often remembered as the selfless champion of humanity whose gift of stolen fire results in his grueling martyrdom, chained to the Caucasus where a vulture forever feeds upon his self-renewing liver. As Charles G. Osgood has noted, in the *Genealogie* Boccaccio reverses the traditional sequence of events by asserting that Prometheus's stay in the Caucasus is not an eternal sentence, but an educational interlude that actually precedes his gift of stolen fire to humanity: 'Quod autem duci et alligari Caucaso Prometheum a Mercurio fecerint, pervertitur ordo, nam prius in Caucaso fuit Prometheus, quam hominem rapto igne animaret' [however, having Prometheus led to and bound on the Caucasus by Mercury perverts the order of things since Prometheus was in the Caucasus before he animated man with the stolen fire] (IV 44, 18).[26] Accordingly, Boccaccio's allegorical interpretation presents us with a Prometheus enchained not by divine ire but devotion to his studies; eviscerated not by eagles but anguished meditation; and healed not through a miraculous regeneration of his viscera but by the discovery of hidden truths. Through such liberal manipulations of the ancient myth Boccaccio achieves the twofold objective of redeeming the gods – who would otherwise stand guilty of requiting a commendable striving for higher things with cruel punishments (an opinion that Boccaccio dismissively ascribes to the 'vulgus iners' [ignorant rabble] [IV 44, 17]) – and enhancing the heroic stature of Prometheus, whose martyrdom is no longer a consequence, so much as a precondition of his mission to improve the human lot.[27] This casting of Prometheus's suffering as elective rather than punitive has the effect of enhancing the martyr-like quality of his travails; whereas the traditional Prometheus is oblivious to the harsh afflictions that await him, the same cannot be said of Boccaccio's revised Prometheus, who embarks upon his excruciating passion with his eyes wide open and in full conscience. Importantly, this new, 'historical,' Prometheus retains the humanitarian impulse of his mythic predecessor, for, having gleaned heavenly truths from the 'gremio Dei' [God's bosom] (IV 44, 14), he sets himself the arduous – and most often thankless – task of educating the ignorant masses.

Boccaccio's activities as an early humanist, avid mythographer, and committed popularizer of learned texts make it all but inevitable that he should view his task in Promethean terms as a rekindling of the long-spent flame of classical culture; one which, like Prometheus's benefaction, entails an element of transgression together with its attendant risks.[28] Though his readiness in the proem of the *Genealogie* to brave a vast sea of literary flotsam in hopes of salvaging the pagan gods may seem praiseworthy from a philological perspective, the resurrection – albeit literary and metaphoric – of those very gods whom Dante's Virgil famously condemns as 'falsi e bugiardi' [false and lying] (*Inf.* I, 72) is more strongly suggestive of pagan idolatry than of Christian piety and consequently casts doubt on the moral integrity of the whole enterprise (a concern addressed in *Genealogie* XV, 9). Moreover, Boccaccio is not content to simply assume the archivist's duty of assembling and cataloguing the relics dredged from this sea of ancient texts; he embraces the pedagogue's far more precarious task of 'unveiling' (most often through historical, naturalistic, and moral exegesis), and publishing for the benefit of the public at large, the divine truths concealed in these precious fragments.

Boccaccio's vernacular translations of Livy (and possibly Valerius Maximus), copious footnotes of the *Teseida*, and public lectures on the literal and allegorical interpretation of the first seventeen cantos of *Inferno* – together with his decisive role in orchestrating Leonzio Pilato's pioneering translation of the Homeric poems – all testify to his humanitarian desire to play the role of a latter-day Prometheus, selflessly mediating between the traditionally discrete spheres of the educated elect and the unlettered multitude. As Boccaccio himself recognizes, it is a mission fraught with troubling ambiguities. Ostracized by the community of scholars for 'exposing' the Muses to the scrutiny of an unworthy rabble, and met with more rancour than gratitude for his efforts to educate the public, the popularizer is a virtual exile – one, Boccaccio would have us believe, whose humanitarian mission and related suffering bear a distinctly Promethean stamp.

No reader familiar with his work will be surprised to discover that Boccaccio most often casts the transgressive component of this Promethean endeavour in terms of an erotic trespass, a literal or metaphoric 'unveiling.' As we shall see, the ostensibly antithetical figures of the pedagogue and the pimp are not so easily distinguished from each other. Though the former may restrict his 'stripping' to Muses and the latter to mortal women, 'le Muse,' to recall Boccaccio's salutary reminder in the *Decameron*, 'son donne' [the Muses are women] (IV, intro, 35), and it stands to reason, therefore, that the disrobing of either is, at least potentially, a means to transcendental knowledge.

In the *Teseida*, Boccaccio tells us that since the Muses first went naked among men, they inspired rhetorical beauty and honesty in some, erotic activities in others:[29]

> Poi che le Muse nude cominciaro
> nel cospetto degli uomini ad andare,
> già fur di quelli i quai l'esercitaro
> con bello stilo in onesto parlare,
> e altri in amoroso l'operaro
> (*Teseida* XII, 84)[30]

> Ever since the Muses first began
> parading naked in the view of men,
> already they inspired in some
> an eloquent and honest speech,
> in others rousing more erotic thoughts

Here, the naked Muse 'parading ... in the view of men' becomes a figure for the Italian vernacular, an idiom that may be viewed as 'undressed' both formally and semantically; it is grammatically simpler than Latin and more universally understood. Inevitably, the application of this trope of undressing to describe the disclosure of knowledge has the effect of making of each poet-pedagogue a potential pimp. It is a trope that, for Boccaccio at least, appears to have its origins in Macrobius's late fourth- or early fifth-century *Commentary on the Dream of Scipio*.[31]

in treating of the other gods and the Soul, as I have said, philosophers make use of fabulous narratives; not without a purpose, however, nor merely to entertain, but because they realize that a frank, open exposition of herself is distasteful to Nature, who, just as she has withheld an understanding of herself from the uncouth senses of men by enveloping herself in variegated garments, has also desired to have her secrets handled by more prudent individuals through fabulous narratives. Accordingly, her sacred rites are veiled in mysterious representations so that she may not have to show herself even to initiates. Only eminent men of superior intelligence gain a revelation of her truths; the others must satisfy their desire for worship with a ritual drama which prevents her secrets from becoming common. Indeed, Numenius, a philosopher with a curiosity for occult things, had revealed to him in a dream the outrage he had committed against the gods by proclaiming his interpretation of the Eleusian mysteries. The Eleusian goddesses themselves, dressed in the garments of courtesans, appeared to him standing before an open brothel, and when in his astonishment he asked the reason for this shocking conduct, they angrily replied that he had driven them from their sanctuary of modesty and had prostituted them to every passer-by. (*Commentary on the Dream of Scipio*, I 2, 17–19)

A vivid dramatization of this passage is found in the proem of *Genealogie* III, where the seafaring Boccaccio encounters the hoary figure of a revivified Numenius who has emerged from amongst the crags and reefs of antiquity to warn him that his, Boccaccio's, foolhardy crusade to elucidate the arcane mysteries of the theologizing poets for the common crowd is like his own: one, he reminds Boccaccio, that long ago provoked the Goddesses (albeit in a dream-vision) to address him as a miscreant pimp, 'leno scelesti,' and accuse him of selling them like whores to the indiscriminate masses. With apparent perplexity, Numenius notes that Boccaccio, far from heeding this warning that certain mysteries should be the patrimony of the few, has dared to take up where he, Numenius, left off: 'Now you, of caution heedless, driven by desire, have entered the vertiginous abyss, daring to do what I had left undone' (III proem, 3). Numenius then seals his admonition with a catalogue of classical exempla illustrating the dire consequences of all such attempts to contend with deity. Undeterred by Numenius's arguments, Boccaccio protests that his intention is not to expose the gods so much as to exalt the classical poets by proving them to have had a grasp of theological truths. Moreover, as the gods in question are those of myth, not the

Christian God, his revelation of their secrets does not, he argues, constitute an act of true impiety.[32]

This question of secular as against sacred knowledge is, of course, at
the crux of all such debates, for the pedagogue is culpable only insofar as
the knowledge he purveys can be qualified as sacred or protected. To
denude and pimp the goddesses is one thing, to 'undress' secular knowledge with purely pedagogical – rather than impious and profane – objectives is quite another. The difficulty, however, lies in distinguishing the
one activity from the other. Numenius's goddesses are, in a sense, Boccaccio's whores, for he readily exposes their most private parts to educate the public and exalt the poets. That exclusionary fraternity of
scholars who held that certain varieties of knowledge were best concealed from the 'ignorant' rabble beneath the veil of allegory had found
an able adversary in the egalitarian Boccaccio, a self-appointed stripper
of Muses for the common weal.

It should be noted that Boccaccio is by no means the first to discern
in Numenius, the ancient desecrator of divine secrets, a classical precursor to those, like himself, committed to the morally dubious task of
popularizing learned Latin texts through vernacular translations and
commentaries. Indeed, in the *Novellino* (LXXVIII) we read an apologue
concerning a kind-hearted philosopher – a Numenius in medieval dress
– who rashly undertakes to translate the sciences into the vernacular for
the laity:

> Fue un filosofo, lo quale era molto cortese di volgarizzare la scienzia per
> cortesia a signori e altre genti. Una notte li venne in visione che le dee della
> scienzia, a guisa di belle donne, stavano al bordello. Ed elli vedendo questo,
> si maravigliò molto e disse: – Che è questo? Non siete voi le dee della scien-
> zia? – Ed elle rispuosero: – Certo sì. – Com'è ciò, voi siete al bordello? Ed
> elle rispuosero: – Ben è vero, perché tu se' quelli che vi ci fai stare. – Isve-
> gliossi, e pensossi che volgarizzare la scienzia si era menomare la deitade.
> Rimasesene, e pentési fortemente. E sappiate che tutte le cose non sono
> licite a ogni persona. (*Novellino*, 104)

There was a philosopher who was so courteous that he translated the sciences as a kindness to the gentry and other people. One night a vision came
to him, where the goddesses of the sciences, in the guise of beautiful women,
were living in a bordello. And he, seeing this, was flabbergasted and said,
'What is this, are you not the goddesses of the sciences?' And they replied,
'Why certainly.' 'How then do you find yourselves in a bordello?' And they

replied, 'Well, this is true because it is you who forces us to remain here.' He awoke and realized that to translate the sciences was to belittle the gods. He remained there, thinking it over, and strongly repented his actions. And know that everyone is not entitled to every thing.[33]

Boccaccio has simply cast himself as the fourteenth-century representative of those praiseworthy populists whose lineage may be traced back through the courteous medieval philosopher of the *Novellino* to its classical progenitor, the venerable Numenius himself. Nor is Boccaccio's role as a literary pimp lost on Filippo Villani, his first biographer, who praises him for having written a delightful and useful book, the *Genealogie*, which made available 'in public' and, as it were, 'to all hands,' the obscure myths of the classical poets:

> Opera certamente dilettevole e utile, e molto necessaria a chi vuole i velami de' poeti conoscere, e senza la quale difficile sarebbe intendere i poeti, e la loro disciplina studiare; perocchè tutti i misteri de' poeti e gli allegorici sensi, i quali o finzione di storia o favolosa composizione occultano, con mirabile acume d'ingegno *in pubblico e quasi alle mani di ciascuno ridusse.* (emphasis mine)[34]

> Certainly a delightful and useful work, and indispensable for those who wish to become familiar with the veils [allegorical fictions] of the poets, and without which it would be difficult to understand the poets or to study their art; for, with miraculous intellectual insight, *he rendered accessible in public and, as it were, to all hands,* the mysteries of the poets and the allegorical meanings hidden beneath historical fictions or imaginary tales.

Towards the end of his digression on vernacular poetry in *Vita nuova* XXV, Dante argues that the precedent set by classical poets authorizes the use of personification allegory by vernacular poets; however, it is essential, he writes, that such allegory be applied in a systematic and rational way such that the allegory is always susceptible to 'undressing':

> E acciò che non ne pigli alcuna baldanza persona grossa, dico che né li poete parlavano così sanza ragione, né quelli che rimano deono parlare così non avendo alcuno ragionamento in loro di quello che dicono; però che grande vergogna sarebbe a colui che rimasse cose sotto vesta di figura o di colore rettorico, e poscia, domandato, non sapesse denudare le sue parole da cotale vesta, in guisa che avessero verace intendimento.

But to prevent any crude persons from drawing any wrong inferences, I say
that the poets did not write this way lacking a purpose, nor should those
who use rhyme write in this manner without there being a purpose behind
what they say. For it would be a disgrace to someone who dressed his rhymes
in the figures or colours of rhetoric if later, on demand, he could not strip
his discourse of this dress to show what he really meant.[35]

Whereas for Dante this idea of a hermeneutic undressing is purely metaphoric, Boccaccio literalizes the metaphor; whereas Dante says only
that such undressing must be possible, Boccaccio, with obvious relish,
assumes the task of undressing the full sisterhood of female personifications – pagan goddesses, Muses, and the like – as a 'moral' imperative, a
civic duty. As Boccaccio declares in *De casibus*, 'ego quidem tenui stilo
plurimum prodesse reor mortalibus' [I hold that I have helped many
men with my humble style] (VI 1, 14). Like the state of physical nudity,
rhetorical undress facilitates a more honest – and productive – communion.

The classical and medieval habit of clothing abstractions in the allur-
ing guise of mortal women had long had the collateral effect of blurring
the distinctions between carnal and spiritual varieties of knowledge. The
further inference that learning consisted in the metaphorical undressing of such lovely personifications only contributed to the confusion. It
was inevitable, therefore, that a person with Boccaccio's satiric wit and
bawdy sensibility should make it a personal mission to plumb the erotic
possibilities of this trope.

In this application of the trope of undressing to secular knowledge
Boccaccio has an authoritative, and well-known, classical precedent. In
the fifth century, the Carthaginian lawyer Martianus Capella introduced
a series of personified Liberal Arts into his *The Marriage of Philology and
Mercury*, a didactic-allegorical treatise concerned with the acquisition of
knowledge, both secular and sacred. In the opening pages of the third
book of this work we are treated to an amusing debate between Martianus and the Muse regarding the appropriate state of dress – or
undress – of Philology's bridesmaids, the personified *Artes*. The ribald
Martianus naturally balks at the Muse's suggestion that the *Artes* be orna-
mented with fabricated stories as 'utility cannot clothe the naked truth,'
and protests that in the previous book he had been assured that the
myths would be put away and replaced with the true precepts of the various arts. The priggish Muse rebuts: 'Let us tell no lies, and yet let the
Arts be clothed. Surely you will not give the band of sisters naked to the

bridal couple?' Martianus, apparently not so sure, hits upon an inspired compromise: 'let them be clothed in incorporeal utterance' (64). By thus personifying and dressing the *Artes* Martianus skillfully tropes the arid business of learning as the metaphoric unveiling of the *Artes*.[36]

One of the earliest and most elaborate parodies of this trope in Boccaccio's works is found in the *Comedia delle ninfe* XVIII where Mopsa, a figure for Wisdom (a devotee of Pallas, nourished, we are told, on the milk of Muses), attempts, with notable lack of success, to seduce the unschooled Affron with the promise of intellectual and spiritual knowledge – that of exploring the ethereal homes of the gods and of understanding the causes of all things (27–30). Recognizing that her young quarry is no philosopher, Mopsa resorts to the more rudimentary strategy of partially undressing. That same rustic imagination unmoved by the invitation to explore the secret regions of Olympus is easily captured by the prospect of investigating the hidden crannies of Mopsa's anatomy.[37] This is not to say that Affron, thus captured, will not be successfully converted to loftier varieties of knowledge; indeed, we are told that soon afterwards he sheds his rusticity and goes on to become an accomplished scholar. In a humourous travesty of the *stilnovista* notion of the 'donna angelicata' – the angelicized lady – Boccaccio has presented us with what is effectively a carnalized angel. Whereas Dante's Beatrice evolves from a historical to an increasingly symbolic entity (from a carnal object of desire with more than a touch of the ethereal in the *Vita nuova* to a spiritual object of desire tinged by carnality in the *Commedia*) Boccaccio's Mopsa, a personification of Wisdom, moves in the opposite direction by voluntarily submitting to the inherently degrading process of incarnation in order to redeem the wayward Affron.[38]

The apparent incongruity between such explicitly sexual episodes and the overriding pattern – one concerned with intellectual, rather than sensual, knowledge – has prompted more than one critic to call into question the artistic integrity and ideological unity of the *Comedia delle ninfe*.[39] However, far from representing an artistic failure, an awkward eruption of youthful brio, such episodes tend to confirm the underlying, and profoundly Boccaccian, philosophy that spiritual salvation and carnal delectation are fundamentally interdependent; though Boccaccio recognizes the superiority of the former, he acknowledges the necessity of the latter. This peculiarity of Boccaccio's texts is one that breeds ambiguities. Though her motives are lofty and her method highly effective, Mopsa's use of erotic techniques for didactic ends – a mingling of pedagogy with prostitution – tends to obscure her achievement. Similarly,

Boccaccio's habit of subjecting women such as Mopsa to a literary strip-tease, albeit for the edification of an ignorant public, results in a blurring of the boundaries between pedagogue and pimp.

Boccaccio's use in the *Teseida* of the metaphor of the naked Muse to describe the Italian vernacular is one that conveys not only the positive notion of linguistic accessibility, but the more problematic idea of a sexual and semantic exploitation: 'Poi che le Muse nude cominciaro / nel cospetto degli uomini ad andare' [Ever since the Muses first began parading naked in the view of men] (*Teseida* XII, 84). The words 'nel cospetto degli uomini' with their emphasis on sight, are less suggestive of a linguistic than of an erotic accessibility: a spectacle designed to please men. It is an image that simultaneously casts suspicion on the Muses, who should not allow themselves to be degraded in this way, and on the vernacular authors, who effectively function as their pimps by making them available to an undiscriminating public.[40]

Troubling ambiguities of this sort are particularly abundant in those passages concerned with the ambivalent figure of the Muse. Nor should this surprise us, for like Prometheus, indeed, like the poet, the Muses are purveyors of divine knowledge to mortals, mediatrixes who bridge an otherwise impassable epistemic divide. Insofar as they commune with the gods they are sacred; insofar as they fraternize with mortals, profane. As Ernst Robert Curtius notes in his brief survey of the Muse topos, 'the search for knowledge – either profane or religious – is a road to immortality and is connected with the cult of the Muses' (234).[41] Muses, as we shall see, occur in one genus but in two species: one honest, the other dishonest, one sacred, the other profane. Since it is Boethius's portrayal of the Muses at the beginning of *The Consolation of Philosophy* that most powerfully informs Boccaccio's many discourses on the Muses, accounting, among other things, for this bifurcation of the Muses into two distinct species, it is useful to recount this episode in some detail.

In the first book of *The Consolation*, Boethius describes how a personified Philosophy suddenly appears to him as he awaits execution (allegedly a victim of trumped-up charges). Upon observing that he is attended by a retinue of poetic Muses who are helping him to compose his lamentations, this imperious Philosophy (clothed, it should be noted, in a gown rent in many places by hands eager to unveil her secrets), treats them to a litany of contemptuous accusations:

Who let these theatrical tarts in with this sick man? Not only have they no cures for his pain, but with their sweet poison they make it worse. These are they who choke the rich harvest of the fruits of reason with the barren thorns of passion [...] Get out you Sirens, beguiling men straight to their destruction! Leave him to my Muses to care for and restore to health. (I, meter 1, 28–41)[42]

In *Genealogie* XI, 2 ('The nine Muses, daughters of Jove') Boccaccio presents various theories concerning the nature of the Muses proposed by such authorities as Isidore (*Etymologies* III 15, 1), Macrobius (*Commentary on the Dream of Scipio* II 3, 1), and Fulgentius (*Mythologies* I, 15ff.),[43] in order to expose the foolish error of those self-righteous misconstruers of Boethius who imagine themselves fully armed by Boethius's slanderous accusations.[44] Once they have given due consideration to the positive assessments of the Muses recorded by such authorities, only then, pronounces Boccaccio, let them say that they have seen such exalted women in the brothels and that they believe that such blessed authors as Isaiah or Job drew them from their squalid whoredom to enlist them in the sacred task of inspiring Holy Writ! May all such cavillers, he concludes, be silent and, enraged, bite themselves!

In *Genealogie* XIV, 20 ('The Muses cannot be contaminated by the defects of lascivious minds'), Boccaccio addresses once again the problem of Boethius's declamation against the Muses in *The Consolation*.[45] Insolent blasphemers of poetry, he writes, 'have dared with unspeakable effrontery to invade the very threshold of the Gorgonian cave, so still, remote, and holy, and thrust themselves into the fair sanctuary [honesta penetralia] of the adorable art where maidens dance together and raise the divine song' (*Genealogie* XIV 20, 1; Osgood 94). The Muses are here not simply cleared of the usual accusations of sexual dishonesty; the charge is turned against those who would denounce them, for it is they who are accused of polluting the sacred precinct by engaging in what is unmistakably a variety of rape – the brutal violation of the 'honesta penetralia' of an implicitly personified Poetry. In defending their reprehensible actions, these blasphemers of poetry gleefully brandish Boethius's condemnation of the Muses:

Thus they shriek in triumph, and fill the place with hubbub ... Little do they understand Boethius's words: they consider them only superficially; wherefore they bawl at the gentle and modest Muses, as if they were women in the flesh, simply because their names are feminine. They call them disreputable, obscene, witches, harlots, and, forcing the meaning of Boethius's diminutive, they would push them to the bottom of society,

nay in the lowest brothel make them supine to the pleasure of the very
dregs of the crowd [in lupanari a fece vulgi prostratas]. (*Genealogie* XIV 20,
1; Osgood, 94–5)

The Muses are not perpetrators, but victims of sexual dishonesty at the
hands of these ignorant whoremongers. Had these maligners of Muses
read *The Consolation* more attentively, they would, observes Boccaccio,
have noted that though there is but one genus of Muse, Boethius distinguishes two species: the one, a chaste Muse of wholesome, healing
poems (and honest poets), the other, a free-wheeling floozy and Muse of
the theatre and 'disreputable comic poets.'

However, the accusation of prostituting the Muses to the very dregs of
the crowd – 'fece vulgi' – can, as we have seen, just as easily be turned
against the vernacular poets, for it is they, after all, who first 'stripped'
the Muses by writing in the vernacular, thus compelling them to go about
naked 'nel cospetto degli uomini' (*Teseida* XII, 64). This is not a new
dilemma but one as ancient as lyric poetry itself. In the *Amores* Ovid concedes – in mournful tones fringed with a sort of pride – that in publishing the charms of his beloved Corinna he has inadvertently prostituted
her: 'Fallimur, an nostris innotuit illa libellis? / sic erit – ingenio prostitit
illa meo' [Could it be my poems made her known? That's it, she was
prostituted by my wit] (*Amores* III 12, 7–8). He is the pimp – 'lenone' (III
12, 11) – whose verse led the way and opened the door to her lover: 'me
lenone placet, duce me perductus amator, / ianua per nostras est ada-
perta manus' [I am the pimp who set out to please, I, the one leading her
lover, by my hand was her door opened up] (*Amores* III 12, 11–12). However, it is not the secular mistress alone who thus risks being pimped by
her lover's poetry; Boccaccio's artful conflation of women with Muses
clears the way for an analogous exploitation of the sacred Muses. If
Corinna's bedchamber was opened to public scrutiny, the Muses have
sustained the even greater indignity of being forced from their Parnassian eyrie into the welter of the public *fornice*.

It is in *Rime* CXXII that we find Boccaccio's most candid acknowledgment of the ambiguous status of the poet – a darling of the Muses who
appears to reciprocate their favours by shamelessly selling them to the
crowd.[46] It is here, too, that Boccaccio most clearly describes the intimate correlation between a pedagogical pimping and a Promethean
punishment. If, says Boccaccio, he prostrated the Muses in the public
brothel and exhibited their hidden parts to the vulgar crowd – 'feccia
plebeia,' a clear echo of the 'fece vulgi' described in the *Genealogie* – he
has been amply punished by Apollo's scourge:

S'io ho le Muse vilmente prostrate
nelle fornice del vulgo dolente,
e le lor parte occulte ho palesate
alla feccia plebeia scioccamente,
non cal che più mi sien rimproverate
sì fatte offese, perché crudelmente
Appollo nel mio corpo l'ha vengiate
in guisa tal, ch'ogni membro ne sente.
(*Rime* CXXII, 1–8)

If I have vilely abased the Muses
beneath the vaulted arches of the wretched crowd,
and recklessly exposed their hidden parts
before the boorish rabble,
for such misdeeds additional reproaches
are not due; so cruelly
has Apollo sought revenge upon my body
that every limb is racked with pain.

If, he continues, he exposed the mysteries of Dante's genius to an unworthy public, he did so largely at the behest of others; their pleas, 'prieghi' moved him to intercede on their behalf:

Se Dante piange, dove ch'el si sia,
che li concetti del suo alto ingegno
aperti sieno stati al vulgo indegno,
come tu di', della lettura mia,
ciò mi dispiace molto, né mai fia
ch'io non ne porti verso me disdegno:
come ch'alquanto pur me ne ritegno,
perché d'altrui, non mia, fu tal follia.
    Vana speranza e vera povertade
e l'abbagliato senno delli amici
e gli lor prieghi ciò mi fecer fare.
Ma non goderan guar di tal derrate
questi ingrati meccanici, nimici
d'ogni leggiadro e caro adoperare.
(*Rime* CXXIII)

If Dante weeps, wherever he may be,
to see the concepts of his towering genius

laid bare to an unworthy crowd,
my lecture, as you say, the means,
this grieves me greatly; may I hold
myself forever in contempt.
Still, I'll spare myself some scorn,
for the folly was of others, not my own.
   Vain hope, true poverty,
and friends' benighted wits
together with their pleas, combined to force my will.
But little pleasure will these thankless hacks,
antagonists of every valued, gracious act,
receive from this defeat.

In launching such accusations of pimping for the Muses against him, the 'ingrati meccanici' (plebians, untrained in the Liberal Arts), enemies of all that is pleasant and worthwhile, have only succeeded in abetting their own ignorance (this, at least, seems to be what Boccaccio is implying). In contrast to Boccaccio, whose *Decameron* is itself, according to the conceit formulated in the Proem, a work prompted by 'gratitudine' and carried out 'per non parere ingrato' [to not appear ungrateful] (Proemio, 7) for benefits received in his hour of need, these 'ingrati meccanici' deserve our censure. Though cloaked in the rhetoric of contrition, these lines are primarily, and most effectively, a harangue of Boccaccio's critics; Boccaccio's misguided generosity elicits our sympathy, his critics' ingratitude, our disgust.[47]

In sum, these bitter verses present Boccaccio as a benefactor of humanity at large (through his work as an explicator of sacred poetic truths to the masses) whose physical and emotional suffering is the direct consequence of this generosity: 'crudelmente / Appollo nel mio corpo l'ha vengiate.' It has long been surmised that these *Rime* were written in response to the highly controversial series of public lectures on the *Commedia* delivered by Boccaccio from the pulpit of the church of St Stephen in Badia in the fall of 1373.[48] Indeed, in his letter of 1374 to Francesco da Brossano (*Epistole*, XXIV, 3–5), Boccaccio writes that it was during his public readings of Dante that he was first stricken by that increasingly excruciating sickness which had, over the course of four months, so reduced him that he seemed another man. What has not, to my knowledge, been noted is the near-perfect correspondence of this distinct pattern of humanitarian transgression and inhuman suffering to the Promethean paradigm.

Whereas this letter of 1374 offers a passing glimpse of Boccaccio's travails contemporary with the Dante lectures, the two letters written to Mainardo Cavalcanti in 1372 describe the far more devastating sickness that beset him in the period just before the lectures were delivered (let us not forget that according to Boccaccio's revised chronology in *Genealogie* IV, 44, Prometheus's suffering precedes his education of the masses). Boccaccio begins the first of these two letters (*Epistole*, XXI) with an apology for his great delay in responding to Mainardo's last letter, a delay, he admits, that would be blameworthy were it not due to a terrible sickness.[49] The remainder of the letter consists of a meticulous and graphic chronicle of the various symptoms that accompany this progressive deterioration. So exorbitant and grandiose is this account that the reader may be tempted to dismiss it all as the delirious blather of a senile hypochondriac. However, a closer examination of the particular images and motifs used throughout this description reveals an underlying pattern – that of martyrdom – and purpose – that of forging a conceptual link between his sufferings and those of such notable figures as Phaethon and Prometheus. It is not by chance, but design that this catalogue of horrifying symptoms and excruciating cures reads more like a martyrology than a medical history.[50] By affiliating himself in this way with an ideal genealogy of culture-hero martyrs, Boccaccio gives us to understand that his agonies, like the notorious torments of these mythic cultural benefactors, have been incurred through acts of supreme generosity. To get a better sense of how it is that Boccaccio accomplishes this task of self-canonization it is necessary to take a closer look at the actual letters.

His life, he tells Mainardo in the first of these (*Epistole*, XXI), was like a sort of death ('simillima morti' [4]) filled with unrelieved afflictions and tedium. His first symptoms were a burning itch ('igneus pruritus') and a dry mange ('scabies sicca' [5]). His fingernails, he adds, barely sufficed to perform the task of scraping off this dry skin: 'abradere squamas aridas et scoria die noctuque vix sufficit unguis assidua' (5). This coarsely descriptive line concerning the bare sufficiency of his fingernails to the loathsome task of 'desquamation' ('abradere squamas') is almost certainly an allusion to the wonderfully crass *captatio benevolentia* used by Dante's Virgil in his effort to coax information from the scab-encrusted alchemists of the tenth bolgia: 'se l'unghia ti basti / eternalmente a cotesto lavoro' [may your nails forever last is this, their labour] (*Inf.* XXIX, 89–90). The tenth bolgia is populated by falsifiers of all stripes of whom the alchemists, falsifiers of metals, constitute just one group. Capocchio, the second of the interviewed alchemists, notes, 'io fui di natura buona scimia' [I was a good ape of nature] (*Inf.* XXIX, 139). By noting that his nails hardly suffice to perform the task of scraping off his scabs, Boccaccio seems to be aligning himself with the falsifiers: like them, he is 'di natura buona scimia' (indeed, among the best). This interpretation is supported by a passage in the *Genealogie* (XIV, 17: 'The poets are not apes of the philosophers') where, clearly rankled by the common accusation that poets are simply the apes of philosophers, Boccaccio notes that had such detractors called them apes of nature, they would have been less far from the truth, for the poets' task is that of describing in verse the effects of Nature.[51] Nevertheless, Boccaccio's affiliation of himself with Capocchio and other 'buone scimie della natura' does not, I would argue, constitute a self-indictment so much as an acknowledgment of the dangerous territory that he, and other imitators of nature, must traverse in the course of realizing their full potential as artist-creators. (Prometheus, let us not forget, represents the prototype of the *homo faber* – and, moreover, the only one, besides God, whose creative act consists in the fashioning of real human beings rather than mere simulacra like Epimetheus's anthropomorphic statues.)

Having furnished Mainardo with this vivid description of his miserable condition, Boccaccio remarks that this is all that he has been able to write in the course of three days, for he has been in the grip of a new, intensely painful bout with sickness. This sickness, he writes, began with a burning fever so sudden and intense that he was sure he would perish at once. Over the course of the night he emitted breaths of fire ('suspiria emictens ignea' [17]) and vainly attempted to lessen the Aetna-like burning ('ethneum incendium' [17]) by rapidly agitating his clothing. Certain that his death was imminent, he turned to meditation on his many sins and, overcome by a great fear, began to cry. As he waited patiently for the end, it seemed to him that a flame was emerging from deep within, shooting first from his navel to the bottom of his stomach and then to the right side of his groin ('dextrum inguen' [21]). At first he sustained this assault patiently, hopeful that the fever would be reduced by this burning. However, upon recognizing that such hopes were vain, he recalled Phaethon's fire and began to fear that he, likewise, would be reduced to ashes: 'Sed cum in cassum cedere expectatum adverti, Phetontis memor incendii cepi michi ipsi timere ne fulmine illo in cinerum iturus essem' (*Epistole* XXI, 22).

Though deeply sceptical of medical science, Boccaccio resolved to consult a doctor the next day. Albeit, Boccaccio remarks, no Apollo, Asclepius, or Hippocrates, this doctor seemed both amiable and prudent. Seeing the fiery mark ('igneam ... maculam' [25]) – a symptom, Boccaccio notes, of an inflamed liver ('epatis ferventis' [25]) – the doctor prescribed a course of repeated cauterization with red-hot irons followed by the excision, with a razor, of the burnt flesh:

> Without delay they prepared the instruments for my excoriation [scarnificationem meam]: the iron and the fire. And the irons, heated till they glowed, were plunged into my flesh, there quenched, then finally removed, and with a razor's edge the skin of these scorched parts was cut with crowded, oft repeated blows [iterum et iterum], not without my greatest torment [maximo cruciato] were they applied. (*Epistole* XXI, 26)[52]

The identification of the fiery mark with an inflammation of the liver, coupled with the description of an excruciating, repetitive excoriation by fire and iron does not simply document the horrors of fourteenth-century medical procedures but evokes a scene of martyrdom carefully designed to combine elements of Phaethon's incineration ('in cinerum iterus essem') with the repeated evisceration of Prometheus's liver.[53] Perhaps it is not coincidental that the expression – 'iterum et iterum' – used to describe the repeated plunging of the incandescent iron into Boccaccio's flesh echoes the words used in the *Genealogie* to depict Prometheus's martyrdom: 'et mox *iterum* restaurari, ac *iterum* ab ave laniari' [and quickly is restored *again*, and *again* lacerated] (IV 44, 5, emphasis mine).

Whereas Prometheus's status as culture-hero and martyr is self-evident, it is less clear how Phaethon fits into this pattern. Fortunately, this apparent obstacle is easily removed by reviewing Boccaccio's description of Phaethon in his youthful *Allegoria mitologica*. As critics have long noted, the second half of this opuscule draws heavily on Ovid's story of Phaethon in the *Metamorphoses*. (Antonio Enzo Quaglio goes so far as to call it a 'pedissequa trascrizione della favola ovidiana' [a servile transcription of the Ovidian tale]). However, the superficial similarities between Ovid's and Boccaccio's stories belie a difference so fundamental that it can be fairly said that the two stories have antithetical aims.[54]

In direct contrast to Ovid's Phaethon, Boccaccio's Phaethon is not concerned with proving that Phoebus Apollo is his father (in Boccaccio's version this divine paternity is taken for granted) but rather with exploiting this affiliation for the generous and lofty end of illuminating a benighted humanity. This Phaethon, we are told, appears to a wayward people just as Mercury appeared to Ulysses when he offered him the precious herb, moly, that would grant him immunity to Circe's enchantments: 'eis apparuit ut Cilenus Ulixi, sibi florem tribuens propter quem Circis pocula non gustavit' (5). It is with Phaethon's illustrious father firmly in mind ('patris fame recoliti' [16]) that this congregation of wretched people approaches him to plead for his intercession on their behalf. It is he, son of the god of stars ('filius stellarum principis' [16]) and giver of light, nourished on Helicon in the company of Muses ('nutritus inter montis Elicone Musas' [16]) to whom they appeal for the 'florum generis novi virtutes' (presumably a variety of knowledge) for which their souls so greatly thirst ('circa quas noster animus ansiatur' [16]). Phaethon agrees, and petitions his father on behalf of the pleading people, who desire that the ignorance enshrouding them be dispersed by his, Apollo's, light ('ut sibi tua luce sui erroris nebulas declararem' [21]). The conclusion of Ovid's and Boccaccio's tales is identical; when Phaethon, unequal to the task of steering the paternal chariot, finds himself careening uncontrollably, leaving in his wake a swathe of desiccated rivers and incinerated earth, Jupiter, concerned for the fate of the Earth, is forced to strike him from the sky with a bolt of lightning.

It is significant that Boccaccio's peculiar reconstruction of Phaethon as a salvific educator is not simply a passing symptom of his youthful whimsy. Attilio Hortis has proposed that Boccaccio's reasons for assigning Phaethon this function in the *Allegoria* may be inferred from the far later, euhemeristic account of Phaethon in *Genealogie* VII, 41, one that retains the same basic pattern of a pedagogue-reformer who sets out to tame the savagery of a rustic people through wisdom:

Perchè il Boccaccio scegliesse Fetonte a rappresentare il riformatore invocato da'Partenopei, possiamo inferire dal libro de *Genealogiis Deorum*, dove parlando di Fetonte cita una storia narratagli dal dotto bibliotecario di re Roberto, da Paolo Perugino, il quale aveva letto che Fetonte, detto anche Eridano, s'era proposto d'incivilire e ammansare i selvaggi e rozzi abitatori del Po.[55]

Boccaccio's reason for selecting Phaethon to represent the reformer petitioned by the Parthenopeians [Neapolitans] we can infer from the book *Genealogy of the Pagan Gods*, where, in speaking of Phaethon, he cites a story related to him by King Robert's learned librarian, Paul of Perugia, who had read that Phaethon, also called Eridanus, had set himself the task of civilizing and domesticating the savage and rustic inhabitants of the Po.

Though precedents for naturalistic and euhemeristic interpretations of the tale of Phaethon abound – Boccaccio mentions those of Eusebius and Orosius in *Genealogie* VII, 41 and another naturalistic explanation was available to Boccaccio in Fulgentius's *Mythologies* I, 16 – a glance at the passage in the *Genealogie* to which Hortis refers us suggests that this positive reevaluation of Phaethon as a pedagogue-reformer central to Boccaccio's innovative portrayal may be traced back to a certain Eustace, whose opinions on the matter were related to Boccaccio by Paul of Perugia:[56]

> Nonetheless, Paul of Perugia asserts, in accordance with I'm not sure which Eustace, that when Sparetus reigned in Assyria, Eridanus, who is also Phaethon, son of the king of Egypt, arrived, guided by the Nile, at the sea with his company and driven by wind-filled sails came to the gulf that we call Ligurian. (*Genealogie* VII 41, 12)[57]

As we read on, we learn that this same Eridanus undertakes an epic voyage that involves a campaign to domesticate hostile and rustic peoples through the application of *ingenium* [intellect] – 'ratus se ingenio superaturum ferociam' [confident of conquering savagery with intellect] (VII 41, 12) – and culminates in the foundation of Torino.

In a recent article, Claude Cazalé Bérard reminds us of the novel quality of Boccaccio's Phaethon, who, in contrast to his Ovidian precursor, serves primarily to exemplify the insufficiency of human artistic creation – in particular poetic composition – in comparison to divine creation. The fearless enterprise of Boccaccio's Phaethon 'si accosta alla versione ovidiana ma attraverso il filtro della sfida poetica: l'aiuto de Fetonte, implorato dall'umanità sofferente, è richiesto in nome delle sue doti poetiche' [approaches the Ovidian version, but through the filter of the poetic challenge: Phaethon's aid, entreated by a suffering humanity, is requested in the name of his poetic gifts] (447).[58] Cazalé Bérard clinches her argument with the observation that Boccaccio ends the Phaethon episode with a reference to the tragic histories of Marsyas and Arachne, two consummate artists traditionally used to illustrate this particular moral.

The latest, and most comprehensive, effort to account for the peculiarities of Boccaccio's Phaethon has been undertaken by Jonathan Usher, whose persuasive arguments leave little doubt that Phaethon may be taken to represent Boccaccio's poetic alter ego, engaged in a mythologized enactment of the dangers inherent in yielding to a vigorous but crude poetic impulse that is neither reined in by technical skill nor guided by cultural knowledge.[59]

However, the redemption of Boccaccio's Phaethon is not yet complete. Though Hortis highlights this reinvented Phaethon's role as culture-hero, Cazalé Bérard observes that Boccaccio's Phaethon represents the figure of the poet (together with the perils inherent in poetic composition), and Usher discerns beneath the Ovidian pastiche a peculiarly Boccaccian concern with the necessity of bridling the innate, but unregulated, disposition for poetry with acquired art, none of these critics specifically addresses what is arguably the most fundamental difference between the traditional, Ovidian, Phaethon and the reconceived version presented in the *Allegoria mitologica*. In contrast to the vainglorious Phaethon of the *Metamorphoses* (I, 747–II, 400), Boccaccio's Phaethon projects an inescapably Christian aura, for he is portrayed as a martyr whose magnanimous spirit ('magnanimus Pheton' [26]) drives him to procure celestial knowledge for his benighted fellows at the cost of his life.

When confronted with the image of an ailing, decrepit Boccaccio assailed in the pulpit of St Stephen in Badia by ungrateful critics for having attempted to unravel the allegories of the *Commedia* in response to his friends' 'prayers' – 'gli lor prieghi ciò mi fecer fare' [their prayers made me do it] (*Rime*, CXXIII) – it is difficult not to view this debacle as the historical fulfillment of Phaethon's sorry fate in the *Allegoria mitologica*, which, likewise, resulted from the generous, if misguided, impulse to answer the 'prayers' of friends: 'Idcirco vestre sotietatis intuitu suscepit anima preces vestras et ad tanti laboris fastigium me disponam' [for this reason, simply upon seeing your company my soul has accepted your prayers, and I will prepare myself to confront such a difficult enterprise] (*Allegoria*, 17).

Though, it is true, this Phaethon bears some relation to such figures as Marsyas and Arachne, his mission, in sharp contrast to theirs, is in no sense self-aggrandizing, for it is motivated from its very inception by the desire to secure the salvation of others. The death of Boccaccio's Phaethon is not simply a personal tragedy, for together with his body is buried the people's hope for illumination: 'Et sic in anxietate priori florum querentes naturam subito reintrarunt' (37). It is one thing to perish in the course of an egocentric mission of self-realization, but quite another to sacrifice one's life in the course of seeking benefits for others. It is, I would argue, this self-sacrificing Phaethon whom Boccaccio recalls in his letter to Mainardo: a magnanimous figure whose premature and dramatic death was the direct consequence of his selfless desire to improve the lot of his fellow humans.

Should we, then, take Boccaccio's studied application to his own life of an artificial, traditional 'Promethean' scheme as an indication that his sufferings were more symbolic than real, more intellectual and spiritual than physical? Not necessarily, for it is by no means unusual for Boccaccio to translate his lived experience into a deceptively conventional tissue of traditional motifs and learned literary allusions.[60] However, that Boccaccio, the greatest mythographer of his age, should invoke this particular selection of culture-heroes and artificer-creator figures in portraying his physical ailments suggests that he would have us view him as a poet-creator, martyred for his transgressive gift of re-creation.

The Prometheus/pimp thematic implicit in so many of Boccaccio's 'minor' works reaches a sort of apotheosis in the *Decameron*, where it becomes fully explicit in the famous sobriquet, *Prencipe Galeotto*, attached to the work both at its beginning and end.[61] According to the formula proposed by Francesca in *Inferno* V – 'Galeotto fu il libro e chi lo scrisse' [a Gallehault the book and he who wrote it, too] – if a book is a Galeotto, it follows that its author is a Galeotto as well. By declaring his book a 'Galeotto,' Boccaccio, as many critics have observed, leaves the reader no choice but to view Boccaccio himself as a Galeotto. This identification receives further confirmation in one of Boccaccio's letters to Mainardo Cavalcanti (*Epistole*, XXII), where he responds to Mainardo's embarrassed confession that he has yet to read Boccaccio's 'libellos' [little books] – usually taken to refer to the *Decameron* – by assuring him that he understands that such literary trifles can hardly be expected to compete with the delights of his new wife. Additionally, since his 'little books' contain much erotic matter that might unduly influence the virtuous women of Mainardo's household, Boccaccio asks that he keep the stories under wraps. Were the women to read them, he observes (not, I think, without a note of irony), they would judge him a filthy pimp: 'Existimabunt enim legentes me spurcidum lenonem' (*Epistole*, XXII, 23).[62]

In the *Decameron* Proem, Boccaccio presents himself as the victim of an unrequited love, preserved from death by the timely intervention of friends and eventually liberated from his painful love through the passage of time. His freedom restored – 'ora che libero dir mi posso' [now that I can call myself free] (Proemio, 7) – he is at liberty to aid others in achieving a similar emancipation from Love's bonds. Since, he argues, a combination of social, psychological, and physiological factors have rendered women particularly susceptible to Love's afflictions, it is they whom he wishes to succour. He concludes his Proem with the request that should he succeed in his efforts on their behalf, they should thank the god of Love, for it is he who, by liberating Boccaccio from his bonds ('legami') has freed him to attend to their pleasure.[63]

Women of a certain refinement and delicacy, observes Boccaccio, subject as they are to fear and shame – as well as social and physical confinement – are forced to conceal the 'amorose fiamme' [amorous flames] of erotic desire in their 'dilicati petti' [delicate bosoms] where it waxes into a 'focoso disio' [fiery desire] that finds a morbid expression in the form of 'malinconia' (melancholy – in the medieval sense of a pathological medical condition).[64] Boccaccio, insofar as he assumes the role of a new Prometheus, is charged with the task not of introducing fire but of teaching humanity – in particular women – how to control it.[65] How does Boccaccio propose that this restoration of erotic self-determination be accomplished? Presumably the 'noia' [anguish] occasioned by women's repressed sexual desire will be alleviated by the medicinal qualities of a text designed to distract them and provide sensual pleasure by proxy.

However, something in this claim does not ring quite true. If the *Decameron* is truly nothing more than harmless diversion and is not invested with some more serious agenda, why does Boccaccio feel it necessary to inaugurate Day IV with his famous apologia? Granted, this forceful declamation of his critics and animated self-defence may amount to little more than rhetorical posturing designed to romanticize the figure of the embattled author, whose decision to continue writing is made to seem an act of such selfless generosity that it assumes the unmistakable guise of martyrdom: a Promethean sacrifice. However, whether or not the attacks upon his work by envious and enraged critics are real, imagined, or simply a rhetorical device hardly matters; it is enough that Boccaccio would have us view him in this light.[66]

If Prometheus was rewarded for his benefaction of humanity by having his liver torn out with a vulture's sharp beak, Boccaccio seems to have fared no better, for by championing the cause of women he has supposedly incurred the wrath of envious critics who are eating him alive, 'infino nel vivo trafitto,' tearing at him with their 'atroci denti' [dreadful teeth] (IV, Intro., 8).[67] Though no one would deny that such stories as that of Alatiel (II, 7), Masetto (III, 1), and Alibech (III, 10) are overtly erotic and may well have provoked real horror in a prudish critic, the allegation that such critics are cannibalizing him – alive no less – is the sort of sensational detail through which Boccaccio transforms the petty antagonisms of a (possibly fictive) conservative backlash into an epic drama with truly radical consequences. By elevating a literary squabble to this epic register Boccaccio forces us to reconsider the nature of his

mediation on behalf of women. Is Boccaccio a 'leno scelestus' – a pornographer – or a 'leno caelestis' – a Promethean pedagogue-martyr?
Since the theme of poet as pimp, as we have seen, is never far from that
of a metaphorical – or literal – undressing, perhaps the most expedient
way of exploring this issue is to consider the way in which the theme of
undressing is presented in the apologia of Day IV.

Despite – or perhaps because of – his deep admiration for Dante, Boccaccio mentions Dante's name only once in the whole of the *Decameron*.
Significantly, it is precisely in the context of the apologia of the Introduction to Day IV that Dante's name is invoked. In response to those critics
who deride him for engaging in an eroticism that they view as ill-becom-
ing a man of his age, Boccaccio first observes that oftentimes beneath
the white-headed leek lurks a green tail and adds:

> io mai a me vergogna non reputerò infino nello stremo della mia vita di
> dover compiacere a quelle cose alle quali Guido Cavalcanti e Dante Ali-
> ghieri già vecchi e messer Cino da Pistoia vecchissimo *onor si tennero*, e fu lor
> caro il piacer loro. (IV, intro., 33, emphasis mine.)

> I shall never feel any compunction in striving to please the ones who were
> so greatly honoured, and whose beauty was so much admired, by Guido
> Cavalcanti and Dante Alighieri in their old age, and by Cino da Pistoia in his
> dotage. (trans. McWilliam, 288)

It has been noted that in addition to naming Dante, Boccaccio uses a
phrase, 'onor si tennero,' most probably modelled on line 76, 'onor mi
tegno,' of Dante's poem 'Tre donne intorno al cor' [Three women
around my heart]:[68]

> l'essilio che m' è dato, onor mi tegno:
> ché, se giudizio o forza di destino
> vuol pur che il mondo versi
> i bianchi fiori in persi,
> cader co' buoni è pur di lode degno.
> (*Rime*, 76–80)

> The exile I must bear, honor I call:
>   For though God's will or vicar Fortune teach
> Earth's valley how to blight
> White blooms to black as night,

It still is best to join the good, and fall.
(trans. Diehl, 193)[69]

'Tre donne intorno al cor' may be described as Dante's meditation on Justice – human and divine – framed by the more specific circumstances of his exile from Florence. The phrase 'onor mi tegno' is a proud declaration that to have been condemned by the corrupt justice of a temporal tribunal is a mark not of ignominy but of honour; in a world turned upside down, an apparent fall is a real elevation. Through this verbal echo, Boccaccio implies that he, likewise, is not chastened, but exalted by the slander of his hypocritical critics.

The 'tre donne' who surround Dante's heart in his poem are none other than a personified Justice (a symbol of divine and natural law) accompanied by her daughters, human law and positive law (legislation): a veritable genealogy of Justice designed to emphasize the continuity between divine and temporal manifestations of law. Despite the protagonizing role of Love, 'here,' Kenelm Foster and Patrick Boyde note in their excellent commentary, 'the erotic sphere is quite transcended,' for this Love represents the 'human love of truth and virtue.'[70] It is no wonder, given his love of virtue and truth, that Love should respond with anger and shame ('pietoso e fello') upon catching a glimpse of Justice's privates through her tattered dress, threadbare from long neglect: 'Come Amor prima per la rotta gonna / la vide in parte che il tacere è bello' (27–30). However, that he should have chosen to direct his sight towards Justice's midriff in the first place does seem to suggest that his interests are not confined to virtue and truth. No less disconcerting is the stanza beginning at line 91, in which the personified Canzone is addressed, and advised that nobody should attempt to lay a hand on her in hopes of disclosing her hidden secrets; let such people be content with those parts (the literal text) that are already exposed:

Canzone, a' panni tuoi non ponga uom mano,
per veder quel che bella donna chiude:
bastin le parti nude;
lo dolce pome a tutta gente niega,
per cui ciascun man piega.
(*Rime*, 91–5)

My song, let none set fingers to your dress
To see those parts which lovely women hide,

Suffice what lies outside,
Deny to all the apple and its sweets
Though hands be at your pleats;
(Diehl, 193)

The hidden secrets, the 'dolce pomo,' should be reserved for the exclusive fruition of the select few, friends of virtue:[71]

Ma s'elli avvien che tu alcun mai truovi
amico di virtù, ed e' ti priega,
fatti di color' novi,
poi li ti mostra; e'l fior, ch'è bel di fori,
fa disïar ne li amorosi cori.
(*Rime*, 96–100)

But if it ever chance, someday, that you
Discover virtue's friend, and he entreats,
Make all your colours new,
Then show yourself – so fair its outer parts,
Your bloom will stir desire in loving hearts.
(Diehl, 195)

When Boccaccio invokes Dante's name, it is presumably to support his argument that erotic passion is not incompatible with or, indeed, inappropriate for older men. It is entirely possible, therefore, that the insertion of the phrase 'onor mi tegno' in this particular context is intended to evoke the allegorical undressing of the three women in 'Tre donne intorno al cor.' If, he seems to be implying, the aged Dante – whose poetic greatness is questioned by none – was permitted to indulge in these erotic fantasies, why should he be denied the same licence? Naturally, this entirely facetious argument is itself no more than a clever strategy for drawing the reader's attention to a more profound analogy between Boccaccio's and Dante's texts; in both, erotic material serves a moral end. Foster and Boyde's assertion that 'the erotic sphere is quite transcended' tends to overlook the exquisite paradox that it is this same 'erotic sphere' that furnishes the means for its own transcendence. Dante's disclosure of Justice's privates is not provoked by a senile prurience but by a recognition that erotic metaphor is among the most effective ways of concretizing abstract notions: an incarnation of doctrine that renders it not only intelligible, but sensible, not only sensible, but seductive.[72]

Implicit in Boccaccio's affiliation of his brand of eroticism with that used by Dante in 'Tre donne' is the belief that the erotic material in his *Decameron* fulfills a similarly educative, even moral, purpose. Though the tribunal of the ignorant public may judge him a 'leno sceleste' [contemptible pimp], the enlightened reader cannot help but recognize that he, like Dante, is not simply in the business of hawking flesh to an indiscriminate crowd but is concerned with revealing the hidden lineaments of Virtue to an audience of initiates in the mysteries of love. Like Dante's *Vita nuova* (which, incidentally, Dante introduces as a 'libello' [I, 1]), Boccaccio's 'libello' (the term used for the *Decameron* in his letter to Mainardi) is directed primarily to women who have 'intelletto d'amore' [an understanding of love]: those 'dilicate donne' [delicate women] for whom such pedestrian diversions as the 'ago e'l fuso e l'arcolaio' [needle, spindle and skein] (Proem, 13) do not suffice. It is, according to this conceit, due to the fact that his book has made its way into the hands of readers, his boorish critics, who are not part of this ideal audience and therefore lack the discernment to savor the true virtue of the 'dolce pomo,' that he has been labeled a pornographer and subjected to the 'atroci denti' [dreadful teeth] of the rabid mob.

In the Introduction to Day IV (just a few lines after alluding to Dante's 'Tre donne intorno al cor') Boccaccio famously declares:

> le Muse son donne, e benché le donne quel che le Muse vagliano non vagliano, pure esse hanno nel primo aspetto simiglianza di quelle, sì che, quando per altro non mi piacessero, per quello mi dovrebber piacere (35)

> The Muses are ladies, and although ladies do not rank as highly as Muses, nevertheless they resemble them at first sight, and hence it is natural, if only for this reason, that I should be fond of them. (McWilliam, 289)

He goes on to say that whereas Muses have never been a source of inspiration to him, women have inspired him to write more than a thousand verses. Given Boccaccio's eagerness to establish this commensurability of women and Muses, is it not possible that the act of unveiling women, like that of stripping Muses, is intended to serve a virtuous end? In the section that follows I will attempt to answer this question by closely examining the enigmatic *Valle delle donne* [Valley of the women] interlude of *Decameron* VI.

Nel Cospetto degli Uomini: **The Prophylactic Peep-show of** *Decameron* **VI**

The randy priest of VIII, 2 and the object of his devotion, Monna Belcolore, though unlettered, display a virtuosity in their deployment of metaphor rarely equalled in the *Decameron*.[73] When Monna Belcolore intimates that the priest, though a man of the cloth, might perform poorly between the sheets, the priest retorts:

> Sì facciam noi meglio che gli altri uomini: o perché no? E dicoti più, che noi facciamo vie miglior lavorio; e sai perché? perché noi maciniamo a raccolta: ma in verità bene a tuo uopo, se tu stai cheta e lascimi fare. (VIII 2, 23)[74]

> 'We certainly do,' replied the priest. 'Why on earth shouldn't we? What's more, we do a much better job of it than other men, and do you know why? It's because we do our grinding when the millpond's full. So if you want to make hay while the sun shines, hold your tongue and let me get on with it.' (McWilliam, 557)

By arguing that the sexual abstinence exacted of the clergy results in an accumulation of sexual desire and enhancement of sexual prowess, the priest foregrounds one of the most pervasive themes of the *Decameron*: libido, like a river, can be dammed up only so long before it tears through the fragile embankments of social decorum.[75]

The priest's figurative use of the word 'raccolta' (holding tank) implies that the mechanics of one's sexual economy is somehow analogous to the more familiar mechanics of the water mill; a millpond – raccolta – cannot be filled indefinitely. Madonna Filippa expresses this idea most memorably during her trial for adultery when she skillfully argues that having fully satisfied her husband's sexual needs she nevertheless finds herself burdened with a surfeit ('quel che gli avanza' [VI 7, 17]) – would they have her cast it to the dogs? Throughout the *Decameron*, sexual desire is treated mechanistically, as the inevitable product of a physiological process, an accumulation that must be periodically eliminated in order to maintain equilibrium within the human organism. When the credulous Catella of Day III chastizes the man whom she mistakenly takes for her husband, she accuses him of refusing her advances because he wished to 'unload his pack' elsewhere ('scaricare le some altrove' [III 6, 37]), but notes, triumphantly, that despite his scurrilous efforts, the 'water' has flowed downwards, as nature intended: 'l'acqua è pur corsa alla ingiù come ella doveva!' (III 6, 38).[76] Indeed, this idea of a sexual economy defined in terms of loading and unloading is introduced in the 'Proem' itself, where Boccaccio states that whereas men are provided with many means of alleviating ('alleggiare,' having the etymological sense of 'lightening') their burden of thoughts ('gravezza di pensieri' [12]) occasioned by erotic frustration, through such activities as hunting and fishing, women have fewer venues for such a 'lightening' of their load.[77] The *Decameron*, Boccaccio claims, is itself designed to fulfill this function for women. Since Boccaccio casts his text in the role of pander, 'galeotto,' the literary success of his book is inextricably bound up with its erotic success: a text engineered to generate erotic tension must at the same time perform the midwife-like function of delivering women of erotic tumescence.[78]

Given Boccaccio's scepticism regarding the ability of conventional social structures to contain such 'surfeit,' it is noteworthy that he endows his *raccolta* of ribald stories with a narrative dyke – the 'frame' – that takes the form of the *brigata* together with its carefully delineated hierarchy and rigorous schedule of activities. Indeed, the tension generated by this peculiar union is confirmed by the repeated insistence on   the 'onestà' [integrity] of the *brigata*. The *Decameron* is thus, in many respects, a methodical study of the interaction of a sophisticated microsociety, the *brigata*, with those very forces – youth, physical beauty, enforced celibacy, freedom from supervision, leisure, isolation, music, wine, and erotic narrative – that even singly might be considered to pose a threat to virtue.[79] How is it that despite Boccaccio's insistence on the fragility of culture in the face of human nature, Panfilo is able, in the conclusion to Day X, to congratulate the *brigata* for having withstood these many temptations to vice? Even those readers reluctant to take Panfilo at his word must concede that the *brigata* never devolves into an orgiastic free-for-all – no small accomplishment under the circumstances. How is it that the *brigata* prevails in a trial that would have tested the resources of St Anthony himself?

The key to this enigma may be found in the third of Boccaccio's 'frame gardens,' the delectable *Valle delle donne* (Valley of Women) of Day VI, which, with its central reservoir, is itself a variety of *raccolta*, one that derives its true importance from its metaphorical value as a model for the sublimation of human sexual desire into socially valuable forms.[80] Whereas the priest's *raccolta* fuels sexual escapades that are potentially socially destabilizing, the *raccolta* that lies in the middle of the *Valle* is one that satiates desire without putting social stability at risk. Indeed, the *raccolta* of the *Valle delle donne* mirrors the narrative 'raccolta' of the one hundred stories; both are concerned with providing erotic pleasure by proxy – the former with an emphasis on image, the latter on text – and both seem to advocate erotica as socially valuable precisely because it not only defuses sexual tension but renders it socially productive.

Like Boccaccio's jocular expression 'the resurrection of the flesh' (*Dec.* III 10, 13), his evaluation of human sexuality in the *Valle* reveals a programmatic attempt to 'redeem' sexual desire. Since rape is among the most radical manifestations of unbridled sexual desire, it is natural that in his quest to redeem sexual desire, Boccaccio should simultaneously renovate three classical *loci* of rape – the theatre, the wooded tarn, and the pleasance – with respect both to the variety of erotic activity that they accommodate and their physical characteristics. In each case the ominous locus is transformed to a *locus amoenus* without, however, entirely effacing its previous connotations. It is no coincidence that the various incentives to sexual activity enumerated above are complemented by a backdrop – the *Valle* – that combines in a single place three of the sites traditionally associated with rape. Indeed, all elements of the drama unfolded on the stage of the *Valle* – nudity, isolation, susceptibility, erotic play, and so forth – are cannily orchestrated with these topographical associations to suggest a single denouement: rape. That the interlude in the *Valle* does not culminate in a rape despite this apparent overdetermination is the most eloquent testimony that Boccaccio is proposing a radical shift away from carnal intercourse to erotic discourse and voyeurism. Erotic titillation through image and text (the *novelle* of Day VII) triumphs over erotic consummation through act in the drama of the *Valle*.

Though in the process of redeeming the theatre, tarn, and wood-girdled pleasance Boccaccio radically alters their form, he makes a point of retaining the original associations of each: their familiar forms provide a foil that serves to highlight their revised function. In the most basic sense, Boccaccio accomplishes this renovation by making the sexually threatening theatre a variety of erotic spectacle, the wooded tarn a fishpond, and the meadow encircled by a threatening forest, a delightful arboretum. In order to give a better idea of the complexity of this process, I will discuss each of the three similes used by Boccaccio to describe the space. First it is likened to a theatre ('teatro'), shortly afterwards to a fishpond ('vivaio'), and finally to a magisterially landscaped arboretum.

Because I am beginning with the image of the theatre, it is appropriate that I first set the stage. Elissa, the queen of the previous day, suggests (out of earshot of the three men of the *brigata*) that the women go to a beautiful spot, the *Valle delle donne*, where she has been wanting to take them since their arrival at the villa. The women, pleased to follow her suggestion, set out together to the *Valle*, which is only slightly more than a mile distant:

> né guari più d'un miglio furono andate, che alla Valle delle donne perven-
> nero. Dentro alla quale per una via assai stretta, dall'una delle parti della
> quale correva un chiarissimo fiumicello, entrarono, e viderla tanto bella e
> tanto dilettevole, e spezialmente in quel tempo che era il caldo grande,
> quanto più si potesse divisare. E secondo che alcuna di loro poi mi ridisse,
> il piano che nella valle era, così era ritondo come se a sesta fosse stato fatto,
> quantunque artificio della natura e non manual paresse; ed era di giro poco
> più che un mezzo miglio, intorniato di sei montagnette di non troppa
> altezza, e in su la sommità di ciascuna si vedeva un palagio quasi in forma
> fatto d'un bel castelletto. (VI 19, 20)

> nor had they gone much more than a mile, when they came to the Valley of
> the Ladies. This they entered by way of a very narrow path, along one side of
> which there flowed a beautifully clear stream, and they found it to be as
> delectable and lovely a place, especially as the weather was so hot, as could
> possibly be imagined. And according to the description I was given later by
> one of their number, the floor of the valley was perfectly circular in shape,
> for all the world as if it had been made with compasses, though it seemed
> the work of Nature rather than of man. It was little more than half a mile in
> circumference, and surrounded by half-a-dozen hills, all comparatively low-
> lying, on each of whose summits one could discern a palace, built more or
> less in the form of a pretty little castle. (McWilliam, 479–80)

Everything about the description of this hidden valley resonates with a subtle variety of containment which masquerades as diaphanous space. The route which the women take to the valley – the only access – is 'assai stretta' [quite narrow], and even the openness of the circular proscenium of the valley itself is illusory for it is surrounded by a series of diminishing circles:

> Le piaggie delle quali montagnette così digradando giù verso'l piano dis-
> cendevano, come ne' teatri veggiamo dalla lor sommità i gradi infino

all'infimo venire successivamente ordinati, sempre ristringendo il cerchio loro. (VI, Concl., 21)

The sides of the hills ranged downwards in a regular series of terraces, concentrically arranged like the tiers of an amphitheatre, their circles gradually diminishing in size from the topmost terrace to the lowest. (McWilliam, 480)

Viewed as a theatre, the perfect circle of the central clearing inevitably takes on the role of a stage – or, better yet, an arena. The terraces that encircle the central arena evoke the form of bleachers, whose familiar contours are only partially disguised by the living trellis of fruit trees, and the six villas symmetrically distributed on the six hills that modulate the outermost perimeter of the 'natural' theatre correspond to viewing stations for the elite.[81]

The idea of a natural theatre is not an innovation on Boccaccio's part. Indeed, Virgil situates the funeral games in honour of Aeneas's father, Anchises, in just such a setting – on a grassy plain of Sicily's Cape Drepanum: 'This contest sped, good Aeneas moves to a grassy plain, girt all about with winding hills, well-wooded, where, at the heart of the valley, ran the circuit of the theatre' (*Aeneid* V, 286–9).[82] This episode, following, as it does, so hard upon Aeneas's erotic entanglement with Dido in Carthage, serves to document a dramatic conversion from erotic to civic concerns. Aeneas's erotic servitude to Dido and neglect of his civic duty is implicitly contrasted with the remarkable self-possession and political skill that he exhibits in his direction of the funeral games – a test, really, of the very skills that will become indispensable to him as he assumes the political stewardship of the scattered peoples destined to form the Roman Empire.

Like the 'theatri circus' of *Aeneid* V, Boccaccio's amphitheatre functions as a variety of testing ground; however, since the test in the *Valle delle donne* interlude is clearly erotic (rather than political or martial) in nature, it seems to me that a more likely source for Boccaccio's valley-amphitheatre is the etiological myth in Ovid's *Ars amatoria* describing the salacious origins of the theatre – one in which rape and representation are violently united:

But the theatre's curving tiers should form your favourite
Hunting ground: here you are sure to find
The richest returns ...

Flitting from flower to flower, so our fashionable ladies
Swarm to the games in such crowds, I often can't
Decide which I like. As spectators they come, come to be
inspected:
Chaste modesty doesn't stand a chance.
Such incidents at the games go back to Romulus –
Men without women, Sabine rape.
No marble theatre then, no awnings, no perfumed saffron
To spray the stage red:
The Palatine woods supplied a leafy backdrop (nature's
Scenery, untouched by art),
While the tiers of seats were plain turf, and spectators shaded
Their shaggy heads with leaves.
Urgently brooding in silence, the men kept glancing
About them, each marking his choice
Among the girls ...
The king gave the sign for which
They'd so eagerly watched. Project Rape was on ...
... Ever since that day, by hallowed
custom,
Our theatres have always held dangers for pretty girls.
(*Ars amatoria* I, 90–134)[83]

For the solemn, pious mood that dominates Virgil's description of
the funeral games at Drepanum, Ovid substitutes an ironic, even flip-
pant, tone as he describes the sexual depredation of the hapless Sabines
by Romulus and his boorish band in the natural amphitheatre of the
Circus Maximus. The sexual violence of Romulus's age has been
replaced by sophisticated erotic games; the urgent brooding of a virile
people bent on securing their biological posterity has been replaced by
the reciprocal oglings and silly flirtations of a decadent people dedicated to pleasure. This juxtaposition – on the same physical site – of the
natural theatre (a place to rape) with the modern theatre (a place
to date), serves as an apt metaphor for the *Ars amatoria* as a whole, a
work concerned with curbing natural passion by subjecting it to the
rein of art. Though the *Decameron*, itself a variety of *Ars amatoria*, is
guided by similar concerns, Boccaccio, as we shall see, goes even further. Physical intercourse is not simply domesticated through subjection
to 'official' rules of erotic engagement; it appears to have been eliminated al-together.

Like Boccaccio's natural amphitheatre, Ovid's too is characterized by the absence of human artifice: 'scena sine arte fuit' (*Ars amatoria* I, 106). The 'plain turf' seats correspond to the horticultural marvel of the *Valle's* terracing. Here, the voyeuristic exploitation of the women that is implicit in the *Valle* is unambiguously fulfilled. However, in marked contrast to the *Valle*, here, voyeurism functions as a prelude to rape. Whereas Dioneo is the symbolic king who regrets that he lacks the authority to force women to engage in sex (for, he maintains, had he the power, he would make them all indulge in that act without which no party can be said to be truly complete [VI, Concl., 3]), Romulus is the king traditionally credited with having conceived and carried out the rape of the Sabine women in the valley of the Circus Maximus.

Consequently, Boccaccio's implication that the *Valle delle donne* is somehow an enclosed and private 'feminine' space, as is suggested by its very name, must be balanced by the observation that this experience of freedom, while subjectively authentic, serves, ironically, as the means for the women's objectification, their unwitting exposure to male scrutiny. The *Valle* is an amphitheatre[84] of the erotic in which the naked women disport for both their own delectation and that of the invisible 'viewers' who look down upon them from the windows of the six villas: 'viewers' who are representative of the readers of Boccaccio's text for they enjoy the same privileged view and the same immunity.[85]

The notion that Boccaccio is fulfilling a pimp-like role by effectively 'prostituting' the young women of the *brigata* – forcing them to walk naked, like the Muses, in the 'cospetto degli uomini' (*Teseida* XII, 84) – is further reinforced by Boccaccio's etymology of 'fornicazione' in the *Esposizioni*. Here, Boccaccio maintains that 'fornicazione' derives from the architectural term 'fornice' [vault], a space long invested with a strongly erotic valence due to the established custom of practicing prostitution beneath the sheltering arches of the ancient theatres:[86]

e 'fornici' eran chiamate propiamente quelle le quali eran fatte a sostenamento de' gradi de' teatri; a' quali teatri per ciò che la moltitudine degli uomini anticamente si ragunava i dì solenni a vedere i giuochi, li quali essi si faceano, predevano in queste fornici le femine volgari loro stanza a dare opera al loro disonesto servigio con quegli a' quali piaceva. (*Esp.* V, alleg., 64–5)

Properly speaking then, the 'fornices' are the vaults that were made to support the graduated seating of a theatre. During ancient times, crowds would gather at these theatres on holidays to watch the games that were held there and women of ill repute would fix up rooms under the vaults in order to perform their dishonest services with whomever was interested. (Papio trans.)

Let us not forget that in the *Rime* Boccaccio tells us that it is in the 'fornice del vulgo,' a figurative vault, that he has, according to his critics, vilely prostrated the Muses and foolishly exposed their hidden parts to the dregs of society (*Rime* CXXII, 1–4).

By transferring the erotic activity from the hidden recesses of the *fornici* that subtend the theatre's *gradi* [tiers] to the open arena at the theatre's centre, Boccaccio simultaneously transforms the nature of the erotic activity from one of private, physical, and compliant intimacy to one of public, visual, and – from the women's perspective – unwitting intimacy. Boccaccio accommodates this interpretation by providing such tantalizing phrases as the following:

In questo adunque venute le giovani donne, poi che per tutto riguardato ebbero e molto commendato il luogo, essendo il caldo grande e vedendosi il pelaghetto chiaro davanti e *senza alcun sospetto d'esser vedute*, deliberaron di volersi bagnare. (VI, Concl., 29, emphasis mine)

Having arrived in this place, looked about, and sung its praises, feeling the great heat, seeing the clear pool in front of them and *having no suspicion of being observed*, the young women decided to go for a swim.

How should one interpret the words, 'senza alcun sospetto d'esser vedute' [having no suspicion of being observed]? Would it not have been easier to simply write, 'senza esser vedute' [without being observed]? The inclusion of the word 'sospetto' [suspicion] suggests that they are being watched and are merely not conscious of the fact. Strong evidence in support of this interpretation is Boccaccio's skillful appropriation of the words 'senza alcun sospetto,' words immortalized by Francesca da Rimini in Canto V of Dante's *Inferno*:

Noi leggiavamo un giorno per diletto
   di Lancialotto come amor lo strinse:
   soli eravamo e *sanza alcun sospetto*.
(127–9, emphasis mine)[87]

One day, to pass the time away, we read
of Lancelot – how love had overcome him.
We were alone, and we suspected nothing.
(*Divine Comedy*, trans. Mandelbaum [hereafter cited as Mandelbaum])

These words imply that it was the enraptured lovers' guileless faith in
their security that finally secured their doom; they should have suspected. We find even firmer confirmation of this reading in Boccaccio's
own work, the *Ninfale fiesolano*, where we are presented with the lusty
young Africo who, disguised as a woman, deliberates his best course of
action upon finding himself obliged to join his fellow nymphs as they
bathe naked in a tarn:

Perch'allor era la maggior calura
che fosse in tutto 'l giorno, e dal diletto
tirate di quell'acqua alla frescura,
e veggendosi *sanz'alcun sospetto*,
e l'acqua tanto chiara e netta e pura,
diliberaron far com'avean detto,
e per bagnarsi ognuna si spogliava
(octave 236, emphasis mine)

It was the hottest hour of the day,
and surely those cool waters lured them all
into their bland refreshment instantly.
Knowing themselves to be quite safe from harm,
and seeing then the pool so clear and pure,
they did at last as they had thought and said.
So while each nymph was getting quick undressed,
sweet Mensola young Africo addressed
(*Giovanni Boccaccio's Nymphs of Fiesole*, trans. Tusiani, [hereafter cited as
Tusiani], 84)

Naturally, his deception does not survive his disrobing and all the terrified nymphs escape but one, Mensola, the object of his unbridled passion whom he rapes without more ado. The *Ninfale fiesolano* was written
before the *Decameron*, and perhaps it is for this reason that it adheres so
closely to the classical paradigm – the culmination of the scene in a rape.

In his account of the rape of Proserpina in the *Esposizioni*, Boccaccio describes how Pluto, suddenly seized by love, directs his chariot towards Proserpina, 'la quale di ciò non sospicava' [who was suspecting no such thing] (VII, alleg., 12). Since the *Valle* episode parallels such scenes in so many details, it is significant that Boccaccio has so radically altered the traditional denoument; in the *Valle*, gape replaces rape.

While the simile of the theatre introduces the basic elements of audience and actor – distorted by the erotic lens of Boccaccio's text in such a way that the spectator is cast as voyeur and the actor as unwitting participant in an erotic spectacle – it is in the second of the three similes used to describe the *Valle*, that of the fish pond, that the theme of voyeuristic exploitation is most clearly articulated. Boccaccio likens the central pond to a fish pond, a vivaio: 'e ivi faceva un picciol laghetto, quale talvolta per modo di vivaio fanno ne' lor giardini i cittadini che di ciò hanno destro' ['where it formed a tiny lake like one of those fishponds that prosperous townspeople occasionally construct in their gardens'] (VI, Concl., 27; McWilliam, 480).

The pool of water in the centre of the valley in which the women bathe is of such supernatural clarity that it hides their fair-skinned bodies as effectively as a thin sheet of glass conceals a pink rose: 'non altrimenti li lor corpi candidi nascondeva, che farebbe una vermiglia rosa un sottil vetro.' Significantly, the image of the complete exposure of the body as of a blossom suspended in clear glass probably derives from Ovid's story of Salmacis and Hermaphroditus in the *Metamorphoses*:

> The Naid [Salmacis] cannot wait; she can't delay
> delight; she aches; she must embrace; she's crazed.
> With hollow palms he claps his sides, then dives
> with grace into the waves; his left, his right
> arms alternating strokes, he glides; the light
> shines through the limpid pool, revealing him –
> as if, within clear glass, one had encased
> white lilies with the white of ivory shapes.
> (Book IV, 352–9)[88]

While Boccaccio's Ovidian source casts a woman as the sexual antagonist, in his *Valle*, it is the women whose bodies are exposed like that of Hermaphroditus and it is, therefore, their security that is implicitly threatened. Boccaccio goes so far as to ensure the accessibility of the image of the women's naked bodies by crediting the waters of his *Valle* with a supernatural trait; the women are able to engage in their playful chasing after fish without disturbing the mirror-smooth surface of

the water: 'né per ciò alcuna turbazion d'acqua nascendone, cominciarono come potevano a andare in qua in là di dietro a' pesci' ['when they
were in the water, which remained as crystal clear as before, they began as
best they could to swim hither and thither in pursuit of the fishes'] (VI,
Concl., 31; McWilliam, 481). While the *Valle* as a whole conveys, in its ide-
alization of natural forms, a slightly supernatural aura, it is, nevertheless,
regulated by natural laws. Here, we find the single exception to this rule
for we are presented with a variety of water that is evidently not subject to
natural law. This type of exemption is something of an anomaly in the
Decameron, where the supernatural intrudes only on rare occasions, and
always in the *novelle*, not the frame.[89] It appears, therefore, that Boccaccio's desire that the women be readily viewed is so pressing that he is willing to risk the verisimilitude of his work itself – expose the fiction of the
brigata – in order to 'undress' the bathing women.

Boccaccio's description of the pleasance corresponds in many particu-
lars to Ovid's description of the site of Proserpina's abduction:[90]

Not far from Henna's walls there is a deep pool of water, Pergus by name ...
A wood crowns the heights around its waters on every side, and with its foli-
age as with an awning keeps off the sun's hot rays. The branches afford a
pleasing coolness, and the well-watered ground bears bright-coloured flowers. (*Metamorphoses*, V, 385–90)[91]

Here, we recognize the wood-encircled valley punctuated by a central
pond and protected by an arbour. Here, too, we see the flowery meadow
and are reminded that Proserpina's gathering of flowers is intimately
associated with her own defloweriing by Hades. A 'flower' herself, she is
plucked from the lovely meadow even as she plucks flowers – just as the
women in the *Valle* are visually 'caught' even as they catch fish. In Claudian's fourth-century reworking of the story of Proserpina (one that was
enormously popular in the Middle Ages) we see these same elements
recycled, though with a significant addition – the extraordinary transparency of the water:

Not far from this spot extends a lake (the Sicani have called it Pergus), and,
being girdled with a leafy border of groves, its nearby waters show pale: it
admits observing eyes into its depths, and the water, transparent afar, leads
the unobstructed gaze under its clear flood and betrays the innermost secrets
of its pellucid depths. (*De raptu Proserpinae* II, 112–17; trans. Gruzelier, 33)[92]

Curiously, having done such a good job evoking the effortless penetrability of the water and helpless revelation of its secrets, Claudian gives no indication of the nature of the exposed secrets. Boccaccio needed little incentive to remedy this 'oversight' on the part of his classical predecessor; he gave the water as many secrets to expose as there were women in it. Although Claudian had something more spiritual in mind when he alluded to the secrets of the pellucid depths, one cannot really fault Boccaccio for exploiting a theme that so ideally suited his own agenda.

The Ovidian intertext here, and elsewhere, serves to conjure up the spectre of rape even as Boccaccio systematically eliminates rape by replacing it with a voyeuristic form of fulfillment. The rape that in Ovid is often viewed as a creational act – the origin of the Romans themselves is traditionally traced back to the rape of the Sabine women – has been displaced in Boccaccio by a re-creational act: voyeurism.

Equally telling in this regard is Boccaccio's assertion that the bottom of the pond 'mostrava d'esser d'una minutissima ghaia, la qual tutta, chi altro non avesse avuto a fare, avrebbe, volendo, potuto annoverare' ['showed up vividly as a stretch of very fine gravel, every fragment of which could have been counted by anyone with sufficient patience and nothing better to do'] (VI, Concl., 27; McWilliam, 480–1).[93]

Significantly, once again the Ovidian intertext is one intimately associated with the threat of imminent sexual violation, the story of Arethusa and Alpheus in the *Metamorphoses*:

> I came upon a stream. Unmurmuring
> and unperturbed it glided, crystalline –
> so clear down to the riverbed that one
> could count each pebble there.
> (Book V, 589–92)[94]

These are Arethusa's words describing the delectable waters where she was tempted to bathe – an inauspicious decision, for shortly afterwards she was raped by Alpheus, the god of the waters that had seemed so benign.

Whereas of the female spectators in the natural theatre of his *Ars amatoria* Ovid says that they came both to see and be seen – 'Spectatum veniunt, veniunt spectentur ut ipsae' – this lovely chiasmus is not maintained in the *Valle*, where it is the women alone who are the subjects of erotic contemplation. Whereas Ovid's chiasmus suggests a kind of reciprocal mirroring between subject and object, Boccaccio goes out of his way to revise the central lake of the *Valle* in such a way that the traditional trope of lake as reflective speculum is deliberately cast aside in favour of transparency; the surface of the water does not reflect image but exposes it (with a laugh, Cupid exchanges the poetic speculum for the medical speculum). Consequently, while no actual rape occurs, one is nevertheless left with the feeling that women are being sexually exploited. However, the invisible 'Actaeons' of Boccaccio's *Valle* incur no wrath, human or divine, and suffer no ill consequence. Boccaccio's revision of these Ovidian myths reveals his goal of preserving women from the outrage of rape and men from the destructive consequences of seeking forbidden knowledge of women.

In examining the central pond I have thus far dealt with it insofar as it resembles its Ovidian prototype. However, just as Boccaccio has altered the activity that takes place in the pond, so too has he changed the nature of the pond itself. The natural pond is here very deliberately replaced by its artificial counterpart, the *vivaio* – a type of man-made fishpond that the Romans called a *piscina*. The classical tradition of the piscina, a fishpond incorporated into the architectural plan of many of the more luxurious Roman villas, was maintained, on a more restrained scale, in the secular homes of Boccaccio's time.[95] As in Classical times, the *vivaio* is associated with wealthy citizens who can afford such a luxury: 'i cittadini che di ciò hanno destro.'[96]

In book IX, chapter 80 of his popular early fourteenth-century treatise on agriculture, the *Liber ruralium commodorum*, the Bolognese lawyer Pietro de' Crescenzi furnishes interesting details concerning the situation, construction, and stocking of such *piscinae*.[97] Significantly, in the concluding paragraph of chapter 80, he stresses the utilitarian advantages of fish farming:

> La utilità della peschiera è grande, percioche di pochi pesci rinchiusi in brevissimo tempo se n'hanno molti , & se ne posson vender & havere molti a uso di mangiare.

> The usefulness of the *piscina* is great, for from the few fish enclosed in it, in a very short time one has many, and some can be sold, and many others eaten.

So great is Piero's enthusiasm for the potential benefits of the *piscina* that it is with something of a wistful tone that he informs us that whales cannot be kept in one! Like the *mulino a raccolta* [millpond driven mill], the *piscina* represented a means of using human ingenuity to harness the forces of nature; it required far less effort to saunter to one's backyard and net a few fish than to set out to sea with hook and bait. Well aware of this particular feature of the *piscina*, Seneca dryly observes that Philosophy had no hand in the invention of 'fish-preserves, which are enclosed for the purpose of saving men's gluttony from having to run the risk of storms, and in order that, no matter how wildly the sea is raging, luxury may have its safe harbours in which to fatten fancy breeds of fish' (*Epistle* XC, 7–8).[98]

Fish farming offered various other advantages as well. The fish's environment could be strictly controlled both with regard to salinity and temperature, the threat of natural – marine – predators could be eliminated, and a constant source of fresh fish was virtually guaranteed to the only predator – man – that remained. However, in order for the *piscina* to successfully fulfil these functions, it had to provide the fish with a convincingly real ersatz marine environment. Though the *piscinae* themselves were often starkly geometric in form – rectangles and circles seem to have been favoured – the sides of the pond generally contained perforations or embedded amphorae to serve as naturalistic hiding places, and bits of natural rock and seaweed were scattered throughout to enhance the illusion: 'quantunque artificio della natura e non manual paresse' [though it seemed a work of Nature, not of man]. In *De re rustica*, Columella recommends that one contrive as best one can 'to represent the appearance of the sea, so that though they are prisoners, the fish may feel the captivity as little as possible' (VIII 17, 6).[99] Indeed, the *piscinae* were often stocked by creating an environment so congenial to the desired species of fish that the fish would actually work their way into the *piscina* through one of the channels used to feed it. Leaving the *piscina* was less easy, for the outlets were covered by bronze grates.[100]

Boccaccio's term, *Valle delle donne*, for the setting of his *vivaio* is marvellously ambiguous for it is by no means clear whether the 'delle' is to be taken as a possessive or a partitive; does the valley somehow belong to the women, or do the women, like the fish, 'belong' to the valley? Like the fish in a *piscina*, have the women been duped by the superficially naturalistic setting into imagining themselves to be in their 'natural' habitat? Perhaps the term 'Valle delle donne' is somehow analogous to more familiar terms such as 'aviario' [aviary] and 'peschiera' [fish pond]. Indeed, given that in the second pleasure garden of the frame the *brigata* is surrounded by animals that are 'quasi dimestichi' [almost tame] (III, Intro., 13), perhaps it is intentional that in the *Valle* – long considered a culmination of the pleasure garden theme – it is the women who are portrayed as the indigenous population of the garden (it is, after all, their garden) and it is they who are 'domesticated.'

In book VIII, chapter 3 – 'De i Giardini de Re, et de gli altri Illustri et ricchi Signori' [On the gardens of Kings and of other illustrious and wealthy Lords] – of his agricultural treatise, Crescenzi advises the prospective designer of a pleasure garden to include both a fishpond, where fish can be raised, and a shelter of tightly-knit boughs to serve as a refuge for the hares, rabbits, and various species of birds that have been introduced into the garden. Significantly, he recommends that the trees be arranged in such a fashion as to ensure a clear view of the animals at play – 'Gli ordini de gli arbori de giardino dal Palagio al bosco non sien per traverso, accio che si possa agevolmente veder dal palagio, ciò che fanno gli animali che son nel giardino' [the rows of garden trees placed between the Palace and the forest should not run transversely, so that one can easily observe from the palace the activities of the animals in the garden]. Is it not possible that the neatly serried trees of Boccaccio's arboretum – the third simile used in describing the *Valle* – serve a similar purpose?

> Il piano appresso, senza aver più entrate che quella donde le donne venute v'erano, era pieno d'abeti, di cipressi, d'allori e d'alcun pini sì ben composti e sì bene ordinati, come se qualunque è di ciò il migliore artefice gli avesse piantati: e fra essi poco sole o niente, allora che egli era alto, entrava infino al suolo, il quale era tutto un prato d'erba minutissima e piena di fiori porporini e d'altri. (VI, Concl., 24)

> The plain itself, to which there was no other means of access than the path by which the ladies had entered, was filled with firs, cypresses, bay-trees, and a number of pines, all of which were so neatly arranged and symmetrically disposed that they looked as if they had been planted by the finest practitioner of the forester's craft. And when the sun was overhead, few or none of its rays penetrated their foliage to the ground beneath, which was one continuous lawn of tiny blades of grass interspersed with flowers, many of them purple in colour. (McWilliam, 480)

The perfect regularity of the topography of Boccaccio's *Valle* does more than underline the artificial, trap-like nature of the construction into which women are lured and secretly observed; it is the most effective device for directing attention to the truly anomalous presence of the bathing women. Whereas the *selva* is the traditional symbol of an intellectual, spiritual, or physical impediment – one which somehow threatens the integrity of the individual – the arboretum, the imposition of rational discipline on nature, suggests accessibility, compliance, and safety.

Boccaccio's observation that the well-ordered trees almost fully block the sunlight from the meadow below seems, at first glance, to weaken the thesis that the *Valle* accommodates voyeurs by presenting an unobstructed view of its occupants. However, if I am correct in seeing in this passage an echo of a convention found in the medieval French romances, such apparent privacy only masks an enhanced accessibility. In Chrétien de Troyes's *Cligés* (a romance that may have been familiar to Boccaccio) we read of an enclosed garden built by the master artificer John, one that surrounds the tower that serves as a sort of erotic prison for Cligés's mistress, Fenice:[101]

> Et desoz l'ante ert li praiax,
> Molt delitables et molt biax,
> Ne ja n'iert tant li solauz chauz
> En esté, quant il est plus hauz,
> Que ja rais i puisse passer,
> Si le sot Jehanz conpasser
> Et les branches mener et duire. (6323–9)[102]

> Beneath this privet was a grassy plot
> Great both in beauty and delight
> Nor, indeed, is the sun so hot
> Even in summer, when it is very high,
> that its rays can penetrate the privet.
> For thus had Jean known to dispose,
> arrange and train its branches.

The 'erba minutissima' corresponds to the 'praiax ... molt biax'; the height of the sun ('sole ... alto' / 'solauz ... hauz'), and the inability of the sun to penetrate the tree canopy are images common to both; and, finally, the idea of the garden being the work of a master artificer – generic in Boccaccio, who simply alludes to 'il migliore artefice' – is prominent in both. In both cases the horticultural artistry is expressed through the artisan's skill in taming nature, ordering ('mener et duire,' 'composti ... ordinati') the recalcitrant product of nature.

In the thirteenth-century *Roman de la Rose*, a book certainly familiar to Boccaccio, the first of the two (antithetical) gardens is endowed with a similarly dense tree canopy:

> Mes li arbre, ce sachiez, furent
> Si loing a loing con estre durent:
> Li uns fu loins de l'autre asis
> Plus de .v. toises ou de .vi.
> Mes li rain furent gent et haut,
> Et por le lieu garder dou chaut
> Furent si espes par deseure
> Que li solauz en nes .i. eure
> Ne pooit a terre descendre
> Ne faire mal a l'erbe tendre.
> (1362–71)[103]

> Know too that these trees were spaced out as they should be; one was placed at a distance of more than five or six fathoms from another. The branches were long and high and, to keep the place from heat, were so thick above that the sun could not shine on the earth or harm the tender grass for even one hour. (trans. Dahlberg, 49)[104]

Significantly, Guillaume de Lorris makes it clear that the canopy's function is to prevent the tender grass from being scorched, for this moist grass serves as an ideal place to bed one's mistress: 'Aussint i poïst l'en sa drue / Couchier con desor une coite / Car la terre ert douce et moite' ['There one could couch his mistress as though on a feather bed, for the earth was sweet and moist ...'] (1391–3; Dahlberg, 49).

If I am correct in associating these two passages with Boccaccio's description, it would be reasonable to see the blocking of the sun's rays not as evidence of sexual inaccessibility but rather as a guarantee of sexual exclusivity – even the sun, the traditional figure of the all-seeing eye, is precluded from seeing what we, the reader – or Cligés – can observe at our leisure and in absolute privacy.[105] In addition to these shared themes, both passages refer to an erotic variety of *hortus conclusus*: one in which women are 'kept' for male delectation. While Boccaccio's classical precursor Ovid cast this sexual accessibility in terms of rape, his medieval precursors Chrétien and Guillaume transformed the locus of rape into one of consensual sex. It remained for Boccaccio to populate the garden with women whose accessibility was limited to the eye alone.

Inherent in Boccaccio's model of the *Valle delle donne* is the idea that the *Valle*, though artificial in appearance, is naturally artificial rather than artificially natural ('quantunque artificio della natura e non manual paresse,' [VI, Concl., 20]); the 'objectification' of woman is implicitly part of the natural – God's – order and her exploitation is therefore divinely condoned.[106] This Boccacesque order of things takes the form of an abbreviated 'food chain,' for the women, aided by the same clarity of water by which they are disclosed, set about chasing the fish, who have nowhere to hide – 'cominciarono come potevano ad andare in qua in là di dietro a' pesci, i quali male avevan dove nascondersi, e a volerne con esso le mani pigliare' ['they began as best they could to swim hither and thither in pursuit of the fishes, which had nowhere to hide, and tried to sieze hold of them with their hands'] (VI, Concl., 31; McWilliam, 481) – while they, likewise, having no means of concealing themselves, are effectively 'seized' by the spectral viewers in their mountain perches: the occupants of the six villas that modulate the valley's perimeter. Whether or not such viewers stand by their windows and gawk is hardly a matter of significance, for by describing the *Valle delle donne*, Boccaccio has effectively transformed each reader of this particular passage of the *Decameron* into one such viewer.[107]

Although the *Valle delle donne* is described in Day VI and forms part of the physical terrain upon which the characters of the *brigata* themselves move, it is recapitulated and to a certain extent glossed by a member of the *brigata*, Fiammetta, in the sixth story of Day X. The story concerns a certain messer Neri degli Uberti, a Ghibelline who, chased from Florence by Charles I and the Guelfs, unaccountably does not leave Guelf territory altogether but builds himself a comfortable home with a lovely garden in an area somewhat removed from any settled populations. The most remarkable feature of his home is his garden, in the centre of which, significantly, is a fishpond:

> un dilettevole giardino, nel mezzo del quale, a nostro modo, avendo d'acqua viva copia, fece un bel vivaio e chiaro, e quello di molto pesce riempié leggiermente. (*Dec.* X 6, 6)

> a delectable garden, in the centre of which, there being a goodly supply of fresh water, he constructed a fine, clear fishpond in the Florentine style, which he stocked in his own good time with abundant supplies of fish. (McWilliam, 732)

It is the widely known beauty of messer Neri's garden that lures King Charles, though a political enemy, into arranging a secret dinner at Neri's home. Although Charles is pleased enough by the garden itself, he soon finds more exalted reasons for rejoicing once he has been regaled by the sight of Neri's two adolescent daughters, clad in diaphanous linen, immersing themselves in the *vivaio* to capture fish for his dinner. Through the able manipulation of a rod, the fish are flushed out of their hiding places and caught in the net (note that unlike the women of the *brigata* they do not attempt to catch the fish with their bare hands!). The scene that follows is a description – infused with erotic innuendo – of the delightful game in which both the girls and their noble guests engage as they playfully toss the fish into the frying pan:[108]

> sì come ammaestrate erano state cominciarono a prendere de' più begli e a gittare su per la tavola davanti al re e al conte Guido e al padre. (X 6, 15)

> but then they began to pick out some of the finest specimens, as they had been instructed, and to throw them up on the table in front of the King, the Count, and their father. (McWilliam, 733)

Like the domesticated animals that populate so many pleasure gardens (including Boccaccio's in the introduction to Day III), the two girls are trained, 'ammaestrate,' to perform, and the performance itself is no more than a thinly disguised variety of erotic foreplay. That this is the case is confirmed by the characterization of the fish course as an 'intramettere'; messer Neri ordered it 'più per uno intramettere che per molto cara o dilettevol vivanda' [more by way of an entremets than as a specially choice or delectable dish] (X 6, 16; McWilliam, 734). The word 'intramettere' derives from the French 'entremets,' a word referring to the appetizers served between courses to titillate the palate and awaken the appetite.[109] Since an appetizer is the culinary equivalent of foreplay, it is likely that in the case of this particular banquet, which is, after all, conceived as a banquet of the senses (and by no means the higher senses), the fish course fulfills precisely this function.

Interestingly, whereas the *Valle delle donne* passage was constructed in such a fashion as to heighten the sense of the women's unwitting entrapment, in this story where the voyeuristic element is so explicit, it is the 'hunter,' a sexual predator – King Charles – who is trapped:

> Quivi, tenendo il re la sua affezion nascosa né per grande affare che

sopravenisse potendo dimenticar la bellezza e la piacevolezza di Ginevra la bella, per amor di cui la sorella a lei simigliante ancora amava, sì nell'amorose panie s'invescò. (X 6, 24)[110]

where the King continued to harbour his secret passion; nor was he able, however weighty the affairs of state which supervened, to forget the charm and beauty of the lovely Ginevra, for whose sake he also loved the sister who resembled her so closely. Indeed, he could think of practically nothing else, so hopelessly had he become entangled in the snares of love. (McWilliam, 735)

Perhaps it is significant that the men of the *brigata* are induced to visit the *Valle* by Pampinea's evocative description – both of the valley and of the 'forbidden' activities that have taken place there. In both of these cases the traditional predators are themselves enslaved by their irrepressible need to fulfill their desire; Charles must conquer himself and the men and women of the *brigata* must substitute discourse – the *novelle* – for intercourse.[111]

Having been treated to the tantalizing spectacle of the young women engaged in their piscatorial pursuit, the king and his company are entertained by the even more beguiling appearance of the sisters as they emerge, their work complete, from the *vivaio*:

Le fanciulle, veggendo il pesce cotto e avendo assai pescato, essendosi tutto il bianco vestimento e sottile loro appiccato alle carni, né quasi cosa alcuna del dilicato lor corpo celando, usciron del vivaio, e ciascuna le cose recate avendo riprese, davanti al re vergognosamente passando, in casa se ne tornarono. (X 6, 17)

On seeing that the fish had been cooked, the girls emerged from the pool, their fishing done, with their thin white dresses clinging to their flesh so as to conceal almost nothing of their dainty bodies. And having taken up each of the things they had brought with them, they walked shyly past the King and made their way back into the house. (McWilliam, 734)

After several such visits inspired less by a desire to gourmandize than to gape, King Charles can resist temptation no longer and resolves to steal the two women from their father. Fortunately, he confesses his plan to his companion, conte Guido, who points out that were he to engage in such an act he would be no better than his adversary, Manfredi, who had

perpetrated similar sexual crimes against the Guelfs. His counsel ends
with the observation that the greatest triumph is that of conquering not
an enemy but oneself, and that he would do well to curb his intemperate
desires. Charles takes conte Guido's advice and in an act of consummate
generosity (as well as astute self protection) marries Neri's daughters to
two noblemen, thereby channeling his initial erotic and socially destructive energies into the productive, socially conciliatory union of Ghibelline brides with Guelf grooms. As can be seen from even this brief
synopsis, Fiammetta's story functions as a recapitulation in miniature of
many of the concerns central to the *Valle delle donne.*

It is significant that in both the *Valle delle donne* passage and X, 6, the
threat of a 'Romulan' variety of rape, which is implicit in the former and
explicit in the latter (when Charles concedes that he intends to steal
[torre] both girls for his pleasure), is ultimately defused through a conversion of the initial antisocial impulse into a socially acceptable variant.
The women of the *Valle* are symbolically domesticated (thereby eliminating the need for violent possession) and rendered a spectacle whereas
the two girls are consigned to a fate that differs from rape only insofar as
it is conventionalized by the ritual of marriage. In his *Ars amatoria* Ovid
treats the theatrical spectacle as a prelude – an 'intramettere' – to the act
of rape, for the seated men 'kept glancing / About them, each marking
his choice / Among the girls' in a gesture that is precisely echoed, many
centuries later, by King Charles – with a critical difference. Whereas
Romulus and his cohorts mark a choice, King Charles finds himself
unable to differentiate between the two girls: 'ne sapeva egli stesso qual
di lor due si fosse quella che più gli piacesse, sì era di tutte cose l'una
simiglievole all'altra' ['nor could he decide which of the two he preferred, so closely did they resemble one another in every particular'] (X
6, 19; McWilliam, 734). This inability to distinguish between the two and
make a choice results in a variety of impotence; like Pentheus stymied by
his vision of two suns, Charles finds his erotic aim thwarted by the presence of twin targets. Similarly, in the *Valle* the women are not differenti-
ated in such a way as to encourage selection. To the contrary, the use
of imagery evocative of animal husbandry and horticulture reinforces
the generic quality of the women – like the trees and the fish, they are
portrayed as a commodity. This generic quality functions as a sort of
anaphrodisiac which blunts the urgency of the sexual appetite, thereby
allowing the viewer to assume a more passive role of spectator.[112]
Whereas rape would obviously present a threat to the fragile social structure established by the *brigata*, passive forms of erotic enjoyment serve to

solidify and preserve this society by safely defusing sexual desire – a particularly pressing objective given the theme of Day VII: the (largely adulterous) tricks that women have played upon their husbands.

While it has been suggested that the *Valle delle donne* marks the apogee of female emancipation from social constraint, I prefer – for the reasons enumerated above – to view the *Valle* as a place whose function is variable in accordance with the perspective from which it is viewed. From the earthbound perspective of the valley the women cannot help but feel themselves free from social constraint, whereas the reader-voyeur, looking from a literal or figurative promontory, sees the women as subject to a rigorous and highly sophisticated variety of constraint. Though the voyeuristic variety of erotic exploitation proposed by Boccaccio is conceived of as an antidote to socially destructive alternatives, it does, nevertheless, adopt – in subtle form – the traditional tools of erotic exploitation. With the relish of an enlightened architect of zoos, Boccaccio has created a terrarium in which women, in their 'natural' state, can be observed engaging in their most 'characteristic' pastime, catching 'fish.' Day VI ends with Elissa's song in which she makes a sad plea to a personified Love that he free her from his artigli [talons]. Indeed, the song abounds with images of entrapment – hooks, chains, and talons among others – and leaves its audience wondering what could possibly have inspired Elissa to choose such a mournful song: 'ancor che tutti si maravigliasser di tali parole, niuno per ciò ve n'ebbe che potesse avvisare che di così cantare fosse cagione' ['albeit everyone puzzled over the words no one was able to say who it was that had caused her to sing such a song'] (VI, Concl., 47; McWilliam, 483). If, as I have argued, the *Valle* is a sort of emblem of culturally productive entrapment inscribed on the landscape – both geographical and literary – of the *Decameron*, it is not surprising that Elissa's plaintive song should issue from such a setting: a kind of anti-epithalamium lamenting the collusion of nature and art to produce erotic bondage, the *Valle*.

When, upon their return from the *Valle*, Pampinea announces 'Oggi vi pure abbiam noi ingannati' [today it is we who have deceived you], it is only natural for Dioneo – for whom language and sex are intimately aligned – to retort with the jocular, 'cominciate voi prima a far de' fatti che a dir delle parole?' [have you begun doing deeds before speaking words?] (VI, Concl., 34).

Teodolinda Barolini has proposed that the antithesis undergirding the whole episode, that of words and deeds, is critical to an understanding of Boccaccio's 'sexual poetics' in the *Decameron*.[113] She begins her argument by invoking the Italian proverb, 'Le parole son femmine e i fatti son maschi' [Words are female, deeds, male] in order to illustrate the distinctly gendered quality of this distinction between words and acts. She then goes on to disclose the unsettling ambiguity that underlies this assertion; 'fatti' is itself a 'parola' and consequently participates in the 'feminine' sphere of the spoken word. Indeed, she sees this ambiguity mirrored in the *Valle delle donne* episode where a similar conflation of these apparently distinct spheres takes place.

However, this model is something of a hermeneutic Pandora's box, for it has the effect of opening the sluicegate between word and act, creating a kind of brackish middle ground. It is by no means clear whether language is assimilated to the 'potent' sphere of action through the linguistic expression of act, 'fatto,' or whether act, 'fatto,' is consigned to the 'impotent' sphere of language. While I would maintain that both of these processes are at play, in the case of the *Valle*, I tend to favour the latter scenario.

In response to Dioneo's playful query, 'cominciate voi prima a far de' fatti che a dir delle parole?' Pampinea responds with an affirmation and goes on to describe the 'fatti' in which the women have engaged. While the three men are treated to Pampinea's discursive re-creation of the valley and the activities in which the women engaged, the reader has had the great privilege of reading the narrator's testimony, one which conveniently circumvents the watchful eyes of their maidservants who have been posted at the entrance and assigned the task of alerting the bathing women to the presence of intruders. In what sense have the women betrayed or fooled the three men? Which of the various activities or 'fatti' could possibly be construed as an 'inganno' [deception]? Certainly Pampinea's use of the word 'inganno' so shortly after Dioneo has constrained the women to accept (by intimating that to do otherwise would be taken as a form of self-indictment) the topic of tricks that women have played on their husbands, suggests that she is self-consciously aligning the women of the *brigata* with the fictional women of Day VII whose stories have yet to be told.[114] Given the context of this use of 'inganno,' and the sexual overtones of 'fatto,' the idea of a sexual variety of betrayal is inevitable. What form does this betrayal take? Are we to understand that the women's dalliance with fish constitutes a sort of cuckolding (after all, they do succeed in catching a few)? The reader alone has been granted a special intimacy with the bathing women. Of the women's acts, 'fatti,' those of making an excursion to the valley, undressing, and catching fish, the last two certainly are infused with a specifically sexual connotation. Even in a well-stocked vivaio, it is no mean feat to catch a fish with one's bare hands – one can as easily catch a bird in flight.

Then again, Boccaccio does provide us an example of the latter, for the hot-blooded Caterina of V, 4 not only succeeds in 'catching' a nightingale with her bare hands but, having formalized her bond with the nightingale's 'keeper,' Ricciardo, spends many years hunting nightingales day and night: 'uccellò agli usignoli e di dì e di notte quanto gli piacque' (49). The jarring inverisimilitude of the image of the women catching fish with their bare hands only confirms the metaphorical cast of this episode that was all too evident to begin with.[115]

In both cases, the metaphors are based on the idea of a hunt. However, whereas Caterina's 'hunt' is fulfilled in true 'fatti' that are registered in the form of sexual metaphor, in the case of the women in the *Valle delle donne* the sexual metaphor is literalized; the women are enacting a sexual metaphor, translating metaphoric 'parole' to symbolic 'fatti' – *not* engaging in sexual activity.

Barolini argues that sexual metaphors that employ the language of 'male' occupations such as those identified in the 'Proem,' namely 'uccellare, cacciare, pescare, cavalcare, giucare o marcatare' [fowling, hunting, fishing, riding, gambling or engaging in commerce] are a linguistic means exploited by Boccaccio to assimilate women to the male sphere.[116] Indeed, we have numerous examples of the female appropriation of specifically male activities. For instance, 'uccellare,' defines the activity of the 'huntress' Caterina, who catches her nightingale. While in the case of Caterina I see a confirmation of this view of metaphor as a means of female empowerment, the same model cannot be applied to the 'fishing' of the women in the *Valle* for, as I argue in this chapter, we are not presented with a textual metaphor used euphemistically to 'cover' a sexual act, but rather an 'enacted' metaphor that actually functions as a substitute for sex. This refinement of Barolini's hypothesis suggests that whereas the use of metaphorical parole empowers women, the participation in metaphorical *fatti* results in their exploitation.

Unlike 'parole' and 'atti' (III 10, 34), used by Alibech in her attempt to describe to the amused townswomen the nature of her service to God (putting the 'Devil' back into 'Hell'), the movements of the women in the *Valle* are not intended as a pantomime of the sexual act itself but rather as an evocation of a popular metaphor for the sexual act. Consequently, the women's sexual 'infraction' is of a very low order indeed for it is at a further remove from the actual act than language itself! The *usignolo* [nightingale] that Caterina 'catches' is part and parcel of her lover, Ricciardo. The same is not true of the fish; here we are witnessing not metaphor in the service of action but action in the service of metaphor.

Surely, within the world of the *novelle*, we are led to believe that a bird in hand of the variety caught by Caterina is better than any number of such fish. Indeed, when Boccaccio desires to convey the idea of an unsatisfactory substitute for sex, he does so through the literalization of a fishing metaphor. In II 10, the story of the corsair Paganino who saves the vivacious young Bartolomea from an abstemious life with her dried-up and decrepit husband, the latter loses his wife when he takes her on a fishing trip, 'per darle alcuna consolazione' [to give her some consolation] (II 10, 12). From the 'Proem' on, we have been sensitized to the highly equivocal nature of the word 'consolazione.' Consequently, it comes as no particular surprise that in the process of fishing the young woman herself is caught, abducted by Paganino, who shortly thereafter consoles her with such skill ('per sì fatta maniera la racconsolò' [II 10, 16]) that she elects to stay with him of her own free will. This passage succinctly makes the point that fishing is a poor substitute for sex.[117]

The 'fatti' of the *Valle delle donne* which are so often touted as evidence that the women have freed themselves from the shackles of convention are actually, like a game of charades, no more than physical activity emulating discourse: that is, foreplay. Indeed, the theme of the game and of artifice predominate in the entire *Valle delle donne* interlude. Dioneo claims that though crowned he has less authority even than the chess piece representing the King. In other words, Dioneo's ability to dictate action is inferior to that of a symbolic 'King.' Upon their return from the *Valle* the women find the men occupied with games, as though time had been suspended during their brief sojourn: 'quivi trovarono i giovani giucando dove lasciati gli aveano' (579). Similarly, the women in the *Valle* engage in a ludic form of erotic activity that derives a literary – artificial – quality from its source in sexual metaphor. No intrusion of reality, no 'Paganino,' materializes to succour them from their insubstantial pleasures – or are such pleasures insubstantial?

In an age such as ours, in which pragmatic, medical, concerns have tended to focus more attention on the voyeuristic aspects of sexual engagement, it is difficult to dismiss the possibility that much of the fetishistic quality of Boccaccio's constructs has a similarly practical rationale; after all, the slightest physical contact was alone sufficient to contract the plague. In the introduction to Day I Boccaccio dwells on the dangers of physical contact with plague victims – so virulent is the plague that even their garments harbour the contagion. In the midst of this social collapse, two contrasting attitudes to sexual contact predominate: there are those who indulge in a carnival of the flesh with no concern for the likely consequences, and those who, terrified, flee physical contact in any form. In short, the middle ground of amorous, courtly, playful physical contact has been largely effaced by the plague. Perhaps the *Valle*, with its conspicuously central location (with respect to its topographic, textual and narrative settings) is intended as a restoration of this lost space.

The move away from Florence is conceived of as an antidote to the dehumanizing effects of the plague, and this spatial distancing is just one of the many symptoms of the *brigata*'s difference from the populace as a whole. However, 'the *brigata*'s behaviour is rigidly premised on what came before; they must establish their difference precisely with respect to the prevailing norm' (524).[118] What, precisely, was the prevailing norm where sexual mores were concerned? In the introduction of Day I Boccaccio claims that when a woman was infected with the plague, it little mattered how young, beautiful or noble she was, for, 'infermando non curava d'avere a' suoi servigi uomo, qual che egli si fosse o giovane o altro, e a lui senza alcuna vergogna ogni parte del corpo aprire' ['when a woman fell ill, no matter how gracious or beautiful or gently bred she might be, she raised no objection to being attended by a male servant, whether he was young or not. Nor did she have any scruples about showing him every part of her body'] (I, Intro., 29; McWilliam, 9). In the 'Conclusion,' he recapitulates this theme of sexual laxity by characterizing the plague years as a time in which 'andar con le brache in capo per iscampo di sé era alli più onesti non disdicevole' ['even the most respectable people saw nothing unseemly in wearing their breeches over their heads'] (Concl., 7; McWilliam, 799). By using this image of complete inversion, in which the seat of our rational being is conflated with that profane seat usually hidden by breeches, Boccaccio invites the reader to surmise that in achieving its radical departure from this 'norm,' the *brigata* must intellectualize the physical aspects of sex; instead of having one's brain in one's breeches, the breeches are under the jurisdiction of the brain (a condition that evokes Augustine's vision of the prelapsarian condition of humanity – or, for that matter, a pre-plague Florence). The sexual element is by no means eliminated thereby; rather, it becomes textual – the erotic *novelle*. If, as Boccaccio claims, the plague years were marked by a kind of sexual incontinence, the sexual act itself must necessarily have become enormously devalued and bereft of an erotic dimension. The fetishistic displacement of sexual energy in the *Decameron* suggests, to me at least, not the elimination of sexual desire, nor merely its sublimation, but the restoration to sex of an erotic – and sophisticated – element that has evanesced in a world turned bordello: the narrative equivalent of foreplay.

While critics have tended to laud the *brigata* for their conspicuous abstinence from sex, this attitude is really tantamount to applauding a shoe fetishist for exhibiting such prodigious fortitude in diverting his or her sexual interest to footwear.[119] What is true of both the *brigata* and the average fetishist (the word 'fetish' is ultimately derived from the Latin *facticium*, meaning 'made by art') is that both have transferred their sexual interest from people (the natural) to artifacts. The sexualized *novella* is just this, an artifact, as, for that matter, is the *Valle* itself. Remember that Boccaccio's phrase, 'quantunque artificio della natura e non manual paresse' (VI, Concl., 20), while ostensibly favouring the idea of Nature as artist, reminds us, by the qualification 'paresse' [it seemed], that it is Boccaccio's industrious hand that, with a dexterity like that of John in *Cligés*, has sculpted the raw material of Nature into the familiar forms of the *Valle*. Certainly it is hard not to identify the mysterious 'migliore artefice' [best artificer] with Boccaccio himself (the words 'migliore artefice' echo the phrase, 'miglior fabbro,' used to describe the provençal poet Arnaut Daniel in the *Divine Comedy* [*Purg.* XXVI, 117]). The *Valle* serves as the most vivid illustration of the poetics of the *Decameron* itself, which, as a self-proclaimed lover's manual, is inherently a union of passion and precept, nature and art.

The hygienic concerns introduced by the plague effectively universalize (at least among the more cautious) an enforced celibacy of the sort that produced such an abundant reserve in the priest of VIII, 9 (who likens his sexuality to a mill with a *raccolta*) without, however, providing people with a comparable means of relieving themselves of the surplus – the 'gravezza' alluded to in the 'Proem' (12). The frame characters succeed in redressing this imbalance through the device of erotic narrative – the vicarious experience of sex.

In his 'Proem,' Boccaccio claims that his intention in writing the *Decameron* is to provide women with a similar outlet – presumably what works for the characters who tell the stories will have a similarly salutary effect on those who read them. He empathizes with women for the sexual frustration and deprivation that afflicts them more than it does men, for they are subject to a series of social restrictions and remain 'il più del tempo nel piccolo circuito delle loro camere racchiuse' ['most of their time cooped up within the narrow confines of their rooms'] ('Proem,' 10; McWilliam, 2). Whereas in the 'Proem,' Boccaccio declares that his motivation in writing the *Decameron* is to fulfill the role of a sort of purveyor of 'consolazione' by relieving women of 'gravezza' [weight/'pregnancy'] (12) and provide 'allegiamento' [a lightening / 'delivery'] (8), in the introduction to Day I, the frame characters reveal that their reason for telling the tales of the *Decameron* is to distance themselves from the circumstances of the plague. We are thus provided with two different motivations that somehow coincide in a single work: a cure for love and for despair. This is not so strange when we consider that in many respects women – as depicted in the 'Proem' – are perennial victims of the very same limitations that have been universally, though temporarily, enforced by the plague.

The removal to the circular proscenium of the *Valle delle donne*, the point geographically furthest removed from the 'piccolo circuito delle loro camere' [the small circuit of their rooms], may not represent a complete emancipation, but it does represent a kind of solution, a *Remedia amoris* for women. In describing the *Valle*, Boccaccio uses images strongly reminiscent of both the second frame garden and of the garden in X 6. Whereas in the second frame garden the abundant water produced by the fountain and gathered in one place (a 'raccolta') finds a fruitful issue (an 'allegiamento') as it is diverted to the mills, thereby suggesting a type of release identified with sexual intercourse in the metaphoric economy of the *Decameron*, what becomes of the similarly abundant water that feeds the *vivaio* in the centre of the *Valle*? It is significant that Boccaccio bothers to tell us what becomes of the inevitable surplus: 'L'acqua la quale alla sua capacità soprabondava un altro canaletto ricevea, per lo qual fuori del valloncello uscendo, alle parti più basse se ne correva' [the water that exceeded its capacity was received by another small culvert, through which, carried from the valley, it flowed into the lower reaches] (VI, Concl., 28). The *Valle* represents a perfect natural self-regulating ecosystem, an autonomous entity. Given the inescapably sexual nature of the *Valle delle donne* (it has been suggested, quite correctly I think, that it could be taken synechdochally as a symbolic vagina; Boccaccio himself makes a jocular allusion to a 'Val Cava,' whose patron saint is San Cresci [II 7, 109]),[120] and of the activities that take place there, it seems not entirely farfetched to suggest that such a display of self-sufficient sexuality ('Oggi vi pure abbiam noi ingannati') as a means of coping with sexual deprivation should be taken as a type of masturbation – the most universally available *remedium amoris* and one intimately associated with erotic text (in the second story of Day IX we are presented with a passage that strongly suggests this idea of masturbation as a means of coping with the inaccessibility of other forms of sexual gratification: 'l'altre che senza amante erano, come seppero il meglio, segretamente procacciaron lor ventura' ['her fellow nuns, without lovers ... consoled themselves in secret as best they could' (IX 2, 19; McWilliam, 658)). How else did Boccaccio imagine that ribald stories would be useful to 'encloistered' women? However, it is not women alone who are succoured by this particular *remedium*, for, by creating a peepshow of the *Valle*, Boccaccio has also attended to men's pleasure. The *Valle delle donne* is the women's valley, but it is also the site of the storytelling during Dioneo's 'reign' and is, consequently, as fully his domain. Since Dioneo is associated by his pseudonym with love (for Dione was the mother of Venus) and by his narrative preferences with erotic text, it is not surprising that his realm – the *Valle* – should epitomize these traits. Whereas the traditional remedium for love can be effected by fulfilment of the desired objective or by a successful diversion away from the desired object, Boccaccio has hit upon a remedium that combines both solutions: in his Valle love is both exorcised and exercised.

chapter 4

The Myth of Historical Foresight:
Babel and Beyond

On the Shoulders of (Blasphemous) Giants: The Limits of Knowledge

In the tenth *novella* of *Il trecentonovelle*, Franco Sacchetti relates the story of Messer Dolcibene's pilgrimage to the Holy Land. When one of his travelling companions draws his attention to the Valley of Josephat, noting that it is there that we must all congregate come Judgment Day, the buffoonish Dolcibene, ever the pragmatist, cannot help expressing some concern: 'O come potrà tutta l'umana generazione stare in sí piccola valle?' [Oh how will the whole human race fit in such a small valley?]. One of his companions, Messer Galeotto, responds: 'Serà per potenza divina' [It will be by divine power].[1] Dolcibene, apparently reluctant to rely on anything as nebulous as God's power, takes matters into his own hands by dropping his pants and relieving himself on a spot in the centre of the valley, explaining to his companions that he is reserving a place in anticipation of the Last Judgment. When it is apparent that his quizzical explanation has done little to satisfy his companions' natural confusion, Dolcibene offers them a sententious definition of prudence: 'Signori, io ve l'ho detto: e' non si può esser savio, se l'uomo non s'argomenta per lo tempo che dee venire' [Gentlemen, as I have told you: a man cannot be deemed wise if he does not make provisions for the future].

The medieval concept of prudence is grounded in this idea of foresight based on knowledge of past events. A prudent person is one who by extrapolating the future from the past is able to avoid personal calamity in the present. The remarkable sobriety of Dolcibene's words to the effect that wisdom consists in preparing for future events is belied by the extravagance and absurdity of the 'providential' actions that he has undertaken. Scatology is elided with eschatology in a single action, the ostensible irreverence of which is actually motivated by a profound reverence; though his desire to get first dibs on a good location in the Valley of Josephat betrays a comic opportunism, it also attests to his orthodox conviction that Scripture *is* history. Beneath this entertaining fiction lies a serious concern; where does one draw the line between a praiseworthy prudence and blasphemous presumption?

In the Proem of the *Cronica* (I 2), Giovanni Villani (following Livy's model) proposes that his chronicle serves to preserve for posterity a record of the 'mutazioni e delle cose passate, e le cagioni, e perchè; accioc-ch'eglino si esercitino adoperando le virtudi e schifando i vizi, e l'avversitadi sostegnano con forte animo a bene e stato della nostra repubblica' [vicissitudes and past events, and the causes, and the end; in order that they might practise adopting virtues and avoiding vices, and sustain adversities with a strong spirit for the good and well-being of our republic]. Though Villani exhibits some optimism with respect to the viability of using historical knowledge to anticipate and thereby prepare for future events, he is careful to remind us that speculative knowledge of future events should by no means be conflated with immunity to 'avversitadi' [adversities]. Such knowledge, though a guide, can offer no guarantees in a universe, the ultimate shape of which corresponds to the inscrutable pattern of divine providence. The armour of virtue conferred upon us through moral activity does not shield our body but fortifies our soul so that we can bear adversities 'con forte animo' [with a strong spirit].

Anxiety that the act of recording history somehow trespasses on the territory of the Holy Spirit – the author of Scripture – is apparent in Eusebius of Caesarea's early attempt to write a universal history, the *Chronicon* (read by Boccaccio in Jerome's translation). In the proem of this work Eusebius is careful to acknowledge that knowledge of the whole is available to God alone, a point that he clarifies by citing Acts 1.7: 'Non est vestrum nosse horas et tempora, quae Pater posuit in sua potestate' [It is not for you to know the times or periods that the Father has set by his own authority].[2] This is precisely the sort of intellectual humility that suffuses the whole of the *Decameron*: the first words, as Teodolinda Barolini has noted in 'The Wheel of the *Decameron*' (521), declare its non-transcendence – 'Umana cosa è l'aver compassione agli afflitti' [it is a human trait to feel compassion for those who are afflicted] – and its concluding pages remind the reader that its imperfections are inevitable, for God alone performs all things well and completely ('per ciò che maestro alcun non si truova, da Dio in fuori, che ogni cosa faccia bene e compiutamente'). It is no accident that the most concise formulation of this principle of non-transcendence is found in the preamble of the very first *novella*, where Panfilo declares that under no circumstances can mortal vision, however keen, penetrate the secrets of the divine mind ('non potendo l'acume dell'occhio mortale nel segreto della divina mente trapassare in alcun modo').[3]

Though the chronicle, that summa of human experience culled from past events, can provide some guidance in conjecturing future experiences, it provides no certainty. It is moral knowledge alone that can be educed with certainty from the example of history. Only a fool would draw from the example of the Noachic Deluge the lesson that it is prudent to build an ark in anticipation of a Universal Flood (indeed, we encounter one such fool in Chaucer's 'Miller's Tale'); the true lesson is that immoral activity cannot be pursued with impunity.

Although the Florentine chroniclers maintain that their histories are not simply a sentimental record of past events, but a useful and vital tool for charting one's own future, they, like Eusebius, make a point of underscoring the shortcomings of history as an instrument for forecasting future events. Both Giovanni Villani and his nephew Filippo illustrate this precept through the imposing figure of Nimrod, king of Babylon and putative architect of the tower of Babel in Genesis 11. Giovanni Villani initiates the second chapter of his first book – the beginning of the history proper – with the story of the tower of Babel:

> Questo Nembrot fu figliuolo di Cus che fu figliuolo di Cam il secondo figliuolo di Noè, e per lo suo orgoglio e forza credette contrastare a Dio, dicendo che Iddio era signore del cielo, ed egli della terra; e acciocchè Dio non gli potesse più nuocere per diluvio d'acqua, come avea fatto alla prima etade, sì ordinò di fare maravigliosa opera della torre di Babel. (*Cronica*, 3)

> This Nimrod was the son of Cus, who was the son of Cam, the second son of Noah, who on account of his pride and strength thought to challenge God, stating that God was the lord of the sky, and he, lord of the earth; and, so that God might not harm him again with a deluge of water as he had done in the first age, he contrived to construct the marvelous work of the tower of Babel.

Whereas in the Genesis account the blasphemy consists in the building of a tower, the peak of which is designed to pierce the very heavens – 'cuius culmen pertingat ad caelum' (Genesis 11.4) – for Villani, blasphemy (the presumptuous desire to contend with God) precedes the construction of the tower. Indeed, for Villani, the construction of the tower represents not an offensive assault but a defensive measure, a precaution lest God resort to the familiar strategy of flooding the earth.

This perspective is not original to the Italian chroniclers, but was already an established, if less often invoked, interpretation of Genesis 11. The most common interpretations of the tower-building episode of Genesis 11 are those that regard it as an apologue illustrating the dangers of blasphemous pride and intellectual vanity; a primal unity – one that is both political and linguistic – cedes to disunity through the spontaneous proliferation of languages and the subsequent scattering of the various peoples to different geographical regions. Representative of this view is the fourth chapter of the sixteenth book of Augustine's *City of God*: 'On the diversity of languages and the foundation of Babylon.'

The alternative view – one in which a causal relation is established between Nimrod's construction of the tower and the episode of the Noachic deluge that precedes it – is at least as ancient as Josephus, who presents the idea of a prophylactic tower in his *Jewish Antiquities* (I, 113–14). Among the Latin Fathers, it is Augustine – as far as I can tell – who first introduces this variant tradition. In his tract on the Gospel of John, Augustine writes: 'And inflated with pride ... they erected a tower, as if to avoid destruction by a deluge if one should happen later.'[4]

A product of this variant tradition, Giovanni Villani's Nimrod exhibits not only the aggressive traits of the arch-traitor (in Hebrew his name means 'let us rebel') but the prudence of a military strategist. For Nimrod, the Great Deluge, the same survived by his great grandfather Noah, was the formative event of his historical epoch. Unfortunately, what Nimrod extracts from this historical knowledge is not a redemptive moral lesson, but rather the brash conviction that human cunning can successfully contend with any scourge visited upon humanity by divine justice. Although Villani retains the traditional function of the tale as an explanation for the diversity of languages, the dispersion of peoples throughout the 'three parts' of the world (Asia, Africa, and Europe), and a moral exemplum concerned with blasphemous pride, the unusual stress on the tower as a prophylactic measure – one, moreover, made possible by historical knowledge (that is, knowledge of past events) – suggests that this Nimrod represents the disastrous results that ensue from the perverse application of historical knowledge to temporal vanities in lieu of worthier, spiritual ends.

In his *De origine civitatis Florentie*, Giovanni's nephew Filippo portrays a Nimrod whose vain obduracy is even more pronounced:

In the time of Phalec [Peleg of Luke 3.35] the giant Nimrod, since he had heard that it had been predicted from Adam that the whole world would be destroyed by fire and water, and it being generally believed at that time that the world would soon be submerged and the waters rise to a certain height, this most stupid of men, thinking it possible to avoid both fire and rising waters, trusting too little in the words of God announced by the prophetic spirit [a reference, no doubt, to the covenant of Genesis 9.8], and fearing lest the human race be destroyed a second time either by fire or by flood, confident in his prodigious strength, while attempting because of this to complete the incredible structure of the tower of Babel, was thwarted by being struck by the division of languages. (*De origine* II, 3)[5]

Fearing prophecies of annihilation and distrustful of divine guarantees, Nimrod elects to take matters into his own hands by constructing the great tower of baked brick mortared with bitumen (the former resistant to fire, the latter to water). This Nimrod is not only prudent but prescient, for he has somehow anticipated the possibility that divine justice could take the form of a conflagration – even before the destruction of Sodom and Gomorrah, indeed, before any Scripturally recorded instance of holocaust.

In addition to reproducing elements of these various established traditions, Boccaccio's account of Nimrod in *De casibus* I 3 adds several significant details.[6] This Nimrod, though an arch traitor with respect to God, is in many respects the first great advocate for and benefactor of human beings: the prototypical culture-hero. It is fitting, Boccaccio notes, that Nimrod be granted the second place after Adam in his history, for whereas Adam was the first man, Nimrod is the first governor of men. When, Boccaccio continues, the human race had been somewhat restored after the salvific ark ('arca iustorum servatrix' [2]) had come to rest on Ararat, the great giant Nimrod was born, a man whose prodigious size and overweening pride supplied him with the means of persuading his contemporaries to conspire against the heavens:

In truth, so that the futility of the projected enterprise might be manifest, following their leader they began to work on that foolish labour in the region of Senaar, girded by the river Euphrates: the construction, that is, of a tower that would rise higher than the clouds to avoid destruction by the waters, and be as wide as seemed necessary to achieve the desired height. (I 3, 3)[7]

If the conception of the tower is itself foolish, 'stultus,' Boccaccio nevertheless expresses great admiration for the unprecedented – and never to be replicated – communal effort exacted by the logistical and architectural challenges of such a monumental project. Indeed, he remarks that most would judge Nimrod not only blessed among men, but another God on earth ('se deum in terris alterum' [4]) upon witnessing the enthusiastic mobilization of almost the whole human race united in their endeavour to construct such a magnificent edifice; one, moreover, still extant and judged 'ingens et admirabile' [prodigious and worthy of admiration] (4) by those who have seen it.

Even more remarkable than this undisguised appreciation for the architectural and social triumph is his account of the destruction of the tower. Boccaccio's is the only account – to the best of my knowledge – in which a rationalistic explanation for the destruction is advanced.[8] According to Boccaccio, the definitive destruction of the tower is adumbrated by a partial collapse; suddenly, whether pushed by wind or by the hand of God he cannot say, the highest portion of the fabric, already practically touching the clouds, comes tumbling down.[9] Though a more circumspect and pious man would no doubt have taken this as a cue to leave well enough alone, Nimrod, his resolve only strengthened by this setback, decides that he will not only rebuild what has fallen, but will actually make the new structure taller:[10]

> The violence against God having, therefore, been renewed by Nimrod, not only was there a reconstruction of what had been presumed shattered by God's wrath, but it was built even higher, almost as though the object were not to avoid future flooding but to filch the heavens from the Creator of all things [quasi non ad evitandas undas in posterum, sed ad surripiendum Opifici rerum celum straretur iter]. (I 3, 7)

Unlike the first construction, which was motivated by the prudent – if misguided – desire to create a safe haven from a prospective deluge, this rebuilding is spurred by a specifically blasphemous desire to usurp God's throne; the human artificer and megalomaniac Nimrod suffers from the tragic delusion that he can surpass the artificer of all things: the 'Opifex rerum.'

It would seem that Boccaccio cannot help expressing support for any endeavour that bespeaks magnanimity, unity, and cooperation – particularly when such praiseworthy qualities are provoked by the natural desire for self-preservation. In the *Decameron* this attitude is given its most eloquent expression by Pampinea who, in arguing that she and her friends are fully justified in their scheme to flee the pestilence of Florence for the relative sanctuary of the surrounding countryside, proclaims that it is their birthright to undertake any reasonable actions ('rimedii') necessary to protect their lives, for 'Natural ragione è di ciascuno che ci nasce, la sua vita quanto può aiutare e conservare e difendere' ['Every person born into this world has a natural right to sustain, preserve, and defend his own life to the best of his ability'] (I, Intro., 53–4; trans. McWilliam, 14).

What was Nimrod's original conception if not one such 'rimedio'? Indeed, the building of the tower is, if anything, a 'rimedio' morally superior to that initially chosen by the *brigata*, for it aims at universal salvation. It is the selfless conception of a political leader concerned with preserving not his own body alone but the body politic. It is only the belated introduction of a truly reprehensible goal – the foolish and ill-augured conspiracy to drive God from the heavens – that tarnishes Nimrod's otherwise heroic status.

It is likely that this ambivalent portrait of Nimrod derives, at least in part, from the need to accommodate the story of Nimrod to the general pattern of a glorious rise and ignominious fall that undergirds each of the exemplary portraits in *De casibus*. However, given the abundance of historical personages whose lives require no adjustments to correspond to this pattern, it is clear that Boccaccio was not obliged to include Nimrod in his catalogue, but had a particular interest in doing so. This is not at all strange when one considers Boccaccio's sustained advocacy of racial, cultural, and political unity. As the first governor, and the first person to create not only a political unity but, even more remarkably, a unity of purpose, Nimrod, it is clear, deserves our praise and respect. Indeed, in the course of the initial construction, before he is seized with the maniacal desire to assault God, Nimrod is in many respects the prototype of Boccaccio's ideal type, that individual whose spirit, like that of Alcibiades, 'bounds forth and with its greatness embraces the whole earth and easily transcends the stars, and driven by the flame, burns with sublime desires' (*De casibus* III 13, 3). What is to be condemned in such men as Nimrod and Alcibiades is not this supernatural thirst for glory but rather the vice, one associated by Boccaccio precisely with magnanimity, of desiring to climb 'to the heights by a route different from that permitted by reason' (*De casibus* III 13, 4). By parsing the construction of the tower into two disparate moments, Boccaccio is simultaneously dramatizing the cleavage between rational and irrational desire. The first construction, one motivated by the reasonable, prudent desire to create a sanctuary from catastrophe is implicitly endorsed by Boccaccio, who associates divine vengeance not so much with this initial building (which may, he observes, have been damaged by natural causes), but rather with the subsequent rebuilding – one motivated by a blasphemous desire to topple God. Had Nimrod adhered to Pampinea's precept that all efforts at self-preservation must be guided by reason, the primal linguistic and genetic unity might, Boccaccio seems to imply, have persevered forever.

By cleaving the traditionally unified episode into these two discrete moments, Boccaccio accomplishes something the importance of which cannot be overstated; he transforms a parable concerned with the vanity of reckless ambition into one concerned with the nobility of reasoned ambition (and the dangers of irrational pride). On the very desert landscape the ruins of which commemorate the devastating consequences of blasphemous pride, Boccaccio has constructed his own towering monument to all human striving that is pursued under the aegis of reason.

Nor is this the first time that Boccaccio has taken advantage of a deserted, rubble-strewn landscape to inaugurate a new building project; indeed, the *Decameron*, as we have seen, conforms perfectly to this pattern of collapse and renewal. In the section that follows I intend to show that the *Decameron* is, in a sense, Boccaccio's own, redemptive, Babel. With ink, parchment, and quill Boccaccio has composed a book destined to far outlast both bricks and bitumen: a literary monument that will forever bear witness to the power of the human spirit to triumph over all afflictions, even death itself.

Through the Literary Looking-glass: The Textual Monument as Mirror

In the *Anticlaudianus*, Alain de Lille's epic of moral regeneration through the creation of a 'new man' (the collaborative effort of God, Nature, the Liberal Arts, Philosophy, Theology, Faith, and Prudence, among others), Prudence is charged with the daunting task of soliciting God's contribution of a human soul. In response to Prudence's request, God replies:

> If I reckoned according to their deserts the vices of the earth, the wickedness of the world, the crimes of the universe and wished to mete out full punishment, I would again cover the land with floods, again envelop the mountains in surging waters and the whole human race would perish in the deluge. No one's merits of life would exempt him from the flood; no second Deucalion would survive and no second Noah would close up the ark. Rather, the world, which lives a life of continuous crime, would, as

its manner of life deserves, perish by a single punishment. (bk. VI, 169–70)[11]

Since, however, God's infinite mercy and love transcend the cold equations of justice, he generously grants Prudence her request. Understood allegorically, Alain's story suggests a process whereby humanity is both redeemed and rendered impervious to disaster through the intercession of secular knowledge (the liberal arts/philosophy), sacred knowledge (theology), and faith; the path to restoration begins with the seven disciplines of the medieval curriculum and ends with a vision of God.[12]

Another author who uses the theme of universal annihilation as a foil for a proposed remedium to all such afflictions is Jean de Meun. In the 'Nature's confession' section of the *Roman de la Rose*, Jean interweaves elements of the pagan, Ovidian, account of the deluge from *Metamorphoses* I with the Christian doctrine of free will. Here, Nature declares the primacy of free will:

> In the same way, if one is not stupid, one can guard against all the other vices, or turn away from virtues if one wants to turn toward evil. For free will is so powerful, if one knows oneself well, that it can always be maintained if one can feel within one's heart that sin wants to be its master, no matter how the heavenly bodies may go. For he who could foreknow the things that heaven wished to do could certainly prevent them. If heaven wanted to dry out the air until all people would die of heat, and if the people knew it beforehand, they would construct new houses in damp places or near rivers, or they would dig out great caverns and hide themselves underground, so that they would not mind the heat.
>
> Or if, however late, it happened that a flood of water came, those who knew the places of refuge would leave the plains beforehand and flee to the mountains. There they would build such strong ships that they would protect their lives against the great inundation, as Deucalion and Pyrrha did in former times when they escaped by the boat into which they entered when they were not seized by the flood. (lines 17569–605)[13]

The thrust of Jean's argument seems to be that if one could forecast calamitous events, one would certainly find a means of avoiding them. This apparently fatuous observation is really just a means of setting up the central paradox that he wishes to illustrate; while perversely devoting untold time and ingenuity to futile attempts to foresee, and thereby avoid, extraordinary, external threats to our physical survival, we blindly neglect the ordinary, internal, and far more insidious dangers to our physical and spiritual health. Whereas we cannot predict deluges, famines, and the like, we have been granted the means – a reasoned application of our free will – to anticipate, and therefore avert, those daily disasters that through ignorance we bring upon our own heads:

> Free will then, by the exercise of good understanding, could better and more easily avoid whatever can make it suffer. It has no concern that it may sorrow over anything, provided that it does not wish to consent to it and that it knows by heart that one is the cause of one's own discomforts. Outside tribulation can only be the occasion of it. (lines 17715–24)

Alain's allegory of a journey through the heavens to God mediated by a full cast of personifications tends to highlight the extrinsic quality of knowledge and divine determinism. Hence it is natural that his remedy to humanity's travails should take the form of a 'new man,' a semi-divine interceder (though, understood allegorically, this 'new man' is no doubt representative of each individual's capacity to achieve spiritual salvation). Jean's emphasis on good understanding and free will as a means of empowering the individual highlights the intrinsic journey; the solution to our afflictions lies within. Importantly, what is true of both Alain and Jean is the pronounced tendency to equate knowledge – in particular, moral knowledge – with an improved capacity for self-determination and a correspondingly enhanced immunity from harm.

In the *Decameron* Boccaccio is essentially following the example of Alain and Jean in his use of a 'universal' catastrophe (the plague) to frame a discourse concerning determinism and free will. Boccaccio's perspective embraces elements of both authors. For Boccaccio the 'new man' is both external (the Promethean pedagogue) and internal (the self, restored through a type of epistemic journey). Insofar as the book/galeotto succeeds in leading us to knowledge, particularly self-knowledge, it furnishes us with a means of better anticipating the consequences of any given action, thereby permitting us to chart, within reasonable limits, our own course through life – in both a physical and a moral sense.[14]

Like Alain and Jean, Boccaccio has chosen the circumstance of a 'universal' cataclysm – the most compelling example of divine determinism – to test the doctrine of free will. However, unlike the scenarios of destruction limned by these authors, Boccaccio's 'universal' cataclysm is not simply a matter of conjecture but a historical reality: the plague of 1348. When Boccaccio poses the question of whether or not free will can be reconciled with divine cataclysm, he is not constrained to look for his answers in the dusty parchments of the literary authorities (though he does not neglect these), for he has been afforded a historically unique opportunity to seek out his answers in the streets of Florence and hills of Fiesole. Does one have the freedom to avoid destruction? Is it possible to flee vice (the plague/Florence) and seek virtue (the *brigata's* microsociety/pastoral Fiesole)? These questions are implicit in the *Decameron* Introduction, and these same questions are answered – both, as we shall see, with a qualified 'yes' – by the conclusion of Day X.

In the introduction to the third book of *De casibus*, Boccaccio tells the tale of a competition between Poverty and Fortune.[15] Poverty, an agile wrestler, easily subjugates Fortune and decrees that she is to sacrifice one half of her empire. Henceforth, ill-Fortune will be fettered and bound to a stake in a public plaza. Good Fortune, meanwhile, is free to roam. Having recounted this entertaining anecdote, Boccaccio claims that he is being summoned back to work by the clamour of that wretched crew of people who have foolishly unloosed their misfortunes from this stake: 'Sed ecce qui solverunt a palo infortunium suis me revocant clamoribus in laborem' (*De casibus* III 1, 23). The Fortune presented here by Boccaccio is neither an agent of divine providence (like Dante's Fortune of *Inferno* VII) nor the traditional personification of inexorable, and arbitrary, change ('blind' Fortune). Her destructive force presents a threat only to those who are perversely induced to loose her from her bondage. The primary effect of this model is that of restoring an element of self-determination – free will – to the individual, who is thus made to shoulder the responsibility for his or her own ill fortune. The challenge, of course, lies in determining which actions will result in this destructive unleashing of Fortune. Certainly, none of the men and women whose rapid rise to greatness and tragic fall are documented in *De casibus* wittingly set out to secure their doom by deliberately untying Fortune from her stake. How, then, does one engage in a propitious exercising of one's free will? It is precisely the ability to distinguish between good and evil that supplies the key to this ancient conundrum.

In the Proem to the *Decameron*, Boccaccio proposes that his text not only provides pleasure, but serves a useful moral-didactic function in that its thematically and chronologically varied – and in some sense exemplary – stories will furnish his readers with a means of recognizing good and fleeing evil: 'diletto delle sollazzevoli cose in quelle mostrate e utile consiglio potranno pigliare, in quanto potranno cognoscere quello che sia da fuggire e che sia similmente da seguitare' (Proem, 14). His application of this formula in the *Decameron* is most commonly viewed as a restatement of the well-known Horatian precept according to which poetry should supply both pleasure and profit, should be 'utile dulci' (*Ars poetica*, 343): Boccaccio's 'diletto' and 'utile consiglio.'[16] Though the possible Horatian influence has long been noted, such a pedigree is, I would argue, far from satisfactory, for Horace neither recommends the use of exemplary models nor specifies the precise nature of poetic utility. By invoking the resonant formula 'cognoscere quello che sia da fuggire e che sia similmente da seguitare' in the *Decameron* proem, Boccaccio is not simply reciting a vague ethical prescription but is reproducing a conventional formula frequently invoked in classical and Christian texts – philosophical, theological, and, as we shall see, historical – concerned with tracing the origins, or prescribing the forms, of moral conduct.

In the seventh book of his *Divine Institutes*, a work much cited by Boccaccio in his scholarly compendia, the fourth-century Christian apologist Lactantius uses this ethical formula in the course of attempting to resolve the thorny question of why it is that a good God would find it expedient to populate the earth with dangerous animals:

> Since man is composed of diverse and opposing notions, body and soul, that is, of heaven and of earth, and since he is tenuous and comprehensible, eternal and temporal, sensible and brute, endowed with light and darkness, reason itself and necessity demand that both good and evils be set before him; goods which he may use [bona, quibus utatur], evils which he may shun and avoid [mala, quae vitet et caveat]. It is for this that wisdom has been given to man, so that the nature of goods and evils having been learned, he may exercise the power of his reason in seeking the goods and avoiding the evils [et in appetendis bonis, et malis declinandis, vim suae rationis exerceat]. (*Divine Institutes* VII, 4)[17]

We find a reprise of Lactantius's strongly dualistic model in Jerome's *Commentarius in Ecclesiam* where we are told once again that harmful things are created for a didactic end, for it is by avoiding them that we acquire wisdom. Solomon, Jerome tells us, recognizing this principle, devoted as much effort to studying ignorance and error as he did to studying knowledge and truth, for true wisdom consists not simply in embracing the latter, but in fleeing the former:[18]

> Opposites are understood through opposites. And wisdom first of all is the

lack of stupidity. On the other hand, it is not possible to lack stupidity
unless you have understood it. For this reason many harmful things were
also created, so that in shunning them, we would be guided toward wisdom.
Thus it was of equal importance to Solomon to learn not only wisdom and
knowledge but their opposites, error and stupidity: in seeking some and
avoiding others, his true wisdom would be tested. (*Patrologia Latina* 23 col.
1023)

Opposites define each other, and since wisdom itself consists in the ability to discern difference and make distinctions, an acquaintance with
harmful things is absolutely fundamental.[19] Viewed through this particular optic, the plague – understood both in a literal and figurative sense –
would logically represent a particularly extreme form of 'harmful thing,'
and thus provide an unprecedented opportunity to gain insight into the
inner workings of nature (insofar as the plague is a natural phenomenon), and of the spirit (insofar as the plague is a moral phenomenon).

The Venerable Bede, placed by Dante among the theologians of the
Heaven of the Sun in *Paradiso* X, gives this ethical fleeing/following for-
mula a prominent place in the preface of his most famous work, the
Ecclesiastical History of the English Nation. His history is dedicated to King
Ceolwulph, whom he commends for his zeal in acquainting himself with
the words and deeds of great men of the past:

> For if history relates good things of good men, the attentive hearer is
> excited to imitate that which is good; or if it mentions evil things of wicked
> persons, nevertheless the religious and pious hearer or reader, shunning
> [devitando] that which is hurtful and perverse, is the more earnestly
> excited to perform [exsequenda] those things which he knows to be good,
> and worthy of God. (Bk I, preface)[20]

Though it is hard to deny the pedagogical value – even necessity – of
illustrating both virtue and vice with vivid exempla, the problem, of
course, is that by illustrating vice one inherently runs the risk of corrupting one's congregation – or reader. It is for this reason that Bede finds it
necessary to introduce the feeble argument that wicked examples do not
corrupt the pious, but rather galvanize their desire to act morally. Distinguishing the sacred, chaste, and salutary desire to gain knowledge of
good and evil from the profane, lustful, and damning ambition for such
knowledge is a notoriously slippery task. The temporal condition is one
of moral flux proceeding from the need to constantly negotiate between
poles of good and evil; the very same homilies and histories that guide

one person on the path to virtue will goad another along the road to perdition. The same images of St Catherine's wheel-wracked body or St Agatha's amputated breasts that inspire Christian piety in one individual will excite a more voluptuous, even prurient piety in another.

Boccaccio's assertion that his text will prove useful by aiding its readers to distinguish 'quello che sia da fuggire e che sia similmente da seguitare' [those things that should be fled and that, likewise, should be followed] appears not only in the *Decameron* but in the exemplary histories of *De mulieribus claris* and the near-hagiographic, exemplary biography of Dante, the *Vita di Dante*. In the proem of *De mulieribus claris* Boccaccio expresses the hope that his readers will not be disturbed by his decision to intersperse his vignettes of women famous for their virtue with those of women like Medea, infamous for their great but 'pernitiosum ... ingenium' [pernicious ... intellect] (6). Tellingly, he feels it necessary to defend this technique of pairing exemplum with counter-exemplum by proposing that it fulfils a useful moral purpose, a 'sacra utilitas':

> An account that praises deeds worthy of commemoration and sometimes heaps reproaches upon crimes will not only drive the noble towards glory and to some degree restrain villains from their wicked acts; it will also restore to this little book the attractiveness lost as a result of the shameful exploits of certain of its heroines. Hence I have decided to insert at various places in these stories some pleasant exhortations to virtue and to add incentives for avoiding and detesting wickedness. Thus holy profit [sacra ... utilitas] will mix with entertainment and so steal insensibly into my readers' minds. (*De mulieribus*, proem, 7; *Famous Women*, trans. Brown [hereafter cited as Brown], 11)[21]

In the *Vita di Dante* Boccaccio claims that the objective of pagan poetry is, like that of Scripture, to illustrate 'le cagioni delle cose, gli effetti delle virtù e de' vizi, e che fuggire dobbiamo e che seguire' [the causes of things, the effects of virtues and of vices, and what we should flee and what follow] (XXII). In this particular case, Boccaccio's primary aim is to validate the claim that Dante's *Commedia* is, like Scripture, a theological work – a sacred poem – concerned with providing moral guidance by illustrating the causes of things ('le cagioni delle cose') and the consequences of virtue and vice. In a strategy much employed in his frequent defences of pagan poetry Boccaccio creates a proportion whereby poetry *is* theology and theology, poetry: 'bene appare, non solamente la poesí essere teologia, ma ancora teologia essere poesia' (*Vita di Dante*, XXII). Indeed, theology is God's poetry: 'la teologia niun'altra cosa è che una poesia di Dio' (*Vita di Dante*, XXII). Boccaccio is not constructing an argument so much as drafting a contract; so long as theologians appropriate poetic means – allegory and the like – to unravel the moral message of Scripture, it is only fair that poets be granted the right to attribute theological, moral ends to their fictions. It is an argument that is more than slightly coercive but marvelously effective. If we allow that the acts of cruelty and sexual debauchery so common in the Old Testament fulfill a morally educative end, upon what grounds can we deny that pagan fictions serve a similar function?

In *De mulieribus* it seems that Boccaccio's primary reason for advertising the moral utility of the technique of pairing exemplum with counter-exemplum is to preempt criticism for having included the lurid bedroom odysseys of such spirited women as Medea, Flora, and Sempronia. Though one might rightly question Boccaccio's sincerity in promoting the medicinal value of such sexually extravagant counter-exempla, his method, as we have seen, has venerable precedents in Christian theological and historical texts.

Importantly, Christian theologians, preachers, and historians are not alone in advocating the didactic efficacy of contrasting exemplum with counter-exemplum. A particularly noteworthy occurrence of the formula 'cognoscere quello che sia da fuggire e che sia similmente da seguitare,' one whose likely influence on Boccaccio has, to my knowledge, gone unnoted, is that found in the proem of Livy's *Ab urbe condita libri*, where it represents nothing less than the guiding principle of the entire work:

> What chiefly makes the study of history wholesome and profitable is this, that you behold the lessons of every kind of experience set forth as on a conspicuous monument [inlustri ... monumento]; from these you may choose for yourself and for your own state [rei publicae] what to imitate [quod imitere capias], from these mark for avoidance [quod vites] what is shameful in the conception and shameful in the result. (*Ab urbe* I, 10–11)[22]

Livy's great history traces Rome's trajectory from its nebulous, mythical origins through its age of world supremacy to the social, political, and moral degeneracy of his own age, one so entrenched that human beings can endure neither their vices nor their cure: 'donec ad haec tempora quibus nec vitia nostra nec remedia pati possumus' (I, 9). Livy aims to write a text which does not simply document a tragic fall but provides a moral lesson and, most importantly, suggests a practical remedy. This remedy takes the form of a bright literary 'monument' ('inlustri ... monumento') composed of historical exempla from which his readers are invited to select those examples worthy of imitation and reject those reprehensible in conception and consequence. The concurrence of this theme of radical collapse (political, social, and moral) with a program for social renovation – grounded, moreover, in an exemplary form of didacticism – cannot help but recall the near-identical concerns expressed by Boccaccio in the *Decameron* proem.

Vittore Branca writes that, in 1348 – that is, in the period directly before starting work on the *Decameron* – Boccaccio was busy finishing up his translation of Livy: 'si pose in questi mesi la conclusione del volgarizzamento liviano (III e IV deca)' ['completed the vernacular translation of Livy (decades III and IV)'] (*Giovanni Boccaccio*, 77; *Boccaccio: The Man and His Work*, trans. Monges [hereafter cited as Monges], 75). He then goes on to note that Boccaccio's close involvement with Livy's text had a decisive influence on the syntax, style, and historical vision of the *Decameron*:

> Fu una esperienza essenziale e decisiva per il 'padre della prosa italiana.' Il quale, superando le strutture valeriane e apuleiane dominanti nel *Filocolo* (e ancora nella *Comedia delle ninfe*), maturò su Livio la sintassi e lo stile che col suo capolavoro doveva imporre alla nostra tradizione letteraria. E maturò anche, in senso narrativo, la visione storica degli uomini e delle loro vicende nel quadro di quella interpretazione risolutamente provvidenziale che ispirerà poi la celebre introduzione al *Decameron*. (Branca, *Giovanni Boccaccio*, 77)

> It was an essential and decisive experience for the 'father of Italian prose.' Rising above the Valerian and Apuleian constructions dominant in the *Filocolo* (and again in the *Comedia*), Boccaccio had mastered the syntax of Livy and the style which he was to impose on Italian literary tradition with his masterpiece. In a narrative sense, he also matured in his historical vision of men and their vicissitudes, as is evident later on in the famous introduction to the *Decameron*. (Monges, 75)

The Livian influence that Branca discerns on both a structural and thematic level in Boccaccio's plague description of the *Decameron* Introduction is, I would argue, even better represented by those critical, and intensely Livian, lines of the proem which establish the moral – and 'medicinal' – aspiration of the work as a whole. Whereas Christian sermons and histories use exempla to restore their parishioners and readers to spiritual health in preparation for the next world, Livy's ambition is to·exploit the didactic potential of the historical past to remedy the personal and political ills of the historical present and even, it is implied, to achieve some degree of influence over the future.[23] That Christian theologians and preachers should have appropriated this formula from the classical tradition and adapted it to their own spiritual agenda is consistent with the usual pattern whereby the intellectual treasures of pagan culture are converted to Christian ends. More interesting is the way in which a Livian, secular, valence is gradually restored to this formula with the 'rediscovery' of Livy's history in the late Middle Ages and early Renaissance.

A century or so before Boccaccio invoked the formula in his *Decameron* proem, this notion of the moral and political value of historical exempla, together with the ethical fleeing/following formula, was applied by Giovanni Villani in the first chapter of his *Cronica*. Like the Christian moralists, Giovanni translates the relatively abstract notion of exempla to be imitated (Livy's 'quod imitere capias') and avoided (Livy's 'quod vites') into the specific, Christian moral vocabulary of virtue and vice: 'adoperando le virtudi e schifando i vizi' [seeking the virtues and avoiding the vices]. However, like Livy, Villani stresses the importance of securing the health of the republic: 'e bene e stato della nostra repubblica' (a phrase strongly reminiscent of Livy's 'inde tibi tuaeque rei publicae quod imitere capias, inde foedum inceptu, foedum exitu, quod vites'; 'from these you may choose for yourself and for your own state what to imitate, from these mark for avoidance what is shameful in the conception and shameful in the result' [*Ab urbe*, I, preface, 10; Foster, Loeb ed.]). A secular historian and a Christian, Villani concerns himself not only with the eternal fate of the individual soul, but with the temporal destiny of the republic at large. The exercise of moral choice is thus restored to the secular, historical arena where it can be of practical utility to both individual and republic.

Villani's introduction of this unmistakably Livian brand of pragmatism into his widely read *Cronica*, together with the increased availability, in the fourteenth century, of new, vernacular translations of Livy's *Ab urbe condita libri* (Boccaccio himself, as has been noted, is credited with a vernacular translation of the first, third, and fourth Decades) suggests the likelihood that most educated readers of the *Decameron* would have recognized in the 'follow/flee' formula of the Proem an implicit affiliation of Boccaccio's work not only with the sacred utility of Christian homily (or sacred history) but with a quintessentially Livian brand of secular history and utility.[24]

Just as Livy uses the pattern of history to bind exempla of human experience into a lustrous monument with pedagogical value, the historical plague and the fictional history of the frame narrative bind the *novelle* of the *Decameron* into a conspicuous monument whose final purpose is somehow – though less overtly – pedagogical.[25] Like Livy, Boccaccio is concerned with the possibilities that exemplarity affords for a political and social reconstruction in this world. Like the Christian preachers, Boccaccio tends to view this reconstruction in moral terms. His invocation of the formula in the *Decameron* implies a synthesis of classical (Livian) and Christian concerns; here, both eternal beatitude (spiritual health), and temporal beatitude (the restoration of health to individual and republic) are at stake.[26] By uniting Livy's secular utility with a Christian 'sacra utilitas,' Boccaccio has produced a generic hybrid, a secular 'scripture' designed to serve as a panacea for all human ills, physical and spiritual: an eminently practical 'remedy for fortunes fair and foul.'

Whereas Boccaccio's invocation of the Livian formula in the *Decameron* Proem introduces the general theme of a moral reorientation based on learning to make the right choice, the diametrically opposed Introduction of Day I and Conclusion of Day X serve to define the terms of this choice. In the Introduction to Day I, Pampinea, the first of the *brigata* leaders, poses, in language that clearly evokes the formula of the Proem, the basic moral dilemma: is it prudent and morally defensible for her and her companions to flee Florence and seek Fiesole?

> Io giudicherei ottimamente fatto che noi ... di questa terra uscissimo, e fuggendo come la morte i disonesti essempli degli altri onestamente a' nostri luoghi in contado, de' quali a ciascuna di noi è gran copia, ce ne andassimo a stare. (I, intro., 65)

> I would consider it an excellent plan for us ... to leave this city, and fleeing like death the dishonest examples of others, honorably set out for our country estates, of which we each have a great number.

In the Conclusion of Day X Panfilo, the last of the *brigata* leaders, poses the opposite question: would it be prudent to flee Fiesole and seek Florence?[27] The clear parallelism of these paradigmatic moments of choice that inaugurate and conclude the framing fiction serves to foreground a basic paradox: confronted with a historical circumstance – the plague in Florence – that remains unchanged, the *brigata* apparently subverts logic by arriving at two seemingly contradictory decisions.

Viewed objectively, the *brigata*'s decision to forsake their fellow Florentines, leaving them to fend for themselves in the worst calamity the world had known as they themselves head off to the well-appointed Fiesolan villas, is akin to the callous behaviour exhibited by the priest or the Levite in Luke's parable of the Good Samaritan. Aware that this is how their actions may be perceived, Pampinea finds it necessary to reiterate the circumstances that distinguish their plan to leave Florence from the morally indefensible desertions of other *brigate*. She further argues that plague-ridden Florence has become little more than a dreadful gallery of 'disonesti essempli' [dishonest examples]; the diversity of moral exempla characteristic of a healthy city has here succumbed to the monotony of vice. Consequently the *brigata* is not so much fleeing to physical safety as it is fleeing from moral danger.

A similar ambivalence underlies the decision to return to Florence in the conclusion of Day X. If we accept Pampinea's original argument that 'l'onestamente andare' [honorable going] is preferable to 'lo star disonestamente' [dishonorable staying] (I, intro., 72), how can we accept that the *brigata*'s decision to return to Florence is in any way virtuous? Yet, despite such ambiguities, we are led to believe that each of these two movements – the progressive move from Florence to Fiesole and the retrogressive move from Fiesole to Florence – represents the morally superior choice. In order to resolve this apparent contradiction we are forced to conclude that whereas the historical and physical circumstances of Florence and Fiesole remain unchanged, the spiritual and moral orientation of the *brigata* members has undergone a perfect conversion. The same circumstance (being in Florence) viewed as morally indefensible in the Introduction has, contrary to expectation, become the only morally defensible option by the conclusion of Day X. The lesson encoded in this paradox is related, no doubt, to the inadequacy of all rigid ethical prescriptions. Though we may all agree that it is good to flee vice and embrace virtue, the problem lies in distinguishing among acts of virtue and acts of vice. By structuring this basic paradox, Boccaccio forces us to redefine moral action itself. If the election to remain in Florence may be viewed as morally indefensible one moment and morally commendable the next, it follows that moral action can be neither securely prescribed through words nor accurately inferred from actions. Boccaccio's is a world without graven laws or moral touchstones. Indeed, this much is clearly stated by Dioneo in the conclusion to Day VI: 'Or non sapete voi che, per la perversità di questa stagione, li giudici hanno lasciati i tribunali? Le leggi, così le divine come le umane tacciono?' ['Are you not aware that because of the chaos of the present age, the judges have deserted the courts, the laws of God and man are in abeyance'] (VI, concl., 9; McWilliam, 478).[28]

When Pampinea argues that the moral imperative to help their fellow Florentines to cope with the plague has been superseded by the moral imperative to shun vice and seek virtue, 'fuggendo come la morte i disonesti essempli degli altri, onestamente a' nostri luoghi in contado,' [fleeing like death the dishonest examples of others, honorably set out for our country estates] (65) she is essentially casting the plague as a crisis in exemplarity. The conspicuous absence of examples of virtue implies nothing less than the foreclosure of knowledge itself; if 'contrariis contraria intelliguntur,' it follows that the absence of such contraries results in the privation of knowledge (in this case, moral knowledge) and, therefore, of choice (moral choice). Somehow, the 'Saïtic' archive of human experience bound in the one hundred *novelle* manages to restore knowledge and, therefore, choice to the *brigata*. The difficulty lies in establishing how, precisely, this end is achieved.

When Boccaccio announces his intention to have his *brigata* tell 'cento novelle, o favole o parabole o istorie' ['a hundred stories or fables or parables or histories'] documenting 'piacevoli e aspri casi d'amore e altri fortunati avvenimenti ... così ne' moderni tempi avvenuti come negli antichi' ['a variety of love adventures, bitter as well as pleasing, and other exciting incidents, which took place in both ancient and modern times'] with the useful end of enabling his readers to recognize 'quello che sia da fuggire e che similmente da seguitare' ['what should be avoided and likewise what should be pursued'] (Proem, 13–14; McWilliam, 3), the exemplary aim of his *novelle* would hardly seem to be contestable. However, critics of recent years, better attuned to Boccaccio's ironic spirit, have convincingly argued that though Boccaccio has indeed pilfered the preacher's handbooks for the traditional exemplary forms, his own use of this material is guided by a different, often subversive, end and infused with a different spirit.[29]

The problem with the traditional didactic use of exemplum and counter-exemplum is the tendency to use exempla as prescriptive models whose vivid illustrations of the cost of vice and the rewards of virtue are designed to set the listener on the right path through fear and desire, not – and this is critical – through self-knowledge and understanding; such prodding from the pulpit engages the emotions, not the intellect, and does not necessarily lead to an intellectual and spiritual conversion to the right path.[30]

Dante's response to the clear deficiencies of this dualistic model is to create a more nuanced, triadic model by adding to the traditional categories of examples to flee (hell) and examples to follow (paradise) a third, intermediate category (purgatory) in which fleeing alternates with following, exemplum with counter-exemplum, in a pattern designed to reproduce the dynamic moral flux of the temporal condition. Whereas hell's static environment is rooted in the eternal privation of knowledge, and paradise's imperturbability in the eternal plenitude of knowledge, purgatory is a place quickened by moral, intellectual, and spiritual dialectic: a place of learning.[31] Here, it is not the parishioner standing in the midst of a crowded congregation who is alternately terrified and assuaged by chronicles of vice punished and virtue rewarded, but the ever-transient pilgrim, Dante, who moves past exemplum and counter-exemplum as he wends his way up through the seven terraces. As Dante and Virgil negotiate the precarious, undulating path that threads the fissured rock and issues onto the first terrace of purgatory, the 'Terrace of Pride,' Virgil warns Dante that he must use some 'art' in clinging first to one side of the rock and then the other. For the preacher's injunction to flee vice and seek virtue, Dante substitutes this physically strenuous careening from side to side. The exempla themselves have acquired a vitality and verisimilitude foreign not only to the preachers but to Dante's poetic predecessors; they are God's art, a 'visibile parlare, / novello a noi perché qui non si trova' [visible speech, new to us because it's not found here] (*Purg.* X, 95–6). So lifelike are these exemplary histories that they are at times indistinguishable from the historical realities that they represent; they are experienced not as literature but as life.[32] Upon completing the moral 'curriculum' of the seven purgatorial terraces, Virgil tells Dante 'libero, dritto e sano è tuo arbitrio' ['your will is free, erect and whole'] (*Purg.* XXVII, 140; *Divine Comedy*, trans. Mandelbaum [hereafter cited as Mandelbaum]). By successfully navigating between exemplum and counter-exemplum on each of the seven terraces, Dante has re-aligned his will and is prepared to enter the terrestrial paradise – the place where God's gift of free will was first granted (and first abused).[33]

Whereas Dante is faced with the task of rendering a supernatural, incredible otherworld experience natural, believable, and 'worldly,' through the studied application of a veneer of realistic detail, Boccaccio assumes the opposite challenge: that of forcing the ever-changing, protean stuff of life, of reality, into conformity with an artificial, supernatural pattern that encodes (or at least appears to encode) a moral lesson.

It is primarily through the device of the frame that Boccaccio succeeds in superimposing a symbolic order on the unruly *novelle*. The much touted naturalism of the plague description in the Introduction to Day I is, paradoxically, enlisted in the task of illustrating the manifestly unnatural state to which human beings have been reduced, one in which even the most sacred natural bond, that between parents and children, has, incredibly, been severed:[34]

> era con sì fatto spavento questa tribulazione entrata ne' petti degli uomini e delle donne, che l'un fratello l'altro abbandonava e il zio il nepote e la sorella il fratello e spesse volte la donna il suo marito; e, che maggior cosa è quasi non credibile, li padri e le madri i figliuoli, quasi loro non fossero, di visitare e di servire schifavano. (I, intro., 27)

> this scourge had implanted so great a terror in the hearts of men and women that brothers abandoned brothers, uncles their nephews, sisters their brothers, and in many cases wives deserted their husbands. But even worse, and almost incredible, was the fact that fathers and mothers refused to nurse and assist their own children, as though they did not belong to them. (McWilliam, 8–9)

If the introductory plague description foregrounds the unnatural vice triggered by the universal (or semi-universal) collapse of nature and reason, the Conclusion to Day X is expressly designed to highlight the unnatural virtue of the *brigata*, achieved through a restoration of these same qualities. As Panfilo proudly proclaims:

> quantunque liete novelle e forse attrattive a concupiscenzia dette ci sieno e del continuo mangiato e bevuto bene e sonato e cantato (cose tutte da incitare le deboli menti a cose meno oneste), *niuno* atto, *niuna* parola, *niuna* cosa né dalla vostra parte né dalla nostra ci ho conosciuta da biasimare: *continua* onestà, *continua* concordia, *continua* fraternal dimestichezza mi ci è paruta vedere e sentire. (X, concl., 4–6, emphasis mine)

> although light-hearted tales have been told, of the sort, perhaps, apt to excite carnal desire, and we have continuously eaten and drunk well, played music and sung (all of which things incite feeble minds to dishonest acts), to my knowledge, *not one* act, *not one* word, *not one* thing has been committed, either on your part or mine, that is blameworthy: it is my impression, rather, that I have seen and heard *continual* seemliness, *continual* concord, *continual* brotherly goodwill.

This glaringly artificial rhetoric constructed of two complementary series of anaphora – 'niuno' [not one] thrice repeated with respect to acts of vice and 'continua' [continual] thrice repeated with respect to acts of virtue (a complex reformulation of the basic formula of vice shunned and virtue sought) – represents a picture every bit as unnatural, and incredible, as that presented in the Introduction. Importantly, though both the abject depravity of the unnatural acts committed in the plague and the perfect virtue of the *brigata* are so improbable as to test our credulity, they are, at least, within the realm of possibility. Bracketed by these extremes of subhuman (unnatural) and superhuman (supernatural) morality – the terrestrial analogues of hell and heaven – we find the morally intermediate, the fully human realm described in the hundred *novelle* of the *Decameron*.

In the *Commedia* the reader is not left to puzzle out how Dante manages to work his way from the dark wood to paradise; the poem is itself an account of this journey. However, such knowledge of the whole is the privilege of eschatological visions alone. Though Boccaccio's overarching pattern of conversion – from bestiality to super-human virtue – is clear enough, it is left to his readers to determine what role, if any, the intervening *novelle* play in this process of conversion. It falls to the reader of the *Decameron* (and to the ideal 'readers' of the *brigata*) to negotiate this middle ground and determine how it is that the *novelle* serve a moral, didactic end.[35]

Whereas the traditional function of exempla is, as we have seen, fundamentally normative – that of prescribing virtuous behaviour – Boccaccio systematically perverts this function in many of his *novelle* by using an exemplary idiom (forms, themes, and so forth) to describe a far from perfect reality, and an imperfect reality to represent exemplary behaviour. This process is epitomized by Boccaccio's radical reevaluation of God's role as divine artificer: one that is best appreciated against the foil of Dante's more traditional perspective.

In the *Convivio* Dante, citing Boethius, locates the supernal exemplum in God's mind: 'Tutte le cose produci da lo superno essemplo, tu, bellissimo, bello mondo ne la mente portante' (*Conv.* III, 2). In the *Commedia* God is cast as the supreme artificer, whose unmediated creations, Adam and Christ, are characterized by their perfection:

Però se'l caldo amor la chiara vista
   de la prima virtú dispone e segna,
   la perfezion quivi s'acquista.
Così fu fatta già la terra degna

di tutta l'animal perfezione;
    così fu fatta la Vergine pregna:
(*Par.* XIII, 79–84)

    Yet where the ardent Love prepares and stamps
the lucid Vision of the primal Power,
a being then acquires complete perfection.
    In that way, earth was once made worthy of
the full perfection of a living being;
thus was the Virgin made to be with child.
(Mandelbaum)

Boccaccio perversely forces God, the 'matrix' of the created order, into the constrictive mould of a human artificer, thereby travestying one of the most sacred tenets of the Christian faith – the belief that humans were made in God's image: 'et creavit Deus hominem ad imaginem suam' [So God created humankind in his image] (Gen. 1.27).

In the *Decameron* it is the witty Michele Scalza of VI, 6 who first introduces this notion with his facetious argument that the proverbial ugliness of the Baronci family confirms their ancient pedigree since it is evident that they were produced before God had mastered his skills. Were such blasphemous allegations confined to the mouths of satiric wags, they might be easily dismissed; however, Boccaccio, as was already noted in the first chapter, formulates a very similar argument in the course of expounding the allegorical meaning of Dante's mysterious Old Man of Crete in the scholarly *Esposizioni*. In a passage that at first glance appears to be little more than a reiteration of the traditional pessimistic motif of epochal degeneration – the sequence of metallic ages – Boccaccio introduces what amounts to an ideological countercurrent through the insertion of various testaments to the extraordinary physiological and cultural advances (technological and intellectual) made by the species over this same period of moral decline. Though the First Parents were, like gold, beautiful and pure, their offspring, like silver, shone with greater clarity and beauty (*Esp.* XIV, alleg., 27–8) – an evolutionary theory of human beauty entirely consistent with that proposed in jest by Michele Scalza (and echoed centuries later by Milton's Satan who, filled with wonder at the beauty of Earth, God's new creation, observes: 'O Earth, how like to Heav'n, if not preferrd / More justly, Seat worthier of Gods, as built / With second thoughts, reforming what was old!' [*Paradise Lost* IX, 99–101]).

By allowing that the creator of the natural world, and the model of the human species, leaves something to be desired both as artist and exemplar, Boccaccio negates the possibility of an absolute scale of values. Indeed, this reevaluation of Adamic beauty heralds a new anti-absolutist attitude toward all traditional forms of exemplarity (both as model to flee and model to follow): the exemplary life, the pictorial exemplum, the historical exemplum (on the model of such authors as Valerius Maximus), and so forth.

Both the practical value and ethical status of the literary genre of the saint's life (the most exemplary life in the Christian view) are scrutinized in the very first story of the *Decameron*, where Cepparello, a counter-exemplum of the first rank, is paradoxically converted into a saint and role model (whether through his own ingenuity or the mysterious workings of providence, to his own spiritual advantage or detriment remains – and will always remain – unresolved). In a world where God wears a workman's smock it should come as no surprise that the picaresque Cepparello should be equipped with a nimbus.

Models of secular virtue fare no better. Zinevra, condemned to death on trumped up charges succeeds, after much travail, in indicting Ambruogiuolo, her false accuser, acquitting Bernabò, her faithless husband, and proving to the satisfaction of the Sultan and all others present that she is a true paragon of female virtue (*Dec.* II, 9). What, then, is one to make of the fact that directly after hearing this story, Dioneo is moved to mock the 'bestialità' [bestiality] of Bernabò and others like him who entertain the absurd 'fantasy' that their wives remain chaste during their absence?

Pictorial exempla exert a no less equivocal influence. In IV, 2, we read of the vain and irremediably ignorant Lisetta, for whom a painted representation of the Annunciation serves not to remind her of the mystery of the Incarnation but rather to suggest the possibility that angels are in the habit of courting mortal women – thereby priming her for Frate Alberto's farcical strategy of wooing her in the guise of the Archangel Gabriel.[36] In the Filippo Balducci story of the Introduction to Day IV, we are reminded once again of the dubious moral efficacy of pictorial exempla. When his father warns him to avoid women, claiming that they are evil, his son responds with incredulity, 'O son così fatte le male cose?' [So is this what evil things look like?] (26), and remarks that he finds them 'più belle che gli agnoli dipinti' [lovelier than painted angels] (28). It is, paradoxically, his acquaintance with such painted images of angels that provides Filippo's son with a standard for judging the beauty of women, their terrestrial counterparts – as well as a basis for presuming the angelic virtue of these carnal 'angels.'

Boccaccio's vision is one that casts divine truths in human forms and human truths in divine forms. God has the failings of a human artisan, and human artisans are touched by divinity; Muses are women and women, Muses; angels too are women and women, as Filippo's son notes, are like angels (indeed, better); the archangel Gabriel is a lover and the scurrilous priest an archangel; Cepparello is both broker of nefarious affairs and divine mediator, a fully ambivalent 'mezzano.' This chiastic structure of Boccaccio's cosmos has the effect of exalting mortals even as it degrades gods. However, the world of the *Decameron* is in no sense a simple travesty, a carnivalesque inversion of an established order. It describes a new order, one in which the usual vertical stratification (political, social, and metaphysical) is collapsed into a single stratum. It is a landscape characterized by biological, moral, semantic – even onto-logical – hybridity. It is no wonder that the days held sacred by the *brigata* members are Friday – in honour of Christ's Passion – and Saturday – in honour of the Virgin Mary (II, concl., 5–6); Christ epitomizes the perfect hybridization of human and divine, and Mary the living medium for this unique synthesis.

By stressing the semantic instability of traditional exempla, Boccaccio proves that exempla have no inherent, immutable meaning, but can be converted to whatever end one desires. They are semantic vessels that authors and readers invest with meaning.[37] Even the soundest doctrine can be skewed to serve corrupt ends. As Cicero's Cotta observes (citing Aristo of Chio's favourite saying), 'philosophers are harmful to their hearers when the hearers put a bad interpretation on doctrines good in themselves' (*De natura deorum* III 31, 77).[38] In the *Decameron* Epilogue, Boccaccio expresses a similar opinion with regard to his *novelle* by assert-ing that their healthful or harmful effects are not intrinsic, but deter-mined by their hearers: 'Le quali [the *novelle*], chenti che elle si sieno, e nuocere e giovar possono, sì come possono tutte l'altre cose, avendo riguardo all'ascoltatore' ['stories, whatever their nature, may be harmful or useful, depending upon the listener'] (Epilogue, 8; McWilliam, 799).

Although this observation is by no means free of the polemical and flip-pant tone characteristic of the Epilogue as a whole, and no one, least of all Boccaccio, would deny fiction's ability to exercise a commanding influence on its readers, it is equally certain that for Boccaccio, it is the reader alone who is finally accountable both for interpreting fiction and for acting upon its suggestions.[39] Among the *brigata*'s central functions is that of dramatizing the production and consumption of literary fictions in order to remind us that though rhetoric may persuade, it does not coerce. By using the sobriquet 'Prencipe Galeotto,' Boccaccio invokes

Francesca's famous crimination of the book in *Inferno* V: a model of reading that serves as a foil for the *brigata*'s more self-conscious, critical way of reading. Francesca's declaration that one point alone defeated her and her lover Paolo, 'un punto fu quel che ci vinse' (*Inf.* V, 132), a variety of semantic determinism, must be contrasted with Boccaccio's poetics, one in which the single point is studiously polysemic – one need only consider the numerous meanings conveyed by the word 'testo' in the story of Lisabetta (IV, 5). By insisting upon a plurality of meanings, Boccaccio brings both choice and moral accountability to the fore. Having relinquished the gift of free will that they abused in life, Dante's damned find their wills forcefully aligned with the divine will (thus producing the dreadful paradox of souls who thirst for punishment). Conversely, Dante's saved freely unite their wills with the divine will. Only the shades of purgatory, those whose condition most clearly parallels that of mortals, continue to struggle with choice, and it should not, therefore, surprise us that it is the poetics of purgatory, of semantic ambiguity and choice, that Boccaccio's own poetics, a poetics of life, most closely resembles.

The *brigata*'s success in fleeing the erotic allurements of the *novelle* and seeking virtue is nothing less than a vindication of fiction itself, proof that texts neither create their readers nor determine their actions. Though Francesca blamed the book, it was she herself who was to blame. The polysemic nature of Boccaccio's *novelle* introduces an interesting conundrum: if no fixed, 'correct,' interpretation can be ascribed to any of the tales, in what sense can they be said to be meaningful? Meaning, it would seem, is not an intrinsic property of the *novelle* but is generated by each individual reader's communion with a given text. Boccaccio's fictions do not shape their readers but, to the contrary, serve as the ideal medium with which to reveal the readers' 'shape.'

It is in this sense that the novella provides the key for the *brigata*'s gradual, methodical recuperation of virtue. The world incrementally constructed through the layering of *novelle* is, finally, a speculum, or mirror, in which the members of the *brigata* gradually come to know themselves.[40] Whereas Livy's polished monument reflects the overarching patterns of a public history, the *Decameron* is a speculum that seeks to penetrate and disclose the hidden particularities of a private, internal history. Whereas Livy presents his history as one inscribed for all time in the neat glyphs of his 'inlustri ... monumento,' a static, monumental 'mirror' (in *Naturales quaestiones* I 17, 5, Seneca notes that polished stone – 'leve saxum' – functions as a mirror), Boccaccio's history, his novelistic archive of human experience, is traced in the ever-fluctuating stuff of life, in 'color d'erba': a literary garden, and a mirror of the soul.

The idea of the collection of *novelle* as a literary 'garden' is ancient. Florilegia, anthologies of literary 'flowers' plucked from their original volumes and gathered together in a single volume, enjoyed a tremendous vogue throughout the late classical period and the Middle Ages. As is well known, it is from one such florilegium, the *Novellino*, that Boccaccio draws material for a number of his tales in the *Decameron*. Interestingly, the *Novellino's* declared objective is that of presenting the notable words and deeds of noble and courtly people as a mirror for the less cultured – 'uno specchio appo i minori': a handbook of social etiquette.[41]

Like the *Novellino*, the *Decameron* is figured as a literary garden, and like the *Novellino* garden, in which the narrative 'flowers' ['belli fiori'] do not exist in splendid isolation but are found jumbled up among less beautiful words ('mischiati intra molte altre parole' [*Novella* 1]) the *Decameron* garden is 'marred' by the odd weed (Boccaccio notes that 'niun campo fu mai si ben coltivato, che in esso o ortica o triboli o alcun pruno non si trovasse mescolato tra l'erbe migliori' ['No field was ever so carefully tended that neither nettles nor brambles nor thistles were found in it, along with all the better grass' (Epilogue, 18; McWilliam, 800)]).[42] However, here the similarities between the *Novellino* and the *Decameron* end, for whereas the garden/mirror of the *Novellino* is a prescriptive guide for social conduct, the garden/mirror of the *Decameron* is not constructed with a normative, but with a transformative end in mind. By holding up a mirror to its readers, Boccaccio's text provides a conduit to self-knowledge and its corollary, virtue. In short, it is a text that promises a moral conversion from vice to virtue – one dramatized by the circular journey of the *brigata* itself.

Those readers who, quite rightly, are prompted to object that the relation between self-knowledge and ethical behaviour is not self-evident should bear in mind that in Boccaccio's view, the original state of each individual is one of innocence; we lose sight of this essential, innate self as we progress through life, trading – to use Boccaccio's colourful metaphor once again – our first wife, 'innocence,' for a second, corrupt, wife (*Genealogie* IV, 59). The acquisition of knowledge of the true, essential self implies a restoration of this initial marriage to innocence. Moreover, as exposure to historical accounts or hypothetical stories (plausible fictions) concerning the 'habits and words' [mores et verba] of a wide variety of men and women in the works of such 'honest' writers of comedy as Plautus and Terence has, according to Boccaccio, an ethical impact insofar as such stories both instruct and admonish their readers ('et interim lectores docere et cautos facere' [*Genealogie* XIV 9, 7]), the *Decameron novelle*, a virtually encyclopedic record of the 'mores et verba' of the most historically, culturally, socially, and ethnically heterogeneous assembly of people imaginable, seems to have been expressly designed to galvanize the ethical consciousness of its readers. This proposition that an ostensibly immoral tale – whether the obscene play of a Plautus or Terence, or a lewd tale in the *Decameron* – can provide ethical instruction will no doubt strike many readers as a bit of casuistry worthy of Boccaccio's Cepparello or Frate Alberto. Such conclusions, though natural enough, may well be based on a misunderstanding of the weird alchemy whereby erotic dross is transmuted into ethical gold. Indeed, Boccaccio's argument is premised on the conviction that we are essentially good and that our unethical behaviour stems less from concerted malice than from ignorance. By providing readers with a means of vicariously experiencing alternate emotions, circumstances, and modes of existence, fiction dilates their understanding of the human experience, heightening their awareness of the wider social repercussions and ethical implications of their actions.

Observing that the (supposed) 'immorality of poetry rests upon a misconception of the manner in which poetry acts to produce the moral improvement of man,' Shelley – in the *Defence of Poetry*, a work that owes much (if, most probably, indirectly) to books XIV and XV of Boccaccio's *Genealogie* – argues that poetry 'awakens and enlarges the mind itself by rendering it the receptacle of a thousand unapprehended combinations of thought,' observing that 'a man, to be greatly good, must imagine intensely and comprehensively; he must put himself in the place of another and of many others; the pains and pleasure of his species must become his own.' Indeed, 'the great instrument of moral good is the imagination; and poetry administers to the effect by acting upon the cause.' 'Poetry,' Shelley concludes, 'strengthens the faculty which is the organ of the moral nature of man, in the same manner as exercise strengthens a limb. A poet therefore would do ill to embody his own conceptions of right and wrong, which are usually those of his place and time, in his poetical creations, which participate in neither.'[43]

Like a mirror, the composite formed of the *Decameron novelle* reflects, but does not create, image; it is descriptive, not prescriptive. Boccaccio does not make the mistake of attempting to 'embody his own conceptions of right and wrong' in his 'poetical creations' (thereby vitiating their eternal relevance by binding them in the temporal and spatial fetters of historical circumstance) but forces readers to exercise and expand their individual imaginations, thereby honing their capacity for moral judgment. The story of Ser Cepparello that inaugurates the work serves to introduce this central tenet. How each of us chooses to resolve the vexed question of whether Cepparello ends up in heaven or hell has absolutely no effect on Cepparello's metaphysical destiny. What matters is that by introducing such ambiguity Boccaccio's story engages our own critical response in a way that cannot help but reveal something about us – perhaps even suggesting whether we ourselves are headed towards heaven or hell. By so often including the reaction of the *brigata* members to the various stories, Boccaccio is not so much directing our own critical response as he is illustrating the central paradox that readers are themselves 'interpreted' by how they chose to interpret what they read (or hear).

When the *brigata* members return to Florence at the end of their fourteen-day sojourn, it is not due to some naive belief that the plague has dissipated and the coast is clear. To the contrary, it is knowledge, not ignorance, that underwrites their return. Is it fair, then, to conclude that the self-knowledge gleaned by staring into the *Decameron* 'mirror' has conferred some sort of immunity on the *brigata* members, that the *Decameron* is not simply a *remedium amoris* (its declared function) but is in some sense a *remedium mortis*? In attempting to resolve this question, it is useful to consider a more traditional example of the 'remedy' genre: Petrarch's stodgy *De remediis utriusque fortune*. In the preface (210) Petrarch informs the reader:

> in its text you might behold your mind as in a looking glass. Yet should you encounter anything lacking in refinement, anything that offends your taste, reshape and adjust it, so as to avoid being overpowered when hereafter your Fortune varies in familiar or in unaccustomed ways, of which she possesses an inexhaustible store – that being prepared for anything, ready for everything, you may despise the sweet as well as the bitter, and counter both most confidently with this verse by Virgil:
>
> > No novel kinds of hardship, no surprises,
> > Loom ahead, Sister. I foresaw them all.
> > Went through them in my mind.[44]

Here, the notion of text-as-mirror that is implicit in the *Decameron* is made explicit. The great benefit that accrues to the individual through self-knowledge is not so much an enhanced ability to determine external events but the ability to confront the inevitable with relative equanimity (by virtue of a psychological preparation). Boccaccio's *remedium*, like

Boccaccio himself, has none of the air of cold, philosophical detachment so pervasive in Petrarch. Impassivity of the sort espoused by Petrarch is not viewed as a triumph of the intellect so much as a failure of the heart – of the distinctively human trait of compassion. In the Introduction Boccaccio wryly observes that the radical and sudden losses caused by the plague had the effect of transforming simpletons to philosophers by endowing them, in a matter of days, with a stoic equanimity that daily tribulations had been unable to teach the wise: 'assai manifestamente apparve che quello che il naturale corso delle cose non avea potuto con piccoli e radi danni a' savi mostrare doversi con pazienza passare, la grandezza de' mali eziandio i semplici far di ciò scorti e non curanti' (I, Intro., 41). On the face of it, this would seem to be a positive development. However – and this is what distinguishes Boccaccio's perspective from that of the philosophers – though patience may indeed be a virtue, abject impassivity is not. Indeed, Boccaccio's outrage upon being labelled 'Iohannem tranquillitatum' (*Epistole* IX, 2) by Niccolò Acciaiuoli – an epithet deliberately calculated to provoke the thin-skinned Boccaccio by implying that he was indifferent to his friends' misfortunes – clearly indicates his abhorrence for all that might be construed as an emotional stinginess or complacence. This accusation, Boccaccio asserts, is more fittingly leveled at Niccolò himself, who, upon hearing that his son Lorenzo had died not only displayed no emotion but, addressing himself to the princes and barons who had gathered to mourn, treated them to a prolix and studied discourse on the senselessness of concerning oneself with the dead! (*Epistole* IX, 25). Boccaccio's 'remedium' is grounded not in impassivity but in compassion, not in the hypocritical morality of the anchorites or isolationists who remain 'pure' because they remain separate but in the genuine virtue of those rare individuals whose moral mettle is tested and proved in the crucible of life.

In *De vulgari eloquentia* II 2, 8 Dante argues that since human beings are compounded from vegetable, animal, and rational components they are destined to follow a threefold path; the vegetative component seeks self-preservation, the animal component, love, and the rational, virtue. This sequence is remarkably similar to that reproduced in the *Decameron*, which likewise begins with the urgency of self-preservation, continues with the intellectual and sensual pleasures of storytelling and culminates in the virtuous return, one that is predicated on a new understanding of the nature of self-preservation – as a spiritual in lieu of a physical salvation. If, as Pampinea argues, 'naturale ragione' [natural right] confers upon all who are born the licence to take whatever measures are necessary to preserve their lives (I, Intro., 53), then it is clearly not 'naturale ragione' that induces the *brigata* to return. Apparently, 'naturale ragione' with its credo of *sauve qui peut* has been supplanted by a different type of 'ragione,' one tutored not by fear but by knowledge and its correlate, virtue. As Boccaccio observes with epigrammatic concision in *De casibus*: 'Se ipsum noscere virtutis exitus et initium est' [to know oneself is the beginning and end of virtue] (V 18, 10).[45]

Boccaccio is not simply preaching a gospel of knowledge in the interest of self-preservation at all cost. Indeed, as Alain and Jean had already established, even the most intimate self-knowledge provides no surety against the possibility of catastrophe or the certainty of death, no guarantee of self-preservation. No doubt the greatest value of knowledge is that it equips us with a means of pursuing virtue, and it is virtue alone that confers true immunity upon its practitioners. In the eighth book of *De casibus* Boccaccio loosely quotes a passage from Cicero's *De officiis* (I 66): 'Virtue does not allow itself to be taken, it knows not the dishonour of subjection, it deems a succumbing to Fortune as the most dismal of destinies; it thinks up novel and showy means of death' (*De casibus* VIII 4, 18) – if, Boccaccio adds parenthetically, it is proper to say that one who has extinguished his life in such a way has actually perished ('si quisquam interit qui sic extinguitur').[46] Suicide, the ultimate act of self-determination in the classical world, is, in a sense, the ultimate remedy – provided that it is motivated by virtue. Just as the pusillanimous forsake life by living under death's shadow, the magnanimous embrace life by disdaining death – a point concretized in the *Commedia*, where the pusillanimous are described as 'sciaurati, che mai non fur vivi' ['wretched ones, who never were alive'] (*Inf.* III, 64; Mandelbaum) and Cato, the great-hearted suicide, is not only saved but granted custodianship of the portal to salvation itself, the island of purgatory.

It is for this reason that the *brigata's* journey begins with a concern for physical self-preservation and ends with a full liberation from such concerns. In the raking light of true knowledge is revealed the moral truth that true 'life' is commensurate to virtue, and true 'death' to vice. The desire for self-preservation has not changed. What has shifted is the understanding of what constitutes the self (a moral, not a physical entity), and preservation (a spiritual rather than a physical permanence). Thus it is that in the Introduction of Day IX, we are told that anybody who encountered the members of the *brigata* – festooned with garlands and bearing flowers – would have been forced to conclude : 'O costor non saranno dalla morte vinti o ella gli ucciderà lieti' ['Either these people will not be vanquished by death, or they will welcome it with joy'] (4–5; McWilliam, 648).[47] A scant eight days of storytelling have succeeded in releasing the members of the *brigata* from Fortune's thrall. The distilled knowledge contained in the *novelle* has furnished them with a means of avoiding those calamities that are evitable and embracing those afflictions that are inevitable (not just with a stoic equanimity, but with a sense of joy). This rhetoric of embracing death joyfully has all the earmarks of a tale of martyrdom. Though philosophical detachment may supply its adherents with the fortitude to accept death with equanimity, the active pursuit of virtue provides something better by far: a joyful extinction – a final victory that is, paradoxically, secured by defeat.[48]

If the *brigata*'s departure is fuelled by the natural desire for self-preservation, their return is effected under the aegis of virtue. For the myopic belief that life is merely the state of being alive is substituted the comforting certainty that life is synonymous with virtue and therefore independent of the caprices of fortune and immune to death. The educative qualities of the *brigata*'s sojourn have effected what amounts to a complete conversion. The physical circularity of the journey documents the internal, philosophical conversion that has gradually taken place in the course of their retreat.[49] Though Florence and the circumstances of the plague have not changed, the members of the *brigata* have. Converted to virtue, the prevalence of 'disonesti essempli' no longer represents a danger to them but rather the opportunity – indeed, the moral imperative – to disseminate their own, virtuous 'essempli.'

Notes

Introduction

1 Singleton asserts that the art of the *Decameron* 'neither illustrated nor proved an idea'; 'On Meaning in the *Decameron*,' *Italica* 21, 3 (Sept., 1944): 121. While he does concede that the frame contains a meaning that goes beyond the literal, Singleton insists that this 'meaning' consists in its function as a 'strategy to protect and justify an art' (122).

2 See Beatrice Corrigan, *Italian Poets and English Critics, 1755–1859* (Chicago: University of Chicago Press, 1969), 67, for Coleridge's jaundiced view of the *Decameron* and its literary legacy. Note, however, that Coleridge – and this is hardly surprising – did appreciate Boccaccio's vernacular romances, which he admired for their psychological acuity and the 'wild and imaginative character of the situations' (66).

3 See *Rime* CVIII, 1–11 and the Introduction to the *Vita di Dante* for other examples of this modesty *topos*.

4 This etiology of wall-eyed individuals is found in *Esposizioni* VII, lit., 33.

5 C.S. Lewis, *The Allegory of Love* (New York: Oxford University Press, 1968), 11.

6 'una trascrizione in cui la tessitura metrica è solo lievemente trasgredita con qualche mutamento nell'ordine delle parole' (*Tutte le opere*, vol. 5, t. II, 1122n46).

7 Among the more striking and better-studied examples of this phenomenon are the Nastagio degli Onesti story of *Dec.* V, 8 (with close analogues in Vincent of Beauvais's *Speculum historiale* and Iacopo Passavanti's *Specchio della vera penitenza*), the 'incomplete' story of Filippo Balducci of *Dec.* Intro. IV (based – if through intermediate sources – on John of Damascus's 'Barlaam and Josaphat' apologue), and the two tales – *Dec.* V, 10 and *Dec.* VII, 2 – taken from Apuleius's *Golden Ass*.

8 In a move that gives the lie to the enduring myth of his passive compliancy in the face of authority (one, as has been noted, promoted by Boccaccio himself), Boccaccio not only omits any reference to Dante's presumably 'definitive' account in the *Commedia* in both *Genealogie* VII, 51 and *De mulieribus* XXX, but also concludes his discussion of Manto in the *Genealogie* with a question designed to simultaneously invoke and negate Dante's bold assertion in *Commedia*: 'who would hesitate to believe the account of such a famous poet [Virgil] with regard to the origin of his own city?' (VII 51, 3). Only readers unfamiliar with the *Commedia* could fail to see that this 'who' is none other than Dante. Boccaccio's objective, however, is not so much to present a definitive version as it is to dismantle Dante's pretensions of providing a definitive version. In short, his reverence for Dante does not prevent him from finding fault with many of Dante's conclusions. Boccaccio's curious comment about Briareus in *Genealogie* IV, 18 (to wit, that Briareus is not in Dite, but elsewhere in hell, reserved by God for future conflicts) has a similar effect – that of casting doubt on the truth claims of Dante's fiction. Other examples of this polemical undercurrent abound.

9 George Eliot, epigraph from chap. 27 of *Middlemarch*. That Eliot had more than a passing interest in Boccaccio is confirmed by her decision to write an adaptation of *Decameron* X, 7, 'How Lisa Loved the King.'

10 Simone Marchesi (*Stratigrafie decameroniane* [Florence: Olschki, 2004], chap. 3) has addressed this fascinating question of dream interpretation in Boccaccio's *Decameron*, proposing that there are important parallels between oneirocritics and hermeneutics, and concluding that the interpretative challenge does not consist in establishing the truth or falsity of a dream, but in interpreting it in accordance with ethics – a principle whose pertinence, he convincingly argues, is not restricted to dreams, but constitutes a more general 'ethic of interpretation.'

11 Boccaccio acknowledges his debt to these authors and defends his use of them in *Genealogie* XV, 6. For Theodontius, see Attilio Hortis, *Studj sulle opere latine del Boccaccio* (Tricote: Julius Dase, 1879), 464–8.

12 Charles G. Osgood, *Boccaccio on Poetry* (New York: Bobbs-Merrill, 1930), xxix.

Chapter 1. Universal Myths of Origin

1 *Giovanni Boccaccio: Eclogues*, trans. Janet Levarie Smarr (New York: Garland, 1987).

2 The theme of Robert's death had already been treated in eclogue form by Petrarch in 'Argus,' the second eclogue of the *Bucolicum carmen*. That Boccaccio was thoroughly familiar with this particular eclogue is proven by a partial

transcription of 'Argus' preserved in his Zibaldone Laurenziano XXIX, 8. Though here, too, we find the political allegory of a falling forest, Petrarch is concerned less with the decadence of the Angevin monarchy in the wake of Robert's death than with the commemoration of Robert, 'Argus.' While Petrarch idealizes the figure of Robert he never explicity identifies him with Saturn, or his reign with the Golden Age. Though the identification of Boccaccio's Tytirus with Robert is, finally, conjectural (it is not among the matters elucidated by Boccaccio in his letter to Fra Martino da Signa [*Epistole* XXIII]), such an identification is supported by Boccaccio's similar treatment of Robert in several other works and is the interpretation most often submitted by scholars. Note, however, that Robert is not always glorified in Boccaccio's works (see, for example *Comedia delle ninfe* XXXV, 32ff; *Amorosa visione* XIV, 22ff) nor is Giovanna always censured (see, for instance, Boccaccio's glowing portrait of Giovanna in *De mulieribus* CVI). In using the bucolic genre as a vehicle to communicate political and personal matters through pastoral allegories, Boccaccio was emulating what he took to be Virgil's method in the *Eclogues* (see *Epistole* XXIII, 1 and *Genealogie* XIV, 2). In the first century AD, Calpurnius Siculus, the first poet to make explicit use of an allegorical method in the bucolic genre, exploits the political dimension of the Golden Age theme through a political allegory celebrating Nero's enlightened reign (that is, before the madcap antics of his later years). That Boccaccio chose to continue this tradition in his fifth *Eclogue* is perhaps not coincidental; it was, after all, through Boccaccio's transcription of Calpurnius's *Eclogues* that Calpurnius's text was popularized among the Tuscan humanists (Branca directs the reader to the relevant articles in his *Boccaccio Medievale* [8th ed.], 282). Boccaccio offers a brief history of the bucolic genre in the beginning of a letter to Fra Martino da Signa (*Epistole* XXIII), the same letter that provides so many valuable glosses on Boccaccio's own eclogues. See chap. 1 of Attilio Hortis, *Studj sulle opere latine del Boccaccio* (Tricote: Julius Dase, 1879), who draws upon his vast erudition to piece together the personal and political events hidden beneath the allegories of Boccaccio's sixteen eclogues; Francesco Torraca, *Per la biografia di Giovanni Boccaccio* (Milan: Albrighi, Segati e C., 1912), 153–93; Giorgio Padoan, *Il Boccaccio, le Muse, il Parnaso e l'Arno* (Florence: Olschki, 1978), 151–98, who discusses Boccaccio's important role in the rebirth of the pastoral genre; Francesco Bruni, *L'invenzione della letteratura mezzana* (Bologna: Il Mulino, 1990), 410–13; and the introduction of Janet Smarr's translation, *Giovanni Boccaccio: Eclogues* (New York: Garland, 1987). For Boccaccio's technique of using fictional surrogates to describe real events in his prose works, see *Fiammetta* I 23, 5ff and the Dedication of the *Teseida* (*Tutte le opere*, vol. 2, 246).

3 This is not to say that Boccaccio is above such applications of the Golden Age motif. Indeed, in his letter to Iacopo Pizzinga (*Epistole* XIX) he quotes Virgil's fourth *Eclogue* with a specifically encomiastic intent (38). However, Boccaccio's fifth *Eclogue* is not an encomium of Robert so much as an elegiac evocation of a paradise lost. As he writes to Fra Martino da Signa in *Epistole* XXIII: 'Quinte egloge titulus est *Silva cadens*, eo quod in ea tractetur de diminutione et quodammodo casu civitatis neapolitane post fugam Lodovici predicti regis' [The title of the fifth *Eclogue* is *The Falling Forest*, for it treats the theme of decadence and, in a way, the fall of the city of Naples after the flight of the previously mentioned King Lodovico] (9).

4 For a more elaborate picture of Boccaccio's Neapolitan education, see Vittore Branca, *Giovanni Boccaccio: Profilo biografico* (Florence: Sansoni, 1977), chaps. 1–4; Thomas Goddard Bergin, *Boccaccio* (New York: Viking, 1981), chap. 1; Padoan, *Il Boccaccio*, chap. 1; Francesco Sabatini, *Napoli Angioina cultura e società* (Cava dei Tirreni: Edizioni scientifiche italiane, 1975), 103–15; Vincenzo Crescini, *Contributo agli studi sul Boccaccio con documenti inediti* (Turin: Ermanno Loescher, 1887), 107ff.

5 In general, Boccaccio stresses the contrast between Florentine disunity and Neapolitan unity; the former, a model of infernal multiplicity, the latter of divine simplicity. Another eulogy to Naples is found in *Fiammetta* V 27, 1. For additional examples, see *Decameron* (III 6, 4); *Epistole* II; and *Comedia delle ninfe* XXXV, 22. Harsh judgments of Florence – often revealing a Dantean pedigree – abound in Boccaccio's work. See, for example, *Epistole* V, 6 and XXIII, 18; *Decameron* III 3, 5; and *Consolatorio a Pino de' Rossi*, 37ff.

6 Though this strategy of situating a spiritual, moral drama on a historical proscenium – sacred history – is a widespread medieval convention, the historical dimension in such schemes is usually subordinated to the spiritual element; for instance, the individual identities of Babylon, Sardanapolis, and Carthage are lost in a generic pastiche of moral decadence. What distinguishes Boccaccio's application of this strategy is the palpable historicity of his moral exempla; an almost perfect balance is achieved between the ideal, exemplary dimension, and the real, historical dimension. Naples is cast as the historical realization of a mythological, metaphysical ideal. Indeed, a similar conflation of moral and historical valences undergirds the whole of the *Decameron*, where a plague-ridden Florence and a pastoral Fiesole fulfill an important symbolic function as the opposed poles of a moral spectrum without, however, losing their historical identity.

7 For a more conventional perspective on Original Sin, see *Esposizioni* IV, alleg., 2ff.

8 The sensualist 'shepherd' Acaten in the *Comedia delle ninfe fiorentine* repre-

sents this facet of Boccaccio in his response to the ascetic 'shepherd' Alcesto: 'quand'io vorrò, da cui mi fia interdetto / il su salire al monte' [when I should wish it, by whom would my ascent of the mountain be forbidden] (XIV, 106–7). As Timothy Kircher notes in *The Poet's Wisdom* (Leiden: Brill, 2006), 'For the Trecento humanists the overwhelming fact of the temporal, historical existence need not divert one's quest for the divine; on the contrary, from the opposition between earthly and spiritual desire a dialectic emerges, which more precisely delineates the contours of both realms, human and divine' (18).

9 For a vigorous repudiation of the 'conversion theory,' see Padoan's *Il Boccaccio*, 88.

10 This is one of the pernicious fallacies that Kurt Flasch investigates in the last chapter of his *Giovanni Boccaccio, Poesie nach der Pest: Der Anfang des 'Decameron'* (available in an Italian translation: *Poesia dopo la peste: Saggio su Boccaccio*).

11 Joan Ferrante, 'The Frame Characters of the *Decameron*: A Progression of Virtues,' *Romance Philology* 19 (1965): 212–26.

12 No doubt Boccaccio's emphasis on the uniqueness of the heifer was influenced by Ovid's insistence, in *Ars amatoria* I, 289ff., on the uniqueness of the bull – for he alone of all the herd incited Pasiphae's lust. Other good examples of this principle of erotic discrimination are found in *Filocolo* I 2, 5 and II 48, 10.

13 In Hesiod's account the first three races are Gold, Silver, and Bronze; the fourth is a race of Heroes, and the fifth of Iron. The race of Gold is identified with the reign of Kronos, whose subjects enjoy a perfectly serene life marked by a succession of festivals and feasts and rounded out by sleep and a painless death, whereas the fifth and last race, that of Iron, represents the most degraded age. A useful and far-ranging treatment of this motif can be found in Arthur Lovejoy and George Boas's seminal *Primitivism and Related Ideas in Antiquity* (New York: Octagon, 1965). For a general survey of the Golden Age theme in Italian literature, see Gustavo Costa, *La leggenda dei secoli d'oro nella letteratura Italiana* (Bari: Laterza, 1972). In *The Myth of the Golden Age in the Renaissance* (Bloomington: Indiana University Press, 1969), Harry Levin devotes little attention to the period that concerns me, and indeed goes so far as to claim that 'the myth had no great currency in the Middle Ages' (Preface, xx). Though we inevitably cover some of the same ground, our emphases are very different; whereas I am primarily concerned with the way this epochal scheme culminating in abject corruption serves as a prelude to regeneration, Levin is more interested in examining the topos as a testament to the eternal myth of original blessedness (and historical belatedness).

14 Though Boccaccio's use of Ovid's and Virgil's models is evident in most of his

works, his application of the others is less obvious. We know that Boccaccio was familiar with Boethius's and Juvenal's versions for he cites both in his *Esposizioni* (VII, alleg., 51 for Boethius; XIV, lit., 61 for Juvenal). Boccaccio's familiarity with Horace's *Epodes* is, at best, dubious, but he cites from the *Satires* frequently and was no doubt familiar with the Lucretian account of cultural evolution in *Satires* I 3, 96ff. While the love poet Tibullus, a contemporary of Virgil, and the pastoral poet Calpurnius (first century AD) both present Golden Age schemes – the former in the third *Elegy* of his first book (ll.36ff) and the latter in his first *Bucolic* (ll.33ff) – Tibullus was probably not known to Boccaccio (see note 2 for Calpurnius). However, as Petrarch does make occasional references to Tibullus (see, for example, *De remediis* I 69, 132) with which he was most likely familiar through a florilegium (see L.D. Reynolds, ed., *Texts and Transmission: A Survey of the Latin Classics*, [Oxford: Clarendon Press, 1983], 423), it is at least possible that Boccaccio knew of Tibullus through Petrarch. (Tibullus is also mentioned by Jean de Meun in the *Roman de la Rose*, line 10, 512.) Boccaccio's use of Seneca's description of the Golden Age in the *Phaedra* is discussed at the end of this chapter.

15 Interestingly, it is in his description of this partial restoration of the original Golden Age that Hesiod first mentions the abundance of acorns and honey – two food sources that become a staple of subsequent golden age descriptions. Hesiod does not identify the foods consumed in the original Golden Age feasting.

16 Elements of Hesiod's original scheme would have been available to Boccaccio through such intermediary sources as Servius's commentary on the *Aeneid*. See, for example, *In Virgilii carmina commentari* VIII, 326, where Servius alludes to the Hesiodic ages of metal.

17 While this view of law as a precondition for political stability dominates the Golden Age model proposed in *Aeneid* VIII, it is a view somewhat discomfited by Latinus's words to Aeneas and his fellow Teucrians in *Aeneid* VII, 192ff, where Latinus boasts that the Latins, descended from Saturn, embrace the righteous way of their own free will, without the constraint of legal edicts: 'Latinos / Saturni gentem, haud vinclo nec legibus aequam, / sponte sua veterisque dei se more tenentem' (VII, 202–4).

18 This euhemeristic view – the belief that what we call 'Gods' are actually exceptional individuals whose cultural, political and other contributions have garnered them a place in the heavens – is described with particular clarity in Cicero's *De natura deorum* II, 23ff. and Isidore's *Etymologies* VIII.xi.1ff.: 'Those who the pagans assert are gods are revealed to have once been humans, and after their death they began to be worshipped among their people because of the life and merit of each of them' (trans. Barney et al.). For a

history of the various metamorphoses undergone by the pagan gods throughout the course of the Middle Ages and Renaissance, see Jean Seznec's seminal
study, *The Survival of the Pagan Gods* (Princeton: Princeton University Press,
1972).

19 Harry Levin (*Myth of the Golden Age*, 16–17) sees this shift from a retrospective
to a prospective model as Virgil's contribution to the myth.

20 Nor has the present age dispensed with this cultural habit; we have simply
shifted the terms from Saturn and Saturnia to Arthur and Camelot.

21 The fourth Hesiodic race, the relatively august race of Heroes, is obviously a
stumbling block for those wishing to moralize the Hesiodic scheme through
a neat correlation of the chronological decadence with the successive stages
of a moral decline. So long as the Bronze race, one marked by the constant
warring of its belligerent men, cedes to a race of righteous, heroic demigods,
it is impossible to see even a convincing causal relation between the two ages,
let alone invest this causality with a moral dimension. By excising this anomaly from the sequence of ages, not only is the causal relationship among the
ages enhanced, but the way is opened for a full-fledged moralization of the
scheme. This, of course, is precisely what Ovid achieves by presenting an
abbreviated four-age scheme. Though this abbreviation and moralization of
the Hesiodic scheme had already been undertaken by the third-century BC
poet Aratus (whose moralization of the scheme in his *Phaenomena* is dramatized by the device of having the ministrations of a personified Justice dimin-
ish with each new race) in a passage available to Boccaccio through Cicero's
translation in *De natura deorum* 2, 41, it seems to be primarily through Ovid
that this moralized version of the ages of humanity is communicated to the
Middle Ages. Strangely, although Boccaccio alludes frequently to Cicero's *De
natura deorum* in the *Genealogie*, he does not, to the best of my knowledge, cite
this particular passage. See Lovejoy and Boas, *Primitivism and Related Ideas*,
34–6 for a discussion of Aratus's moralization of Hesiod.

22 Ovid actually provides two different etiologies of human degeneration in the
Metamorphoses: the mythical account of Book I and the rationalistic account of
Book XV. Curiously, in both cases degeneration is associated with the consumption of meat. In the first book Ovid is concerned less with the moral
implications of eating meat than with the moral outrage of serving human
flesh to the gods – an act which is overtly blasphemous and metaphorically, if
not technically, cannibalistic. In Book XV Pythagoras proposes a scheme
according to which the Golden Age, an age of strict vegetarianism, is brought
to an end by gluttonous cravings that have rendered us, originally happy and
sinless, violent carnivores with an insatiable blood lust. Elements of both
these etiologies crop up with notable regularity in Boccaccio's accounts. In

the *Esposizioni*, for example, we find accounts reminiscent of Ovid's *Met.* I (*Esp.* VII, alleg., 45ff) and of *Met.* XV (*Esp.* VI, alleg.) Boccaccio's preoccupation with the role of cannibalism in primitive societies is also evident in his three euhemeristic accounts of Jupiter in the *Genealogie* (II, 2; V, 1; XI, 1).

23 Though this aspect of the moral dimension is not entirely absent in Hesiod – impiety accounts for the demise of the second, Silver, race – it is apparent that in Hesiod's model, such moral infractions do not alone account for the process of degeneration. (Indeed, as we have seen, the causal relations among the ages are, at best, nebulous.)

24 This is the method followed by Boccaccio in the *Allegoria mitologica*. For a more detailed discussion of this phenomenon, see A. Bartlett Giamatti, *The Earthly Paradise and the Renaissance Epic* (Princeton: Princeton University Press, 1966), chap. 1; Levin, *Myth of the Golden Age*, chap. 2. Remember, however, that whereas Hesiod's Golden Age was one of community and identity with divinity – 'both gods and men began the same' – in the Old Testament Eden, it was precisely the desire of the first parents to be godlike – the serpent promised Eve that by eating the apple she would become 'sicut dii' (Gen. 3.5) – that precipitated the Fall.

25 A concise overview of this strategy of ascribing a shadowy glimpse of Christian truths to the classical poets and philosophers so frequently employed by such Greek and Latin apologists as Clement, Origen, Tertullian, and Lactantius is provided in chapter 1 of Don Cameron Allen, *Mysteriously Meant: The Rediscovery of Pagan Symbolism and Allegorical Interpretation in the Renaissance* (Baltimore: Johns Hopkins Press, 1970). In *De canaria*, an ethnographic account of the exploration of the Canary Islands transcribed by Boccaccio in the Zibaldone Magliabechiano, is preserved evidence of the contemporary practice of such 'primitive' monotheism; the indigenous peoples worship in temples that are unadorned except for a single stone statue representing a naked man (whose genitals, however, are modestly covered with a palm frond) holding a staff in one hand (5).

26 For more on Lactantius and the Golden Age, see Giamatti, *Earthly Paradise*, chap 1; George Boas, *Primitivism and Related Ideas in the Middle Ages* (Baltimore: Johns Hopkins University Press, 1997), 33–41; Louis J. Swift, 'Lactantius and the Golden Age,' *American Journal of Philology* 89, 2 (1968): 129–56.

27 In Romans 7.9 Paul applies the historical model of a time before law to his own life by stating: 'I was once alive apart from the law.' The period before the law is one of innocence to sin and the period after law of redemption for sin, grace – law alone nourishes sin. Hugh of St Victor uses this tripartite model of history extensively in his two tracts on Noah's Ark. In the fifth chapter of *De arca Noe mystica* he writes of the division of the ark into three parts:

the first corresponding to a period of natural law from the beginning of time to the age of the Patriarchs; the second, to a period, bracketed by the patriarchal age and that of the Incarnation, regulated by positive law; the third, to a time of grace ranging from the Incarnation to the End-Time (*PL.* 176, cap.V, col.688B). Hugh cites several passages from Romans to support this scheme. Boccaccio discusses related issues of law and universal history in *Esposizioni* IV, alleg., 24ff.

28 Another North African, Fulgentius Planciades, furnishes a similar scheme in his *De aetatibus mundi et hominis*. Though the convention of parsing universal history into six discrete ages appears to be very widespread in later times, Bede's version in *De temporibus* chap. 16 (*PL* 90, col. 288), and Isidore's in his *Etymologiae* (V 38, 39; XI 2) and *Chronica* appear to have been particularly influential. (It is taken up again by Rabanus in *De universo* ('De sex aetatibus saeculi' *PL* 111, col. 307.) In the sixth book of Paul the Deacon's *History of the Lombards* – the same work that Branca believes influenced Boccaccio's description of the plague in the Introduction of the *Decameron* – can be found a similar description of the six ages (chap. 33). Brunetto Latini uses the scheme of the six ages in his account of sacred history in the first book of *Li livres dou tresor* (I, 20ff). For a brief discussion of this motif see Boas, *Primitivism and Related Ideas*, 177–85. The preoccupation with the number six (one already evident in Philo's works) reaches a sort of apogee in Augustine, who devotes chapter 30 of Book XI of *The City of God* to a discussion of the 'perfection' of the number six.

29 Philippe of Harveng's *De somnis Nabuchodonosor* can be found in the *PL* 203, col. 585–92. For Philippe's use of the Old Testament colossus of metals as a model for the Augustinian ages of the world, see Boas, *Primitivism and Related Ideas*, 181. For a discussion of Philippe's model in relation to Dante's 'Old Man of Crete' of *Inf.* XIV, see Anthony Cassell, *Dante's Fearful Art of Justice* (Toronto: University of Toronto Press, 1984), chap. 5 ('The *Gran Veglio*'). Richard of St Victor's *De eruditione hominis interioris libri tres, occasione accepta ex somnio Nabuchodonosor apud Danielem* (*PL* 196, col. 1229–1366), a tropological interpretation of Daniel's statue, provides an interesting contrast to Philippe's interpretation. A particularly innovative and rewarding approach to the enigma of the Veglio is to be found in Giuseppe Mazzotta, *Dante, Poet of the Desert: History and Allegory in the* Divine Comedy (Princeton: Princeton University Press, 1979), chap. 1.

30 Most early commentators agree that Dante's selection of Crete for the statue's 'pedestal' is due to the notion in Dante's time that Crete was at the very centre of the three main divisions of the known world: equidistant from Asia, Europe, and Africa. Crete was also considered to have been not only the

site of the original Kingdom of Saturn, but the birthplace of Jupiter and the womb of humanity – indeed, according to poetic tradition, the provenance of time itself (a possibility strengthened by the habit of conflating Cronos with Chronos [see, for example, *Genealogie* III, 23; *De natura deorum* II, 25] and, of course, with the etiological nature of the Golden Age itself). In his gloss to Canto XIV in the *Esposizioni*, Boccaccio refines this essence of 'centrality' by noting that as Crete is 'posta in mezzo il mare' [situated in the middle of the sea], it signifies, 'l'universale corpo di tutta la terra' [the universal body of the whole earth] and then goes on to point out the phonological similarity between 'terra' and 'creta,' which he adduces as further evidence that Crete denotes not only the Earth in a generic sense, but that particular earth of which God made human beings (XIV, alleg., 16). The island of Crete, then, comes to stand in a microcosmic fashion for both the Earth and the homonymous material out of which the human body is formed.

31 Though this observation is directed to Dante, Virgil, and Statius, it is, of course, to Virgil that these words are primarily addressed. Matelda's affectedly casual conjecture belies a bitter irony; had Virgil but known that Parnassus was a dream of Eden, he would have had the means of salvation. No mere cartographer's slip, this misidentification of Eden as Parnassus represents nothing less than the absolute difference between salvation and perdition. For more on Dante's view of the Golden Age, see Gustavo Costa, *La leggenda dei secoli d'oro nella letteratura Italiana* (Bari: Laterza, 1972), 4–15. Matelda's words are echoed by Olympia's description of Elysium in Boccaccio's fourteenth *Eclogue*.

32 As Boccaccio observes in *Esposizioni* XIV, the allusion to the reign of Saturn – like that of the golden head of the statue itself – is simply an allusion to the primitive purity of the First Parents in Eden.

33 See, for example, *De monarchia* I, 11: 'Moreover, the world is best ordered when justice is its greatest power. Thus Virgil, seeking to praise an age which seemed to be arising in his day, sang in his *Bucolics*: *Iam redit et Virgo, redeunt Saturnia regna* [Now the Virgin returns, now return the Kingdoms of Saturn; my translation]. By "Virgo" he meant justice, sometimes called "the starry." By "Saturnia regna" he meant the best ages, sometimes called "the golden." Justice has the greatest power under a unitary government; therefore the best order of the world demands world-government or empire' (*De monarchia* I, 11; trans. Herbert W. Schneider [Indianapolis: Bobbs-Merrill, 1984]).

34 The most recent version of the *Allegoria mitologica*, edited by Manlio Pastore Stocchi, is included, with facing Italian translation, in the fifth volume of the new Mondadori edition of the collected works of Boccaccio (Milan: Monda-

dori, 1994). An earlier version of the same text and translation is more widely accessible in *Studi sul Boccaccio* 19 (1990): 1–18.

35 In *Boccaccio* (New York: Viking, 1981), a highly readable and lucid introduction to Boccaccio's complete works, Thomas G. Bergin reiterates Branca's judgment, calling the *Allegoria* an 'Ovidian catalog overlaid with moralizing interpretations' and adds that it is of 'slight intrinsic merit' (66). I will refer frequently to the *Allegoria*, and hope to show that this judgment, though understandable (the *Allegoria* is irritatingly obscure), is undeserved. For example, Boccaccio's careful reworking of the Ovidian figures of Prometheus and Phaethon in the *Allegoria* does not, I would argue, suggest a 'confusa contaminazione' of myth and history, paganism and Christianity, so much as a programmatic attempt to redeem the figure of the transgressive culture-hero; the former, a prototypical transgressor, is sanctified through a typological affiliation with Christ, and the latter, infamous for wreaking devastation on the earth in his rash quest to prove himself Apollo's son, is recast as a culture-hero who sacrifices his life to bring enlightenment to his fellow humans. Boccaccio's 'reinvention' of these two figures will be discussed at length below.

36 Though Pastore Stocchi only indicates that this Prometheus is assigned a role analogous to that of Jove in *Met.* I, I would argue that the traditional conflation of the Golden Age with Eden together with the use of the periphrasis 'qui propriis manibus plasmaverat Prometheum' [who had shaped Prometheus with his own hands] (*Allegoria*, 9) for God support the additional identification of Prometheus with Adam. See *Filocolo* I 3, 2, where Boccaccio's use of Prometheus as a figure for Adam is less ambiguous. For a brief description of the Ovidian ages see *Comedia delle ninfe* XXIX, 28.

37 In the *Esposizioni*, Boccaccio locates the Golden Age neither in an antediluvial, nor, like Dante, in a prelapsarian, 'Eden,' but in a postdiluvial era of ascetic virtue: 'per molti secoli si nutricò e visse inocua l'umana generazione *dopo'l diluvio universale*, i cibi della quale furono le ghiandi' [for many centuries *after the Great Deluge*, human beings lived and nourished themselves innocently; their food was acorns] (*Esposizioni* VI, alleg., 4; emphasis mine).

38 'illius pietatis ineffabili gratia, qui propriis manibus plasmaverat Prometheum, via salutis omnibus est parata. Ipse enim aperiens suas delitias nobis concessit thesaurum cariorem et Saturnia regna restaurans Àstree virginis gladium reparavit' (*Allegoria mitologica*, 9).

39 In *Esposizioni* IV, lit., 30, Boccaccio discusses this Christological association of the fourth *Eclogue*. An almost identical use of the model of the fourth *Eclogue* to describe the Incarnation is found in Boccaccio's fourteenth *Eclogue*, 'Olympia,' where it is the irrefragable testimony of Boccaccio's dead daughter,

Violante, that confirms Christ's (here, 'Codrus's') restoration of the Golden
Age: 'We live eternal life by Codrus' merits / and by his power divine, who
recently, / sent down from heaven to a virgin's lap, / brought back the
Golden Age; who having suffered / the shepherds' shameful mocking, to a
cedar / affixed, then freely granted death a triumph' (91–5; Smarr, 161).

Augustine's depiction of the Athenian King Codrus as one who willingly
sacrifices his life to deliver his country from harm may be the basis for this
Codrus/Christ typology (*City of God* XVIII, 19). See also Valerius Maximus,
Factorum et dictorum memorabilium V, 6 ext. 1. In the *Chronicon*, Isidore notes:
'Codrus, Atheniensum rex, sponte se pro salute patriae hostibus offerens'
[Codrus, King of Athens, voluntarily giving himself up to the enemy for the
welfare of the fatherland] (*PL* 83, col. 1030A).

In the *Commedia*, Statius credits Virgil's fourth *Eclogue* with having illumi-
nated him concerning the nature of the true God and goes so far as to supply
a vernacular rendition of the critical passage: 'Secol si rinova; / torna giusti-
zia e primo tempo umano, / e progenïe scende da ciel nova' [The ages are
renewed; / justice and man's first time on earth return; / from Heaven a new
progeny descends] (*Purg.* XXII, 70–2; Mandelbaum).

40 From *Il Filocolo*, trans. Donald Cheney and Thomas G. Bergin (New York: Garland, 1985).

41 Additionally, Boccaccio follows the Christian/classical pastiche of ages with a
more specifically Judeo-Christian history of gluttony based on Scripture
(*Esposizioni* VI, alleg., 31–5). Elements of Chaucer's Golden Age references in
the 'Pardoner's Tale' (lines 170ff.) bear an uncanny resemblance to this passage in *Esposizioni* VI.

42 See *De casibus* III 17, 1ff for a Golden Age recollection with a similar
emphasis.

43 This echoes Dante's analogous assertion in *De vulgari eloquentia* I 2, 1: 'nam
eorum que sunt omnium soli homini datum est loqui cum solum sibi neces-
sarium fuit' ['for man alone among all existing things was given the capacity
for speech, since he alone needed it'] (Haller, 4). A similarly positive evaluation of speech – though not of overwrought speech – is found in Lucilius Bal-
bus's stoic disquisition on the gods in Cicero's *De natura deorum* II, 59.

44 Boccaccio presents similar arguments in *Esposizioni* IV lit., 190ff. and *Genealogie* XV, 1, 'Minus oportuna preciosa fore non numquam' [Unnecessary things
are sometimes precious], where he observes that Nature itself is by no means
free of such embellishments; since such natural features as hair, horns,
brightly coloured feathers and so forth are not, strictly speaking, necessary, it
follows that Nature has supplied these for purely ornamental ends (XV 1, 4).
See Vitruvius *De architectura* II 1, 6–7 for a comparable view of architectural

embellishment and the role of increasingly sophisticated craftsmanship in promoting a peaceful civilization. Like Boccaccio, Fulgentius (Planciades) views ornament as evidence of human advancement: 'first, there is given by nature that courage of soul which may serve for advancement, for no creature is taught that is not born capable of being taught; second, there is the learning which adorns nature as it advances, just like gold, for it is the nature of gold to be improved and become ornamental, and it advances to its perfect state through the workman's beating it out with his hammer' (*Expositio continentiae Virgilianae* 10; trans. *Fulgentius the Mythographer*, by Leslie George Whitbread [(Columbus: Ohio State University Press, 1971)]).

45 Citations of Seneca are from Richard M. Gummere's translation in the Loeb edition of Seneca's *Epistles* (Cambridge, MA: Harvard University Press, 1920). I find it somewhat perplexing that though Boccaccio cites Seneca's *Epistles* several times in the *Esposizioni* and twice in the *Genealogie* – and a volume containing all 124 letters is listed in the inventory of the 'Parva libreria' (see Antonia Mazza, 'L'inventario della "Parva libreria," "Parva Libreria" di Santo Spirito e la biblioteca del Boccaccio,' *Italia medioevale e umanistica* 9 [1966]: 16) – his citations are taken almost exclusively from the first sixty or so letters (the exception is a reference to *Epistle* 107 in *Genealogie* I 5, 2) and he never, to my knowledge, directly cites letter XC despite his keen interest in the Golden Age topos. This enigma is partially resolved by Aldo Maria Costantini's hypothesis that a complete copy of Seneca's letters was not available to Boccaccio until he was editing his last work, the *Esposizioni*, between the fall of 1373 and the spring of 1374; see Costantini, 'Studi sullo Zibaldone Magliabechiano. II. Il florilegio senechiano,' *Studi sul Boccaccio* 8 (1975): 84–6. Although this certainly helps to account for the nearly complete absence of references to Seneca's *Epistles* in Boccaccio's other works, I nevertheless find it strange that Boccaccio does not make greater use of *Epistle* XC in his various excurses on the Golden Age in the *Esposizioni*. Evidence of Boccaccio's familiarity with the later Senecan letters (in particular the ninety-fifth, to Lucilius) is provided by Jonathan Usher in 'Apicius, Seneca, and Surfeit: Boccaccio's Sonnet 95,' *MLN* 118 (2003): 46–59, where he discusses Boccaccio's ironic inversion of conventional social categories and expectations by granting the dissolute 'artes' of the kitchen (Apicius) and boudoir (Sardanapalus) the authority usually reserved for academic disciplines; in a world that has no appreciation for poets and intellectuals, gluttons and sensualists reign supreme.

46 Concern about this aspect of the Golden Age diet is expressed by Lucretius, who attempts to solve the dilemma by stressing the succulent quality of Golden Age acorns. Boccaccio notes that Isidore (*Etymologies* XVII; 7, 21)

believes that it is not the acorn-bearing oak, but the walnut that is sacred to Jupiter, for the fruit of the latter is famously nourishing (*Genealogie* XI, 1). Dante betrays a similar scepticism regarding the alleged pleasures of the Golden Age diet (*Purg.* XXII, 148) for even as Dante, pilgrim, approaches Eden, the historical site of Golden Age sobriety, he has a disembodied voice on the terrace of gluttony offer the exemplum of the Golden Age, an age when hunger sufficed to render the acorns savory and thirst to make the water seem like nectar. Clearly if even a poet as famously abstemious as Dante finds it necessary to account for this implausible delight in eating acorns, such poets as Ovid and Boccaccio who revel in cosmopolitan sophistication must have even stronger opinions on the subject – as indeed they do.

47 Morton W. Bloomfield, 'The Source of Boccaccio's *Filostrato* III, 74–79 and Its Bearing on the MS Tradition of Lucretius, *De rerum natura*,' *Classical Philology* 47 (1952): 162–5, provides evidence suggesting that Boccaccio may have had access to a manuscript of *De rerum natura*. A brief history of the transmission of Lucretius's *De rerum natura* is provided in L.D. Reynolds, ed., *Texts and Transmission*, 218–22.

48 See E. Bignone, 'Per la fortuna di Lucrezio e dell'epicureismo nel medioevo' (*Rivista di filologia e di istruzione classica*, XLI, 1913). For evidence that Boccaccio actually owned a manuscript of Vitruvius's *De architectura*, see Mazza 'L'inventario della "Parva Libreria,"' 42.

49 The works of the mysterious Theodontius were known to Boccaccio exclusively by way of the *Collectionum*, a vast collection of notices related to the Pagan world compiled by Paul of Perugia, Robert of Anjou's librarian, with the help of the Calabrian scholar Barlaam (see *Genealogie* XV 6, 8). In his erudite and engaging discussion of Boccaccio's use of this passage from Vitruvius, Erwin Panofsky (*Studies on Iconology*, chap. 2) states that this Sintian/simian confusion derives from Servius's *Commentary on Virgil*. See also H.W. Janson, *Apes and Ape Lore in the Middle Ages and Renaissance* (London: Warburg Institute, 1952), 291–2.

50 This translation is taken from Attilio Hortis, *Studj sulle opere latine*, 560, where the first books of Leonzio's translations of both the *Iliad* and the *Odyssey* (as preserved in the Paris. Lat. 7880, an early transcription) are reproduced. In *Genealogie* XV 7, 2 Boccaccio claims to have heard Leontius read aloud his Latin rendition of the *Iliad* and adds, 'Erant Omeri libri michi et adhuc sunt, a quibus multa operi nostro accommoda sumpta sunt' [I had, and still have, the books of Homer from which many notices useful to my work were taken]. For an inventory of Boccaccio's citations from Leontius's translation in his *Genealogie*, see Hortis's long footnote (pp. 371–2) and the 'authors cited' index in the Mondadori edition of the *Genealogie*, ed. Vittorio Zaccaria.

Agostino Pertusi, *Leonzio Pilato fra Petrarca e Boccaccio* (Venice and Rome: Istituto per la collaborazione culturale, 1964) provides an in-depth examination of the complex matter of the identification and transmission of Leontius's translation.

51 Horace, *Satires, Epistles, Ars Poetica,* trans. H.R. Fairclough, Loeb edition (Cambridge, MA: Harvard University Press, 1932). This Horatian precept is most wittily exemplified in the story of the Babylonian princess Alatiel (*Dec.* II, 7). Boccaccio further explores the nexus of women and war in *Genealogie* IX, 3, where he analyses the traditional affiliation of Venus with Mars.

52 See Ovid's *Amores* III, 8 and 10 for additional elegiac recollections of the Golden Age.

53 Trans. J.H. Mozley, Loeb edition (Cambridge, MA: Harvard University Press, 1985). See also *Fasti* II, 289–302 and *Heroides* IV, 131–2 where Phaedra says to Hippolytus: 'ista vetus pietas, aevo moritura futuro, rustica Saturno regna tenente fuit' [such old-fashioned piety, destined to perish in the future, was rustic even during Saturn's reign]. However, Ovid is not always so optimistic. In a particularly caustic assessment of his times, Ovid proclaims his own age the true Golden Age – 'aurea sunt vere nunc saecula' (*Ars amatoria* II, 277) – neither because it abounds in virtue nor because it offers the pleasures of vice, but, rather, because it is an age controlled by wealth.

54 Trans. Richard M. Gummere, Loeb edition (Cambridge, MA: Harvard University Press, 1996).

55 This Aristotelian model of the life-arc was available to the Middle Ages through Latin translations of Aristotle's treatise 'On Youth and Old Age.' In *Convivio* IV, 23, Dante provides an involved discussion of the arc of human life, in the course of which it is established that whereas the exact length of this life-arc varies from individual to individual, its apex, 'punto sommo' (*Conv.*, IV, 23, 9), falls somewhere between the thirtieth and fortieth year of life.

56 A similar conflict arises from his relation to his contemporary authorities, Dante and Petrarch, for both are, in very different ways, models of ascetic virtue. Whatever else may be true of Dante's Beatrice and Petrarch's Laura, it is clear that in a carnal sense at least they remain elusive objects of desire. Indeed, the very notion of sleeping with one's muse is entirely at odds with the unwritten code that guides the conduct of poets and muses. Yet in the *Amorosa visione* Boccaccio appears to describe nothing less than the ecstatic moment of sexual consummation with his own muse, Fiammetta – one, moreover, that is underwritten by his celestial guide!

57 Quotations are from Aldo S. Bernardo's translation, *Letters of Old Age I–XVIII* (Baltimore: Johns Hopkins University Press, 1992); for more on the lugubri-

ous Petroni, see Branca, *Profilo biografico*, 123. Boccaccio treats such enemies of poetry at length in *Genealogie* XIV, 5 and 18.

58 Boccaccio, *Famous Women* [*De mulieribus*], ed. and trans. Virginia Brown (Cambridge, MA: Harvard University Press, 2001).

59 For more on this revised concept of the hero, see Branca, 'Il mito e il concetto dell'eroe nel Boccaccio,' in *Essays in Honor of John Humphreys Whitfield Presented to Him on His Retirement from the Serena Chair of Italian at the University of Birmingham* (London: St George's, 1975).

60 For an earlier and equally glowing assessment of Giotto in Boccaccio's works, see *Amorosa visione* IV, 10. Boccaccio's enthusiastic appraisal of Dante and Giotto is shared by his contemporary, the historian Filippo Villani, who writes of Dante that he was the first to rescue poetry from the shadowy abyss where it had resided since the days of Claudian ('Ea igitur iacente sine cultu, sine decore, vir maximus Dantes Allegherii quasi ex abisso tenebrarum erutam evocavit in lucem dataque manu prostratam erexit in pedes' [*De origine civitatis* II, 5]), and of Giotto that he was not simply as accomplished as his classical predecessors, but had actually surpassed them ('Giottus, non solum illustris fame decore antiquis pictoribus comparandus, sed arte et ingenio preferendus, in pristinam dignitatem nomenque maximum picturam restituit' [*De origine civitatis* XXVI, 8]).

61 These ideas are repeated in *Vita di Dante*, XXII: 'assai leggiermente potremo vedere gli antichi poeti avere imitate, tanto quanto a lo 'ngegno umano è possibile, le vestigie dello Spirito santo; il quale, sí come noi nella divina Scrittura veggiamo, per la bocca di molti, i suoi altissimi secreti revelò a' futuri, facendo loro sotto velame parlare ciò che a debito tempo per opera, senza alcuno velo, intendeva di dimostrare' [and we can see easily enough that the ancient poets followed, to the extent that the human mind is capable of such a thing, the traces of the Holy Ghost; who, as we see in Holy Scripture, revealed his most recondite secrets to future generations through many mouths, demanding that they relay in veiled form those things which in due season, through works and without a veil, he intended to reveal]. For another encomium to Dante see *Amorosa visione* V through VI. Whatever one's opinion may be concerning the actual sanctity of Dante's 'sacro poema,' it is sufficient to acknowledge that Dante makes a point of associating his poetry with Scripture, God's poetry. In his brief biographies of Florentine citizens, Filippo Villani observes: 'ipsasque vatum fictiones naturali atque morali phylosophie coerentes adeo cum christianis licteris concordavit, ut obstenderet veteres poetas, quasi Sancto afflatos Spiritu, quedam fidei nostre vaticinasse misteria' (*De origine civitatis* II, 6). For more on the theme of the poet theologian, see Craig Kallendorf, 'From Virgil to Vida: The Poeta Theologus in

Italian Renaissance Commentary,' *Journal of the History of Ideas* 56 (1995): 41–62; and Ronald G. Witt, 'Coluccio Salutati and the Conception of the *Poeta Theologus* in the Fourteenth Century,' *Renaissance Quarterly* 30, 4 (winter 1997): 538–63.

62 The original sentence reads: 'ipse id nempe omnibus visum puto, iam multo ante lapsa felicia tempora ac regna saturnia rediisse' (16–17). For more in praise of Petrarch, see *Genealogie* XV, 6.

63 'Longe notior per maria agitatus Ulixes, ocioso Egysto sub celo patrio lasci-viente, cuius libidinosam damnamus desidiam, ubi illius laudamus et admira-mur errores' (*De casibus* III 13, 9).

64 'Raro sua sorte contentum comperio aliquem; nec mirum: divino quidem munere nobis animus insitus est, cui ignea vis et origo celestis et glorie inex-plebilis est cupido. Hic, generosus ubi sit, non ignavia attritus corporea, parvo pectoris carcere claudi nec detineri potest: exilit, et magnitudine sua orbem terrarum complectitur, et facilitate transcendit sydera, actusque incendio sublimi cupidine incenditur' (*De casibus* III 13, 2–3). The revolu-tionary quality of Boccaccio's vindication of Alcibiades is best appreciated by comparing it to such contemporary views as that expressed by Iacopo Passa-vanti in the *Specchio della vera penitenza* (which is based on Valerius Maximus's *Memorable Doings and Sayings* VI 9, ext. par. 4).

65 For a similar evocation of the 'picciola orazione,' see also Theseus's speech in the *Teseida* (II, 44ff). A partial inventory of such echoes of Dante's Ulysses in Boccaccio's work is provided by Aldo Rossi, 'Dante nella prospettiva del Boc-caccio,' *Studi danteschi* 37 (1960): 81–3.

66 Non ergo negligenda est, non ocio calcanda, non tanquam inane et super-fluum detestanda, sed propter Deum totis exquirenda viribus est (*De casibus* VIII 1, 18).

67 See *Aeneid* VI, 730–2, for a possible source for this notion of the igneous spirit of celestial origin.

68 This restlessness characteristic of the merchant's life is presented in a nega-tive light in *Esposizioni* III, alleg., 26ff, where the insecurity inherent in a life spent tossed about on the sea, forever subject to the whim of atmospheric and political disturbances, is used to epitomize the uncertainty inherent in all temporal things. See also *Esposizioni* VII, alleg., 18 for a restless chariot ride in search of wealth.

69 In chapter 5, 'L'epopea dei mercatanti,' of his influential study, *Boccaccio medievale*, Branca provides a thorough examination of the way that the mer-cantile experience both informs and is given form by Boccaccio's works. For autobiographical references to Boccaccio's training as a merchant see *Corbac-cio* 125 and *Genealogie* XV, 10.

70 In *Esposizioni* II, lit., 70 Boccaccio reproduces Aristotle's definition of magnanimity: 'sì come Aristotile nel IIII della sua *Etica* dimostra, colui è da dire
"magnanimo" il quale si fa degno d'imprendere e d'adoperare le gran cose.'
Boccaccio associates the term 'magnanimo' not so much with the quality of
generosity as with that of enterprise.

71 Horace, *Odes and Epodes*, trans. C.E. Bennet, Loeb edition.

72 Trans. H.F. Stewart, E.K. Rand, and S.J. Tester, Loeb edition. Similar denunciations of navigation are found in Hesiod, *Works and Days*, 224ff; Aratus,
Phaenomena 110–11; Lucretius, *De rerum natura*, V, 1000ff; Virgil, *Eclogue* IV,
32ff and *Georgics* 1, 136ff.; Tibullus, *Elegies* I 3, 37ff; Ovid *Met.* I, 94–5; and Seneca, *Epistles* XC, 24. In Boccaccio's works, see also *Fiammetta* V 30, 21; *Esposizioni* VI, alleg., 7. This conventional perspective is parodied by Ovid who,
undone by the thought of Corinna's imminent departure declares: 'The trou-
ble began when they felled those pines on Pelion / And the barren sea-lanes
beheld / Argo, amazing Argo, on her reckless quest for the Golden / Fleece,
threading the Clashing Rocks. / Why didn't she spring a fatal leak? If only no
man / Had ever bothered the wide / Seas with an oar!' (*Amores* II 11, 1–6;
trans. Green).

73 In a Golden Age description of *Esposizioni* VII, alleg., 461, Boccaccio presents
the traditional, moralizing view.

74 For Boccaccio's peripatetic lifestyle – and that of his adventuring compatriots
like Marco Polo – see Attilio Hortis, *Accenni alle scienze naturali nelle opere di
Giovanni Boccaccio* (Trieste: Tipografia del Lloyd Austro-Ungarico, 1877),
43ff.

75 Trans. Thomas H. Corcoran, Loeb edition.

76 Though Boccaccio mistakenly believes Seneca the philosopher (Seneca
'morale') and Seneca the tragedian to be two different authors, he is familiar
with – and frequently cites – both the *Naturales quaestiones* and the *Medea*.

77 Translation from Lovejoy and Boas, *Primitivism and Related Ideas in Antiquity*,
280.

78 See *Natural Questions* III 29, 8–9 for a fuller description of this catastrophe.

79 'Bonum mare . . . quo distantes populi copulantur, quo praeliorum removen-
tur pericula, quo barbaricus furor clauditur, subsidium in necessitatibus, ref-
ugium in periculis, gratia in voluptatibus, salubritas valetudinis, separatorum
conjunctio, itineris compendium, transfugium laborantium, subsidium vecti-
galium, sterilitatis alimentum' (*Hexameron* III, v, 22; *PL* 14, col. 165). The corresponding passage in Basil's Greek *Hexameron*, the precursor to and model
for Ambrose's Latin *Hexameron*, is actually much closer in spirit to Boccaccio's
encomium to navigation in the *Genealogie*: 'Moreover the sea is beautiful in
God's view because it embraces the islands, serving these as both an adorn-

ment and a source of security; and then also because the sea draws together the most distant lands, providing a free exchange among sailors: by means of these [sailors] the sea acquaints us with stories of events unknown to us, it procures wealth for merchants, easily supplies life's necessities, providing the wealthy with a means of transporting their excess goods, and helping the poor to furnish their own needs' (*Homily* IV, 7, 3–4; English translation based on the Italian translation in *Sulla Genesi* (*Omelie sull'*Esamerone) ed. Mario Naldini [Milan: Mondadori, 1990]).

80 See also *Genealogie* VII, Proem. While much of the ethnographic and geographic information presented here by Boccaccio was available from such texts as Pomponius Mela's *De chorographia* (see also Solinus's *Collectanea rerum memorabilium*, Book I of Orosius's *Seven Books Against the Pagans*, Fazio degli Uberti's *Dittamondo* and the 'virtual' tour of the Mediterranean in Brunetto Latini's *Tesoretto* [1027ff.]), this positive assessment of navigation, if not peculiarly Boccaccian, is, at least, a relatively unusual stance. Though this theme of navigation as a civilizing force is a leitmotif of the *Odyssey* (where ignorance of shipbuilding is associated with the cannibalistic Cyclopes [IX, 125ff.] and virtuosic shipbuilding with their relatives, the highly civilized Phaiakians), Boccaccio does not – to the best of my knowledge – invoke Homer's poem in support of his argument. Of the works I have examined, only in Basil's and Ambrose's *Hexameron* and Vincent de Beauvais *Speculum historiale* have I found a similar optimism with regard to the cultural benefits of sea journeying. Vincent de Beauvais writes: 'Navigatio est mechanicae species, ad quam pertinet omnis industria venendi & emendi, haec invisa littora addit: pacem & familiaritatem cum exteris nationibus componit, & privata communia facit' (I, 54, 'De praticis, & mechanicis artibus').

81 Trans. H.F. Stewart et al., Loeb edition.

82 Boccaccio's ambivalence towards Boethius is most amusingly exemplified by a passage in *De casibus* (VIII 18, 6ff) in which he briefly deliberates whether or not to present a portrait of Boethius but decides instead to describe King Arthur and the knights of the Round Table! As noted above, Horace, in his *Odes*, presents the ideas of exploratory navigation and Prometheus's theft of divine fire as complementary manifestations of human impiety. For an application of the Ciceronian 'Dream of Scipio' motif in Boccaccio's work (possibly mediated, as C.S. Lewis argues in *The Discarded Image*, by Lucan's description of the ascent of Pompey's soul in the *Pharsalia* [VI, 507 ff.]), see *Teseida* XI, 1–3, where Arcita's soul flies up to the heavens and, looking back on the distant Earth, sees 'il poco / globo terreno' [the slight terrestrial sphere], judges it insignificant in comparison with the heavens, and laughs contemptuously at the absurdity of human vanity.

83 Giuseppe Chiecchi, the editor of the Mondadori edition of the *Consolatoria a Pino de' Rossi*, identifies Cicero's *Tusculan Disputations* as the 'nucleo aneddotico' [anecdotal nucleus] elaborated by Boccaccio 'mediante la tecnica retorica della *interpretatio*' [by means of the rhetorical technique of *interpretatio*] (note 18). A similar advocacy of cultural syncretism may be inferred from Boccaccio's letter of 1348 to his friend and teacher Zanobi da Strada. The letter, *Epistole* VI, begins with a rapturous tribute to the numen of friendship ('amicitie numen'), whose bond-forging skills exceed even those of Nature herself, for friendship not only draws together such temperamentally incompatible peoples as 'the unyeilding Parthians, difficult Getae, antisocial Iberians, uncivilized Mauretanians, unruly Numidians' and 'easy-going Ethiopians,' but also, by means of virtue, unites them into a single whole 'unum et solidum faciet ex duobus' [makes out of two, one single and solid] (*Epistole* VI, 2).

84 Boccaccio, *Famous Women*, trans. Virginia Brown, 109 (XXVII, 9–11).

85 Virgil, *Eclogues, Georgics, Aeneid, 1–6*, trans. H.R. Fairclough, Loeb edition (Cambridge, MA: Harvard University Press, 1916).

86 A similar perspective is provided by Hesiod's *Works and Days*, though not in the specific context of the Ages of the World *topos* but in his description of the dyadic Strife, who is responsible not only for the destructive desire to engage in war but also for the constructive goading of lazy mortals to work. Hesiod also maintains that the earth's natural bounty is hidden by divine design with the specific aim of discouraging complacency.

87 Citation from Claudian, *De Raptu Proserpinae*, trans. and commentary by Claire Gruzelier (Oxford: Oxford University Press, Clarendon Press, 1993).

88 In other passages, Boccaccio advances a model of Golden Age chastity reminiscent of the opening lines of Juvenal's sixth *Satire*. See also *Esposizioni* VI, 3–8; XIV, 61ff. A similar view is expressed in the *Roman de la Rose*, 8359ff.

89 No doubt part of this confusion regarding the moral virtues of the Golden Age derives from the coexistence of two conflicting etiologies: in one Jupiter's castration of Saturn spells the end of the Golden Age (e.g., *Metamorphoses* I); in the other the exiled Saturn establishes a Golden Age kingdom in exile (e.g., *Aeneid*, VIII). However, the ambivalence regarding the moral status of the Golden Age that pervades so many of Boccaccio's works appears to be rooted less in such conflicting accounts than in the belief that any circumstance that promotes idleness is inherently susceptible to moral decadence. G. Villani alludes to Saturn's exilic kingdom in chapters VI and XXIII of the *Cronica*.

90 For more on Saturnian cannibalism, see *Genealogie* VIII, 1.

91 Boccaccio lampoons this belief in the moral, prophylactic virtues of

agricultural labour in the story of Masetto (*Decameron* III, 1), perhaps the most industrious cultivator of gardens on record.

92 The theme of eros provoked by indolence is extremely common in Boccaccio's works. See, for example, *De mulieribus* XXIII, 11; *Teseida* VII, 54; *De casibus* III, 13. As I will argue in chapter 4, much of the dynamism of the *Decameron* derives precisely from the tension generated by situating a virtuous, chaste *brigata* in a setting which neatly combines all of those elements – the *locus amoenus*, leisure, song, dance, wine, story-telling, etc. – commonly reputed to incite erotic activity. For this theme, see in particular *Esposizioni* V, lit., 181.

93 From Mariangela Causa-Steindler and Thomas Mauch, trans., *The Elegy of Lady Fiammetta* (Chicago: University of Chicago Press, 1990).

94 Nevertheless, see *Esposizioni* VI, 3–8 and XIV, 61ff, where Golden Age chastity is lauded.

95 This model represents a synthesis of what Lovejoy and Boas refer to as 'chronological primitivism' and 'anti-primitivism,' two starkly opposed ways of conceiving historical change – a coupling of antithetical ideas already prominent in Hesiod's *Works and Days*.

96 For Boccaccio's profile of Vulcan, see *Genealogie* XI, 70.

97 This allegorical interpretation of the Church as garden is that advanced by Pastore Stocchi in his notes to the *Allegoria mitologica*.

98 In Horace's *Odes* (I, 16) Prometheus is represented as one who fashions human beings through a Frankenstein-like assemblage of the physical and temperamental attributes of other animals: 'Prometheus, as goes the tale, when forced to add to our primeval clay a portion drawn from every creature, put also in our breasts the fury of the ravening lion' (13–16, trans. C.E. Bennet, Loeb edition). Boccaccio cites this passage in *Genealogie* IV, 44. For a full discussion of Boccaccio's use of the figure of Prometheus, see Lucia Marino, 'Prometheus, or the Mythographer's Self-Image,' *Studi sul Boccaccio* 12 (1980): 263–73.

99 In *De mulieribus* I, 4 Boccaccio expresses the more traditional view. See also *Decameron*, Epilogue 17 and *Genealogie* XV 4, 2: 'Et quis ex imperfecto homine perfectum exquiret opus? Solius Dei est, opus perfectum componere, quoniam et ipse perfectus est!' [And who would expect a perfect work from an imperfect man? It is for God alone to compose perfect works, for he is himself perfect!].

100 See, however, St Thomas, *Summa* CI.

101 Quotations are from vol. 1 of the translation by Aldo S. Bernardo et al., *Letters of Old Age I–XVIII*.

102 Though Boccaccio frequently cites passages from Horace's *Ars poetica*,

Satires, Epistles and *Odes*, I cannot find any reference to the *Epodes*. Indeed, in the *Esposizioni*, Boccaccio, having mentioned the *Odes, Ars poetica, Epistles* and *Satires* goes on to say, 'Altri libri de' suoi, che i quatro predetti, non credo si truovino' [I don't believe that other books of his, besides these four already mentioned, are to be found] (*Esp.* IV, lit., 115). Strangely enough, Petrarch does seem to have had access to the *Epodes* – whether direct or indirect I cannot say – for he makes references to them in the *De remediis*.

103 Trans. C.E. Bennett, Loeb edition.

104 Trans. Frank Justus Miller, Loeb edition.

105 For Boccaccio's knowledge of Seneca's works, see Vincenzo Crescini, *Contributo agli studi sul Boccaccio con documenti inediti* (Turin: Loescher, 1887), 160–4; Albert Cook, 'Boccaccio and Seneca,' *American Journal of Philology* 28 (1908): 200–4; Aldo Maria Costantini, 'Studi sullo Zibaldone Magliabechiano. II. Il florilegio senechiano,' *Studi sul Boccaccio* 8 (1975): 79–126; Mario Serafini, 'Le tragedie di Seneca nella *Fiammetta* di Giovanni Boccaccio,' *Giornale storico della letteratura italiana* 126 (1949): 95–105.

106 Some of Boccaccio's views on monarchy and tyranny can be found in the following passages: *Esposizioni* VIII, lit., 61; *Esposizioni* XII, alleg., 25; *Genealogie* IX, XXVII; and *De casibus* II, V.

107 Like Virgil, Boccaccio here views the Saturnian reign as a reproducible phenomenon; it is sufficient that a given king be like Saturn for him to preside over a Golden Age. See *Esposizioni* I, alleg., 171 where this view is fully developed. For additional paeans to the country life – particularly as an aid to contemplation and the composition of poetry, see *Genealogie* XI, 2; XIV, 11 and *De casibus* XIV, 6.

108 Boccaccio, *Famous Women*, trans. Brown, 61 (XIII, 14).

109 Other examples of such metaphorical applications of the word 'peste' in Boccaccio's work abound: in *Filocolo* V, 28, 1, pride is a plague; in *Fiammetta* 15, 4, love is a plague; in *De mulieribus* XIII, XIV, XXIII sensual passion is a plague, and so forth. The association of plague with sexual trespass is most vividly illustrated by the story of Oedipus, one available to Boccaccio through Seneca's *Oedipus*, a Latin adaptation of Sophocles's play. For more on Boccaccio's thematization of the plague as a metaphor for passion, see Jessica Levenstein, 'Out of Bounds: Passion and the Plague in Boccaccio's *Decameron*,' *Italica* 73, 3 (autumn 1996): 313–35.

110 Though this account is strongly influenced by Ovid – even Lycaon and Deucalion's flood are worked into the scheme – it departs significantly from Ovid in granting Saturn the role of lawgiver, for Ovid's Saturnian reign is characterized by the absence of law. In this respect, Pomena's account is closer to the Virgilian model, for her Saturn, like Virgil's, is credited with

governing 'sotto caste leggi' [with chaste laws] (XXVI, 47) whereas Jupiter's legal laxity is associated with a period of moral dissolution.

111 In her article 'Il giardino di Pomena,' *Studi sul Boccaccio* 15 (1985–6): 235–52, Marina Massaglia notes the way this theme of garden as sanctuary anticipates the function of the gardens in the *Decameron*. In the *Amorosa visione* we find another instance of the garden as a place for recreation – in the sense of restoration: '"Entriàn" diss'io "in questo orto vicino, / donna, se piace a voi, ché poi, alquanto / ricreati, terrem nostro cammino"' ['Let us enter,' I said, 'this nearby garden, / if, my lady, it pleases you to do so, for afterwards, somewhat refreshed, we can continue our journey'] (XXXVII, 65).

Chapter 2. Local Myths of Origin

1 Though Dante displays a marked ambivalence regarding the ancient population of Fiesole (consider, for example, the memorable condemnation of the 'ingrato popolo maligno' [that malicious, ungrateful people] in *Inf.* XV, 61–62 as contrasted with the more positive assessment of *Par.* XV, 124–126, XVI, 121–122), he, too, views it as a place of origin. Vanni Fucci's prophetic words to Dante in *Inf.* XXIV, 'poi Fiorenza rinnova gente e modi' [then Florence renews men and manners] (144) within the context of Fucci's travesty of a phoenix-like rebirth from ashes are a bleak, parodic confirmation of this regenerative quality. In the *Ninfale fiesolano* Boccaccio devotes many octaves (436ff) to a mytho-historical account of the mixing of the pure indigenous stock – the 'schiatta africhea' – initially with a group of invaders headed up by Atalante (identical with G. Villani's 'Attalante') and later with the Romans, who, having razed Fiesole, found the city of Florence in the plain below.

2 All citations from Giovanni Villani are from the *Cronica di Giovanni Villani* (Florence: Magheri, 1823).

3 This history of Fiesole is most conveniently found (together with parallel transcriptions of two other early histories) in Otto Hartwig, *Quellen und Forschungen zur altesten Geschichte der Stadt Florenz* (Marburg: N.G. Elwert, 1875–80). The extract is from page 39; the emphasis is mine. Many details of the last octaves of the *Ninfale fiesolano* – those containing a synopsis based on such traditional accounts of Fiesole's origin – attest to Boccaccio's familiarity with these histories. Indeed, the version of the *Cronica de origine civitatis* presented in Hartwig's book is taken from the Laurentian Library's Plut. XXIX, 8: one of Boccaccio's own notebooks – the so-called Zibaldone Laurenziano. A critical edition of the *Chronica de origine civitatis florentie* based, in part, on the version found in Boccaccio's Laurentian notebook, has been published

by Anna Maria Cesari in *Atti e memorie dell'Accademia Toscana di Scienze e Lettere: La Colombaria*, vol. 58 (Florece: Olschki, 1993).

While the absolute, universal primacy granted the city of Fiesole in the *Libro fiesolano* is not found in the other accounts that I have read, most do at least agree in according Fiesole the status of first postdiluvial city in Europe (one third of the inhabited world according to the ancient convention of dividing the land masses of the Northern Hemisphere into Europe, Africa, and Asia). Though Boccaccio was clearly familiar with this tradition – and ready enough to recycle its basic elements when it served his purpose (see, for example, *Amorosa visione* VII/XXXV, 73ff; *Genealogie*, Proem to VI; *Filocolo* V, 38–49; *Ninfale*, octaves 436ff), an observation in his *Esposizioni* reveals a more sceptical assessment of such popular notions: 'Fiesole, secondo che alcuni vogliono, è antichissima città, e quella dicono essere stata edificata da non so quale Atalante, de' discendenti di Iafèt, figliuolo di Noè, prima che altra città d'Europa: *la qual cosa creder non posso che vera sia*' [Fiesole, according the the opinion of some, is a most ancient city, built, they claim, by I don't know which Atalante, one of the descendants of Noah's son Japheth, before the other European cities: *an account which I cannot believe to be true*] (XV, lit., 40–1, emphasis mine). See *Esposizioni* IV, lit., 159. See also Charles T. Davis, 'Topographical and Historical Propaganda in Early Florentine Chronicles and in Villani,' *Medioevo e rinascimento* 2 (1988): 33–51.

4 Since this mountain has certain features that recur in Boccaccio's descriptions of Certaldo – see 'Elsa' in *De montibus* [*De fluminibus*] – it is impossible to establish its identity with certainty. However, a passage in *Comedia delle ninfe* (III, 1), reinforces possible identification of this *picciolo poggio* with Fiesole by dwelling on the centrality of Fiesole, which is described as being 'almost in the centre and most prosperous part of its [Etruria's] blessed bosom' (Serafini-Sauli, 5).

5 'Multas preterea et diversarum spetierum, maritimarum tamen omnium, radens cursu solum detegit concas vacuas et vetustate candidas et ut plurimum aut fractas aut semesas. Quas ego arbitror diluvium illud ingens quo genus humanum fere deletum est, dum agitatu aquarum maximo terras circumvolveret fundo, illis reliquit in partibus' (*De fluminibus*, 368). The deluge as a historical event – empirically 'proven' by the evidence of seashells stranded on mountain tops – is a leitmotif of Boccaccio's works. See, for instance, *Filocolo* III 33, 12; V 42, 2, *Comedia delle ninfe* XXIII, 25, and *Eclogue* XVI. Branca alludes to Boccaccio's interest in the blanched seashells of Certaldo in the initial pages of *Giovanni Boccaccio: Profilo biografico* (Florence: Sansoni, 1997); Attilio Hortis discusses the theme in *Accenni alle scienze naturali*

nelle opere di Giovanni Boccaccio (Trieste: Tipografia de Lloyd Austro-Urgarico, 1877), 22–3, and *Studj sulle opere latine del Boccaccio* (Trieste: Julian Dase, 1879), 251.

6 Boccaccio's confidence in such allegedly empiric evidence of marvelous occurrences is supported by several passages in the *Genealogie*. See, for example, his description of the discovery of a human colossus at Drepanum that turns to dust upon being touched – empiric evidence of the existence of Giants in ancient times. In *Genealogie* XII, 25 we are told that the bones of the sea monster from whose gaping maw Perseus snatched Andromeda are still extant (an account, he adds, corroborated by such authorities as Jerome and Pliny), and in XII, 60 we read of the discovery of the enormous, fully embalmed body of the Arcadian prince Pallas – incontestable proof, Boccaccio notes, of the even more prodigious size of the Rutulian king, Turnus, who killed him. While there is something distinctly quixotic in Boccaccio's uncritical acceptance of such relics (I am reminded of Quixote's similar argument that the historical veracity of Roland is 'proven' by the existence of his famous horn, still on view in Rencesvals), we are given no particular reason to believe that such arguments are facetious or insincere – despite the delight that Boccaccio takes in lampooning the Christian cult of relics throughout the *Decameron*. Ugo Foscolo (*Discorso storico sul testo del* Decamerone [Lugano: G. Ruggia 1828], 18) and Henri Hauvette (*Boccace: Étude biographique et littéraire* [Paris: Armand Colin, 1914], 463) are among the critics who have remarked the irony that Boccaccio's will includes a bequest to Santa Maria del Santo Sepolcro consisting of his personal collection of relics, gathered, Boccaccio writes (in a phrase that inevitably recalls Frate Cipolla's pilgrimage) from all over the world with much effort.

7 Boccaccio generally refers to the *Etymologiae* as the *Origines*. An incomplete transcription of Orosius's *Historiae* in Boccaccio's hand is preserved in the Riccardiano 627. (Giorgio Padoan discusses this autograph in *Il Boccaccio, le muse, il Parnaso e l'Arno* [Florence: Olschki, 1978], 249). See also Pliny, *Naturalis historia* IX, 36.

8 From *The Etymologies of Isidore of Seville*, trans. Stephen A. Barney, W.J. Lewis, et al. (New York: Cambridge University Press, 2006). Rabanus's section on floods in *De universo* (*De diluvio* XI, 21; *PL* 111, col. 53) repeats, almost word-for-word, Isidore's notice in the *Etymologiae*. Augustine had already made a point of distinguishing among these various deluges in the *City of God* XVIII, 8: 'And historical writers are not agreed when Ogyges flourished, in whose time also a great flood occurred – not that greatest one from which no man escaped except those who could get into the ark, for neither Greek nor Latin history knew of it, yet a greater flood than that which happened after-

ward in Deucalion's time' (trans. Marcus Dods [New York: Random House, 1950]). See also the Eusebius-Jerome *Chronicon* I, 16 (*PL* 27, col. 53).

9 *Dartmouth Dante Project* (*DDP*), Lana (1324), *Purg.* 21. 130–6. For further evidence of this Deucalion/Noah typology one need only glance at the various medieval moralizations of Ovid.

10 Lucan, *The Civil War* (*Pharsalia*), trans. J.D. Duff.

11 Granted, this 'historical' account of the preservation of a Tuscan hill is delivered by Idalogos, a talking tree (and, critics seem to concur, a stand-in for Boccaccio); however, if Virgil's Polydorus and Dante's Pier delle Vigne have taught us anything, it is that one can safely heed the testimony of trees.

12 Arturo Graf observes: 'Che Dante, ponendo il Paradiso terrestre sulla cime del monte del Purgatorio, fece cosa non caduta in mente a nessuno dei Padri e Dottori della Chiesa, fu notato già da parecchi; ma che, quanto alla situazione del Paradiso, l'opinione di lui s'accorda con quella dei Padri e Dottori che lo posero nell' antictone, non fu, ch'io sappia, fatto osservare da alcuno' [That Dante, in placing his terrestrial paradise on the peak of the purgatorial mountain, did something that had not occurred to any of the church Fathers and Doctors, has already been noted by many; but that, with regard to the situation of Paradise, his view coincides with that of the Fathers and Doctors who placed it in the antipodes, has not, to my knowledge, been noted by anybody] (*Miti, leggende e superstizioni del medio evo* [Rome: Plurima, 1989], 19). See Graf 27ff. for a discussion of the tradition that the terrestrial paradise was preserved from devastation by the deluge. In 'Intorno al sito del 'Purgatorio' e al mito dantesco dell'Eden,' *Il giornale dantesco*, anno XXV, quad. 4 (October–December, 1922), Bruno Nardi also addresses these peculiar patristic and scholastic traditions concerning the location and physical characteristics of the terrestrial paradise. See also *Dante and the Medieval Other World* (Cambridge: Cambridge University Press, 1990), 160–2 where Alison Morgan provides an interesting review of authors who anticipated – and may well have influenced – Dante's decision to locate Eden on a mountain summit.

13 In the exquisitely lyrical *De phoenice* Lactantius Firmianus (the attribution is dubious), like Boccaccio, combines the theme of a place of immunity from universal catastrophe with that of rebirth. Also like Boccaccio, Lactantius uses the figure of Deucalion to recall the deluge (with the attendant threat of extinction) and Phaethon to recall the theme of a celestial conflagration (with the associated threat of death by desiccation). Extensive as these parallels are, the absence of any precise allusion to Lactantius's poem in Boccaccio's works (I, at least, have found none) suggests that Boccaccio's knowledge of Lactantius was limited to his *Divinae institutiones* (a work alluded to in both the *Genealogie* and the *Esposizioni*). For the *De phoenice*, see *Minor Latin Poets II*, Loeb edition.

14 Trans. T.H. Corcoran, Loeb edition.

15 In *Genealogie* IV, 68 Boccaccio presents Varro's theory concerning the 'historical' truth behind the myth of the gigantomachy, or revolt of the giants against the Olympian gods (an interpretation available to him through Servius's commentary on the *Aeneid*). According to Varro, the so-called revolt took place in the wake of the deluge and involved not gods and giants, but rather those diverse groups of people who had weathered the deluge by seeking refuge in the mountain tops. In any given conflict, Boccaccio continues, those who dominated the heights of the mountain had a distinct advantage and were thus viewed as 'gods' with respect to their earthbound adversaries, the 'giants.' Though Varro's strained historicization of a standard mythological *topos* may fail to convince, it does, at least, convey a rationalistic attitude towards myth entirely consonant with Boccaccio's own perspective – particularly with regard to the process of postcataclysmic regeneration. For related theories concerning hilltops and deluge survival, see Orosius's *Historia* I, 8 and the *Origo gestis romanae* (a work, according to Hortis, known to Boccaccio [*Opere latine*, 413]).

16 For Boccaccio's views on *Venus genetrix*, see *Genealogie* III, 22 and V, 26. In *De mulieribus* XIII (Tisbe) sexual passion is described as a plague that must be borne patiently for Nature herself inflicts it upon us so that we may procreate and perpetuate the species. For expressions of similar ambivalence towards human sexuality, see *Esposizioni* V, alleg., 25; V, alleg., 77. Simone Marchesi discusses this passage from the *Genealogie* in *Stratigrafie decameroniane*, 128.

17 This belief is already implicit in *Natural History* VII, lvi, 57 where Pliny provides a lengthy catalogue of inventors, for it is not unusual to find two or more inventors of different nationalities credited with the same discovery. Dante expresses a similar attitude in *De vulgari eloquentia* I 6, 3.

18 Luciano Rossi has argued that the plague description of the *Decameron* introduction may owe more than has been generally acknowledged to the Myrmidon episode in the *Metamorphoses* – one that includes a fairly extensive account of the Aeginian plague. See Luciano Rossi, 'Presenze ovidiane nel *Decameron*,' *Studi sul Boccaccio* 21 (1993): 132–4.

19 From *The Book of Theseus*, Bernadette Marie McCoy's translation of the *Teseida* (New York: Medieval Text Association, 1974).

20 From David Anderson, 'Boccaccio's Glosses on Statius,' *Studi sul Boccaccio* 22 (1994): 3–128.

21 'Fesule mons est biceps Florentie inclite Tuscie civitatis supereminens, olivetis plenus, ex quo si lapides qui plumbei sunt excidantur brevi tempore spatio novis incrementis restaurari compertissimum est. Fuit et in culmine huius eiusdem nominis vetustissima civitas, ruinis semesis testantibus' (*De montibus*, 234). The image of Fiesole in ruins is invoked in the *Amorosa visione* (XXXV,

73–5) in a passage strongly reminiscent of the 'tombe terragne' [pavement tombs] of Dante's 'Terrace of Pride' in *Purgatorio* XII.

22 *DDP*, Benvenuto (1373), *Inf.* 15.61–4: 'Scribit modernus poeta eorum Boccatius de Certaldo, quod lapides Faesularum sunt plumbei, et dicit mirabile de eis, quod si excidantur, in brevi temporis spatio certissime novis incrementis restaurantur: quod, si verum est, satis attestatur naturae ipsorum florentinorum, quorum semen continuo germinat de radice.'

23 From *Ovid Metamorphoses*, trans. Rolfe Humphries (Bloomington: Indiana University Press, 1955).

24 Citations of Filippo Villani are from *Philippi Villani de origine civitatis Florentie et de eiusdem famosis civibus*, ed. Giuliano Tanturli (Padua: Antenore, 1997). Parnassus's twin peaks are commemorated in the first canto of Dante's *Paradiso*: 'Infino a qui l'un giogo di Parnaso / assai mi fu; ma or con amendue / m'è uopo intrar ne l'aringo rimaso' ['Until this point, one of Parnassus' peaks / sufficed for me; but now I face the test'] (*Par* I, 16–18; Mandelbaum). Boccaccio's entry for 'Parnaso' in *De montibus* also dwells on this attribute. In the same entry he identifies Parnassus as the site for the preservation of Deucalion and Pyrrha during the deluge. In describing the port of Carthage, Virgil remarks that the harbour is bracketed by twin peaks (*Aeneid* I, 162–4), perhaps to underscore Carthage's role as a false 'Rome' – a seductive distraction from Aeneas's true mission as nation-founder.

25 'Est et Musis consecratus fons Castalius et alii insuper plures, et hoc quia habeat limpidus fons, non solum delectare intuentis oculos, sed eius etiam ingenium quadam virtute abscondita in meditationem trahere, et componendi desiderio urgere. Nemus autem ideo illis sacrum est, ut per hoc intelligamus solitudinem, qua uti debent poete, quorum est poemata meditari, quod quidem nunquam bene fit inter strepitus civitatum, aut compita etiam ruralia' (*Genealogie* XI 2, 14).

26 These peaks are more fully described in *De montibus*. 'Ianiculus is one of the mountains of Rome located in Tuscany, adjacent to the Sublician Bridge. It is believed that it takes its name from Janus, a former god of the Romans' (*De montibus*, 274). 'Saturnius is a mountain in the city of Rome called both the Capitoline and the Tarpeian Rock' (*De montibus*, 485). As for Boccaccio's assertion that Ianicolo, the Roman mountain, is actually located in Tuscany, this geopolitical continuity between Rome and Tuscany (though already implicit in the *Aeneid*, where Virgil uses the adjective 'Tuscan' to describe the Tiber [VIII, 368] and in the *Metamorphoses* [XIV, 615]), is clearly delineated by G. Villani in the *Cronica* I, 43, where he maps out the province of Tuscany – one which includes part of Rome itself. For the Italic kingship of Janus and Saturn, see *Amorosa Visione* VII.

27 'Aiunt insuper cum concors una cum Iano regnaret, et vicina communi opere constructa haberent oppida, Saturniam scilicet et Ianiculum, aurea fuisse secula, eo quod libera tunc esset omnibus vita, nemo servus, nemo alteri obnoxius, nullum etiam fertur in eius finibus furtum factum, nec sub illo fuit alicuius privatum' (*Genealogie* VIII 1, 15–20).

28 A good illustration of Boccaccio's methodology is found in *Genealogie* XII, 45 where he offers a naturalistic explanation of the story of Aecus, the devastation of the plague, and the subsequent replenishment of the population through the marvelous transformation of ants into people: the Myrmidons.

29 Importantly, the rape of the Sabine women, though premeditated, was not, at least according to Livy, a gratuitously violent act but was prompted by the refusal of the Sabine people (who were not alone in their refusal) to grant the Romans the right to intermarry with them – a pressing concern as the Roman population was fast diminishing for lack of women. See *Ab urbe condita libri* I, 9.

30 From *The Aeneid*, trans. Robert Fitzgerald (New York: Vintage, 1983).

31 This passage is in *Ab urbe condita libri* I 2, 5. For Boccaccio's translation into the vernacular of decades 1, 3, and 4, see Maria Teresa Casella, *Tra Boccaccio e Petrarca: I volgarizzamenti di Tito Livio e di Valerio Massimo* (Padua: Antenore, 1982). Boccaccio alludes to Livy with great frequency in the *Esposizioni* and *Genealogie.* That only these three decades (1, 3 and 4) were available to Boccaccio may be inferred from Petrarch's letter to Livy (*Familiares* XXIV, 8) where he laments the loss of all but twenty-nine of the original 142 books, corresponding to the 'first, the third, and the fourth' decades of Livy's history. In addition to actual manuscripts of these decades of *Ab urbe condita libri,* Boccaccio would have had access to a number of medieval histories modelled on Livy's work (among them that of the Paduan notary Albertino Mussato, the epitome of Livy attributed to Lucius Annaeus Florius and even the strongly Livian *Romuleo,* a Roman history written by his friend, the well known Dante commentator Benvenuto da Imola), commentaries such as Nicola Trevet's *Ad historias Titi Livii* (cited in *Esp.* I, alleg., 66) as well as numerous florilegia containing Livian excerpts. See G. Billanovich, 'Il Boccaccio, il Petrarca e le più antiche traduzioni in Italiano delle Decadi di Tito Livio,' *Giornale storico della letteratura italiana* 130 (1953): 311–37; and *La tradizione del testo di Livio e le origini dell'umanesimo* (Padua: Antenore, 1981). For a catalogue of Boccaccio's references to Livy, see Attilio Hortis, *Cenni di Giovanni Boccaccio intorno a Tito Livio* (Trieste: Tipografia del Lloyd Austro-Ungarico, 1877), in which Hortis cites Boccaccio's well-known lines in praise of Livy in the *Amorosa visione* and provides a transcription of Boccaccio's biographical vignette of Livy from the Zibaldone Laurenziano (now available in vol. V, tome 2 of

the Mondadori edition of the complete works). More recently, Emilio Lippi has written two studies on Boccaccio's vernacular translations of Livy: 'Una redazione particolare del volgarizzamento liviano,' *Studi sul Boccaccio* 10 (1978): 27–40; and 'Per l'edizione critica del volgarizzamento liviano,' *Studi sul Boccaccio* 11 (1980): 125–98. For Trevet and Boccaccio, see L. Van Acker, 'L'oeuvre Latin de Boccace et Nicholas Trevet,' *L'Antiquité classique* 33 (1964): 414–18.

32 This, and all other English citations of Livy are from *The Early History of Rome,* Aubrey de Sélincourt's translation of the first five books of *Ab urbe condita libri* (New York: Penguin, 1960). The quote is from p. 36. A similar pattern obtains in the case of the Sabine women. The conflict sparked by their rape is, according to Livy, initially quelled by the heroic intervention of the Sabine women themselves and finally resolved through the political expedient of joining the two peoples under a single government, thereby doubling the population of Rome (p. 48).

33 Lucius Annaeus Florus, *Epitomae de Tito Livio,* trans. Edward Seymour Forster, Loeb edition (Cambridge, MA: Harvard University Press, 1984). Though Boccaccio uses information taken from Florus's *Epitomae* in both the *Genealogie* and the *Esposizioni,* the *Epitomae,* as Hortis notes (*Studj,* 430), is cited by name only once, in *Genealogie* XII 65, 4. A manuscript of Florus is included in the inventory of Boccaccio's library. See Antonia Mazza, 'L'inventario della "Parva Libreria,"' 51.

34 From Justin, *Epitome of the Philippic History of Pompeius Trogus,* trans. J.C. Yardley (Atlanta, GA: Scholars Press, 1994).

35 Hortis (*Studj,* 158) discusses Boccaccio's dedication of the *Genealogie* to Hugh, King of Cyprus. In the *Aeneid* Virgil briefly alludes to the conquest of Cyprus by Dido's father Belus (I, 621–2). Other authors who influenced Boccaccio's views on Cypriot sexual customs include Augustine (*City of God* 4, 10) and Lactantius (*Divine Institutes* I, 17, 10), both of whom are mentioned in the context of the story of Adonis in *Genealogie* II, 52, 4–5. In the Lactantius passage we read that Venus instituted the prostitutes' art and essentially authorized the Cypriot custom.

36 Giovanni Villani writes that Florence was populated by the cream of Roman citizenry who welcomed those Fiesolans who so wished to live and dwell there with them ['e accolsono con loro quelli Fiesolani che vi vollono dimorare e abitare'] (*Cronica* I, 38). The theme of Fiesolan/Florentine mixing is foregrounded again in Villani's description of Arrigo's reign (III, 6), where the Fiesolans, routed by the Florentines, are invited to surrender and resettle, without prejudice, in Florence.

37 A similar elevation of the mechanical arts is found in *Genealogie* XV, 10, where

Boccaccio argues that all human offices are equally valuable to the preservation of the human race. Without farmers, where would theologians find the nutrition to continue with their studies? Although Boccaccio's concern in this passage is primarily that of defending his own decision to pursue a career in poetry, his belief that the diversification of the parts contributes to rather than diminishes the strength of the whole is a notion that recurs throughout his works and of which miscegeny is just one example – albeit an important one – among many. In *De casibus* he reminds us that those who govern have a responsibility to remember that their subjects are not slaves but collaborators: 'Meminisse quippe presidentes debent non esse populos servos, sed conservos' (II 5, 2). Scaglione discusses Boccaccio's social egalitarianism in *Nature and Love in the Middle Ages* (Westport, CT: Greenwood, 1976), 68–75. For Boccaccio's political ideas see also Hauvette, *Boccace*, 386; Hortis, *Studj*, 140–5.

38 This pseudo-Greek etymology is noted by Antonio Enzo Quaglio in his edition of *Filocolo*, vol. 1 of *Tutte le opere de Giovanni Boccaccio* (Milan: Mondadori, 1967), V, 48n3.

39 This discussion of the Caloni and Cireti episode is in the fifth section, 'Breve digressione su Boccaccio, la critica delle fonti e le antichità toscane,' [A brief digression on Boccaccio, source criticism and Tuscan antiquities] of chapter 4 of Bruni's *Boccaccio: l'invenzione della letteratura mezzana* (Bologna: Il Mulino, 1990). In considering these histories, Bruni gives particular emphasis to the popular tradition that Florence was originally constituted from an artificial, uneasy union of hostile Fiesolan and Roman factions (the 'historical' root of the ongoing civil conflict of Florence). He remarks that Giovanni Villani, the most authoritative exponent of this tradition, describes the first and second foundations of Florence as having resulted 'grazie a un nucleo romano che si unisce, senza amalgamarsi, a una componente fiesolana' [thanks to a Roman nucleus which unites itself, without amalgamation, to a Fiesolan component] (282), and cites the following passage from Villani to corroborate this point: 'E nota, perchè i Fiorentini sono sempre in guerra e in dissensione tra loro, che non è da maravigliare, essendo stratti e nati di due popoli cosí contrarii e nemici e diversi di costumi, come furono gli nobili Romani virtudiosi, e' Fiesolani ruddi e aspri di guerra' [And note it is no wonder that the Florentines are always at war and in a state of internal conflict, given that they are extracted and born of two such contrary and incompatible peoples, of such different ways of life as are the noble, virtuous Romans and the rough, war-toughened Fiesolans] (*Cronica* I, 38). It seems to me, however, that this passage does not necessarily support Bruni's argument of 'non-amalgamation' ['senza amalgamarsi'], as the phrase 'essendo stratti e nati di due popoli' may

just as easily be taken to imply a genetic 'marriage' of the two peoples. More-over, other passages in Villani strongly support the notion that racial mixing does take place. In *Cronica* III, VI Villani discusses the post-Carolingian recon-struction (the second construction) of Florence and the intermarriage of Fiesolan and Florentine families which preceded a period of sustained civic growth: 'molta buona gente di Fiesole lasciaro l'abitare della città del poggio, e tornaro all'agio del piano e del fiume ad abitare in Firenze, *imparentandosi* co' Fiorentini' [many good people of Fiesole stopped living in the city on the mountain peak and went to live in Florence, to the comforts of its plain and river, *intermarrying* with the Florentines] (III, V, emphasis mine). It is signifi-cant that in the historical 'appendix' of the *Ninfale fiesolano*, Boccaccio chooses to stress this intermarriage of Roman Florentines with native Fiesolans in words that clearly echo Villani's chronicle: 'si furo insieme tutti *imparentati*, / e fatti cittadin con grande amore, / avendo la lor parte d'ogni onore' (octave 457, emphasis mine). Morevoer, in the *Ninfale* this intermar-riage is described as being pre-Carolingian. In his sixth epistle (24) Dante refers to the Florentines as a 'miserrima Fesulanorum propago' [wretched offshoot of the Fiesolans] – a phrase that unambiguously casts the Florentines as a genetic offshoot of the Fiesolans. See also Fazio degli Uberti's *Il dittamondo* III, 7 ('E se del tutto allor fossero espolsi, / E non raccolto l'un con l'altro sangue, / Forse tal canterebbe, ch'ora duolsi' [and had they been completely driven out / and the one blood not united with the other / perhaps he would rejoice, who now laments]), and Ser Giovanni's *Il pecorone* XI 1, 230.

40 On the question of Boccaccio's birthplace, see Branca, *Boccaccio: profilo biografico*, chap. 1 and the notes to chap. 7 on p. 247.

41 'a dextro modico elatum tumulo Certaldum vetus castrum linquit, cuius ego libens memoriam celebro, sedes quippe et natale solum maiorum meorum fuit antequam illos susciperet Florentia cives' (*De fluminibus*, 368).

42 In *De casibus* II 19, 5 Boccaccio ascribes a Lydian ancestry to the Tuscans – no doubt on the authority of Virgil's *Aeneid* where, at the beginning of book IX, we are told that the Tuscan town of Corythus (birthplace of Dardanus) was populated by Lydians.

43 *DDP, Paradiso* 16.49–51.

44 Hauvette, *Boccace*, 71

45 The Ovidian narrative is reproduced at length in *Genealogie* X, 14. Though Achaemenides is mentioned several times in the *Genealogie* (X, 14; XII, 36; XIV, 15), here, no trace is to be found of this youthful tale of Achaemenides as a nation founder. Indeed, what little genealogical information is supplied is in direct contradiction of this youthful fiction. In his commentary on the first six books of the *Aeneid*, Bernardus Silvestris supplies an 'etymological'

evaluation of Achaemenides's name, linking it with joylessness and sorrow: 'Achemenides dicitur quasi acheremenes, id est sine gaudio et hilaritate, quod est tristicia' (bk 3, 691). Achaemenides is also mentioned briefly in Ovid's *Ex ponto* (II 2, 25) and *Ibis* (415–16) – a text transcribed by Boccaccio in the so-called *Miscellanea laurenziana*. As I have not been able to find any source for Boccaccio's further elaboration of the story of Achaemenides I am assuming that it is his own invention.

46 Trans. Frank Justus Miller, Loeb edition.

47 Indeed, Virgil has carefully shaped Achaemenides as an 'in bono' avatar of the notorious Sinon, whose false claim to have transferred his allegiance to Aeneas and his men proved so detrimental to the Trojans.

48 In fact Francesco Bruni is the only critic I know of who has addressed the subject of Boccaccio's reinvented Achaemenides. Bruni (*Boccaccio*, 286) notes the new, Theban, genealogy assigned to Achaemenides and observes that Boccaccio thereby calls to mind the epic greatness of Thebes together with the poet, Statius, who immortalized the history of Thebes. He stresses the interesting chronological and historical implications of Boccaccio's appropriation of Achaemenides: according to Boccaccio's revised history, Florence would have been founded after Fiesole but before Rome – thereby, Bruni notes, much enhancing the antiquity of Florence. Though Bruni proposes that the figure of Achaemenides serves to somehow recapitulate the 'Theban' and 'Trojan' moments of Boccaccio's literary career – the *Teseida* and the *Filostrato* respectively – he does not further elaborate upon the cultural, intellectual, and genetic synthesis of Greek and Roman so pervasive in this revised history.

49 While Boccaccio did not have direct access to the texts of the Greek tragedians Sophocles and Euripides, the story of the Theban dynasty was readily available to him through Seneca's *Oedipus* (Boccaccio's primary source for the account of Oedipus in the *Genealogie*), Statius's *Thebaid*, and Lactantius Placidus's commentary, *In Statii thebaida commentum*.

50 Boccaccio's decision to associate Achaemenides with Orcamo is, no doubt, related to the tradition (one recorded in *Genealogie* XII, 38) that a man called Orcamus was king of the great Persian dynasty of the Acheamenidae. The name of Achaemenides's mother, 'Ionia' (a name associated with the ancient Greek colonies scattered along the Aegean coast of Turkey) may well have been chosen to emphasize the genetic purity of Achaemenides's Greek ancestry.

51 For Cadmus in general, see *Genealogie* II, 63. For a partial catalogue of the afflictions visited upon Cadmus and his progeny, see the historical vignette of Cadmus in *De casibus* I, 6. An earlier account (though one not available to

Boccaccio) of Cadmus's pivotal role vis-à-vis the importation of the Phoenician alphabet is found in bk. V, ll. 57–9 of Herodotus's *Histories*. A more involved description of the unsavory details of Oedipus's misfortunes is found in *De casibus* I, 8. Other notices regarding the ill-starred Thebans would have been known to Boccaccio from *Metamorphoses* IV, 512ff. and the *Commedia, Inf.* XXX, 1ff. and XXXIII, 88–9.

52 Trans. Frank Justus Miller, Loeb edition.

53 This story, recorded by Herodotus (5C BC) in the first book of his *Histories*, was available to Boccaccio through Valerius Maximus's first-century *Factorum et dictorum memorabilium* (a work popularized by Boccaccio through his vernacular translation) and Justin's *Epitome* of Pompeius Trogus's *Historiae Philippicae* (I, 4). In *Genealogie* I, 31, Boccaccio alludes to both the story of Astyages's dream and his source, Valerius. Boccaccio also refers to this prophetic dream in *Esposizioni* VI, lit., 62 and VII, lit., 68; however, the fullest account is found in *De casibus* II, 17. In *Genealogie* VI, 22 and *Esposizioni* V, lit., 124, Boccaccio alludes to Cicero's account of Hecuba's prophetic dream that she is giving birth to a firebrand destined to burn all of Troy (*De divinatione* [I, 21, 42]). For Boccaccio's take on dreams in general, see *De casibus* II 8, 'Pauca de somniis.'

54 In *Aeneid* VII, 210, we learn that Dardanus came from the Tuscan home of Corythus. In the *Comedia delle ninfe* Boccaccio observes that there are those who maintain that it was not Atlas (Atalante), but Corythus who married Electra and fathered Italus, Dardanus, and Siculus – a variant which Boccaccio ascribes to Paul of Perugia in *Genealogie* VI 1, 1–3 and reproduces in *Esposizioni* I, lit., 136; IV lit., 165 etc. The more usual view – one found in G. Villani's *Cronica*, the *Libro fiesolano*, and the *Chronica de origine civitatis* – is that Electra was married to Atlas. In books VI and VII of his *De origine civitatis florentie*, Filippo Villani identifies Corythus as one of Dardanus's brothers. In the entry for 'Cortona' in Repetti's *Dizionario geografico*, we are reminded of Cortona's extremely remote origin, and told that it was considered to have been at one point in its history the home of Dardanus, who named it 'Corito' in honor of his father.

55 Though a similar synthesis is already implicit in the *Aeneid* where Evander's Arcadians form an alliance with Aeneas, it is the genetic reunion of the Trojans with their Dardan ancestry that is granted priority by Virgil.

56 Literary precedents for the colonization of Italy by Greeks abound. In *Aeneid* III, 398ff. the seer Helenus warns Aeneas to avoid the coastal towns of Southern Italy for they are colonized by evil Greeks. In *Aeneid* VI the Sibyl of Cumae informs Aeneas that he will first receive help from a most unexpected source: a Greek city (Pallantium). In *Genealogie* XI, 42, Boccaccio records the tradi-

tion that Ulysses has a child by Circe, Telegonus, who, after unwittingly killing his own father, travels to Italy where he founds the city of Tibur or Tusculum (Boccaccio identifies Ovid as his source for the account of Telegonus as founder of Tibur [*Fasti* IV, 71ff.] and Papias [in the *Lexicum*] as his source for Telegonus as founder of Tusculum). The following entry, XI, 43, provides an account of yet another son of Ulysses, Ausonius, after whom Italy was named Ausonia. In *Esposizioni* IV, lit., 213, Boccaccio alludes to the tradition that the Laurentian king Latinus was the son of Ulysses and Circe. (However, in *Genealogie* XII, 68 Boccaccio tells the story of Palantia, Evander's daughter who, raped by Hercules, gives birth to Latinus.) Almost identical stories are told of the sons produced by the unions of Ulysses with Calypso. In *Genealogie* XII, 19, we read of Alesus, one of Agamemnon's sons, who settles in Italy where he continues to wage war against the Trojans. In *Metamorphoses* XV, Ovid records the foundation of the Italian city of Croton by the Greek Myscelus and Vitruvius writes that Diomedes founded the town of Salpia in Apulia upon his return from Troy (*De architectura*, I 4, 11). See the Eusebius/Jerome *Chronicon* (I, 43) for more on the colonization of Italy by Greeks.

However, G. Villani – motivated, no doubt, by a desire to distance Italians from this spectre of Greek ancestry (Virgil's unflattering depiction of Greeks in the *Aeneid* [perpetuated by the medieval versions of the Trojan cycle] together with the mistrust generated by the eleventh century Roman Catholic/Greek Orthodox schism did much to discredit Greek culture) – maintains that after the Trojan war, the large majority of returning Greeks came to harm, whereas the fleeing Trojans (descendants of Dardano, son of Attalante, the founder of Fiesole) colonized Italy where their descendants became the future Romans and Florentines (*Cronica* I, 15). This perspective is replicated by Boccaccio in *De casibus* (I 15, 13; IV 8, 2). Among the medieval versions of the story of Troy available to Boccaccio would have been those by Benoit de Sainte-Maure (*Roman de Troie*), Guido delle Colonne (*Historia destructionis Troiae*), Dares the Phrygian (*De excidio Troiae historia*), and Dictys the Cretan (*Ephemeridos belli troiani libri sex*). Giorgio Padoan (*Il Boccaccio le muse*, 249) notes that we have a transcription of the *Ylias Frigii Daretis* in Boccaccio's hand. Other sources of Trojan lore would, of course, have included Virgil's *Aeneid* and Ovid's *Heroides* and *Metamorphoses*.

57   See G. Villani's *Cronica*, chapters XXXVIII–XL. In these chapters we read of Caesar's construction of the first city of Florence on the site of the Roman general Fiorino's slaughter in order that Fiesole might never be rebuilt. Here, also, is the description of the divisive process of naming Florence. The name 'Cesaria,' favoured, for obvious reasons, by Caesar, is rejected by the Roman Senate which, instead, recommends the organization of a contest

involving the construction of the civic infrastructure of the new city; the win-
ner is to be granted the privilege of choosing the city's new name. Amazingly,
all the contestants complete their work simultaneously, and, therefore, none
is granted this privilege. Hence, the new city is at first simply called 'piccola
Roma' by some, while others call it 'Floria,' after the martyr Fiorino or
because of the local abundance of flowers, or, finally, because it contains the
'flower' of the Roman population. This population, notes Villani, is mixed
with that of those Fiesolans who choose to remain. Thus, we are told, it is no
wonder that Florence is such a divisive city: an uneasy synthesis of noble
Romans and rude, war-like Fiesolans. (Caesar, miffed because the new city is
not named after him, leaves them to dither about nomenclature and, going
off in search of new victories, soon becomes consul, defeats Pompey, and
establishes the Empire.)

The theme of a competition to name a city is perhaps best known from the
ancient story of Minerva and Neptune's competition to name Athens, one
remembered by Boccaccio in *Genealogie* V, 48. See *Metamorphoses* VI, 70ff. and
Mythographi Vaticani II, 142, *De certamine Neptuni et Minerve* for accounts of this
contest that would have been familiar to Boccaccio.

58 In the Jerome-Eusebius *Chronicon* we read: 'Sphingam vero, scribit Palaephatus, uxorem Cadmi, propter zelum Harmoniae a viro recedentem contra
Cadmios iniisse bellum' (*PL* 27, col. 243). Palaephatus, like Euhemerus, was
known for his rationalization of myths. Palaephatus's versions of the Theban
myths are among the tales that Orosius declares he will pass over as he
endeavours to hasten through the endless butcheries of pre-Christian history
(*Seven Books against the Pagans* I, 12). Cadmus's good judgment – that is, with
regard to his choice of a wife – is brought under scrutiny by the notice related
by Solinus in the *Collectanea rerum memorabilium* (chap. 39) that the Sphinx
was a variety of deep-chested ape! Other traditions record that the Sphinx
was actually Laius's daughter (hence Oedipus's sister). For more information
on this variant, see the entry for 'Sphinx' in Pierre Grimal's excellent *Dictionary of Classical Mythology.*

59 Further evidence of this intermarriage of aborigines and colonizers is supplied by the well-known tradition that Echion, one of the five Spartoi, marries
Cadmus's daughter Agave. Born of this ill-augured union is Pentheus. Boccaccio's familiarity with this story is clear from *Genealogie* II, 65, where the
basic elements of the tale are reproduced. Curiously, the account of Cadmus
in *De casibus* I, 6 makes no mention of the peculiar story of Cadmus's original
marriage to the Sphinx. Indeed, here, the Spartoi are presented as an obstacle that must be eliminated and nothing more.

60 It would seem that Boccaccio is here implicitly acknowledging the role of vio-

lence in the birth both of the *polis* and of poetry. Boccaccio himself retells the complete story of Perseus, Pegasus, and the Hippocrene fountain – referred to by Boccaccio as the 'gorgoneo fonte' since its origin can actually be traced to the drops of blood which fell from Medusa's severed head – in his footnotes to the *Teseida* (I, 1).

61 'Yppocrene fons est Boetie. Hunc aliqui fingunt ob equi Pegasi percussionem factum, et hinc denominatum. Quod quidem figmentum facile detegitur si secundum quosdam inspiciatur hystoria. Volunt quidam Cadmum equo insidentem, dum sedem sibi sociisque perquireret primo apud hunc fontem constitisse, et quia licterarum grecarum repertor fuit, quarum forsan meditacionem ibidem sumpsit, illum Musis sacer esse voluit' (*De fontibus*, 71).

62 See Pier Giorgio Ricci, 'Studi sulle opere latine e volgari del Boccaccio,' *Rinascimento*, seconda serie, vol. 2 (Florence: Sansoni, 1962), 15, for a brief notice regarding Boccaccio's identification of this font with the 'libetridem fonte' only in the second version of *De casibus*.

63 'Sunt preterea qui velint eum secum Yppocrenen fontem sedentem, atque meditantem, XVI licterarum caracteres adinvenisse, quibus postea omnis Grecia usa est' (*Genealogie* II 63, 4).

64 See, in particular, *Genealogie* XI 2, 14.

65 For Nicostrata, see *De mulieribus* XXVII and *Genealogie* V, 51. For Evander, see *Genealogie* XII, 66. Among the mythical personages credited with similar roles are the city-founder Agenor, his son Phoenix (*Genealogie* II, 55), and the great Athenian poet-legislator Solon.

66 Since Evander, the Arcadian king, is traditionally credited with both the foundation of Pallanteum and the introduction of the Greek alphabet to Italy – a myth, moreover, presented in *Genealogie* XII, 66 – it is likely that Boccaccio's Achaemenides owes much to this tradition as well. Whereas the Arcadian King Evander and his mother Nicostrata ('Carmenta' in the tongue that she herself invented) are often praised by Boccaccio for their role in inventing a new alphabet, the Roman alphabet, and a new tongue, Latin, to commemorate their foundation of a new, Italian, city, Pallantium, Achaemenides (despite his typological connection with Cadmus) is not, it would seem, associated with cultural innovation but rather with the importation of Greek culture to Italy. This interpenetration of the themes of city-founding and poetic creation is particularly evident in yet another one of Boccaccio's etiological accounts relating to Florence. In the *Vita di Dante* (II) where Boccaccio provides a brief outline of Dante's genealogy, we learn that Dante is related to Eliseo, a young nobleman of the Frangiapani family, to whom Boccaccio grants a central role in the Carolingian reconstruction of Florence; he is 'ordinatore della reedificazione, partitore delle abitazioni e delle strade, e

datore al nuovo popolo delle leggi opportune' [orchestrator of the rebuilding, designator of the dwelling places and of the streets, and giver of suitable
laws to the new people]. That the poet who gave the Italians their *volgare illustre* is thus affiliated with a city-founder and law-giver is no simple coincidence;
as the story of the tower of Babel attests, cities are built of language and,
accordingly, the corruption or decay of language implies a corresponding
collapse of the physical city.

67 See also *De mulieribus* C, Zenobia (14).
68 Translation from Norton Critical Edition of the *Decameron*, ed. Mark Musa
and Peter E. Bondanella (New York: Norton, 1967), 194.
69 Translation from Beatrice Corrigan, *Italian Poets and English Critics, 1755–
1859* (Chicago: University of Chicago Press, 1969), 110.
70 Hortis, *Studj*, 384.
71 For Boccaccio's tendency to embrace Homer as a literary model even in his
youthful works, before he had access to the actual Homeric poems (in
Leonzio Pilato's translation), see in particular Hortis, *Studj*, 366ff.; and Manlio Pastore Stocchi, 'Il primo Omero del Boccaccio,' *Studi sul Boccaccio* 5
(1968): 99–122. In 'Venezia, la cultura greca e il Boccaccio,' *Studi sul Boccaccio*
10 (1977–8): 217–34, Agostino Pertusi identifies the 'Homer' of the 'second
grade' mentioned by Petrarch in *Familiares* XXIV, 12 with Boccaccio rather
than Leonzio Pilato. For more on Pilato's critical role in this renaissance of
Greek studies, see Pertusi, *Leonzio Pilato fra Petrarca e Boccaccio* (Venice: Istituto
per la Collaborazione Culturale, 1964); and Pier Giorgio Ricci, *Studi sulla vita
e le opere del Boccaccio* (Milan: Riccardo Ricciardi, 1985), chap. 12 ('La prima
cattedra di greco in Firenze').
72 I have likened the area circumscribed by these geographical features to an
informal trapezoid because the Mugnone runs a southwesterly course past
the westernmost of the three mountains that make up Fiesole before merging with the Arno near *Le Cascine*, while the Mensola originates in the valley at
the eastern base of Mount Céceri, the easternmost of the three mountains,
and runs towards the southeast where it too enters the Arno, near Róvezzano.
While the relatively short top of the trapezoid is crowned by the three mountains of Fiesole, the Southern boundary lies in the Arno valley. Pier Giorgio
Ricci's edition of the *Decameron* provides many useful details regarding the
topography of the area corresponding to the action of the *Ninfale*. Even more
germane to this topic is Ricci, 'I luoghi del "Ninfale fiesolano,"' in his *Studi
sulla vita e le opere del Boccaccio* (Milan: Ricciardo Ricciardi, 1985).
73 Like Ovid's Daphne in the *Metamorphoses* (I, 530), Mensola is 'lovely even in
flight' – one of the numerous Ovidian motifs scattered throughout the
Ninfale. A similar circumstance occurs in the Ovidian story of the nymph

Arethusa and the river god Alpheus, for as Arethusa attempts to escape from Alpheus's watery grasp, she is forced to leave her dress on the opposite bank and her nudity in flight only stokes his desire (*Met.* V, 601–5).

74 Hauvette notes that the discipline imposed by Diana on her society of nymphs recalls in many ways the rules imposed on religious communities (*Boccace*, 169). Boccaccio's choice of the name 'Mensola' may have been influenced by the existence of a Benedictine convent, S. Martino a Mensola, named after the Mensola river: 'verso l'anno 1070 costà [an abbot named Pietro] in Mensola instituì un monastero di donne della regola di S. Benedetto' [towards the year 1070 an abbot named Pietro founded a Benedictine convent adjacent to the Mensola] (E. Repetti, *Dizionario geografico fisico della Toscana*, 3: 193). In 'Un peccato del Boccaccio,' *Giornale storico della letteratura italiana* 36 (1900): 123ff. Enrico Carrara boldly carries the torch of positivist conviction into the twentieth century by arguing that the erotic drama of the *Ninfale* cloaks a torrid autobiographical interlude: Boccaccio's seduction of a nun from one of the local Benedictine convents. Though much less ready to spin 'authentic' histories from such flimsy poetic tow, even readers of these comparatively secular times would find it difficult not to notice the conventual aura of the society created by Diana and her nymphs. It may be supposed therefore that the association of the name 'Mensola' with one of the local Benedictine convents, though never stated in the *Ninfale*, may well have occurred to readers of Boccaccio's time. (The other Benedictine convent associated with the *Ninfale*, San Martino a Maiano, was, according to Boccaccio's fiction, built by Pruneo after his mother's death [see octave 449].)

75 From *Boccaccio, The Nymph of Fiesole* [*Ninfale fiesolano*], trans. Daniel J. Donno (New York: Columbia University Press, 1960).

76 See, for instance, Isidore's *Etymologies* XI.i.143: '... all offspring is made of two kinds of seed, and the greater portion, because it predominates, determines the similarity of the sex' (Barney et al., 241). In his *Dragmaticon*, the twelfth-century philosopher William of Conches uses this embryological theory to prove that some women actually enjoy being raped. If this were not so, he argues, why is it that rape victims occasionally get pregnant? (*Dragmaticon Philosphiae* [*Corpus Christianorum, Continuatio Medievalis*, CLII, 1997]). As Pier Massimo Forni points out in his introduction to the Mursia edition of the *Ninfale*, Africo's violent possession of Mensola in many respects fits the template established by Andreas Capellanus in *The Art of Courtly Love*, where he advises those who have accidentally fallen in love with some peasant woman to first smother them with flattery and then take them by force the moment a convenient opportunity presents itself! (bk. I, dialogue 11). Also in Capellanus is the relevant observation that a woman taken by force is blameless

provided that she does not subsequently consent to a repetition of the act (bk. 1, dialogue 6).

77 Ovid's Acis has a fate that in certain respects is similar, for having been crushed by a rock thrown by Polyphemus, his blood trickles down from the rock and is gradually clarified until it becomes a clear river and Acis a river god: 'Though larger now, and with a dark-blue face, / Acis had certainly not been erased: / a river-god – that was his newfound shape – / a river that retained his former name' (XIII, 485–8, trans. Allen Mandelbaum [New York: Harcourt Brace, 1993]).

78 Boccaccio makes a point of emphasizing Mensola's 'death' by having her collapse, apparently lifeless, into Africo's arms (octave 251). While he laments, her soul temporarily leaves her body and wanders about: 'Gli spiriti di Mensola, errando / eran per l'aria buona pezza andati, / e dopo molto nel corpo tornando nelli lor luoghi si fûr rientrati' [Mensola's spirits, wandering, had gone a long distance through the air, and after a long while returned to their dwelling places] (octave 254). Furthermore, it is clear that in Mensola's mind the loss of virginity was equated with death not only on a symbolic level but in the most literal sense, for Diana made a pastime of killing those nymphs who transgressed the most sacred law of her order by losing their virginity.

79 In Ovid's tale of Pyramus and Thisbe (*Met.* IV, 55ff.) this mixing of blood is never made quite so explicit. A similar fetishistic displacement is found in the *Valle delle donne* interlude of *Decameron* VI, where we are told that the *brigata* men head off to bathe in the same mountain lake in which the *brigata* women had recently bathed; the 'contact' of the naked bodies of the men and women is implicitly mediated by the water.

80 For different – and generally more sympathetic – accounts of the foundation history of the Amazons, see the profiles of the Amazon queens Marpesia and Lampedusa in *De mulieribus* (XI/XII respectively) and that of Penthesilea in *Esposizioni* IV, lit., 203ff.

81 This use of architectural evolution – from mud and wattle *capanne* to the *nobil casamento* – as an index of cultural progress suggests that in a sense, the cultural history traced in the *Ninfale* is loosely modelled on the Vitruvian etiology of architecture available to Boccaccio in *De architectura* II 1, 7: 'Then, however, building up themselves in spirit, and looking out and forward with larger ideas born from the variety of their crafts, they began to build, not huts, but houses, on foundations, and with brick walls, or built of stone ...' (trans. Granger, Loeb edition). For an interesting discussion of this theme of primitive architecture, see Rykwert's *On Adam's House in Paradise* (New York: Museum of Modern Art, 1972).

82 In 'Dubbi gravi intorno al "Ninfale fiesolano",' the second chapter of his

Studi sulla vita e le opere del Boccaccio, Pier Giorgio Ricci examines the question of Boccaccio's authorship of the *Ninfale.* In his introduction to the *Ninfale fiesolano* in the Mondadori edition, Armando Balduino evaluates the evidence both for and against Boccaccio's authorship.

83 See Armando Balduino's introduction (278) and notes to octave 436 (840) in the Mondadori edition for evidence that G. Villani's *Cronica* was Boccaccio's main source for the historical lore in this curious appendix. Pier Massimo Forni concurs with Balduino's view (see p. 10 of his introduction to the Mursia edition of the *Ninfale fiesolano*). Francesco Bruni, on the other hand, while admitting the possibility that Boccaccio may have had access to Villani's chronicle, thinks it unlikely (*Boccaccio,* 284).

84 Page number references are to Francesco Bruni's *Boccaccio.* Hauvette (*Boccace,* 164) views the historical 'appendix' of the *Ninfale* as awkward and unnecessary: 'l'intérêt poétique de cette addition est nul, d'autant plus qu'elle n'ajoute rien à ce que nous savons par ailleurs de ces legends' [this addition has no poetic value, all the more so as it adds nothing to what we know of these legends from other sources].

85 *Boccaccio, L'Ameto,* trans. Judith Serafini-Sauli (New York: Garland, 1985).

86 As Dante's son Pietro notes in his commentary to the *Commedia,* Cacciaguida's words recall those used by St Thomas in *De regimine principum* II, 7: 'extraneorum autem conversatio corrumpit civium mores.' In his *De vulgari eloquentia* Dante baits the reader by initially seeming to advocate the use of the 'volgare illustre' by even mediocre writers, arguing that 'if something which is the best of its kind is mixed with something inferior to it, the superior thing does not simply not detract from the inferior, it actually improves it' (*De vulgari* II 1, 3; Haller's trans.), only to pronounce this argument false in the following paragraph, with the assertion that the illustrious vernacular 'demands men of its own level, just like our other customs and fashions ... and, by the same token, this vernacular seeks out those with the greatest natural talent and learning' (*De vulgari* II 1, 4–5; trans. Haller). Matters are complicated by Dante's further qualification of this statement several paragraphs later: 'Concerning the statement that a superior thing mixed with an inferior thing brings it assistance, I say that it is true whenever the distinction between the two is broken down, as when we melt gold and silver together' (*De vulgari* II 1, 10; Haller's trans.). Dante seems to be implying that the resulting alloy does not represent an improvement on its constituent metals, but a compromise between them; the baser metal is exalted and the more noble metal debased. Like such an amalgamation of metals the genetic mixing of 'noble' Romans and 'base' Fiesolans has, in Dante's view, a twofold effect: it simultaneously enhances the Fiesolan stock and corrupts the Roman stock.

87 The association of poetry with hybridity is, of course, one of the dominant
    themes of Horace's *Ars poetica*. If a painter, remarks Horace at the beginning
    of his *Ars*, were to join the head of a beautiful woman to the body of an ugly,
    black fish, would we not be induced to laugh? Poets wishing to avoid such
    derision are therefore advised to exhibit restraint in their inventions, never
    venturing beyond the bounds of propriety. Horace openly acknowledges that
    the invention and portrayal of such hybrids is one of the special privileges of
    poets and painters. His concern is that this licence is too often abused: 'this
    licence we poets claim and in our turn we grant the like; but not so far that
    savage should mate with tame, or serpents couple with birds, lambs with
    tigers' (*Ars poetica*, 11–13, trans. H.R. Fairclough [Cambridge, MA: Harvard
    University Press, 1926]). As we have seen, Boccaccio's political miscegeny
    and social intermarriage all, in a way, represent a flouting of this Horatian
    precept. For a passage in Boccaccio strongly reminiscent of these opening
    lines of the *Ars*, see *Genealogie* XIV, 7 ff.

88 The identity of Boccaccio's biological mother is one of the enduring myster-
    ies surrounding Boccaccio's life. (Hauvette actually dedicates his *Boccace* to
    the memory of 'la parisienne inconnue qui donna le jour à l'auteur du
    Décaméron en 1313' [the unknown Parisian woman who gave birth to the
    author of the *Decameron* in 1313].) It is, therefore, particularly interesting to
    note that in the *Genealogie*, Boccaccio rebuts the cynical view that Aeneas's
    mother is called Venus simply because he is the child of a venereal union
    between Anchises and an unknown woman by asserting that there are many
    great men – among them Priam and Agamemnon – about whose mothers
    nothing is known (VI, 53). There is something in the slightly defensive tenor
    of this comment indicating that perhaps Boccaccio himself did not know the
    identity of his biological mother, and that this deficit of knowledge should
    not be viewed as proof of illegitimacy. Boccaccio never mentions his mother;
    curiously, neither does Ovid, the author whose poetic career Boccaccio's
    most closely resembles. The last paragraph of Thomas Hyde's excellent arti-
    cle on the *Genealogie*, 'Boccaccio: The Genealogies of Myth,' *PMLA* 100, 4–6
    (1985): 737–45, advances the suggestive thesis that Boccaccio's choice of
    genealogy as the structuring principle for his mythological handbook was
    influenced by his own illegitimacy and the questions surrounding his biolog-
    ical origin.

89 Janet Levarie Smarr provides a brief history of this type of criticism in the
    introduction of *Boccaccio and Fiammetta: The Narrator as Lover* (Urbana: Uni-
    versity of Illinois Press, 1986). See also the concise bibliography supplied by
    Branca in his *Profilo biografico*, 6n13.

90 See *De origine civitatis florentie det de eiusdem famosis civibus*, ed. Giuliano Tan-

turli (Antenore: Padua, 1997) for the various redactions of F. Villani's work; and G. Billanovich, *Restauri Boccacceschi* (Rome: Istituto Grafico Tiberino, 1947), 33.

91 From Francesco Torraca, *Per la biografia di Giovanni Boccaccio* (Milan, Rome, and Naples: Società Editrice Dante Alighieri di Albrighi, Segati e C., 1912), 56.

92 Branca acknowledges that his campaign to purge Boccaccio's biography of these romantic accretions has, of necessity, been somewhat uncompromising and does not, finally, negate the possibility that beneath these suggestive details, in fragmentary form, lurks some element of truth ('non può far negare in modo assoluto e totale che qualcosa di vero non si possa celare frammentariamente sotto quei dati sospetti'); the difficulty consists in distinguishing such elements from those of the inherited schemes – particularly in those circumstances where the patterns of literary motif and lived romantic experience coincide ('specialmente quando, coincidendo essi con le vicende più comuni ad ogni esperienza amorosa, la discriminazione fra schemi a posteriori e naturali ripetizioni è più difficile per non dire impossibile') (*Boccaccio medievale*, 243).

93 For Boccaccio's own definition of allegory, see *Genealogie* I, 3.

94 Branca, *Boccaccio medievale*, 231–2. Among the notable examples of this pattern in the *Decameron* are Proemio, 3; I 5, 4; II 3; and III 2.

95 For a fairly exact echo of Capellanus's precept in Boccaccio's work see *Decameron* VII 8, 4. Question eight of the 'questioni d'amore' of *Filocolo* IV essentially reiterates this idea from *De amore*.

96 For more on this notion of the half-caste see the story of Peleus in *Genealogie* XII, 50, where Achilles's status as a half-caste is discussed.

97 This passage is filled with allusions to Dante's Pier della Vigna and is initiated with a *captatio benevolentia* so egregiously tasteless – and yet so clearly modelled on those found in the *Commedia* – that the whole interview starts to feel like a parody. Boccaccio's intention to model Idalogos's transformation on an Ovidian variety of metamorphosis, though clear enough from the obvious parallels with the fate of Daphne (among others), is further confirmed by the rather jarring insertion of Idalogos in catalogue of predominantly Ovidian characters in the *Comedia delle ninfe* XXVI, 35. Both Polydorus and Pier serve in part to thematize the intimate bond between language and pain – speech issues together with blood through the ersatz orifices of their wounds – and this pain somehow accredits the truth-value of their words. In the case of Polydorus, the truth thus voiced concerns the circumstances of his death; he was cruelly murdered by his alleged guardian, Polymestor. Pier's speech consists in a clarification of the events surrounding his ignominious fall from

Frederick's favour – one which allows him to clear himself of the allegation of treachery that has long clouded his good name.

98 Talking trees seem to have found their ideal advocate in Boccaccio, who not only recurs to the *topos* himself, but submits the talking trees of Judges 9.8–15 as evidence that the use of such extravagant figures is not necessarily incompatible with the conveyance of truth (*Genealogie* XIV, 9). Though there is nothing remotely verisimilar in such limber-tongued trees, this tradition demands not only that we believe that trees can speak, but that such trees as do speak, confirm, and even illuminate the truth. Since Polydorus uses his gift of speech to condemn Polymestor, and Pier uses his to clear his own reputation, it is reasonable to consider that an analogous agenda informs Idalogos's autobiographical vignette. Other talking trees would have been familiar to Boccaccio from the pseudo-Ovidian *Nux*, whose protagonist is a lamenting walnut tree, and from the *Epistola Alexandri ad Aristotelem* (of which there was a transcription – though not in Boccaccio's own hand – in the Zibaldone Laurenziano) where the oracular trees of the Sun and Moon predict Alexander's death by treachery.

99 E.H. Wilkins identifies Calmeta with Andalò del Negro in 'Calmeta,' *Modern Language Notes* 21, 7 (1906). Quaglio treats this subject at length in *Scienza e mito nel Boccaccio* (Padua: Liviana, 1967), 153ff.

100 The transformation of a lovelorn young man into a tree whose fruit – the pine nut – Boccaccio credits with aphrodisiac properties seems cruel but has the virtue of conforming to a clear, albeit perverse, logic: a *contrapasso*-like form of retributive justice. Lucia Battaglia Ricci notes the association of pine trees, both in the *Roman de la Rose* and in Boccaccio's footnotes to the *Teseida*, with Venus and the sphere of erotic activity; *Boccaccio* (Roma: Salerno, 2000), 158. This image of the nut is frequently invoked by medieval authors wishing to illustrate the layered nature of allegory, whose nourishing, spiritual truths are, like the sweet pith of a nut, secreted within a historical or literal 'shell.' See also Ovid, *Art of Love* II, 424.

101 Vincenzo Crescini, *Contributo agli studi sul Boccaccio* (Turin: Ermanno Loescher, 1887), 15–16n2.

102 See the Mondadori edition, 916n17.

103 Perhaps – and this is pure speculation – this association of Ida with beauty is related to Boccaccio's belief that Ida was the site of the judgment of Paris (*Filocolo* IV, 15).

104 See also *Esposizioni* I, lit., 74 where Boccaccio makes the same association – though in the vernacular, 'esquisito parlare.' Osgood remarks in the notes to this passage in his translation that Boccaccio is here following the lead of Isidore of Seville (*Etym.* 8.7.2). Luigi Sasso, 'L'"interpretatio nominis" in

Boccaccio,' *Studi sul Boccaccio* 12 (1980): 129–74, briefly discusses the name 'Idalogos' in a footnote on 145.

105 In *Genealogie* XV 10 Boccaccio speaks of his innate need to pursue a life of poetry and of his father's condemnation of this yearning. Here, he maintains that his father's sustained effort to turn him from poetry to business ultimately prevented him from fulfilling his true potential as a poet: ' it came to pass that I turned out neither a business man, nor a canon-lawyer, and missed being a good poet besides' (Osgood, 132). Here, the hybridism that is viewed as a source of poetic fecundity in his youthful works is invested with a purely negative valence; this particular hybrid is vitiated, not strengthened, by the diversity of its components. See also *De casibus* III, 14, where Boccaccio discusses the question of whether he should be considered a poet.

106 Trans. H.R. Fairclough, Loeb edition. For Boccaccio's familiarity with the *Culex*, see Jonathan Usher, 'A Quotation from the *Culex* in Boccaccio's *De casibus*,' *Modern Language Review* 97, 2 (Apr. 2002): 312–23.

107 'Praegnans eum mater somniauit enixam se laureum ramum, quem contactu terrae coaluisse et excreuisse ilico in speciem maturae arbouris refertaeque uariis pomis et floribus' (3). That Boccaccio was familiar with Donatus's *Life of Virgil* is confirmed by his occasional use of details from Donatus's life for his own description of Virgil's life and works in the *Esposizioni*, an allusion to the occupation of Virgil's father in *Genealogie* XIV, 4, and is suggested by his inclusion of a similar dream in his *Vita di Dante*. For a discussion of Boccaccio' s familiarity with the early *Vitae Virgilianae*, see Osgood, 'Boccaccio's Knowledge of the Life of Virgil,' *Classical Philology* 25 (1930): 27–36.

108 There is, however, another detail of the classical *Vitae Virgilianae* that suggests an additional affiliation between Idalogos and the great Augustan poet; the 'biographies' of both give special importance to their humble origins. Whereas Idalogos was fathered by a rustic shepherd, Virgil, according to Donatus's account, was fathered by a potter, 'figulus' (see *Vita Donatiana* 1 in *Vitae Virgilianae antiquae* [Rome: Typis Officinae Polygraphicae, 1997]). This detail is mentioned in *Genealogie* XIV, 4 and *Esposizioni* XV, 94. In his *Life of Horace*, Suetonius stresses the menial occupation of Horace's father (see *Esposizioni* IV, lit., 112). Valerius Maximus devotes the fourth chapter of the third book of *Facta et dicta memorabilia* to the theme: 'De humili loco natis qui clari evaserunt' [Of those born in a humble situation who became famous]. Here it is primarily Cicero's humble origin which is discussed. In *Esposizioni* IV, lit., 255, Boccaccio acknowledges Valerius's 'De humili ...' as his source for an account of Socrates's modest beginnings. For other examples of this topos in Boccaccio, see *Esposizioni* I, alleg., 169ff and IV, lit., 91ff (Homer).

109 Giuseppe Billanovich, *Restauri Boccacceschi*, 157.

110 Vincenzo Crescini, *Contributo agli studi sul Boccaccio*, 11.

111 The entry for 'bis' in Uguccione da Pisa's *Magnae derivationes* reads: 'hoc big-ens – tis, qui ex duabus gentibus est natus, sicut ex patre tusco et matre franca.' (!) For Boccaccio on biological hybridism, see *Esposizioni* I, lit., 132.

112 *Memorable Doings and Sayings* VIII 6, 4, trans. D.R. Shackleton Bailey, Loeb edition.

113 This is just one of a number of such 'nocturnal ambush' scenes (see, for example *Filocolo*, IV, 118, 5ff). For many centuries, the recurrence of such scenes in Boccaccio's work was taken as evidence that the youthful Boccaccio had actually engaged in an episode of this sort. Branca's convincing argument that far from being original and peculiar to Boccaccio, such scenes were actually a stock motif of popular romances, poems and ballads, did much to squelch the positivistic fantasy that would have Boccaccio clinging to a gutter spout at his mistress's window. Since Branca's arguments reflect the practical necessity of tempering the excesses of positivist criticism, they sometimes lean too far in the other direction. Certainly, the conventional, literary, characteristic of these night sorties does not preclude the possibility that Boccaccio truly engaged in some such activity – one which, after all, continues to be a staple of collegiate life. However, it seems to me that all such speculation is really beside the point; real or imagined, this erotic scenario clearly exerted great fascination on Boccaccio.

114 See the Mondadori edition, notes 47 and 48 for XXIII.

115 Boccaccio's development of this motif of artistic hubris in the Ibrida passage – in particular the consequences of yielding to poetic inspiration that is not sufficiently reined in and governed by technique – has been treated at length by Jonathan Usher in 'Global Warming in the Sonnet: The Phaethon Myth in Boccaccio and Petrarch,' *Studi sul Boccaccio* 28 (2000): 125–83.

116 There is some ambiguity attached to the adjective 'duri' as it does not necessarily refer to the charioteers, but may refer to the 'high towers' and 'embattled' walls which successfully resist their assault.

117 This theme is discussed at greater length in my article '"O vendetta di Dio": The Motif of Rape and Retaliation in Dante's *Inferno*,' *MLN* 120, 1, Italian Issue (Jan. 2005): 1–29.

118 Other occurrences of the word 'cresta' in Boccaccio's works tend to confirm these associations with sexual arrogance and pride. In Elissa's invective against priestly vanity in *Decameron* VII 3, she likens Rinaldo and his fellow clerics to 'galli tronfi con la cresta levata' [conceited cocks with raised up crests] (VII 3, 9). In her paean to the Golden Age in *Elegia di Madonna Fiammetta* (V 30, 22), Fiammetta laments the demise of a more wholesome age of

natural sobriety, before 'la comante cresta ornava i lucenti elmi' [the frilly crest decorated the shining helmets].

119 Trans. Grant Showerman, Loeb edition.

120 There are numerous literary precedents for both the erotic night sortie and the 'necrophilic' interlude. In the *Genealogie* IX, 40, Boccaccio retells Ovid's story of the rape of the sleeping Silvia by Mars, which resulted in the conception of Romulus and Remus (*Fasti*, III, 11ff), and in *Genealogie* XI, 17 he tells the tale of Mercury's rape of the sleeping Lychione. In *De casibus* II, 19, Boccaccio retells Herodotus's story of the Lydian king Candaules's ill-advised decision to expose his sleeping wife's naked body to his companion Gyges (available to him in Justin's *Epitome* I, 7) – a plot recycled by Boccaccio in the Alatiel tale of *Decameron* (II 7, 56). The fondling of a dead woman – though without a subsequent resuscitation – is a prominent element of Ovid's Story of the Raven (*Met.* II, 617ff). Quaglio (like Francesco Mazzoni in 'In una presunta fonte del Boccaccio,' *Studi danteschi* 29 [1950]: 192–6) proposes the popular *Historia Apollonii regis Tyrii* as a literary precedent for the scene of necrophilia in *Filocolo* IV 67, 7ff. (a motif reprised in *Decameron* X, 4). Pio Rajna discusses the contemporary Florentine tale of Ginevra degli Almieri (whether fictional or historical is left in doubt) which, he suggests, may have originated from the same unidentified historical source that inspired Boccaccio's necrophilic narrative in *Filocolo* IV (and the Gentile de' Carisendi novella of *Decameron* X, 4; see Rajna, 'L'episodio delle questioni d'amore nel *Filocolo*,' *Romania* 31 [1902]: 62–3). See also the end of the *Amorosa visione* where Boccaccio tries to foist himself on his sleeping lover. Pier Massimo Forni discusses Boccaccio's significant manipulation of the narrative elements borrowed from the *Historia Apollonio* in Forni, *Adventures in Speech: Rhetoric and Narration in Boccaccio's* Decameron (Philadelphia: University of Pennsylvania Press, 1996), 80. For an iconic expression of these intertwined themes of sex, death, and bondage, see the genito-botanic pomegranate of *Filocolo* V 25, 3.

121 Such concerns of poetic impotence abound in Boccaccio's work. Consider, for instance, *Rime* CVIII, 1–11. The association of poetry with thwarted desire, the sublimation of erotic feeling into love lyric is, of course, an ancient one. It is a phenomenon exquisitely conveyed by Sappho's haunting lyrics, which often seem to issue from the vacuum left by absent or inaccessible lovers. In a sense, the hundred tales of the *Decameron* may be viewed as the product of one such thwarted love, for by retracing the various events that culminated in Boccaccio's decision to write these *novelle*, it is revealed that the 'first cause' in this series of concatenated events was Boccaccio's failure in love: had he not failed, he would not have required the consolation of

friends; had he not received this consolation, he would not have felt gratitude; had he not experienced gratitude, he would have felt no urge to
return the favour by providing consolation to women in the form of his collection of *novelle*.

122 'Agnosco quidem non esse pennas volucres michi, quarum adiutus suffragio
celos penetrare queam, ibidem Dei lustraturus archana et demum mortalibus visa relaturus ...' (*De casibus* VI 1, 9).

123 In *Genealogie* IX, alleg., 32, in the course of discussing the various terms used
to denote the Furies, Boccaccio observes that among the inhabitants of hell,
that is, he explains, men of a base and despicable condition, the Furies are
called 'cani'; among us, that is, men of a middle state, 'in mezzo tra'l cielo e
lo 'nferno,' they are called 'Furie' and 'Eumenide'; and among the gods,
that is, superior and grand men, they are called 'Dire.' Hell, Purgatory, and
Heaven are thus collapsed into a single, terrestrial, plane.

Chapter 3. The Myth of a New Beginning

1 Pio Rajna ('L'Episodio delle questioni d'amore,' *Romania* 31 [1902], 80)
notes that as Körting had already observed in his *Boccaccio's Leben und Werke*
(1880), Boccaccio draws his title from those treatises, the *hexamera*, having to
do with the creation of the world. Having summarily rejected the possibility
that Boccaccio's choice of title reflects a hidden agenda of some sort, Rajna
does not, unfortunately, offer any explanation for Boccaccio's decision to
model the title of his glaringly secular work on that of a sacred genre.
Giuseppe Mazzotta argues that Boccaccio's decision to pattern his title,
Decameron, on the medieval *hexamera* signals his intention to secularize a
sacred genre. Mazzotta notes that 'in medieval numerical symbolism ... ten is
the number of temporal perfection, of self-enclosed totality' and adds the
important observation that this implied self-sufficiency has the effect of casting the *Decameron* as 'an antiworld, an atemporal esthetic garden juxtaposed
to the history of mutability and death' (*The World at Play in Boccaccio's*
Decameron [Princeton: Princeton University Press, 1986], 53). Kurt Flasch
observes that Boccaccio has transformed the venerable six-day creation narrative of the theologians into a personal ten-day creation narrative infused
with a poetic levity (*Poesia dopo la peste: Saggio su Boccaccio*, trans. Rosa Taliani
[Bari: Laterza, 1995], 18). Lucia Battaglia Ricci briefly addresses the question of Boccaccio's title in *Ragionare nel giardino* (Rome: Salerno, 2000), 28.
See also Giovanni Getto, *Vita di forme e forme di vita nel* Decameron (Turin:
G.B. Petrini, 1972), 6.

2 Barberi Squarotti, 'La "cornice" del "Decameron" o il mito di Robinson,' in

Il potere della parola: studi sul 'Decameron' (Naples: Federico & Ardia, 1983), 28. Vittore Branca notes in passing that the members of the *brigata* 'sono gli eletti a ritirarsi e a raccogliersi nella villa fiesolana, come in un'arca di salvezza durante il nuovo diluvio' [are those chosen to withdraw and gather together in the Fiesolan villa, as though in a salvific ark during the new deluge] (*Boccaccio medievale e nuovi studi sul Decameron* [Florence: Sansoni, 1986], 39), but the implications of this association are not further explored.

3 Antonia Mazza notes that although Attilio Hortis maintained that Boccaccio was not familiar with Chalcidius, in truth, Boccaccio cites Chalcidius 'sia come traduttore che come commentatore del *Timeo*' [both as a translator and as a commentator of the *Timaeus*] in both the *Genealogie* and the *Esposizioni*; for Hortis's argument see, *Studj sulle opere latine del Boccaccio* (Trieste: Julius Dase, 1879), 374–5. A manuscript of the *Timaeus* is among the volumes listed in the inventory of the 'little library' of Santo Spirito and may well have been part of Boccaccio's own library; see Mazza, 'L'inventario della "Parva Libreria" di Santo Spirito e la biblioteca del Boccaccio,' *Italia medioevale e umanistica* 9 (1966): 23. Mazza points out, moreover, that Petrarch actually owned the text and commentary by Chalcidius now in the Parisian lat. 6280.

4 For a similar use of this mountain/plain metaphor in Boccaccio, see the *Filocolo* V 31, 3.

5 The allegorical interpretation of the Church as ark was a commonplace in the Middle Ages. Augustine devotes *City of God* XV, 26 to the development of this Church/ark analogy. The Christian-Latin poet Avitus provides a particularly dynamic image of the Church as ark in which the Church is depicted pitching and yawing in the torrential waters of the Deluge (*De spiritalis historiae gestis* IV). Boccaccio alludes to the allegorical interpretation of the Church as ark in *De Genealogie* and Hugh of St Victor, an author familiar to Boccaccio, wrote two much-read tracts on the ark, one moral, *De arca Noe morali*, and the other mystical, *De arca Noe mystica*, in which the Church/ark correspondence is developed at length.

6 From *Fulgentius the Mythographer*, trans. Leslie George Whitbread (Columbus: Ohio State University Press, 1971), 192.

7 *Biblia sacrata iuxta vulgatam versionem*, 3rd ed., ed. Robertus Weber, Bonifatius Fischer, et al. (Stuttgart: Deutsche Biblegesellschaft, 1983).

8 *Rerum familiarium libri* I–VIII, trans. Aldo S. Bernardo (Albany: State University of New York Press, 1975). For a discussion of Petrarch's attitude towards the plague, see Renee Neu Watkins, 'Petrarch and the Black Death: From Fear to Monuments,' *Studies in the Renaissance* 19 (1972): 196–223.

9 *Epistolae de rebus familiaribus et variae*, ed. Iosephi Fracassetti (Florence: Le Monnier, 1859).

10 Matteo Villani, *Cronica* (con la continuazione di Filippo Villani). Ed. Giuseppe Porta. Fondazione Pietro Bembo, Parma: Ugo Guanda 1995.

11 This reading (one already proposed in my dissertation of 2000) is supported by a passage in Timothy Kircher's fine discussion of responses to the plague by fourteenth-century historians, mendicants, and humanists in *The Poet's Wisdom* (Leiden: Brill, 2000), chap. 2: 'This "renewal" [rinovellamento] should not be interpreted to mean for Villani simply the dawn of a new cultural era, or of a social or political recovery ... It must be understood in the Biblical post-diluvian framework that he introduces at the chapter's outset: the term rather suggests a regeneration of human activity after the sentence of death, waste, and devastation' (57).

12 Boccaccio's irresolution concerning whether the plague is to be ascribed to astral influence or to the just ire of God stoked by human iniquity is worth remarking – particularly since Boccaccio, like Dante, generally portrays the stars as agents of divine providence. That Boccaccio should distinguish in this way between astral and divine determinacy seems to indicate his desire to integrate the moralized idea of such cataclysms as manifestations of divine justice (the Judeo-Christian and Ovidian model of divine causation) with the more mechanistic, Platonic notion that natural catastrophes derive from the periodic variation in the movement of heavenly bodies (the model proposed in the *Timaeus*). In the introduction of *De casibus*, Boccaccio states that astral influence, like Fortuna, is simply the classical term for providence; a truth concerning which the pagans were ignorant by dint of their historic anteriority to Christian truth as revealed in the Incarnation. For celestial bodies viewed as ministers of God, see for example *Esposizioni* I, 12ff. and *Vita di Dante* II. See also Giovanni Villani, *La Cronica*, III 1.

13 Though the collapsing of the boundaries between secular and sacred varieties of creation implied by this appropriation of a sacred genre (the *hexaemeron*), for a secular 'creation' text (the *Decameron*) is problematic insofar as it suggests a sort of contest with deity – an act of artistic pride of the sort illustrated by Ovid's stories of Arachne and Marsyas and Dante's exempla of pride punished on the 'Terrace of Pride' in *Purgatorio* – this type of imitation may just as easily be taken as a form of pious emulation of God's original creative act. This apparent conflict is defused, if not fully resolved, by Boccaccio's contention that poetic creation is itself divinely inspired. See for example *Genealogie* XIV and the *Vita di Dante* XXI.

14 In his *Discorso storico sul testo del* Decamerone, Ugo Foscolo draws to the reader's attention a wonderful anecdote from Benvenuto da Imola's commentary on the *Commedia* which describes Boccaccio's distress upon discovering that the monks of Monte Cassino had, with no apparent sense of shame, mutilated the great old codices to make covers for their prayer books; see

Beatrice Corrigan, ed., *Italian Poets and English Critics, 1755–1859* (Chicago: University of Chicago Press, 1969), 11, for an English translation of this passage. A similar concern with issues of textual preservation is evident in Ovid's description in *Met.* XV 809ff. of the Fates' archives of destiny, engraved with adamant points on tablets of iron and bronze, a passage paraphrased by Boccaccio in *Genealogie* I, V and *Esposizioni.* IX, lit.; 65.

15 Hortis, *Studj,* 364

16 Plato, *Timaeus and Critias,* trans. Desmond Lee (New York: Penguin, 1983), 35. Even if Boccaccio did not – as Attilio Hortis maintains – have direct access to a copy of Chalcidius's translation and commentary of Plato's *Timaeus,* he would nevertheless have been familiar with this particular passage since it is reproduced in the Eusebius-Jerome *Chronicon,* a work cited with great frequency in his Latin works (see *PL,* vol. 27, col. 14).

17 In many respects Boccaccio anticipates the concerns of Diderot and his fellow eighteenth-century encyclopedists. In the manifesto-like prospectus of his *Encyclopédie,* Diderot writes: 'Nous osons dire que si les anciens eussent exécuté une Encyclopédie comme ils ont exécuté tant de grandes choses, et que ce manuscrit se fût échappé seul de la fameuse bibliotèque d'Alexandrie, il eût été capable de nous consoler de la perte des autres' [We venture to claim that had the ancients produced an encyclopedia just as they produced so many great things, and had this manuscript alone escaped from the famous library of Alexandria, if would have sufficed to compensate the loss of the others] (citation from the University of Chicago on-line ARTFL *Encyclopédie* project).

18 Macrobius, *Commentary on the Dream of Scipio,* trans. William Harris Stahl (New York: Columbia University Press, 1952). Macrobius's commentary (fourth- or possibly fifth-century) was solely responsible for preserving Cicero's 'Dream of Scipio' for scholars of the Middle Ages, for though elements of Cicero's *De republica* were available indirectly (through the works of Augustine and other patristic authors), it was not until 1822 that the work was recovered in its entirety; see L.D. Reynolds and N.G. Wilson, *Scribes and Scholars* (Oxford: Clarendon Press, 1991), 194. See also Mazza, 'L'inventario della "Parva Libreria,"' 19. Similar sentiments regarding the transitory nature of fame are expressed by Boccaccio in *De casibus* VIII, 1.

19 English citations are from T.H. Corcoran's translation in the Loeb edition.

20 The emperor Nero is among Boccaccio's better known precursors in this idea of imposing a rational plan on the ashes of a razed culture; only, in contrast to Nero, Boccaccio does not actually take the initiative to personally oversee the destruction of the prevailing culture. It is interesting that despite Nero's prodigious turpitude, Boccaccio cannot help but admire both his intellectual gifts and his extensive building projects (see *De casibus* VII, 4).

21 From Guido da Pisa, *Expositiones et glose super Comediam Dantis*, ed. Vincenzo Cioffari (Albany: State University of New York Press, 1974).

22 A slightly different version of this section, 'St Boccaccio: The Poet as Pander and Martyr,' was previously published in *Studi sul Boccaccio* 30 (2002): 125–57.

23 For Boccaccio's application in the *Genealogie* of this trope of the author as a new Prometheus, see Lucia Marino, 'Prometheus, or the Mythographer's Self-Image,' in *Studi sul Boccaccio* 12 (1980), 263–73. In this fine article (the first, I believe, to address Boccaccio's decision to cast himself as a sort of Prometheus redivivus), Marino argues that in Boccaccio's revised version of the myth, Prometheus 'appears to conform substantially to the paradigm for learning, or nine-part theory of cognition proposed by Fulgentius' (269). Accordingly, she views the excoriation of Prometheus's liver in Fulgentian terms as a symbolic representation of the extreme effort exacted by study – the interpretation most often supplied by Boccaccio – but does not investigate the related theme of the pedagogue as a Promethean variety of culture-hero whose suffering is undertaken on behalf of others.

24 Curiously, Melville proposes a very similar allegorization of the Prometheus myth in chap. 44 of *Moby-Dick*: 'he whose intense thinking thus makes him a Prometheus; a vulture feeds upon that heart for ever; that vulture the very creature he creates.'

25 'Eos tanquam lapideos suscipiens quasi de novo creet, docet et instruit, et demonstrationibus suis ex naturalibus hominibus civiles facit, moribus scientia et virtutibus insignes, adeo ut liquido pateat alios produxisse naturam et alios reformasse doctrinam' (*Genealogie* IV 44, 12).

26 See Charles Grosvenor Osgood, *Boccaccio on Poetry* (New York: Bobbs-Merrill, 1930), xxv. Osgood (xxiii–xxiv) uses Boccaccio's exemplary elaboration of the Prometheus myth in the *Genealogie* to cast light on Boccaccio's general methodology.

27 That Boccaccio should find it hard to stomach the notion of a God who rewards human striving with cruel punishments is hardly surprising; one need only consider his lively defence of Alcibiades and virtual redemption of Ulysses – who epitomizes the figure of the transgressor in Dante's *Inferno* – in *De casibus* III, 13. For Boccaccio the yardstick by which transgression is measured is neither divine nor positive law but reason.

28 Both Prometheus and Phaethon represent aspects of Boccaccio: the former both as a compiler/creator (one whose creation is not *ex nihilo* but consists in the constitution or re-constitution of a given entity through the task of compilation) and as purveyor of intellectual knowledge (the stolen fire), and the latter – according to the peculiarly Boccaccian interpretation presented in the *Allegoria mitologica* – as a mediator figure who aims to redeem humanity.

Augustine writes 'The reason why they say that he moulded men out of mud is that he is supposed to have been the best teacher of wisdom' (*City of God*, XVIII, viii; trans. Sanford, Green [Loeb]).

29 The *Teseida*, Boccaccio boasts, is the first martial epic to be written in the (Italian) vernacular: 'ma tu, o libro, primo a lor cantare / di Marte fai gli affanni sostenuti, / nel volgar lazio più mai non veduti' (*Teseida* XII, 84). The ungainly full title of the work, *Teseida della nozze di Emilia*, seems to announce both an epic and an epithalamium: a variety of generic hybridization that pervades all of Boccaccio's work. In *De vulgari eloquentia*, Dante argues that the vernacular should be used to write of such august matters as prowess in arms, the flames of love, and the direction of the will (a revision of his stance in the *Vita nuova* where he deems the vernacular appropriate for love lyric alone). Though, he tells us, the latter two topics have been ably treated by vernacular poets, the first, prowess in arms, has not: 'Arma vero nullum latium adhuc invenio poetasse' (*De vulgari* II 2, 8). As has often been observed, Boccaccio's assertion that his *Teseida* is the first vernacular martial epic would appear to be a direct response to Dante's implied 'challenge.'

30 Boccaccio uses a similar phrase, 'nel cospetto di tutti' [in everybody's sight], in relation to his use of the vernacular in the *Filocolo* (V 97, 10).

31 Macrobius, *Commentary on the Dream of Scipio*, trans. Stahl. This very passage is frequently cited in Boccaccio's works, sometimes at great length. See for instance *Carmine* V, *Esposizioni* I, alleg., 8–9 and *Genealogie* I, 3. See Antonia Mazza, 'L'inventario della "parva libraria,"' 19, for evidence that Boccaccio owned a copy of Macrobius's commentary.

32 This stance is very like that taken by Fulgentius in the *Mitologiarum* where, upon being reproved by the Muse for his intellectual presumption – one that consists in the belief that he is equal to the task of extracting truth from the ancient myths – he responds: 'If one happens to have at least some knowledge in matters where a degree of ignorance is expected, how much more satisfactory has it been to happen not to have been born to such things, rather than to have been born to them in all their futility. For I consider I have awareness of a new threshold of knowledge denied to you' (I, prologue, 22; English translation from *Fulgentius the Mythographer*, trans, Leslie George Whitbread [Columbus: Ohio State University Press, 1971], 45). See *Genealogie*, I, proem, where this pattern is first introduced, most likely on Fulgentius's model.

33 Citation from *The Novellino or One Hundred Ancient Tales*. Based on the 1525 Gualteruzzi editio princeps, ed. and trans. J.P. Consoli (New York: Garland, 1997). Hauvette links the Numenius and *Novellino* narratives in his *Boccace*, but is less concerned with tracing the continuity between these two stories

than he is with distinguishing between the acceptable revelation of pagan secrets in the *Genealogie* as contrasted with the morally questionable revelation of Christian secrets in the lectures on Dante's 'sacro poema.' Henri Hauvette views Boccaccio's expression of regret (in the *Rime*) for having 'prostrated the Muses' and elucidated Dante's sublime concepts for the unworthy rabble as entirely sincere. See *Boccace: Étude biographique et littéraire* (Paris: Armand Colin, 1914), 456. Whereas pagan cultic practices reveal a penchant for secret rituals and privileged knowledge of one sort or another, it seems to me that the Christian religion (at least in its primitive form), with its fundamentally democratic quality and emphasis on revelation, far from being anxious that sacred truths might be exposed to the masses, is actually dedicated to revealing these truths. Consequently, I find it hard to believe that Boccaccio had any genuine religious misgivings about glossing Dante's poem.

34 *Le vite d'uomini illustri fiorentini scritte da Filippo Villani*, ed. Giammaria Mazzuchelli (Florence: Sansone Coen, 1847), 17; my emphasis. The same idiom concerning availability to all hands is present in Villani's original Latin recension.

35 Translation from *Literary Criticism of Dante Alighieri*, ed. and trans. Robert S. Haller (Lincoln: University of Nebraska Press, 1973), 117–18.

36 Citations are from *Martianus Capella and the Seven Liberal Arts*: vol. 2, *The Marriage of Philology and Mercury*, trans. William Harris Stahl and Richard Johnson (New York: Columbia University Press, 1977). For Boccaccio's familiarity with Martianus's work, see Hortis, *Studj*, 459–60. More doubt is cast on the virtue of the personified *Artes* by Hugh of St Victor, who equates the mechanical arts with adultery in his *Didiscalicon*: 'human work, because it is not nature but only imitative of nature, is fitly called mechanical, that is adulterate' (I, 9; *The Didiscalicon of Hugh of St Victor*, trans. J. Taylor [New York: Columbia University Press, 1961], 56).

37 For a survey of such episodes of voyeurism and striptease in Boccaccio's works see Michel David, 'Boccaccio pornoscopo?' in *Medioevo e rinascimento veneto con altri studi in onore di Lino Lazzarini*, vol. 1, ed. R. Avesani, G. Billanovich, and G. Pozzi (Padua: Antenore, 1979), 215–43. Boccaccio's tendency to parody stilnovista models is explored by M. Bevilacqua in 'L'amore come sublimazione e degradazione: il denudamento della donna angelicata nel *Decameron*,' *Rassegna della letteratura italiana* 79 (1975): 415–32.

38 Similarly entertaining parodies of traditional *topoi* abound in the *Comedia delle ninfe*. In Dante's memorable parenthesis to the imagination in the *Commedia*, he marvels at the ability of our imagination to generate, without the imput of the senses, an alternate reality so powerful that we would be oblivious even to

the blare of a thousand bugles (*Purg.* XVII, 13–15). In the *Comedia delle ninfe*, far from separating one from externals, the imagination becomes the medium of choice for exploring the hidden recesses of the external world – and, more particularly, those of its delectable inhabitants. Ameto, surrounded by a surfeit of female beauty, finds himself engaging in 'diverse imaginazioni concordevoli a' suoi disii' [various imaginings concordant with his desires] (XXVIII, 5); an imaginative pilgrimage that allows him to peruse their hidden charms at leisure – even to the point of imagining that he is savoring their 'saporita saliva' [tasty saliva] (5). Though the *Comedia delle ninfe* does, finally, correspond to the traditional pattern – Ameto goes from being a rustic animal ('animale bruto') to a man ('uomo divenuto') when he sees with the intellect rather than the eyes (XLVI, 3–5) – Boccaccio obviously did little to expedite the journey, preferring, it would seem, to dally in the valley with his nymphs.

39 For examples of this critical response, see Thomas G. Bergin, *Boccaccio* (New York: Viking, 1981), 144; and Lucia Battaglia Ricci, *Boccaccio* (Rome: Salerno, 2000), 104.

40 In Apollodorus's *Bibliotheca* (I 1, 3) we have the example of the prurient bard Thamyris who competes with the Muses on the condition that should he win, he be granted their favours in succession (he loses, and is both blinded and deprived of his poetic skills). In his *Naturalis historia* (1C AD), Pliny preserves Varro's anecdote concerning the sorry plight of a Roman knight, Junius Pisciculus, who falls in love with the statues of the Muses of Helicon that grace the Temple of Prosperity (XXXVI 4, 39) – true 'donne petrose'!

41 Ernst Robert Curtius, *European Literature and the Latin Middle Ages*, trans. W.R. Trask (New York: Bollingen, 1953).

42 *The Consolation of Philosophy*, trans. S.J. Tester, Loeb edition (Cambridge, MA: Harvard University Press, 1918).

43 In addition to presenting a scholarly exposition on the various attributes of the Muses, Fulgentius actually provides some support for the Boethian view by suggesting, in the entertaining prologue to the *Mitologiae*, that personifications are sexual entities. When the Muses, in response to his invocation, appear in person to provide their services, he expresses some doubt regarding the wisdom of housing a personified Satire under his roof for, he remarks, his wife would 'be livid with envy because of her, so much so that, should she discover her in the house acting like my mistress with wanton ways, she would feel herself obliged to send her back to Helicon with her cheeks furrowed with scratches' (*Mitol.* I, Prol., 22; 46, *Fulgentius the Mythographer*).

44 This précis of the authoritative perspectives concerning the Muses is

repeated in nearly identical form – though without the defence of Muses – in *Esposizioni* II, lit., 11–34.

45 *Esposizioni* I, lit., 108.

46 Boccaccio's ambivalence regarding the act of popularizing texts through vernacular glosses and translations is described by Vittore Branca in *Giovanni Boccaccio: Profilo biografico* (Milan: Sansoni, Nuova edizione riveduta e aggiornata al 1997): 'Più delle incomprensioni e delle sciocche pretese dell'"ingrato vulgo," dovettero preoccupare il Boccaccio queste accuse di voler prostituire le Muse e i loro alti messaggi, specialmente quando si affermava che Dante stesso avrebbe sdegnato simili volgarizzazioni. È questa la situazione che in quattro sonetti (CXXII–CXXV) sentiamo dibattuta e sofferta profondamente, proprio perché il trepido, religioso culto della poesia aveva fatto alle volte assumere al Boccaccio attegiamenti apparentemente analoghi a quelli di chi ora aspramente lo rimprovava' (186) ['More than the lack of understanding and the foolish stones cast by the "ingrato vulgo," the ungrateful herd, the accusations that he was prostituting the Muses and their exalted messages must have worried Boccaccio, especially when it seemed that Dante himself would have scorned such vulgarizations. The question of vulgarization is debated with profound suffering in four sonnets (CXXII–CXXV), precisely because his tremulous religious attitude towards poetry had often caused Boccaccio to assume positions apparently analogous to those of the man who now was scolding him harshly'] (Branca, *Boccaccio: The Man and His Works*, trans. Richard Monges [New York: New York University Press, 1976], 185).

47 In *Boccaccio: L'invenzione della letteratura mezzana* (Bologna: Il Mulino, 1990), Francesco Bruni notes the contradiction implicit in Boccaccio's promotion of allegory as a means of preventing the devaluation of sublime knowledge through wide dissemination even as he industriously sets about unveiling the allegorical meanings of the *Commedia* to the general public: 'nell'interpretazione del Boccaccio la poesia seleziona i propri utenti grazie al procedimento allegorico, ed è dedicata a un'aristocrazia spirituale; ma nello spiegare pubblicamente le allegorie riposte nella *Commedia*, il Boccaccio non contraveniva a quei principi?' [according to Boccaccio's interpretation, poetry selects its own consumers thanks to the allegorical procedure and is dedicated to a spiritual aristocracy; but in publicly expounding the hidden allegories of the *Comedy*, doesn't Boccaccio contravene these principles?] (470). Having noted this contradiction, Boccaccio's critics confronted him and Boccaccio, continues Bruni: 'sensibile, in questo come in altri casi, agli attacchi ... non si ribellò ma finí per capitolare, come risulta dai quattro sonetti (CXXII–CXXV) nei quali si autoaccusa di aver prostituito le Muse al "vulgo" (CXXII

2), e addirittura attribuisce a giusta punizione divina (di "Appollo") la propria malattia' [sensitive, in this case as in others, to attacks ... did not fight
back, but yielded in the end as can be seen from the four sonnets (CXXII–
CXXV) in which he accuses himself of having prostituted the Muses to the
'crowd' (CXXII 2), going so far as to attribute his own sickness to a justified
divine retribution (of 'Apollo')] (470). Where Bruni sees capitulation and
self-accusation I am more inclined, as I have argued above, to see a sophisticated bid to displace blame from himself to his critics while simultaneously
enhancing his own stature – to be punished by Apollo has a certain cachet.
After all, Marsyas was no amateur.

48 The *Esposizioni* represent, in somewhat revised form, a transcript of these
public lectures.

49 Only with the 1962 publication of Pier Giorgio Ricci's article offering substantial documentary evidence to support a date of 1372 for these letters to
Mainardo was their dating finally resolved. Before then critics had oscillated
between the dates of 1372 and 1373. In the absence of such documentary evidence, the subject matter of the letters taken together with Boccaccio's tendency to associate his sickness with the public lectures – both in his *Rime* (in
particular CXXII and CXXIII) and in his letter of 1374 to Francesco da Brossano (*Epistole* XXIV) – would offer strong support for a date somewhere in
the fall of 1373, and more precisely, during the period of the public lectures
that began in October of 1373 and ended, most likely, in the early months of
1374 due to Boccaccio's sickness recorded in his letter to Brossano; for more
details, see Giorgio Padoan, *Il Boccaccio, le Muse, il Parnasso e l'Arno* (Florence:
Olschki, 1978), 234–9. Indeed, the instinct to assign them this later date is so
strong that Ginetta Auzzas, the editor of the *Epistole* in the Mondadori edition, has actually assigned the year 1373 in the rubric to both letters, though
her footnotes, following Ricci's lead, insist on a date of 1372: 'questa epistola
è sicuramente del 1372' (*Epistole* XXI, footnote 3). For Ricci's argument in
favour of the earlier date, see 'Studi sulle opere latine e volgari del Boccaccio'
in *Rinascimento*, 2nd ser., vol. 2 (1962): 3–29; reprinted in his *Studi sulla vita e
le opere del Boccaccio* (Milan: Riccardo Ricciardi, 1985), 163–71.

50 Hortis not only takes this all at face value but notes the usefulness of this passage to students of medieval medicine – in particular those interested in sur-
gical techniques; see *Accenni alle scienze naturali nelle opere di Giovanni Boccaccio*
(Trieste: Tipografia del Lloyd Austro-Ungarico, 1877), 36.

51 Boccaccio writes: 'If they called them apes of nature, the epithet might be less
irritating, since the poet tries with all his powers to set forth in noble verse the
effects, either of Nature herself, or of her eternal and unalterable operation
... In this sense, I admit, the poets are apes ... It would be better for such crit-

ics if they would use their best efforts to make us all become apes of Christ, rather than jeer at the labors of poets, which they do not understand. Sometimes people who try to scratch another's itching back ['pruritum scalpere'] feel someone's bloody nails ['cruentas ungues'] in their own skin – and not so pleasantly either!' (*Genealogie* XIV 17, 5; Osgood, 79–80). On the strength of this passage, H.W. Janson has argued that 'the author of the *Genealogie* must be regarded as the originator of the Renaissance concept of *ars simia naturae*, as against the mediaeval *simia veri* with its invidious distinction between reality and representational art, the "forgery of reality"' (*Apes and Ape Lore in the Middle Ages and Renaissance* [London: Warburg Institute, University of London, 1952], 293); see also Curtius, *European Literature and the Latin Middle Ages*, chap. 19 ('The Ape as Metaphor'). For Janson, such *in malo* imitators as Capocchio and his spiritual kin are represented in the *Genealogie* by the figure of Epimetheus, Prometheus's brother, whom Boccaccio (on the authority of the mysterious Theodontius) credits with having been the first man to shape a human form from mud: 'hominis statuam primus ex luto finxit' (*Genealogie* IV 42, 1). Jupiter, offended by Epimetheus's presumption, punishes him by transforming him into an ape and relegating him to the Pithecusae islands. Janson sees Boccaccio as distinguishing sharply between plastic and poetic forms of mimesis; the former, epitomized by the figure of Epimetheus, is deemed a transgressive, damnable aping of divine creation – that is, the created world – whereas the latter, represented by the figure of the Poet, is viewed as a pious and praiseworthy imitation of the divine act of creation. Indeed, there would be little reason to question the soundness of this conclusion were one to consider these passages alone. However, we must not forget that this resolutely positive view of poetic imitation occurs in the fourteenth book of the *Genealogie*, Boccaccio's most impassioned defence of poetry. A close consideration of the imagery in the letter to Mainardi suggests that the mimetic qualities of poetry and the plastic arts cannot be so easily distinguished: 'ut pictura poesis.' If in the apologia of *Genealogie* XIV it is the poet's critics who must fear 'bloody nails in their own skin,' in the letter to Mainardo it is clear that the poet's nails have turned upon himself. Petrarch adresses the ape/imitation theme in *Familiares* XXIII 19, 11–12.

52 'Nec mora: parantur in scarnificationem meam instrumenta, ferrum et ignis; et accensis lampadibus et in meam carnem extinctis atque infixis et demum sublatis, et crebris cultro tonsorio, eisdem locis ante preustis, ictibus fracta cute, iterum et iterum apponuntur non absque maximo cruciato meo' (*Epistole* XXI, 26).

53 For Prometheus's recrescent liver see *Genealogie* IV 44, 5. The objection may be raised that all of this material relating to livers and excoriation could just

as fittingly be applied to the Titan Tityus who was condemned to a punishment identical to that of Prometheus for his attempt to rape Apollo's mother, Latona (indeed, the allusion to Aetna in the letter to Mainardi cannot help but recall Tityus, whose vast body, so the Ovidian legend goes, is pinned beneath Aetna's mass). However, it is noteworthy that Boccaccio also presents Tityus as a magnanimous sort whose interest in Latona he interprets not as a sexual infraction but as evidence of a commendable thirst for celestial things: 'Quod Latonam Apollinis matrem amaverit, ingentem eius demonstrat animum, celsitudinem enim appetiit, que claritatis mater est' (*Genealogie* V 25, 3). See also *Esposizioni*, 'Accessus,' 54.

54 For A.E. Quaglio's severe judgment see *Scienza e mito nel Boccaccio* (Padua: Liviana, 1967), 168–75. As noted in chapter 1, M. Pastore Stocchi, the editor of the *Allegoria mitologica* in the Mondadori edition, also stresses Boccaccio's close adherence to Ovid's text.

55 Hortis, *Studj*, 327.

56 Indeed, Boccaccio's Phaethon is so perfect an inversion of that portrayed by Dante, that it is hard not to view the former as a 'response' to the latter. Dante's applications of the tale of Phaethon consistently use the story for the more traditional, moralizing end of illustrating the limitations of human *ingegno* and the consequences of human arrogance. In the *Commedia* Phaethon is primarily remembered for his failure to successfully negotiate the celestial path of his father: 'Fetòn abandonò li freni, / per ch'l ciel, come pare ancor, si cosse' ['Phaethon when he let his reins go free – / for which the sky, as one still sees, was scorched'] (*Inf.* XVII, 107–8; trans. Mandelbaum); 'la strada / che mal non seppe carreggiar Fetòn' ['that same path which Phaethon drove so poorly'] (*Purg.* IV, 72; trans. Mandelbaum); 'e come quivi ove s'aspetta il temo / che mal guidò Feton' ['And as, on earth, the point where we await / the shaft that Phaethon had misguided'] (*Par.* XXXI, 124–5; trans. Mandelbaum). Insofar as the Phaethon of the *Commedia* is one of a select group of strivers whose questing serves as a moral, spiritual, and intellectual touchstone for defining Dante's own literary journeying through the heavens in search of knowledge, it is necessary to view Phaethon's failure, in the *Commedia* at least, as an epistemological failure. For an excellent discussion of Dante's use of such figures see Teodolinda Barolini, *The Undivine Comedy* (Princeton: Princeton University Press, 1992), chap. 3. In *Convivio* II, 14 we encounter a passage where Phaethon is – in the most elliptical fashion – associated with the acquisition of knowledge; here, Dante suggests that the Pythagorean philosophers' speculation that the Milky Way was created by a wandering of the sun from its path was probably influenced by the story of Phaethon. Given all this, it is perhaps sensible to view Boccac-

cio's account of Leonzio Pilato's death – struck down, he claims, by lightning – with some scepticism; such a Phaethon-like death is, after all, all too fitting for the man who reintroduced the Homeric poems to the Latin West! For Petrarch's vivid description of Leonzio's untimely death, see *Seniles* VI, 1.

57 'Asserit tamen Paulus Perusinus, secundum nescio quem Eustachium, quod, regnante Spareto apud Assyrios, Eridanus qui et Pheton Solis egyptii filius, cum copia suorum, duce Nylo navigiis devenit in mare, et ventis adiutus in sinum, quem Lygustinum dicimus, venit ...' (*Genealogie* VII 41, 12).

58 Claude Cazalé Bérard, 'Riscrittura della poetica della riscrittura negli Zibaldoni di Boccaccio,' in *Gli Zibaldoni di Boccaccio: Memoria, scrittura, riscrittura*, Atti del seminario internazionale di Firenze – Certaldo, ed. M. Picone and C. Cazalé Bérard (Florence: Franco Cesati, 1998). Cazalé Bérard highlights the novelty of Boccaccio's conception of Phaethon by viewing it against the background of Ovid's version and contemporary allegorical interpretations of the same myth: 'Un confronto con l'opera più vicina per argomento e cronologia – anche per la presenza di varie testimonianze testuali dell'autore nello stesso corpus – cioè le *Metamorfosi* di Ovidio commentate da Giovanni del Virgilio, invece di fare risaltare somiglianze nella riscrittura e nell'interpretazione allegorica degli episodi permette di misurare la distanza che separa Boccaccio dai commentatori tradizionali del poeta latino: manca assolutamente qualsiasi allusione ad una impresa poetica nel commento delvirgiliano che propone invece una lettura in chiave filosofica del mito, contrapponendo al sapere pratico limitato (Fetonte) la scienza speculativa (Apollo), e mettendo in guardia sul piano morale contro gli errori dovuti alla vanagloria e all'ignoranza' [a comparison with the work closest to it both chronologically and thematically – also for the presence of various textual testimonies of the author in the same work – that is, Ovid's *Metamorphoses* with Giovanni del Virgilio's commentary, instead of making similarities in the rewriting and in the allegorical interpretation of the episode stand out, allows one to gauge the distance that separates Boccaccio from the Latin poet's traditional commentators: there is absolutely no allusion to a poetic undertaking in del Virgilio's commentary, which instead proposes an interpretation of the myth in a philosophic key, counterpoising limited practical know-how (Phaethon) against speculative knowledge (Apollo), and, on the moral plane, guarding against errors proceeding from vainglory and ignorance'] (448).

59 Jonathan Usher, 'Global Warming in the Sonnet: The Phaethon Myth in Boccaccio and Petrarch,' *Studi sul Boccaccio* 28 (2000): 125–83. Usher provides ample and compelling evidence that Boccaccio's revised Phaethon in the *Allegoria* should be considered in the larger context of a group of passages in

Boccaccio's works united by their common concern with this theme of poetic arrogance and inadequacy.

60 For more on Boccaccio's sophisticated use of literary motifs both to idealize real events (for instance the plague of 1348) and to counterfeit real events (the embedded 'biographies' of Boccaccio's youthful works) see Vittore Branca, *Boccaccio medievale*, particularly chap. 7 ('Schemi letterari e schemi autobiografici') and in the appendix, 'Un modello medievale per l'introduzione.'

61 As D. Delcorno Branca has cogently argued in '"Cognominato prencipe Galeotto," Il sottotitolo illustrato del Parigino It. 482,' *Studi sul Boccaccio* 23 (1995): 79–88, Boccaccio's implicit identification with the Galeotto of the Old French romances is further corroborated by the choice of subject and placement of the illuminations in a *Decameron* manuscript (the Parisian It. 482) produced while Boccaccio was still alive. Among the most remarkable features of this manuscript is a series of seventeen extremely expressive ink drawings executed not by a professional artist working from a conventional program but by an accomplished amateur with an unusually keen understanding of the text. Indeed, these drawings reveal such an intimate grasp of the text that Vittore Branca has suggested that they may have been penned by Boccaccio himself. A survey of the iconographic programs found in contemporary manuscripts of Arthurian Romances allows Delcorno Branca to conclude that one of the two couples depicted in the frontispiece of the Parisian It. 482 may represent Galeotto and the lady of Malehaut. Were this the case, she argues, the conspicuous location of the figure of Galeotto just above the famous subtitle bearing his name, and the slightly lower, but no less prominent, illustration of the author (embraced by a storiated initial) would function as a canny pictorial evocation of the famous words 'Galeotto fu il libro e chi lo scrisse' – one, importantly, in which the Galeotto figure is no longer viewed as a 'veicolo di peccato' [vehicle of sin] (87), but is effectively redeemed.

Boccaccio ends both the *Filostrato* and the *Elegia di Madonna Fiammetta* (for the *Teseida*, see footnote 6) with an apostrophe to the book itself; in both cases the spurned lover-author views the book as a medium for conveying a history of romantic torment to the callous object of his and her affection (a motif that runs throughout Ovid's *Amores*). By personifying the book and assigning it the function of erotic ambassador, Boccaccio effectively declares both books *galeotti*. What is implicit in these two works is finally made fully explicit in the *Decameron*.

In the *Esposizioni*, Boccaccio explains that in the French romances one finds the character of a 'prencipe Galeotto' (*Esp.* V, lit., 183), a man of gigantic proportions who, by dint of his sheer size is able to provide Lancelot and Guinevere with a measure of privacy – even in a public room – thereby facilitating their illicit dalliance. Of Francesca's words, Boccaccio notes: 'E così vuol questa donna dire che quello libro, il quale leggevano Polo ed ella, quello officio adoperasse tra lor due che adoperò Galeotto tra Lancialotto e la reina Ginevra; e quel medesimo dice essere stato colui che lo scrisse, per ciò che, se scritto non l'avesse, non ne potrebbe esser seguito quello che ne seguì' ['Thus, the woman means that that book, which she and Paolo were reading, performed the same task for the two of them that Gallehault fulfilled for Lancelot and Queen Guinevere. She also says that that same man was the one who wrote it. This is because, were it not he who wrote it, what happened would never have taken place'] (*Esp.* V, lit., 184 [Papio's trans.]). The implication would seem to be that the prodigious size of the *Decameron* serves, like that of the original Galeotto, as a sort of screen to facilitate erotic activity by carving out a place for private recreation in the very midst of the public eye (a theme that reaches a culminating point in the *Valle delle donne* of *Dec.* VI).

62 See Aldo Scaglione, *Nature and Love in the Late Middle Ages* (Westport, CT: Greenwood, 1976), 117–18; and Giorgio Padoan, *Il Boccaccio, le muse*. Scaglione takes Boccaccio at his word, whereas Padoan argues that Boccaccio is acknowledging the indecorous quality of aspects of the *Decameron*, but that 'la dichiarazione è inficiata da una certa antifrastica posa letteraria' [the declaration is undermined by a certain antiphrastic literary pose] (32). Padoan points out that it was precisely during this period that Boccaccio was busy transcribing the *Decameron* anew and directs the reader to Vittore Branca, 'Non sconfessato il "Decameron,"' *La fiera letteraria* 40, 49 (1965). Cfr. Branca, *Giovanni Boccaccio: Profilo biografico*, 177 and 209.

63 Boccaccio's *Remedia amoris* essentially takes the form of a liberation narrative: one concerned not with a political and social but a psychological enslavement. It is from no 'Egyptian,' political, bondage, but from subjection to a destructive Eros that Boccaccio – himself newly freed – proposes to free others. Here, the promised land is not defined geographically or politically, but psychologically and spiritually; true freedom consists neither in unregulated passion nor in abject impassivity, but in a middle ground where the individual is granted the freedom to choose the objects of his or her affection rather than be chosen by them. It is the Promethean task of the author to somehow restore this element of self-determination to those subject to erotic bondage.

64 See Esther Zago, 'Women, Medicine, and the Law in Boccaccio's *Decameron*,' in *Women Healers and Physicians: Climbing a Long Hill*, ed. L.R. Furst (Lexington: University Press of Kentucky, 1997).

65 Given Boccaccio's tendency to align himself with the figure of Prometheus, it is fitting indeed that he should choose 'Fiammetta' as the *senhal* for the elusive object of his desire for in a sense it is she who comes to embody the 'flame,' the spark of divinity, that animates each one of us by awakening that desire which spurs us on in our quest for knowledge.

66 It is notable that many critics – among them Foscolo. Padoan, and Scaglione – take this at face value. See Ugo Foscolo, *Discorso storico sul testo del* Decamerone (Lugano: G. Ruggia, 1828), 9; Padoan, *Il Boccaccio, le muse*, 97–9; and Scaglione, *Nature and Love*, 102. See also M.P. Simonelli, 'Prima diffusione e tradizione manoscritta del *Decameron*,' in *Boccaccio: Secoli di vita. Atti del Congresso Internazionale Boccaccio*, ed. M. Cottino-Jones and Edward F. Tuttle (Ravenna: Longo, 1977), 136–40, and G. Padoan, 'Sulla genesi del *Decameron*,' ibid., 144–8.

67 For the trope of Envy's tooth, see, for example, Horace, *Odes* IV, 3; Ovid, *Remedia amoris*, ll.365ff. The conventional nature of Boccaccio's defence is suggested by the very similar language used by Alanus de Insulis in the Epilogue of his *Anticlaudianus*: 'Long life to you, o book, over which I have toiled and sweated long and continuously, you whose fame slander already impairs [...] However, the mariner, after negotiating the heaving sea, trembles and fears attacks on land; he fears that, though he has been safe asea, he may be shipwrecked and lost ashore, that spite may rage against him or slander sink her teeth in him who, as he brings his work to a fitting conclusion, has drained his energy in writing and borne the burden of the toil' (*Anticlaudianus*, trans. James J. Sheridan [Toronto: Pontifical Institute of Medieval Studies, 1973]).

68 Kenelm Foster and Patrick Boyde, *Dante's Lyric Poetry* (Oxford: Clarendon Press, 1967), and M. Barbi and F. Maggini, *Rime della 'Vita nuova' e della giovinezza* (Florence: 1956). In his notes to the *Decameron*, Vittore Branca directs the reader to *Rime* CIV, 76 in connection with the phrase 'onor si tennero.' This poem is among the fifteen of Dante's *canzoni* that Boccaccio chose to transcribe in the *Chigiano* L.V. 176. A similar theme dominates 'Se vedi li occhi miei di pianger vaghi' (Foster and Boyde 82; Barbi CV).

69 From *Dante's Rime*, trans. Patrick S. Diehl (Princeton: Princeton University Press, 1979), 193.

70 Foster and Boyde, *Dante's Lyric Poetry*, 283

71 Dante, despite such protestations, was himself undoubtedly the greatest denuder of Wisdom of his age. Not only does he insist in *Vita nuova* XXV that allegory should be susceptible to unveiling, but in both the *Vita Nuova* and the *Convivio* he actually provides a prose auto-exegesis (or, more accurately an auto-allegoresis) of his poetry, an unusual strategy prompted, perhaps, by his concern that he would otherwise by susceptible to misinterpretation

(Boccaccio imitates this technique in the *Teseida*, by providing extensive authorial glosses on the text). In his *Trattatello in laude di Dante*, Boccaccio argues that Dante's decision to write the *Commedia* in the vernacular was motivated by two concerns: the first, that if it were written in Latin it would only be accessible to the learned and not to the uneducated, left to welter in their ignorance ('idioti, abandonati per addietro da ciascheduno'), and the second, that since princes and other great men had forsaken the study of the liberal arts, they, like the common masses, would be excluded from his readership were he to write in Latin (*Trattatelo*, 191–2).

72 Of course, 'Tre donne' is by no means the only example of Dante's use of erotic material; however, the use of the phrase 'onor mi tegno' together with the application of the trope of undressing suggests that it is this particular poem that Boccaccio has in mind. A brief discussion of erotic elements of Dante's poetry (though no mention is made here of 'Tre donne') is to be found in Christopher Kleinhenz's useful survey of erotism in medieval Italian literature: 'Texts, Naked and Thinly Veiled: Erotic Elements in Medieval Italian Literature,' in *Sex in the Middle Ages: A Book of Essays*, ed. Joyce Salisbury (New York: Garland, 1991).

73 A somewhat shorter version of this section, 'Boccaccio's "Valley of Women": Fetishized Foreplay in *Decameron VI*,' was previously published in *Italica* 76, 2 (1999): 147–74.

74 This same metaphor is used by Boccaccio in the 'Conclusion,' in his sardonic defence of his unflattering characterization of monks, who, after all, are 'buone persone e fuggano il disagio per l'amor di Dio e macinano a raccolta' [good people who flee discomfort for the love of God and do their grinding with a full millpond] (26).

75 This theme is provided as an empiric, historical basis in the account of the plague which introduces the work, an exemplary, anecdotal, expression in the Filippo Balducci story of Day IV, and is actually legally ratified by the court proceedings of VI, 7 through madonna Filippa's skilful arguments in defence of adultery.

76 A similar use of this loading/unloading metaphor is to be found in the *Ninfale fiesolano* where Africo, referring to Mensola, affirms: 'Amor m'ha qui per lei carche le some!' [Here, for her, Love's packed me with a burden!] (octave 32). In the *Decameron*, a specifically hydraulic model for human sexuality is also evoked in the sexual metaphor, 'L'acqua corre la borrana' (VIII 2, 9), favoured by Monna Belcolore. The lesson is clear: just as water is subject to its nature, so too are human beings. It is significant in this regard that the homosexual Pietro da Vinciolo is accused by his neglected wife of preferring to go 'in zoccoli per l'asciutto' [in clogs through the dry] thereby forcing her to

strive to 'portare altrui in nave per lo piovoso' [take someone else on a boat through the wet] (V 10, 9). See *De mulieribus* XXIII, 11 (Iole) and *Fiammetta* VIII 9, 12 for the the theme of sexual desire as a natural, inexorable force.

Boccaccio's application of a hydraulic model is by no means limited to sexual flux and reflux. In *Corbaccio* 133–4 he applies a similar model to the elimination of digestive and menstrual superfluity (see also *Corbaccio* 290: 'scaricare la vescica' [empty the bladder]) and in *Decameron* II 5, 37 he describes Andreuccio's ill-augured attempt to eliminate the 'superfluo peso' [superfluous weight] from his 'ventre' [stomach]. For a contemporary use of the notion of a fecal 'unloading,' see *novella* XXIV, 4 of Franco Sacchetti's *Il trecentonovelle*.

77 This passage reiterates the concerns found in Ovid's *Ars amatoria* III, 381ff.
78 See *Esposizioni* III, lit., 61: 'non altrimenti che la femina dispone il peso del ventre suo partorendo' [in much the same way that a woman dispels the weight from her womb in giving birth]. In *Comedia delle ninfe* XXI, Emilia uses a similar expression: 'con maschia progenie poi dal peso diliberandomi.'
79 For a complete catalogue of such incitements to eros, see Boccaccio's fiftieth footnote to *Teseida* VII, where, among other things, he lists: pine nuts, fine foods and wines; a beautiful setting graced by rabbits, sparrows, and doves; and other amenities such as flowers, music, songs, shady places, and fountains. All of these features 'possono, secondo le forze naturali, provocare a l'atto venereo ciascuno' [can, in accordance with natural forces, incite each person to the sexual act]. He then goes on to list the personal qualities (both of physique and character) to which lovers are particularly susceptible: youth, beauty, gentility etc. Likewise, in *Fiammetta* V 17, 1 we read of Fiammetta's husband's counterproductive attempts to cure his lovesick wife by applying remedies that only exacerbate her 'disease.' He takes her to a seaside sanatorium where 'la maggiore parte del tempo ozioso trapassa' [she spends the greater part of her time being idle] and the women pass their days conversing about love and consuming fine foods and aged wines, the combined effect of which would suffice not only to stimulate 'la dormente Venere' [the sleeping Venus] but 'risuscitare la morte in ciascuno uomo' [to revive the dead one in every man]. See also *Dec.* I, Intro., 90.

Chapter 4 of Giuseppe Mazzotta, *The World at Play in Boccaccio's Decameron*, discusses this matter of the indeterminate realm inhabited by the *brigata*: 'It is the imaginative domain where the allegory and the letter are alluded to and equally superseded, where the young people of the *brigata* indulge in esthetic pastimes and are drawn into the artifice: they dance, play, read romances and tell stories. Within this illusory context, their stories evoke a world of sexuality which superficially appear to be an ironic counterpoint to the garden of the introduction but, in a real sense, they end up by exposing the dangers of the esthetic imagination' (110).

80 Hereafter, the *Valle delle donne* is generally referred to as the *Valle.*

81 Branca refers the reader to Boccaccio's *Teseida* VII, 108 ff., in which are described the arena in which Arcita and Palemone duel for Emilia's hand: 'Il teatro ritondo ... nel mezzo aveva un pian ritondo a sesta' [the circular theatre ... had, in in its centre, a field round as by compass scribed]. It is worth noting that in the *Teseida*, Boccaccio does describe such bleachers. For another natural theatre hemmed in by mountains in Boccaccio's work, see the entry for 'Annius' in *De montibus* [*De lacubus*].

82 Pliny the Younger, in describing his Tuscan Villa (*Letters*, Book V, Letter 6) uses the image of the amphitheatre to evoke the form of the landscape surrounding his home: 'Picture to yourself a vast amphitheatre such as could only be the work of nature [quale sola rerum natura possit effingere]; the great spreading plain is ringed round by mountains, their summits crowned by ancient woods of tall trees' (*The Letters of the Younger Pliny*, trans. and introduction by Betty Radice [Penguin Classics, 1963], 7–8). In his discussion of the topos of the pleasance in *European Literature and the Latin Middle Ages* Curtius attributes to this passage from Pliny the introduction of circularity into the structure of the *locus amoenus* of medieval literature. That Pliny may have been among Boccaccio's sources for the theatre simile is supported by the emphasis in both Pliny's and Boccaccio's descriptions on the landscape as a work of nature rather than art.

We encounter another natural amphitheatre in the sixth book of his *Thebaid*, where Statius describes the Nemean Games: 'Set in a green ring of curving hills and embraced by woodland lies a vale; rough ridges stand about it, and the twin summits of a mound make a barrier and forbid issue from the plain, which running long and level rises with gentle slope to grassy brows and winding heights soft with living turf' (*Thebaid* VI, 255–60, trans. J.H. Mozley, Loeb edition [Cambridge, MA: Harvard University Press, 1928]).

One of the most important examples of the natural amphitheatre is the Celestial Rose of *Paradiso* XXX–XXXII, which similarly combines the organic (the rose) with the artificial (the amphitheatre). Thomas Stillinger discusses Boccaccio's use of Dante's rose in 'The Language of Gardens: Boccaccio's *Valle delle donne,*' *Traditio* 39 (1983): 310–21, and sees Boccacio's *Valle* as a place where Dante's two paradises – the terrestrial and the celestial – are 'collapsed.' He proposes that Boccaccio makes a similar use of the two gardens – terrestrial and celestial – found in the *Roman de la Rose.*

Although Virgil, Statius, and Pliny may be the sources of this particular image where the Middle Ages are concerned, the circular pleasance is suggested by Plato's description of Atlantis in the *Critias*, Herodotus's earlier account of Ecbatana in the *Histories*, and Homer's even earlier description of a circular grove of black poplars in the *Iliad*.

83 Here and elsewhere I use Peter Green's translation of the *Ars amatoria* in *Ovid: The Erotic Poems* (New York: Penguin Books, 1982). Citations in Latin are from the Loeb edition (Cambridge, MA: Harvard University Press, 1985). Much remains to be written concerning the influence of Ovid's *Ars amatoria* and *Remedia amoris* on the *Decameron* – a work that, like Ovid's, is presented as both a love manual and a 'remedy' for the lovelorn. Like Ovid, who interrupts his narrative in *Remedia* 362 to address the accusations of those critics who 'brand [his] muse as wanton,' Boccaccio breaks into his frame narrative to provide his famous self-defence in the Introduction of Day IV (IV, Intro., 35). Like Ovid in *Remedia* 369, Boccaccio uses the metaphor of wind to describe the envy of his critics, which, like wind, strikes the summits. Like Ovid in *Remedia* 135, Boccaccio stresses the dangers of leisure as an inducement to love. Like Ovid, Boccaccio displaces responsibility for the lascivious nature of his work by arguing that its alleged obscenity is a quality inherent in the genre, not the author. Boccaccio's strategy of addressing his work to an audience of women may well have been inspired by Ovid's sardonic dedication of the third book of his *Ars amatoria* to a female audience ('Amazons'). These are just some of many such verbal and formal echoes that confirm that Boccaccio had Ovid's erotic poems firmly in mind as he undertook his own erotic handbook. For a useful overview of the striking correspondences between Boccaccio's apologia in the 'Conclusion' of the *Decameron* and Ovid's defences of the *Ars amatoria* in his *Tristia* and *Remedia*, see Janet Smarr, 'Ovid and Boccaccio: A Note on Self-Defense,' *Medievalia* 13 (1987): 247–53. For a study that addresses the Ovidian influence on Boccaccio's *Genealogie*, see Thomas Hyde's thought provoking 'Boccaccio: The Genealogies of Myth,' *PMLA* 100, 4–6 (1985): 737–45. See also Hortis, *Studj*, 400–1, and Scaglione, *Nature and Love*, 112. For more on Ovid and Boccaccio, see Robert Hollander, 'The Proem of the *Decameron*: Boccaccio between Ovid and Dante,' in *Miscellanea di studi danteschi in memoria di Silvio Pasquazi* (Naples: Federico & Ardia, 1993); Victoria Kirkham, 'Boccaccio's Dedication to Women in Love,' in *The Sign of Reason in Boccaccio's Fiction* (Florence: Olschki, 1993); and Luciano Rossi, 'Presenze ovidiane nel *Decameron*,' *Studi sul Boccaccio* 21 (1993): 125–37.

84 Though Boccaccio's insistence on the pervasive circularity of the setup causes one to conjure up a perfectly coherent circular girdle of bleachers, the fact that one must enter the valley through a passage – albeit a narrow passage – breaches the perfect symmetry of his construct and violates the perimeter of

the *Valle delle donne* in a way that cannot help but recall the sexual violation of a feminized architectural precinct (like the castle of *Roman de la Rose*), or of a woman's body.

The association of theatres with erotic engagement, which in Ovid becomes an intrinsic characteristic of theatre from its very inception, is taken up later by Augustine in the *Confessions* where the theatrical spectacle becomes the dominant example of '*cupiditas oculorum*' [cupidity of the eyes]. Tertullian makes much of the dangers of the theatre in *De spectaculis*. Isodore (*Etymologiarum* XVIII, 42) claims that the theatre is also called a *prostibulum* because it is the place where women prostitute themselves, and *lupanar* because such prostitutes resemble wolves (*lupae*) in their rapacity. Finally, Petrarch devotes a section to spectacles – and the moral shortcomings of the theatre – in his *De remediis utriusque fortune*. For another example of this attitude towards the theatre in Ovid, see *Remedia amoris*, 750 ff.

85 Thomas C. Stillinger ('The Language of Gardens') proposes the idea of an absent viewer – one that he too identifies with the reader. However, his emphasis seems to be on the absence of the onlooker and the ultimate frustration of the erotic experience whereas I locate the 'onlooker' in the villas and view the inaccessibility of the women not as an impediment but rather as a precondition to the fetishistic type of fulfillment supplied by Boccaccio's *Valle* – a theme that I take up in my conclusion. Stillinger feels that the voyeuristic promise of the passage is disappointed by the very transparency that would seem to guarantee a full revelation of the women's naked bodies, for the similes used to thematize this transparency supply us with no detail more substantial than that of the two colours: the white and red of 'corpi candidi' and 'vermiglia rosa.' However, where Stillinger sees the white and red as discrete hues separated by difference, I cannot help but see an invitation to participate in the process of combining the two colours into the more inviting rosy hue of pinkish flesh.

86 In his *Glossarium eroticum linguae Latinae* (Paris: Aug.-Fr. & Pr. Dondey-Dupré, Bibliopolas (1826), Pierrugues offers the following definition of 'fornix': '*Fornices* dicebantur angustae illae cellulae arcuatae, quibus singula scorta sub singulis titulis viris dabant. Inde *fornix* pro lupanare.'

87 I owe this observation of the verbal echo with *Inf.* V to Teodolinda Barolini. As Sapegno notes in his commentary to this passage (*La Divina Commedia*, [Florence: La Nuova Italia, 1955]): 'Gli antichi oscillano fra due interpretazioni diverse, così riassunte dal Buti: "non aveano sospetto d'essere al dì compresi [sorpresi] da alcuno,"' ovvero: "non aveano sospetto l'uno dell'altro di tale amore"' [the early critics oscillate between two different interpretations, summed up as follows by Buti: 'They didn't expect to be caught (surprised)

by anybody on that day,' or 'neither suspected the other of such a love'].
While Sapegno favours the latter of these interpretations, it is clear that Boc-
caccio, at least in this particular allusion, is exploiting the voyeuristic conno-
tations of the former. Note that Petrarch engages in a similar echoing of *Inf.*
V in poems three and eight of his *Rime.* In sonnet 3, it is the eyes of the pro-
tagonist's lady that bind him with love while he goes, 'secur, senza sospetto.'
Other occurrences of this motif in Boccaccio's works may be found in *Teseida*
I, 103; V, 78; IX, 75 and *Decameron* IX 8, 12.

88 Trans. Allen Mandelbaum (New York: Harcourt Brace, 1993). The similarity
of Ovid's image in this passage and Boccaccio's description has been frequently noted – without, however, exploring the possible implications. Stillinger's essay, 'The Language of Gardens' is an exception in this regard for he
explores the verbal echoes not only of Ovid, but of Dante's *Commedia* and the
Roman de la Rose. See *Comedia ninfe* XXXII, 50 for a similar image of bodies in
limpid water – here, infused with ominous Dantean undertones deriving
from its similarity to Dante's description of the ice-encased sinners of *Inf.*
XXXIV, 12.

89 Hauvette observes that by the time Boccaccio came to write the *Decameron:*
'Telle est devenue la répulsion du conteur pour tout ce qui sort de l'ordre
naturel, qu'il a entièrement renoncé, dans les nouvelles, à évoquer ces visions
mythologiques, dont il avait été si friand au temps de sa jeunesse, pour
s'enfermer dans le monde des réalités tangibles' [Such had become the storyteller's revulsion for all that strayed from the natural order, that he had
fully renounced, in his novellas, the evocation of those mythological visions
that he had been so fond of in his youth, confining himself to the world of
tangible realities] (*Boccace*, 288). In 'The Gardens of the *Decameron* Cornice,'
PMLA 66 (1951): 505–23, Edith Kern stresses the absence of the supernatural
in Boccaccio's frame-story gardens: 'If we compare the gardens of the
Decameron with those of French, classical Provençal, or Celtic origin or even
those used by Boccaccio in previous works, one general fact appears quite
clear: Boccaccio stripped the *Decameron* gardens of all supernatural elements'
(514).

90 Boccaccio alludes to the abduction of Proserpina with great frequency
throughout his works. See, for example, *Fiammetta* I, 3; III 10, 5; *Teseida* V, 31;
VIII, 108; *Amorosa visione* XX, 25; and *Genealogie* VIII, 6.

91 From *Metamorphoses*, trans. Frank Justus Miller, Loeb. edition (Cambridge,
MA: Harvard University Press, 1916).

92 Claudian's *De raptu Proserpinae*, ed., with trans. and commentary by Claire
Gruzelier (Oxford: Clarendon Press, 1993). Claudian's well-known description of Venus's garden in the *Epithalamium de nuptiis honorii Augusti* – one that

has some features in common with Boccaccio's *Valle delle donne* – was also apparently known to Boccaccio (see *Genealogie* XI 4, 2).

93 An association of this image with a pleasure garden is to be found in *Le Roman de la Rose*, lines 116–20 and 1522–4. For other evidence of influence from the *Roman de la Rose*, see Kern, 'The Gardens.' Boccaccio's use of the image of fine gravel to convey the extraordinary clarity of the waters clearly implies what Boiardo, without recurring to the fetishistic strategy of displacement so appealing in Boccaccio, states directly in Book III of *Orlando innamorato* in his description of the 'Fonte de la fata': 'Era la fonte tutta lavorata / Di marmo verde, rosso, azurro e giallo/ E l'acqua tanto chiara e riposata, / Che traspareva a guisa de cristallo; / Onde la dama che entro era spogliata, / Così mostrava aperto senza fallo / Le poppe e il petto e ogni minimo pelo, / Come se intorno avesse un sotil velo' (III 1, 22) [The fountain had been worked of green, red, blue, and yellow marble, and the water was so clear and still, it was transparent as a crystal. So that the naked maid within showed openly, without a flaw, breasts, chest and every little hair, as though enveloped by a gauzy veil]. Where Boiardo uses the phrase 'ogni minimo pelo' [every little hair] to describe the visual accessibility of the naiad, Boccaccio speaks of the 'minutissima ghiaia' [very fine gravel]. While I would not insist on establishing a strict equivalence between Boccaccio's 'minutissima ghiaia' and Boiardo's 'ogni minimo pelo,' it is true that Boccaccio recurs to similar types of displacement with great frequency. Nor are all of these occurrences of a strictly metaphoric cast. Consider, for example the lovely interlude described in octave 33 of the *Ninfale fiesolano* in which a lovelorn Africo sits on, and shortly afterwards kisses, the same spot occupied just moments before by Mensola. Ovid too delights in this sort of fetishism. See for example *Heroides* X, 51–5: XV, 147–50.

94 *Metamorphosis*, trans. Mandelbaum, 170.

95 Monastic *piscinae* were quite common. Many are recorded in the *Doomsday Book* and Cassiodorus's monastery took its name, Vivariensis, from its *vivaria*. A particularly lovely depiction of a medieval *piscina* is to be found among the fourteenth-century murals that decorate the Papal Palace at Avignon.

96 In Roman times, a great deal of ingenuity was devoted to fish husbandry, and Varro, Columella, Pliny, and Palladius are among the ancient authorities who address the subject of pisciculture. For a thorough study of Roman pisciculture and a catalogue of all extant Roman *piscinae*, see James Higginbotham, *Piscinae: Artificial Fishponds in Roman Italy* (Chapel Hill: University of North Carolina Press, 1997).

97 My citations are from Francesco Sansovino's 1561 translation of Pietro de' Crescenzi's extremely influential fourteenth-century agricultural handbook, the *Opus ruralium commodorum*, available in an anastatic reprint (Perugia:

Quattroemme Editore, 1998). Despite the great importance of this text (it is considered by many to be the single most important agricultural treatise of the Middle Ages) no reprints or critical editions of Pietro's original Latin text are (to my knowledge) available. For a discussion of the various editions and the more general reception of Piero de' Crescenzi's treatise, see Robert G. Calkin, 'Piero de' Crescenzi and the Medieval Garden,' in *Medieval Gardens*, ed. Elisabeth B. Macdougall (Washington, DC: Dumbarton Oaks Research Library and Collection, 1983).

 98 Translation by Richard M. Gummere, Loeb. edition (Cambridge, MA: Harvard University Press, 1920).

 99 Translation by E.S. Forster and E. Heffner, Loeb edition (Cambridge, MA.: Harvard University Press, 1954).

100 Antonia Mazza addresses the question of Boccaccio's familiarity with Columella in 'L'inventario della "Parva Libreria,"' 65, where she notes that Boccaccio cites Columella at length in *Genealogie* XI.

101 For a discussion of the transmission of French romances in Boccaccio's time see Daniela Delcorno Branca, *Boccaccio e le storie di Re Artù* (Bologna: Il Mulino, 1991); for the likelihood that *Cligés* was read in fourteenth-century Italy, see in particular the notes on 48. It is a seductive – but no doubt specious – theory that Boccaccio deliberately strengthened the connection of Elissa with the *Valle* because her name, as Boccaccio was well aware (he says as much in his *De mulieribus claris*), was an alternate name for Dido, the great Phoenician queen – *fenicia* in Italian.

102 From *Les Romans de Chrétien de Troyes: Cligés* (Paris: Champion, 1982).

103 Kern ('The Gardens'), compares this passage from the *Roman de la Rose* to the description of the impenetrable tree canopy of Boccaccio's second frame garden as part of her extended treatment of the influence of the *Roman de la Rose* on Boccaccio's gardens. For related images see also *Decameron* Intro., 109 ff., and Dante *Purg.* XXVIII, 31–3. For an intriguing discussion of Boccaccio's appropriation of elements of Guillaume's garden for his novella concerning that prodigious cultivator of gardens, Masetto (III 1), see Mazzotta, *The World at Play*, chap. 4, where the author argues that Masetto's garden parodies medieval allegories of Eden.

104 Guillaume de Lorris and Jean de Meun, *The Romance of the Rose*, trans. Charles Dahlberg (Hanover, NH: University Press of New England, 1983).

105 For this attribute of the Sun, see Ovid, *Metamorphoses* IV, 170 ff., where the Sun, who 'sees all things first' (videt hic deus omnia primus [172]), discloses Venus's affair with Mars to Vulcan.

106 The image of the artificial looking natural space is one which curiously enough is used by Ovid (*Metamorphoses* III, 151–159) in describing Gar-

gaphia, Diana's grove and the site of her famous fountain where she was observed by Actaeon – an association that does much to enhance the voyeuristic tenor of this interlude. A similar image appears in Ovid's story of Thetis and Peleus (*Metamorphoses,* Book XI, 242–5) in which the site thus described is the locus of Peleus's forced possession of Thetis. The idea of a space in which Nature imitates Art is thereby associated with both voyeurism and rape. See Stillinger, 'The Language of Gardens,' for an interesting discussion of the Ovidian allusions; he addresses the theme of voyeurism and relates it to the Ovidian intertexts – in particular the Actaeon and Narcissus legends (313–14).

107 For an obliquely related idea see *Filostrato* VII 63, 64, and 65, where Troiolo observes the bitter irony that such inanimate objects as the flowers, sky, and mountains are all privy to a vision of his beloved denied him. The mountains, he says, are oblivious to the 'vista amorosa' of her lovely eyes and adds, 'or foss'io un di loro, o sopra un d'essi / or dimorass'io, sì ch'io la vedessi' [would that I were one of them, or lived on top of one, that I might see her] (64).

108 In his lengthy analysis of this *novella* Umberto Olobardi characterizes the girls' activities as flirtatious and notes that this display is a 'civetteria naturale, innata in tutte le donne' [a natural flirtatiousness, innate in all women] (!) – one, moreover, that accounts for their irresistible appeal ('Lettura di una novella del Boccaccio,' *Leonardo* 21 [1943]: 95–103).

109 I am using the etymology that Branca provides in the notes to his edition.

110 I am reminded of Shakespeare's *Winter's Tale* (I, ii, 190ff.), where the idea of 'fishing' in other men's 'ponds' is used in the context of cuckoldry, and the first stanza of Abraham Cowley's 'Bathing in the River': 'The fish around her crowded, as they do / To the false light that treacherous fisher shew / And all with as much ease might taken be, / As she at first took me.'

111 In a *novella* that so deliberately attempts to evoke the medieval romances and the theme of courtly love, it is indeed possible to see this story as a sort of *tableau vivant* illustrating the etymology of 'love' proposed by Andreas Capellanus in *The Art of Courtly Love,* chap. 3, an observation already made by Mazzotta in *The World at Play.*

112 We see a similar strategy applied by the Marchesa of Monferrato [*Dec.* I, 5], who succeeds in discouraging the King of France from foisting himself upon her by serving him a nauseating succession of chicken dishes, each with a different dressing, thereby implying that stripped of such social 'condiments' as status and dress, women, like chickens, are much the same – a lesson that is not lost on the king, who realizes that by persisting in his suit, he would gain nothing that he could not get elsewhere without risk.

113 In '"Le parole son femmine e i fatti sono maschi": Toward a Sexual Poetics of the *Decameron* (*Dec.* II 10),' *Studi sul Boccaccio* 21 (1993): 175–97.

114 See Marshall Brown, 'In the Valley of the Ladies,' *Italian Quarterly* 18 (1975): 33–52, for a more extensive discussion of this complicity.

115 Jonathan Usher maintains that Boccaccio uses this fishing episode as a sexual metaphor and directs the reader to a passage in the *Teseida* (XII) where the use of fishing as a sexual metaphor is even more explicit: see 'Frame and Novella Gardens in the *Decameron*,' *Medium Aevum* 58 (1989): 274–85. Ovid's *Ars amatoria* abounds in examples of this particular sexual metaphor. See for example *AA*, I, 48 ff; I, 763 ff and III, 425 ff. In *De casibus* VII 3, 27 Boccaccio uses the term 'pisciculis' to refer to Tiberius's young male concubines. The editors of the Mondadori edition of *De casibus*, Pier Giorgio Ricci and Vittorio Zaccaria, refer the reader to Suetonius's *De vita Caesarum* where he describes Tiberius's custom of training young boys – whom he called 'little fish' [*pisciculos*] – to swim in between his legs and nibble him (*De vita* III, 44).

116 In '"Le parole son femmine e i fatti sono maschi."' This passage may well have been influenced by *Ars amatoria* 3, 381 ff. where Ovid notes that 'men have richer material for their sport. Swift balls have they, and javelins and hoops and armour, and the horse that is trained to go in circles,' and contrasts these 'male' activities with those available to women. While social conventions prevent women from frequenting the sites of male sporting activities (the Campus, the aqueduct, etc.) they can, Ovid observes, make profitable excursions to the temples, theatres, and other places where they are likely to be seen by men, for 'what is hidden is unknown; what is unknown, none desires; naught is gained when a comely face has none to see it' (397–8, Mozley's trans., Loeb edition). The connection between this passage and Boccaccio's brief catalogue of male activities in the *Decameron* Proem deserves further investigation – particularly in light of Boccaccio's characterization of his *Decameron* as a 'galeotto.' Chaucer, in the 'Wife of Bath' 552ff., alludes to this passage from Ovid and suggests his own series of 'places' and activities designed to fulfill women's desires. Chaucer contemporizes Ovid; Boccaccio proposes a very different solution, one that involves a sublimated sexuality.

117 Ovid, like Boccaccio in his 'Proem,' sees the literal hunt as an antidote to an unsuccessful metaphorical hunt. In the *Remedia amoris* Ovid counsels the jilted or unsuccessful lover to 'take up hunting: Venus has often been shamefully forced to quit the field by Diana' (199–200, Green's translation). However, what neither author attempts to disguise is the fact that such activities are designed as means of enduring the loss of the true objective and are not themselves primary objectives. For a wide-ranging and illuminating dis-

cussion of Boccaccio's narrative strategy of actualizing metaphors in the *Decameron* see Pier Massimo Forni, *Adventures in Speech: Rhetoric and Narration in Boccaccio's* Decameron (Philadelphia: University of Pennsylvania Press, 1996), chap. 4 ('The Poetics of Realization').

118 Teodolinda Barolini, 'The Wheel of the *Decameron*,' *Romance Philology* 36 (1983): 521–39.

119 In 'Frame and Novella Gardens,' Usher holds that Boccaccio's gardens as a whole are conceived as places where moral resolve and virtue are tested by sensual temptations. According to this theory, the *Valle delle donne* represents the culminating test in a series, and the fact that the *brigata* does not succumb to sexual activity even though this particular *locus amoenus* seems to be particularly amenable to sexual activities is evidence of the moral fortitude achieved in the course of their sojourn. He sees the bathing that occurs in the conclusion of Day VI as marking a 'ritual of purification' which attests to their transcendence – their immunity to the seduction of sex.

120 The idea of the valley as the female genitalia is as common as that of the garden as the female genitalia. The classical expression *Vallis femorum* (used as a euphemism for the pudenda) attests to this tradition. Stillinger ('The Language of Gardens') writes, 'If the Valley resembles a divine *omphalos*, it also resembles – with its wooded slopes, its single entrance, its penetrable centre – a vagina' (317). Bandello uses the delightfully pious metaphor 'fishing in the Valley of Josephat' to describe sexual intercourse (novella II, 45) in a context that leaves no doubt that the word 'valley' is a euphemism for 'vagina.' For a general discussion of eroticized landscapes in Boccaccio's works see Regina Psaki, 'Boccaccio and Female Sexuality: Gendered and Eroticized Landscapes,' in *The Flight of Ulysses: Studies in Memory of Emmanuel Hatzantonis*, ed. Augustus A. Mastri (Chapel Hill, NC: Annali d'Italianistica, 1997).

Chapter 4. The Myth of Historical Foresight

1 Valerio Marucci's footnotes to his edition of *Il trecentonovelle* (Rome: Salerno, 1996) identify this messer Galeotto as the historical Galeotto Malatesta of Rimini (a relative by marriage of Dante's Francesca).

2 English translation of Acts 1.7 is from the New Revised Standard Version. The whole passage from the *Chronicon* is: 'Sed enim jam inde ab exordio palam cunctis edico, ne quis unquam arroganter contendat, quasi fieri possit ut temporum certissima cognitio acquiratur. Quod sane quisque sibi persuadebit, si primo veracem Magistrum cogitet familiaribus suis dicentem: "Non est vestrum nosse horas et tempora, quae Pater posuit in sua potestate"' (*Chronicon*, I, 3; *PL*, vol. 27, col. 13). For a discussion of the manu-

script tradition of the Eusebius-Jerome *Chronicon* (particularly as it relates to Petrarch) see Giuseppe Billanovich, *Petrarca e il primo umanesimo* (Padua: Antenore, 1996), chap. 12.

3 Kurt Flasch comments that taken at face value, Panfilo's assertion that God's mind is filled with benevolence actually contradicts this principle. If God's mind is indeed inscrutable to humans, by what special privilege has Panfilo been granted this insight? (*Poesia dopo la peste*, 84). Flasch also notes that while Panfilo's statement reflects views current in the thirteenth century, the more prominent scholastic theologians would have taken issue with his categorical assertion that insight into the divine mind is under no circumstances ('in alcun modo') possible. In their view, metaphysical reasoning could lead to some understanding, however hazy or incomplete, of divine truths. As Flasch shrewdly observes, Panfilo's pious insistence on this absolute disjunction between human acumen and divine truth has the (no doubt intended) effect of undermining a church hierarchy whose authority derives from its mediating function as interpreter and disseminator of God's will.

4 'At editi, aut aliquid tutum, superbia erexerunt turrim; quasi ne diluvio si postea fieret, delerentur' (*In Joannis evangelium tractatus* CXXIV, *PL* vol. 35, col. 1430). Though this view of the tower as prophylactic consistently takes second place to the traditional exegesis, it nevertheless recurs with some frequency in Augustine's works. In his explication of the Psalms, we read: 'Turrem illam recordare superborum factam post diluvium: quid dixerunt superbi? Ne pereamus diluvio, faciamus altam turrem' [Remember the tower of the proud ones, built after the deluge: what did the proud ones say? In order not to perish in a deluge, let us build a high tower] (*Enarrationes in Psalmos, PL*, vol. 36, col. 636). In the twelfth century this view is recapitulated in Peter Comestor's *Historia scholastica*, a work on sacred history very popular throughout the Middle Ages: 'Post obitum vero Noe, moventes pedes suos ab Oriente, convenerunt duces in unum, in campum Sennaar, et timentes diluvium, consilio Nemrod volentis regnare, coeperunt aedificare turrim, quae pertingeret usque ad coelos, habentes lateres pro saxis, et bitumen pro caemento' (Cap. XXXVIII, 'De turre babylon,' *PL*, vol. 198, col. 1089A).

5 'Tempore vero Phalec Nembroth gigas, cum audisset ex Adam fore predictum orbem terrarum igni aquaque delendum, iamque eo constaret tempore mundum sub undis fore demersum aquasque ad certas methas altitudinis pervenisse, existimans stultissimus hominum eousque ingnem evasurum quo aque salierant, parum fidens verbis Dei profetico enumptiante spiritu, timensque ne iterum genus humanum vel ingni vel aquarum inundatione iterum deperiret superbia fretus ingenti, hedifitium incredibile turris Babel dum ob id consumare contenderet, percussus scissione linguarum

inpeditus est' (*De origine* II, 3). This passage is taken from the first of several transcriptions of early manuscripts of *De origine* published in Giuliano Tanturli's critical edition: Philippi Villani, *De origine civitatis Florentie et de eiusdem famosis civibus* (Padua: Antenore, 1997).

6 Nimrod is frequently used in a more traditional exemplary fashion in Boccaccio's works. See *Genealogie* IV, 68ff where Josephus I, 4, 2 (Flavio Giuseppe) is mentioned; *Filocolo* V, 53; *Teseida* I, 7; *Amorosa visione* VII, 7–9; and *De mulieribus* I, 8.

7 'Verum, ut appareret consilii cepti vanitas, ducem suum secuti, in Senaar regione, ab Eufrate fluvio circundata, stulto labori dari operam ceptum est, ut turris scilicet excessura altitudine nubes, ne amplius undis delerentur, edificaretur, ea in amplitudine quam excogitata celsitudo videbatur appetere' (*De casibus* I 3, 3).

8 The pattern of building, collapse and rebuilding may have been suggested to Boccaccio by the tendency of the Latin Fathers to elide the story of the construction of the tower of Babel on the plain of Senaar with that of Semiramis's building of Babylon's fortifications – mentioned by Ovid in the tale of the Babylonian youths Pyramus and Thisbe who lived 'Next door to each other, in the brick-walled city / Built by Semiramis' (*Met.* IV, 58; Humphries, 83). In his *Hexameron*, Bede states that in the wake of the tower's destruction Nimrod remains in Babylon, 'quamvis eamdem urbem Babyloniam postea Ninus vel Semiramis conjux illius majorem ex tempore et augustiorem reddidisse ferantur' (III; *PL*, vol. 91, col. 126 C [Bede cites the passage from Ovid to support his point]). That this pattern of building and rebuilding could be collapsed into a single episode is suggested by Guido da Pisa, who, in his gloss of *Inferno* XXXI, 77–8, observes: 'Nembrot autem non dimisit propter turris destructionem civitatem edificare, quam postea Semiramis cocto latere circumdedit, idest muravit' (*Commentary on Dante's* Inferno, ed. Vincenzo Cioffari [Albany: State Univerity of New York Press, 1974], 639). Interestingly, in Boccaccio's brief biography of Semiramis in *De mulieribus* II, he maintains that she rebuilt Nimrod's ancient city of Babylon (8), a version consistent with his account in *De casibus*.

9 Though Genesis provides no information regarding the fate of the physical fabric of the tower in the wake of the linguistic and geographical division, a long-standing tradition maintained that the tower had collapsed or been razed by God. In Josephus, *Antiquities* (I, 118) and the book of *Jubilees* (10. 26), it is specifically a wrathful wind loosed by God that is assigned responsibility for the collapse. For more on such early exegetical traditions see James L. Kugel, *The Bible As It Was* (Cambridge, MA: Harvard University Press, 1997).

10 'Reintegratis ergo a Nembroth adversus Deum viribus, non solum quod
excussum ira Dei creditur resarcitum est, verum ad excelsiora processum,
quasi non ad evitandas undas in posterum, sed ad surripiendum Opifici
rerum celum straretur iter.' (*De casibus* I 3, 7) In the *De vulgari eloquentia* (I 7,
4), Dante presents Nimrod's building project as a sort of artistic agon – on
the model of Arachne/Minerva, Marsyas/Apollo, etc., and marvels at the
supreme charity of a God who shows such fatherly forbearance towards the
perpetrator of this blasphemous assault. The description of the actual building of the tower that follows is a rare, and valuable portrait of medieval building practices. For other allusions to Nimrod in Dante's works see *Inf.* XXXI,
46ff; *Purg.* XII, 34–46; and *Par.* XXVI, 126.

In this glowing assessment of the architectural qualities of Nimrod's tower
Boccaccio may have been influenced by Jerome (who believes that the tower
was the Capitol of Babylon and describes the marble, gold statues, and other
treasures of the ancient city [*Commentaria in Isiam*; *PL*, vol. 24, col. 163]) and
the Jewish historian Josephus (who expresses admiration for the prodigious
width and height of the structure [*Antiquities* I, 9]) – perhaps by way of Isidore who reproduces both Jerome's and Josephus's views on the matter in
the *Chronicon* ('Secunda aetas saeculi,' 9; *PL*, vol. 83, col. 1022D). Though a
transcription of pseudo-Egesippo's medieval Latin translation of Josephus's
work is to be found in the Zibaldone Magliabechiano, this transcription is
lacking – as noted by Aldo Maria Costantini, ('Studi sullo Zibaldone Magliabechiano,' *Studi sul Boccaccio* 7 [1973]: 21–58) – the entire first book. See also
Orosius, *Seven Books against the Pagans* II, 6.

11 Alain de Lille, *Anticlaudianus*, trans. James J. Sheridan (Toronto: Pontifical
Institute of Mediaeval Studies, 1973). For Boccaccio's likely familiarity with
the *Anticlaudianus*, see Antonia Mazza, 'L'inventario della "Parva Libreria" di
Santo Spirito e la biblioteca del Boccaccio.' *Italia medioevale e umanistica* 9
(1966): 1–74. See also Francesco Bruni, *Boccaccio: L'invenzione della letteratura
mezzana* (Bologna: Il Mulino, 1990), 57–8.

12 Whereas Paul makes it clear that in the earth's infancy faith alone was sufficient to grant Noah immunity to the universal purging of the deluge
(Hebrews 11.7), in an earth no longer young, both secular and sacred knowledge must also be recruited in the journey to God and salvation.

13 Guillaume de Lorris and Jean de Meun, *The Romance of the Rose*, trans. Charles
Dahlberg (Hanover, NH: University Press of New England, 1983).

14 The notion that knowledge is the best route to self-determination is a plati-
tude of the Middle Ages: one most often associated with the figure of Prudence. In the *Genealogie*, Boccaccio notes 'we are taught by the wise that from
the past we may infer the future' (XIV, Proem, 15). The same idea is

expressed by Panfilo in the conclusion to Day X: 'Addorne donne, come io credo che voi conosciate, il senno de' mortali non consiste solamente nell'avere a memoria le cose preterite o conoscere le presenti, ma per l'una e per l'altra di queste sapere antiveder le future è da' solenni uomini senno grandissimo riputato' ['Graceful ladies, the wisdom of mortals consists, as I think you know, not only in remembering the past and apprehending the present, but in being able, through a knowledge of each, to anticipate the future, which grave men regard as the acme of human intelligence'] (*Dec.* X, concl., 2; McWilliam, 795). Other occurrences of this theme of prudence are to be found in *Genealogie* XIV, proem; *Genealogie* V 48 (where Minerva is cast as a symbol of prudence) and *Genealogie* VII, 9.

15 This ancient tale, the truth of which, Boccaccio tells us, he has come to accept, was originally told him in his distant youth by his wise tutor in astrology, Andalò del Negro. The notion that poverty renders immunity to fortune is powerfully dramatized in *Dec.* X, 10, the tale of Griselda, and is frequently found in the Latin works (see, for instance, *Genealogie* XIV 4, 21ff.).

16 In '"Utilità" in Boccaccio's "Decameron",' *Studi sul Boccaccio* 15 (1985–6): 215–31, Robert Hollander argues that this passage echoes both the familiar Horatian precept regarding profit and pleasure and Ovid's advice at the end of the *Remedia amoris* concerning what foods to seek for their aphrodisiac qualities and what foods to flee for their anaphrodisiac characteristics: 'quos fugias quosque sequare'; 'what to flee and what to follow' (*Remedia amoris*, 796). For Boccaccio's use of a similar formula in a less ambiguously moral context see, for example, *De casibus* I, Proem, 3 ('vitia reprimantur et extollantur virtutes' [reprimand vices and extol virtues]); 9 ('morsus in vitia et ad virtutem suasiones' [incitements to virtue and denouncements of vice]); VI 3, 1 ('spernendi vitia imitandeque virtutis' [despise vices and imitate virtues]), etc. The use of this formula in Christian moral literature derives, no doubt, from its earlier application in pagan texts concerned with moral philosophy (see, for instance, Cicero's *De natura deorum*, III 13, 33). In *Literature as Recreation in the Middle Ages* (Ithaca, NY: Cornell University Press, 1982), Glending Olson proposes that the Horatian distinction between pleasure and profit is perhaps too starkly drawn. Entertainment of the sort provided by such texts as the *Decameron* – a temporary respite from the ordinary or extraordinary duties and afflictions of life – has the beneficial, hygienic effect of restoring the mind's faculties, allowing one to not only draw more pleasure, but greater 'profit' from the text (see *Literature as Recreation*, 211).

17 From *The Divine Institutes*, trans. Sister Mary Francis McDonald, O.P. (Washington: Catholic University of America Press, 1964). For the Latin passage see

PL 6, col. 748. For Boccaccio and Lactantius's *Divine Institutes* see Antonia Mazza's 'L'inventario della "Parva Libreria", 32.

18 'Contrariis contraria intelliguntur. Et sapientia prima est, stultitia caruisse. Stultitia autem carere non potest, nisi qui intellexerit eam. Unde et plurima in rebus noxia sunt creata, ut dum vitamus ea, ad sapientiam erudiamur. Aequalis ergo studii fuit Salamoni scire sapientiam et scientiam, et e regione errores et stultitiam: ut in aliis appetendis et aliis declinandis, vera ejus sapientia probaretur' (*Commentarius in Ecclesiam, PL* 23 col. 1023). In I Kings 3 we read that God appeared to Solomon and offered him the gift of his choice. In response Solomon requested that he be given a discerning mind and the ability to distinguish between good and evil (3.9).

19 Given this attitude, it is not surprising that in another work Jerome characterizes the good, educative sermon as one that instructs its audience which virtues are to be embraced and which vices shunned: 'Bonus sermo est ad aedificationem opportunitas, dans gratiam audientibus qui docet virtutes sequendas, vitia fugienda' (*PL* 26, col. 513). See also Augustine *Confessions* X, 40: 'Ubi non mecum ambulasti, veritas, docens, quid caveam et quid appetam' [Where have you not come with me, Truth, showing me what to fear and what to desire].

20 From Bede, *Ecclesiastical History of the English Nation*, trans. J. Stevens, rev. J.A. Giles (New York: Dutton, 1975). For the original Latin version, see *Historia ecclesiastica, PL* 95, col. 21A.

21 Boccaccio, *Famous Women* [*De mulieribus*], ed. and trans. Virginia Brown (Cambridge, MA: Harvard University Press, 2001).

22 Translation by B.O. Foster, from the Loeb edition (Cambridge, MA: Harvard University Press, 1988).

23 Livy's likely source for this passage, Thucydides's *History of the Peloponnesian War*, places even greater emphasis on the value of history as a predictive model: 'It will be enough for me, however, if these words of mine are judged useful by those who want to understand clearly the events which happened in the past and which (human nature being what it is) will, at some time or other and in much the same ways, be repeated in the future' (I 22, trans. Rex Warner [New York: Penguin, 1954]).

24 A brief survey of the early Florentine chroniclers may be found in Eric Cochrane, *Historians and Historiography in the Italian Renaissance* (Chicago: Chicago University Press, 1981). Curiously, Cochrane maintains that 'none of the chroniclers ever suggested that a study of the past might enable their readers to create something better in the future' (11).

25 Two excellent studies of Boccaccio, published since the publication of the original version of this chapter as part of my Columbia dissertation in 2000,

arrive – though by different routes and with different emphases – at similar conclusions. See Simone Marchesi, *Stratigrafie decameroniane* (Florence: Olschki, 2004), 4 and 102–3, and Timothy Kircher, *The Poet's Wisdom: The Humanists, the Church, and the Formation of Philosophy in the Early Renaissance* (Leiden: Brill, 2006), chap. 3 ('Morality's Hazy Mirror: The Humanist Modality of Moral Communication in the *Decameron*').

26 Interestingly Boccaccio addresses accusations that poetry is not useful by affiliating poetry with history – both secular and sacred – thereby declaring its usefulness in a practical sense. See in particular *Genealogie* XIV, 6.

27 The reversal of this pattern is so important to Boccaccio that he has Panfilo introduce an apparently nonsensical argument for returning to Florence. Were they to continue their pastoral sojourn, argues Panfilo, they would risk being joined by outsiders – a horrible prospect indeed, but infinitely preferable, one would have thought, to the prospect of returning to a plague-ravaged Florence.

28 Dioneo is simply confirming what Boccaccio has already stated in the Introduction (I, intro., 23). Giuseppe Mazzotta discusses legal issues of the *Decameron* in *The World at Play in Boccaccio's* Decameron (Princeton, NJ: Princeton University Press, 1986), chap. 8, 'The Law and Its Transgressions.' See also Robert Hóllander and Courtney Cahill, 'Day Ten of the *Decameron*: The Myth of Order,' in *Studi sul Boccaccio* 23 (1995): 113–70.

29 As Vittore Branca and Chiara Degani observe in their study on Boccaccio's use of exempla in the *Decameron*: 'Non è, la novella boccacciana, un *anti-exemplum*, come vogliono certi critici pur preparatissimi ... È se mai un *exemplum*, sempre a carattere dimostrativo e con pretesa di autenticità, ma sviluppato in senso diverso e con finalità e ispirazione diverse da quelli preparati e raccolti al servizio della predicazione o della trattatistica morale e ascetica [The Boccaccian novella is not an *anti-exemplum*, as certain, even quite accomplished, critics hold ... It is more accurately an *exemplum*, still with a demonstrative scope and with the pretence of authenticity, but developed with a different orientation and with a final objective and inspiration different from those prepared and gathered for the purpose of preaching or for moral and ascetic treatises] ('Studi sugli "exempla" e il "Decameron",' *Studi sul Boccaccio* 14 [1983–4]: 185).

In addition to a number of studies exploring the parodic use of specific exemplary tales in the *Decameron novelle* (for example the travestied exemplum of the Nastagio degli Onesti story [V, 8] and the Filippo Balducci apologue of the Intro. to Day IV), an attempt has been made by Carlo Delcorno to illustrate Boccaccio's technique of parodying generic classes of exempla: 'Egli infatti non si limita a utilizzare in chiave parodistica alcune fonti parti-

colari, ma punta le armi dell'ironia contro intere classi di exempla subordi-
nate ai grandi temi della religione popolare, modellata e guidata dalla
predicazione dei Mendicanti' [He does not, in fact, limit himself to using certain particular sources in a parodic key, but turns the weapon of irony against
entire classes of exempla subordinated to the great themes of popular religion, shaped and guided by the preaching of the Mendicants] (Delcorno,
'Studi sugli esempla e il "Decameron". II. Modelli esemplari in tre novelle
(I 1, III 8., II 2).' *Studi sul Boccaccio* 15 [1985–6]: 194).

30 The shortcomings of this strategy are best illustrated by drawing an analogy
with the figurative arts. In the period between the decadence of classical culture and its gradual resurgence in the age of Giotto, artists did not look to the
natural world for their models but to the conventional, highly stylized images
that filled the pattern books of their artistic forbears. In short, the collections
of moral exempla drawn upon by the preachers are analogous to the pattern
books of the artists; neither one corresponds to experiential, empirical reality
and both are based on the imposition of a prescriptive model – of action in
the case of the moral exemplum, and of form in the case of the pictorial
exemplum. Giotto succeeds in breaking away from this conventional language by diverting his gaze from the pattern book to the natural world. The
literary verisimilitude achieved by Dante in the *Commedia* represents a no less
remarkable achievement. If Giotto's ultramarine strokes restored the exquisite blue of the natural sky, Dante's masterful verses restored the expressive
flexibility of his natural tongue, the Italian vernacular. It is necessary, however, to emphasize that insofar as both of these artists are at the vanguard of
their respective revolutions, they are constrained to pour their new wine in
old bottles; it is a realism packaged in medieval dress and coloured by a medieval sensibility.

31 In 'Dante e l'"exemplum" medievale,' *Lettere italiane* 35, 1 [Jan.–Mar. 1983]:
3–28, Carlo Delcorno describes the *Comedy* as the greatest summa of exemplarity, the influence of which extended to the *Decameron*. He also notes the
'doppio sistema esemplare' [double system of exemplarity] that prevails in
purgatory and describes the structure of this system – the alternation of classical with Christian exempla, and so forth – at length.

32 For the most comprehensive treatment of the notoriously complex issues of
artistic representation and verisimilitude in *Purgatorio* X, see Teodolinda
Barolini, *Undivine Comedy* (Princeton: Princeton University Press, 1992),
chap. 6.

33 The exemplary method – particularly in its use of exemplary lives – is weakened by another critical flaw: for most of us it is all too easy to avoid the pitfalls of a Judas or Cataline, and far too hard to even approximate the virtues

of a Lawrence or Cato. The same radical quality of these exempla that makes them so memorable and unambiguous simultaneously renders them irrelevant to the average human being. Recognizing this shortcoming, preachers often supplemented their stock of traditional exempla with anecdotes based on contemporary figures and events. Carlo Delcorno observes: 'Vien sempre il momento in cui il paziente collezionista di racconti edificanti proclama l'efficacia particolare della "tranche de vie" personalmente testimoniata: "Sed quid per antiqua discurrimus?" – esclama Servasanto da Faenza nella sua Summa, scritta nel convento di S. Croce nella seconda metà del Duecento' [The moment always comes when the patient collector of edifying tales declares the particular efficacy of the personally witnessed 'slice of life': 'But why do we go chasing after ancient things?' – exclaims Servasanto da Faenza in his Summa, written in the convent of S. Croce in the second half of the thirteenth century] (Delcorno, 'Dante e l'"Exemplum" medievale,' 6). A comparable effect is achieved in the *Comedy* through the numerous encounters with shades whose historical, ethnic, and moral status bears some relation to that of Dante. As he progresses through the *cornici* of purgatory, Dante is not left to wander aimlessly through the uncharted moral landscape delimited on either end by such absolutes as the Virgin Mary and Satan, but encounters a succession of morally intermediate entities: shades in the process of purging their sinful tendencies. However, Dante does not dispense with the exemplary method; he has simply filled its old forms with a new content by supplementing its stark moral antitheses with a full range of intermediate terms.

34 See Marilyn Migiel, *A Rhetoric of the Decameron* (Toronto: University of Toronto Press, 2003), chap. 1, for an insightful analysis of the subtle, and significant, ways that Boccaccio reworks his source material (Paul the Deacon's *History of the Lombards*) to shift the balance of blame for these acts of abandonment to women.

35 It is notable that the church and Dante's purgatorial mountain – two iconic *loci* of exemplary didacticism – are both recalled in the Introduction of the *Decameron*. We are told to view the 'orrido cominciamento' [horrible beginning] (4) of the plague description in the way a hiker views a steep mountain whose punishing slopes must first be traversed if he or she wishes to enjoy the pleasures that await at the summit, an image, as Branca and others have noted, that cannot help but recall the forest and mountain of the *Commedia's* proem (in the notes to the Mondadori edition Branca writes: 'Non si può non pensare alla selva "aspra" e al "dilettoso" monte del canto introduttivo della *Divina Commedia*' [It is impossible not to think of the 'savage' wood and the 'delightful' mountain of the introductory canto of the *Divine Comedy*]. I

would add that since the forest and mountain of Dante's proem are themselves used, in accordance with the familiar typological scheme, to prefigure
the mountain of purgatory, Boccaccio may well have the latter – a 'monument of exemplarity' – more firmly in mind than the former, the 'colle'
[mountain] of the first canto. That other great locus of exemplarity, the
church, is represented by Santa Maria Novella, which assumes a symbolic centrality as the place in which the *brigata* first congregates, from which it emi-
grates, and to which it finally returns, thus serving as a virtual portal between
Florence and Fiesole. Insofar as the church marks the place of departure and
of return, the sojourn itself may, in a sense, be viewed as having taken place
'within' the church. However, if Boccaccio invokes these canonical places of
exemplarity he does so largely with the aim of indicating his divergence from
such models. Whereas the purgatorial mountain in Dante functions as a
means of accessing not only Eden but the celestial paradise itself, Boccaccio's
journey is quite literally a round trip; the experience of temporal beatitude
serves as preparation not for paradise but for a return to an infernal Florence. Like the purgatorial mountain, the church, the traditional place of
moral education, serves largely to provide a foil for Boccaccio's new brand of
exemplarity, one that in attempting to overcome the limitations of the traditional method strikes out beyond the church and into the hills of Fiesole.

36 In the *Genealogie* XIV, 18, Boccaccio notes the irony that whereas the Fathers
grant painters free licence to decorate princely palaces with pictures of
crimes – human and divine – poets are vituperated for exercising the same
freedoms, as though 'a poet's creations, blazoned in ornate letters' were
'more vicious to the wise than are pictures to the ignorant' (Osgood, 83). In
the story of Giotto and Messer Forese of Day VI, pictures that appeal to the
eyes of the ignorant – represented by the 'old' school of painting by pattern
– are contrasted with Giotto's marvelously verisimilar paintings; images that
appeal to the intellect of the learned (VI 5, 6). It is not by chance that Giotto,
an 'example' of God's failed artwork (he is expressly likened to a Baronci),
assumes the role of the consummate human artificer.

37 Millicent Marcus has argued convincingly that the *Decameron* represents nothing less than the death knell of the exemplary method. In her gloss on I, 3,
the story of Melchisedech, she asserts that the numerous logical inconsistencies and susceptibility to contradictory interpretations that are such inescapable features of both this tale and that of Abraham the Jew that follows it,
serve to illustrate the impossibility of exemplifying 'providential truths in
human constructs' and remarks: 'If man is so woefully inept at reconciling
the human order with the divine, how can he possibly hope to embody God's
truth in stories? The 'exemplum,' which presses fiction into the service of

theological teachings, is thus rejected as a viable literary mode' (Marcus, 'Faith's Fiction: A Gloss on the Tale of Melchisedech [*Dec.* I, 3],' *Canadian Journal of Italian Studies* 2 [1978–9]: 44). In what is essentially an epitaph to the traditional exemplary method, Marcus concludes: 'The tale of Melchisedech thus renders obsolete the notion that human stories can exemplify divine wisdom. Once and for all, Boccaccio rejects the genre of the "exemplum" with its supposed continuity between the Logos and the human word' (47). A valuable discussion of the broader implications of this important phenomenon may be found in Karlheinz Stierle, 'Three Moments in the Crisis of Exemplarity: Boccaccio, Petrarch, Montaigne, and Cervantes,' *Journal of the History of Ideas* 59, 4 (Oct. 1998): 581–95.

38 Translation by H. Rackham, from the Loeb edition.

39 As noted by Janet Smarr in 'Ovid and Boccaccio: A Note on Self-Defense,' *Mediaevalia* 13 (1987: 247–53), Boccaccio's self-defence in the Epilogue draws extensively on Ovid's self-defence in the second book of the *Tristia.*

40 The association of mirrors with self-knowledge is inevitable and ancient. In *Naturales quaestiones* I 17, 4, Seneca observes: 'Mirrors were invented in order that man may know himself, destined to attain many benefits from this: first, knowledge of himself; next, in certain directions, wisdom' (trans. Corcoran, Loeb edition). This salutary use of mirrors follows an entertaining excursus on the perverted use of mirrors by Hostius Quadra, who used mirrors as sexual props; in particular, he delighted in the use of magnifying mirrors to exaggerate the size of his, and his lovers,' genitals. In Martianus Capella's *Marriage of Mercury and Philology,* we read: 'Urania with gentle kindness gave her a gleaming mirror which Wisdom had hung in Urania's rooms amongst her gifts – a mirror in which Psyche could recognize herself and learn her origins' (*De nuptiis* I, 7; trans. Stahl and Johnson).

41 From Novella 1 of *The Novellino or One Hundred Ancient Tales,* ed. and trans. Joseph P. Consoli (New York: Garland, 1997).

42 The members of the *brigata* too make occasional use of the field/garden metaphor in describing the literary space provided by the assigned theme of a given day. In II, 8, Elissa likens the day's assigned theme to an 'ampissimo campo' [very wide field] (II 8, 3) – though one which her further comments reveal to be a jousting field (the site of a literary tourney) rather than a garden variety garden. See IX 1, 2 for a similar use of 'campo.'

   In the shadow of Eden, literary gardens often serve as a proscenium for the dramatic enactment of a test – usually one with a strongly ethical tenor. Eden, at least in Dante's figuration, is the most concise expression of this motif of the garden as an ethical testing ground. Humanity is granted the greatest of all gifts, free will, and within a matter of hours succeeds in abusing this gift through an act of transgression. A common allegorical interpretation of the tree of the knowledge of good and evil saw it as a sort of touchstone for judging the control of free will (Augustine, *City of God* XIII, 11). Dante's terrestrial paradise represents a renewal of the primitive paradise redeemed by Christ's passion. Consequently, the reenactment of this ethical test in *Purgatorio* XXXII is one in which the Gryphon, a Christ figure and hence a 'new' Adam, is congratulated for his self-control in resisting the tree: 'Beato se', grifon, che non discindi / col becco d'esto legno dolce al gusto' (43–4). It is no coincidence that a similarly congratulatory sentiment is expressed by Panfilo in the conclusion to the tenth, and last, day of storytelling. By returning to a garden setting, deliberately exposing themselves to activities notorious for their ability to incite erotic feelings and, finally, proving themselves immune to this sustained attack on their virtue, the *brigata* has succeeded in passing not just any test, but has effectively reenacted the primal test – one which, likewise, took place in a garden, and, likewise, consisted in a contest between virtuous obedience and the powers of seduction.

43 From *Percy Bysshe Shelley: The Major Works* (Oxford: Oxford University Press, 2003), 681–2. For the question of Shelley's acquaintance with Boccaccio's works, see Herbert G. Wright, *Boccaccio in England from Chaucer to Tennyson* (Bristol: Athlon, 1957), 40–1 and 336; and Albert J. Kuhn, 'Shelley's Demogorgon and Eternal Necessity,' *Modern Language Notes* 74, 7 (Nov. 1959): 596–9.

44 These words are spoken by Aeneas to the Cumean Sybil in *Aeneid* VI, 103–5. The citation of Petrarch is from Conrad H. Rawski's translation (and extensive commentary), *Petrarch's Remedies for Fortune Fair and Foul* (Bloomington: Indian University Press, 1991), 9.

45 For a discussion of this concept of 'natural law' in the *Decameron*, see Mazzotta, *World at Play*, 221ff.

46 'Non vetus illud et romani hominis verbum aspexeras: "Capi virtus nescit, patientie dedecus ignorat, Fortune subcumbere omni fato tristius ducit; nova et speciosa genera interitus excogitat" (si quisquam interit qui sic extinguitur)' (*De casibus* VIII 4, 18).

47 In *De casibus* IV 12, 36 Boccaccio declares that nothing, in his opinion, is more beautiful than the act of accepting an inexorable fate with that same countenance and spirit with which we fearlessly confront the instability of life. See also *De casibus* IX, 22.

48 Viewed from this perspective, it becomes apparent that the escape to Fiesole that had appeared to be a manifestation of freedom from constraint is actually more accurately an expression of servitude – to fear of death. Conversely, the *brigata's* return to Florence, one framed by the recurrent image of assuming the yoke, is actually an expression of true emancipation – from fear of

death. Whereas the *brigata*'s decision to depart from Florence was dictated by external factors, their election to return, to reassume the yoke of civic duty, was entirely unconstrained. See *De casibus* I 2, 8 for a comparable image of the yoke of obedience voluntarily assumed.

The freedom that is ultimately acquired by the *brigata* is not freedom from moral constraint but rather the freedom to assume the yoke of morality, freedom to submit to order: Augustine's *libera servitus*. This oxymoronic notion of free servitude represents the prelapsarian condition of the will, one in which the individual will freely elects to conform to divine will. Indeed, true freedom is, like free will, none other than that movement within the yoke of providence, the poetic universe created by Dante within the generic constraints of *terza rima*, the temporal paradise created by Boccaccio within the plague itself – between the departure of the *brigata* from plague-ridden Florence in Day I to their return in Day X. Though this concept of *libera servitus* is most dramatically revealed by the transgressive/regressive pattern of the *brigata's* sojourn, it is a guiding principle of the *Decameron*. In the proem, Boccaccio announces that, having been freed by the god of love, he has freely committed himself to the service of women; in the Introduction, the women, unconstrained, resolve to be ruled by men; and Dioneo, who voluntarily abides by the daily theme despite his exemption, and so forth.

49 It is to Teodolinda Barolini that we owe the first rigorous examination of the circular structure of the *Decameron* frame. Previous to her seminal study, 'The Wheel of the *Decameron*,' *Romance Philology* 36, 4 (1983): 521–39, linear models of the *Decameron* frame structure (most often charting a moral trajectory from vice to virtue) prevailed. Though it certainly had not escaped critics' notice that the frame narrative begins and ends in the same place (see, for instance, Barberi Squarotti, 'La cornice del *Decameron*,' 58), none had previously succeeded in articulating the internal anatomy – the specific stages – of the physical and psychological revolution undergone by the *brigata* over the course of their fourteen-day sojourn.

Works Consulted

Boccaccio's Works

Tutte le opere di Giovanni Boccaccio. Ed. Vittore Branca. 10 vols. Milan: Mondadori, 1994. [Critical edition of Boccaccio's complete works]

Other Editions and Translations Consulted

– *L'Ameto* [*Comedia delle ninfe fiorentine*]. Trans. Judith Serafini-Sauli. New York: Garland, 1985.
– *Boccaccio on Poetry, Being the Preface and Fourteenth and Fifteenth Book of Boccaccio's 'Genealogia Deorum'* Trans. Charles G. Osgood. New York: Liberal Ports Press, 1956.
– *The Book of Theseus.* [*Teseida delle nozze d'Emilia*]. Trans. Bernadette Marie McCoy. New York: Medieval Text Association, 1974.
– *De casibus virorum illustrium.* Laurent de Premierfait's *Des cas des nobles hommes et femmes, Book I: Translated from Boccaccio: A Critical Edition Based on Six Manuscripts.* Ed. Patricia May Gathercole. Chapel Hill: University of North Carolina Press, 1968. [early-fifteenth-century French translation of *De casibus virorum illustrium*]
– *Il codice Chigiano L. V. 176.* Intro. Domenico De Robertis. Rome: Archivi Edizioni, 1974. [facsimile of the Chigian codex autograph]
– *The Decameron.* Norton Critical Edition. Ed. and trans. Mark Musa and Peter E. Bondanella. New York: Norton, 1967.
– *The Decameron.* Trans. G.H. McWilliam. Harmondsworth: Penguin, 1972.
– *Dizionario geografico.* Trans. Nicolò Liburnio. Turin: Fògola, 1978. [sixteenth-century Italian translation of *De montibus*]

– *The Elegy of Lady Fiammetta* [*Elegia di madonna Fiammetta*]. Ed. and trans. Mari-
  angela Causa-Steindler and Thomas Mauch. Chicago: University of Chicago
  Press, 1990.
– *Famous Women* [*De mulieribus*]. Ed. and trans. Virginia Brown. Cambridge, MA:
  Harvard University Press, 2001.
– *Il Filocolo*. Trans. Donald Cheney with the collaboration of Thomas G. Bergin.
  New York: Garland, 1985.
– *Genealogia de los dioses paganos*. Spanish trans. of Romano's ed. Ed. M.ª Con-
  suelo Alvarez and Rosa M.ª Iglesia. *Clasicos para una biblioteca contemporanea*.
  Madrid: Editora National, 1983.
– *Genealogie deorum gentilium libri*. Ed. Vincenzo Romano. Bari: Laterza, 1951.
– *Giovanni Boccaccio: Eclogues*. Trans. Janet Levarie Smarr. New York: Garland,
  1987.
– *Giovanni Boccaccio: Nymph of Fiesole* [*Ninfale fiesolano*]. Trans. Joseph Tusiani.
  Cranbury, NJ: Associated University Presses, 1971.
– *The Nymph of Fiesole* [*Ninfale fiesolano*]. Trans. Daniel J. Donno. New York:
  Columbia University Press, 1960.
– *Zibaldone Laurenziano*. Ed. G. Biagi. Facsimile edition. Florence: Olschki,
  1913.

Other Primary Sources

Alain de Lille. *Anticlaudianus*. Trans. and commentary by James J. Sheridan.
  Toronto: Pontifical Institute of Mediaeval Studies, 1973.
– *Plaint of Nature*. Trans. and commentary by James J. Sheridan. Toronto: Pontif-
  ical Institute of Mediaeval Studies, 1980.
Ambrose. *Hexameron*. *PL*. 14, cols. 123–274.
Andreas Capellanus. *The Art of Courtly Love*. Introduction, translation and notes
  by John Jay Parry. New York: Columbia University Press, 1960.
Augustine. *The City of God*. Trans. Marcus Dods, D.D. New York: Random House,
  1950.
– *Confessions*. Trans. Henry Chadwick. New York: Oxford University Press,
  1991.
Basil of Caesarea. *Hexameron*. Italian translation in *Sulla Genesi (Omelie sull'Esa-
  merone)*. Ed. Mario Naldini. Milan: Mondadori, 1990.
Bede. *De temporibus*. *PL*. 90, cols. 277–92.
– *The Ecclesiastical History of the English Nation*. Trans. J. Stevens, rev. J.A. Giles.
  New York: Dutton, 1975.
– *Hexameron*. *PL*. 91, cols. 9–190.
Benvenuto da Imola. *Il Romuleo*. Italian translation in *Collezione di opere inedite o*

rare dei primi secoli della lingua. Giuseppe Guatteri. Bologna: Gaetano Roma-gnoli, 1867.

Bernardus Silvestris. *The Commentary on the First Six Books of the* Aeneid *of Virgil Commonly Attributed to Bernardus Silvestris.* A critical edition by Julian Ward Jones and Elizabeth Frances Jones. Lincoln: University of Nebraska Press, 1977.

– *The Cosmographia of Bernardus Silvestris.* Trans. with introduction and notes by Winthrop Wetherbee. New York: Columbia University Press, 1973.

Biblia sacra iuxta vulgatam versionem. 3rd ed. Ed. Robertus Weber, Bonifatius Fis-cher, et al. Stuttgart: Deutsche Bibelgesellschaft, 1983.

Boethius. *The Consolation of Philosophy.* Trans. H.F. Stewart, E.K. Rand, and S.J. Tester. Loeb Classical Library. Cambridge, MA: Harvard University Press, 1918.

Boiardo, Matteo Maria. *Orlando Innamorato: Amorum Libri di Matteo Maria Boiardo.* 2nd ed. Ed. Aldo Scaglione. Turin: UTET, 1963.

Brunetto Latini. *The Book of the Treasure (Li livres dou tresor).* Trans. Paul Barrette and Spurgeon Baldwin. New York: Garland, 1993.

– *Il Tesoretto (The Little Treasure).* Ed. and trans. Julia Bolton Holloway. New York: Garland, 1981.

Chrétien de Troyes. *Les Romans de Chrétien de Troyes II: Cligés.* Ed. Alexandre Micha. Paris: Champion, 1982.

Chronica de Origine Civitatis Florentie. Critical edition by Anna Maria Cesari [based, in part, on the version of this chronicle – *Antiquarum historiarum libellus* – in Boccaccio's Laurentian notebook (Laur. XXIX, 8)]. In *Atti e memorie dell'Acca-demia Toscana di Scienze e Lettere. La Colombaria,* vol. 58. Florence: Olschki, 1993.

Claudian. *De raptu Proserpinae.* Edited with introduction, translation, and com-mentary by Claire Gruzelier. New York: Oxford University Press, 1993.

Columella. *On Agriculture (De re rustica).* Ed. and trans. Harrison Boyd Ash. Loeb Classical Library. Cambridge, MA: Harvard University Press, 1941.

Crescenzi, Pietro de'. *Pietro Crescentio Bolognese tradotto nuovamente per Francesco Sansovino.* Sansovino's 1561 translation of the *Opus ruralium commodorum* (1304–1309). Facsimile edition. Perugia: Quattroemme editore: 1998.

– *Trattato della agricoltura.* Trans. and ed. 'Nferigno of La Crusca. Milan: Società Tipografica de' Classici Italiani, 1805.

Dante Alighieri. *Commedia.* Ed. Anna Maria Chiavacci Leonardi. Milan: Monda-dori, 1991–7.

– *Commedia. La Divina Commedia.* Ed. Natalino Sapegno. Florence: La Nuova Italia, 1955.

– *Convivio.* Ed. Cesare Vasoli and Domenico de Robertis. Milan: Riccardo Riccardi, 1995.

– *The Divine Comedy of Dante Alighieri.* Trans. Allen Mandelbaum. 3 vols. New York: Bantam Books, 1986.

– *Literary Criticism of Dante Alighieri.* Trans. and ed. Robert S. Haller. Lincoln: University of Nebraska Press, 1973.
– *Monarchia.* Ed. and trans. Prue Shaw. Cambridge: Cambridge University Press, 1995.
– *On World Government (De Monarchia).* Trans. Herbert W. Schneider. Indianapolis: Bobbs-Merrill, 1949.
– *Rime. Dante's Rime.* Trans. Patrick S. Diehl. Princeton: Princeton University Press, 1979.
Donatus. *Life of Virgil.* In *Interpretationes Vergilianae: Vitae Vergilianae.* Ed. Brummer, I. Stuttgart: Teubner, 1969.
– *Vitae Vergilianae antiquae.* Ed. G. Brugnoli and F. Stok. Rome: Typis Officinae Polygraphicae, 1997.
Eusebius-Jerome. *Chronicon. PL* 27, cols. 675–702.
Fazio degli Uberti. *Il dittamondo.* Milan: Giovanni Silvestri, 1826.
Fulgentius. *Fabii Planciadis Fulgentii V. C. Opera: Mitologiarum libri tres.* Stuttgart: Teubner, 1970. Trans. Leslie George Whitbread, *Fulgentius the Mythographer.* Columbus: Ohio State University Press, 1971.
Guido da Pisa. *Expositiones et glose super Comediam Dantis or Commentary on Dante's Inferno.* Ed. with notes and an introduction by Vincenzo Cioffari. Albany: State University of New York Press, 1974.
Guido delle Colonne. *Historia destructionis Troiae.* Trans. with an introduction and notes by Mary Elizabeth Meek. Bloomington: Indiana University Press, 1974.
Guillaume de Lorris and Jean de Meun. *Le Roman de la Rose.* Ed. Ernest Langlois. Paris: Société des anciens textes français, 1914–24.
– *The Romance of the Rose.* Trans. Charles Dahlberg. Hanover, NH: University Press of New England, 1983.
Hesiod. *Works and Days.* In *Hesiod Theogony, Works and Days: Theognis, Elegies.* Trans. with introductions by Dorothea Wender. New York: Penguin, 1973.
Horace. *Odes and Epodes.* Trans. C.E. Bennett. Loeb Classical Library. Cambridge, MA: Harvard University Press, 1968.
– *Satires, Epistles, Ars Poetica.* Trans. H.R. Fairclough. Loeb Classical Library. Cambridge, MA: Harvard University Press, 1932.
Hugh of St Victor. *De arca Noe moralii. PL.* 176, cols. 617–80.
– *De arca Noe mystica. PL.* 176, cols. 681–704.
– *The Didascalicon of Hugh of St Victor.* Trans. with an introduction and notes by Jerome Taylor. New York: Columbia University Press, 1961.
Isidore of Seville. *Chronicon. PL.* 83, cols. 1017–58.
– *Etymologiae. PL.* 82, cols. 73–443.
– *The Etymologies of Isidore of Seville.* Trans. Stephen A. Barney, W.J. Lewis, et al. New York: Cambridge University Press, 2006.

Jerome. *Commentarius in Ecclesiam. PL.* 23, col. 1023.

Josephus. *Jewish Antiquities.* Trans. H. St J. Thackeray, M.A. Loeb Classical Library. Cambridge, MA: Harvard University Press, 1978.

Justin. *Epitome of the Philippic History of Pompeius Trogus.* Trans. J.C. Yardley. Intro. and notes by R. Develin. Atlanta, GA: Scholars Press, 1994.

Lactantius (Lucius Caelius Firmianus Lactantius). *De phoenice.* In *Minor Latin Poets II.* Ed. and trans. J. Wight Duft. Loeb Classical Library. Cambridge, MA: Harvard University Press, 1968.

– *The Divine Institutes.* Trans. Sister Mary Francis McDonald, O.P. Washington, DC: Catholic University of America Press, 1964.

Lactantius Placidus. *In statii thebaida commentum.* Vol 1. Ed. R.D. Sweeney. Stuttgart: Teubner, 1997.

Livy. *Ab urbe condita libri. Livy: The Early History of Rome.* Trans. Aubrey de Sélincourt. New York: Penguin, 1981.

– *Livy I: Books I and II.* Trans. B.O. Foster. Loeb Classical Library. Cambridge, MA: Harvard University Press, 1988.

Lucan. *The Civil War* [*Pharsalia*]. Trans. J.D. Duff. Loeb Classical Library. Cambridge, MA: Harvard University Press, 1988.

Lucius Annaeus Florus. *Epitomae de Tito Livio.* Trans. Edward Seymour Forster. Loeb Classical Library. Cambridge, MA: Harvard University Press, 1984.

Macrobius. *Commentary on the Dream of Scipio.* With an introduction, translation, and commentary by William Harris Stahl. New York: Columbia University Press, 1952.

– *The Saturnalia.* Translated with an introduction and notes by Percival Vaughan Davies. New York: Columbia University Press, 1969.

Malispini, Ricordano. *Storia Fiorentina.* Rome: Multigrafica Editrice, 1976.

Martianus Capella. *Martianus Capella and the Seven Liberal Arts.* Vol. 2: *The Marriage of Philology and Mercury.* Trans. William Harris Stahl and Richard Johnson with E.L. Burge. New York: Columbia University Press, 1977.

Milton, John. *Paradise Lost and Regained.* Ed. Christopher Ricks. Intro. Suzanne Woods. New York: Signet, 2001.

Montaigne, Michel de. *Essais.* Ed. Albert Thibaudet. Paris. Gallimard, 1950.

Mythographi vaticani. Ed. Péter Kulcsár. *Corpus Christianorum.* Series Latina. XCIc. Turnholt: Brepols, 1987.

The Novellino or One Hundred Ancient Tales. Based on the 1525 Gualteruzzi editio princeps. Ed. and trans. Joseph P. Consoli. New York: Garland, 1997.

Orosius, Paulus. *The Seven Books of History against the Pagans.* Trans. Roy J. Deferrari. Washington, DC: Catholic University of America Press, 1964.

Ovid. *Ars amatoria; Amores; Remedia amoris.* Trans. Peter Green in *Ovid: The Erotic Poems.* New York: Penguin, 1982. [includes *Amores, Art of Love, Cures for Love,* and *On Facial Treatment for Ladies*]

- *The Art of Love and Other Poems.* Trans. J.H. Mozley. Loeb Classical Library. Cambridge, MA: Harvard University Press, 1985.
- *Ovid IV: Metamorphoses II.* Trans. Frank Justus Miller. 2nd ed. Revised by G.P. Gould. Loeb Classical Library. Cambridge, MA: Harvard University Press, 1984.
- *Metamorphoses.* Trans. Rolfe Humphries. Bloomington: Indiana University Press, 1955.
- *The Metamorphoses of Ovid.* Trans. Allen Mandelbaum. New York: Harcourt Brace, 1993.

Passavanti, Iacopo. *Lo specchio della vera penitenza.* Ed. F.L. Polidori. Florence: Le Monnier, 1863.

Patrologia Latina. Ed. J.-P. Migne. 221 vols. Paris: Garnier, 1841–1905.

Paul the Deacon. *Historia Langobardorum.* Latin with facing Italian trans. Ed. Lidia Capo. *Storia dei Longobardi.* Milan: Mondadori, 1993.
- *History of the Lombards.* Trans. William Dudley Foulke. Philadelphia: University of Pennsylvania Press, 2003.

Petrus Comestor. *Historia scholastica. PL.* 198, cols. 1053–1722.

Petrarch. *Epistolae de rebus familiaribus et variae.* Ed. J. Fracassetti. Florence: Le Monnier, 1863.
- *Letters on Family Matters* [*Rerum familiarium libri*]. Trans. Aldo S. Bernardo. Albany: State University of New York Press, 1975.
- *Letters of Old Age* [*Rerum senilium libri*]. Trans. Aldo S. Bernardo, Saul Levin, and Reta A. Bernardo. Baltimore: Johns Hopkins University Press, 1992.
- *Remedies for Fortune Fair and Foul.* A translation and commentary of *De remediis utriusque Fortune* by Conrad H. Rawski. Bloomington: Indiana University Press, 1991.

Philippe of Harveng. *De somnis Nabuchodonosor. PL.* 203, col. 585–92.

Plato. *Timaeus and Critias.* With a translation, introduction, and appendix on Atlantis by Desmond Lee. New York: Penguin, 1983.

Pliny. *Naturalis historia.* Various translators. Loeb Classical Library. Cambridge, MA: Harvard University Press, 1997.

Pompeius Trogus. *Historiae Philippicae.* See Justin.

Pomponius Mela. *De chorographia.* Trans. F.E. Romer. *Pomponius Mela's Description of the World.* Ann Arbor: University of Michigan Press, 1998.

Rabanus Maurus. *De universo. PL.* 111.

Richard of St Victor. *De eruditione hominis interioris libri tres, occasione accepta ex somnio Nabuchodonosor apud Danielem. PL.* 196, cols. 1229–1366.

Sacchetti, Franco. *Il trecentonovelle.* Ed. Valerio Marucci. Rome: Salerno, 1996.

Seneca. *Epistles.* Trans. Richard M. Gummere. Loeb Classical Library. Cambridge, MA: Harvard University Press, 1920.

– *Hercules, Trojan Women, Phoenician Women, Medea, Phaedra.* Ed. and trans. John G. Fitch. Loeb Classical Library. Cambridge, MA: Harvard University Press, 2002.

– *Naturales quaestiones.* Trans. T.H. Corcoran. Loeb Classical Library. Cambridge, MA: Harvard University Press, 1972.

Servius. *In Virgilii carmina commentari.* Ed. Georgius Thilo and Hermannus Hagen. Hildesheim: Georg Olms, 1961.

Solinus, Caius Julius. *The Excellent and Pleasant Worke. Collectanea rerum memorabilium.* Trans. Arthur Golding (1587). Facsimile reproduction with introduction by George Kish, Gainsville, FL: Scholars' Facsimiles and Reprints, 1955.

Uguccione da Pisa. *Derivationes.* Edizione critica princeps a cura di Enzo Cecchini et al. Florence: Edizioni del Galluzzo, 2004

Valerius Maximus. *Facta et dicta memorabilia.* Ed. John Briscoe. Stuttgart: Teubner, 1998.

– *Memorable Doings and Sayings.* Ed. and trans. D.R. Shackleton Bailey. Loeb Classical Library. Cambridge, MA: Harvard University Press, 2000.

Villani, Filippo. *De origine civitatis Florentie et de eiusdem famosis civibus.* Ed. Giuliano Tanturli. Padua: Antenore, 1997.

– *Le vite d'uomini illustrati fiorentini scritte da Filippo Villani.* Ed. Giammaria Mazzuchelli. Florence: Sansoni Coen, 1847.

Villani, Giovanni. *Cronica di Giovanni Villani.* Florence: Il Magheri, 1823.

Villani, Matteo. *Cronica (con la continuazione di Filippo Villani).* Critical edition, ed. Giuseppe Porta. Fondazione Pietro Bembo. Parma: Ugo Guanda, 1995.

Vincent of Beauvais. *Speculum quadruplex, sive Speculum maius: naturale, doctrinale, morale, historiale.* Douai, 1624. 4 vols. Reprint, Graz, Austria: Akademische Druck-u. Verlagsanstalt, 1964–5.

Virgil. *Aeneid.* Trans. Robert Fitzgerald. New York: Vintage, 1983.

– *Aeneid 7–12, The Minor Poems.* Trans. H.R. Fairclough. Loeb Classical Library. Cambridge, MA: Harvard University Press, 1986.

– *Eclogues, Georgics, Aeneid, 1–6.* Trans. H.R. Fairclough. Loeb Classical Library. Cambridge, MA: Harvard University Press, 1986.

Vitruvius. *De architectura.* Trans. Frank Granger. Loeb Classical Library. Cambridge: Harvard University Press, 1985.

William of Conches. *Dragmaticon Philosophiae. Corpus Christianorum.* Continuatio Medievalis, CLII, 1997.

Secondary Sources

Allen, Don Cameron. *Mysteriously Meant: The Rediscovery of Pagan Symbolism and Allegorical Interpretation in the Renaissance.* Baltimore: Johns Hopkins Press, 1970.

Anderson, David. 'Boccaccio's Glosses on Statius.' *Studi sul Boccaccio* 22 (1994): 3–128.

Auerbach, Erich. 'Frate Alberto.' In *Mimesis: The Representation of Reality in Western Literature*. Trans. William R. Trask. Princeton University Press, 1953. 203–31.

Baratto, Mario. *Realtà e stile nel* 'Decameron.' Rome: Riuniti, 1984.

Barberi Squarotti, Giorgio. 'La "cornice" del "Decameron" o il mito di Robinson.' In *Il potere della parola*. Naples: Federico & Ardia, 1983. 5–63.

Barbi, M., and F. Maggini, *Rime della 'Vita nuova' della giovinezza*. Florence: Le Monnier, 1956.

Barolini, Teodolinda. *Dante's Poets: Textuality and Truth in the* Comedy. Princeton: Princeton University Press, 1984.

– '"Le parole son femmine e i fatti sono maschi": Toward a Sexual Poetics of the *Decameron* (*Decameron* II 10).' *Studi sul Boccaccio* 21 (1993): 175–97.

– *The Undivine Comedy: Detheologizing Dante*. Princeton: Princeton University Press, 1992.

– 'The Wheel of the *Decameron*.' *Romance Philology* 36, 4 (1983): 521–39.

Barsella, Susanna. 'The Myth of Prometheus in Giovanni Boccaccio's *Decameron*.' *Modern Language Notes* 119, 1 (Jan. 2004): S120–S141.

Batard, Yvonne. 'Le cosmopolitanism du *Décaméron*.' In *Proceedings of the IV Congress of the International Comparative Literature Association*. The Hague: Mouton, 1966. 114–18.

Battaglia, Salvatore. *Giovanni Boccaccio e la riforma della narrativa*. Naples: Liguori, 1969.

Battaglia Ricci, Lucia. *Boccaccio*. Rome: Salerno, 2000.

– *Ragionare nel giardino*. 2nd ed. Rome: Salerno, 2000.

Bec, Christian. 'Sur le message du Décaméron.' *Revue de études italiennes*, 21 (1975): 284–303.

Bergin, Thomas G. *Boccaccio*. New York: Viking, 1981.

Bevilacqua, Mirko. 'L'amore come sublimazione e degradazione: il denudamento della donna angelicata nel *Decameron*.' *Rassegna della letteratura italiana* 79 (1975): 415–32. Reprinted in *L'ideologia letteraria del Decameron*. Rome: Bulzoni, 1978. 37–62.

– 'Il giardino come struttura ideologico-formale del *Decameron*.' *Rassegna della letteratura italiana* 80 (1976): 70–9. Reprinted in *L'ideologia letteraria del* Decameron. Rome: Bulzoni, 1978. 65–78.

Bignone, E. 'Per la fortuna di Lucrezio e dell'epicureismo nel medioevo.' *Rivista di filologia e di istruzione classica* 41 (1913).

Billanovich, G. 'Il Boccaccio, il Petrarca e le più antiche traduzioni in Italiano delle Decadi di Tito Livio.' *Giornale storico della letteratura Italiana* 130 (1953): 311–37.

– *Petrarca e il primo umanesimo.* Padua: Antenore, 1996.
– 'Petrarch and the Textual Tradition of Livy.' *Journal of the Warburg and Courtauld Institutes* 14 (1951): 137–208.
– *Restauri Boccacceschi.* Rome: Istituto Grafico Tiberino, 1947.
– *La tradizione del testo di Livio e le origini dell'umanesimo.* Padua: Antenore, 1981.
Bloomfield, Morton W. 'The Source of Boccaccio's *Filostrato* III, 74–79 and Its Bearing on the MS Tradition of Lucretius, *De rerum natura.' Classical Philology* 47 (1952): 162–65.
Boas, George. *Primitivism and Related Ideas in the Middle Ages.* Baltimore: Johns Hopkins University Press, 1997.
Boitani, Piero. 'Chaucer and Lists of Trees.' *Reading Medieval Studies* 2 (1976): 28–44.
Branca, Vittore. *Boccaccio: The Man and His Works.* Trans. Richard Monges, co-trans. and ed. Dennis J. McAuliffe. New York : New York University Press, 1976.
– 'Boccaccio e le tradizioni letterarie.' *Il Boccaccio nelle culture e letterature nazionali.* Florence: Olschki, 1978, 473–96.
– *Boccaccio medievale e nuovi studi sul Decameron.* Florence: Sansoni, 1986.
– 'Boccaccio rinnovatore.' *Il Veltro* 20 (1976): 263–81.
– *Giovanni Boccaccio: Profilo biografico.* Nuova edizione riveduta e aggiornata. Milan: Sansoni, 1997.
– *Linee di una storia critica al* Decameron *con bibliografia boccaccesca completamente aggiornata.* Milan: Società anonima editrice Dante Alighieri, 1939.
– 'Il mito e il concetto dell'eroe nel Boccaccio.' In *Essays in Honour of John Humphreys Whitfield Presented to Him on His Retirement from the Serena Chair of Italian at the University of Birmingham.* London: St George's, 1975.
– 'Non sconfessato il "Decameron."' *La fiera letteraria* 40, 49 (1965): 70.
Branca, Vittore, and Chiara Degani. 'Studi sugli "exempla" e il "Decameron."' *Studi sul Boccaccio* 14 (1983–4): 178–89.
Brown, Marshall. 'In the Valley of the Ladies.' *Italian Quarterly* 18 (1975): 33–52.
Brugnoli, G., and Stok, F. *Vitae Virgilianae antiquae.* Rome: Typis Officinae Polygraphicae, 1997.
Bruni, Francesco. *Boccaccio: L'invenzione della letteratura mezzana.* Bologna: Il Mulino. 1990.
– 'Il *Filocolo* e lo spazio della letteratura volgare.' In *Boccaccio e dintorni.* Florence: Olschki, 1983. 1–22.
Bullough, Vern L., and James A. Brundage, eds. *Handbook of Medieval Sexuality.* New York: Garland, 1996.
Cachey, Theodore J. 'Petrarch, Boccaccio and the New-World Encounter.' *Stanford Italian Review* 10 (1991): 45–59.

Calkin, Robert G. 'Piero de' Crescenzi and the Medieval Garden.' In *Medieval Gardens*, ed. Elisabeth B. Macdougall. Dumbarton Oaks Colloquium on the History of Landscape Architecture IX. Washington, DC: Dumbarton Oaks Research Library and Collection, 1983. 157–73.

Carrara, Enrico. 'Un peccato del Boccaccio.' *Giornale storico della letteratura italiana* 36 (1900): 123ff.

Casella, Maria Teresa. *Tra Boccaccio e Petrarca: I volgarizzamenti di Tito Livio e di Valerio Massimo*. Padua: Antenore, 1982.

Cassell, Anthony K. *Dante's Fearful Art of Justice*. Toronto: University of Toronto Press, 1984.

Cazalé Bérard, Claude. 'Riscrittura della poetica della riscrittura negli Zibaldoni di Boccaccio.' In *Gli Zibaldoni di Boccaccio: Memoria, scrittura, riscrittura*. Atti del seminario internazionale di Firenze – Certaldo, ed. M. Picone and C. Cazalé Bérard. Florence: Franco Cesati, 1998.

Celli Olivagnoli, Franca. 'Spazialità nel *Decameron*.' *Stanford Italian Review* 3, 1 (1983): 91–106.

Cerisola, Pier Luigi. 'La questione della cornice del *Decameron*.' *Aevum* 49, 1–2 (1975): 137–56.

Cochrane, Eric. *Historians and Historiography in the Italian Renaissance*. Chicago: University of Chicago Press, 1981.

Comparetti, Domenico. *Virgilio nel medioevo*. Ed. Giorgio Pasquali. Florence: La Nuova Italia, 1937.

Consoli, Joseph P. *Giovanni Boccaccio: An Annotated Bibliography*. New York: Garland, 1992.

Cook, Albert. 'Boccaccio and Seneca.' *American Journal of Philology* 28 (1908): 200–4.

Corrigan, Beatrice, ed. *Italian Poets and English Critics, 1755–1859*. Chicago: University of Chicago Press, 1969.

Costa, Gustavo. *La leggenda dei secoli d'oro nella letteratura italiana*. Bari: Laterza, 1972.

Costantini, Aldo Maria. 'Studi sullo Zibaldone Magliabechiano.' *Studi sul Boccaccio* 7 (1973): 21–58.

– 'Studi sullo zibaldone Magliabechiano, II: Il florilegio senechiano.' *Studi sul Boccaccio* 8 (1975): 79–126.

Cottino-Jones, Marga. 'Boccaccio e la scienza.' In *Atti del IX congresso dell'associazione internazionale per gli studi di lingua e letteratura italiana*. Palermo: Manfredi, 1978. 356–70.

– *Order from Chaos: Social and Aesthetic Harmonies in Boccaccio's Decameron*. Washington, DC: University Press of America, 1982.

– 'Saggio di lettura della prima giornata del *Decameron*.' *Teoria.e critica* 1 (1972): 111–38.

Cottino-Jones, Marga, and Edward F. Tuttle, eds. *Boccaccio: Secoli di vita. Atti del Congresso Internazionale Boccaccio*. Ravenna: Longo, 1977.

Coulter, Cornelia C. 'The Genealogy of the Gods.' *Vassar Medieval Studies*, ed. Christabel Forsyth Fiske. New Haven, CT: Yale University Press, 1923. 315–41.

– 'The Manuscripts of Tacitus and Livy in the Parva Libreria.' *Italia medioevale e umanistica* 3 (1940): 281–86.

– 'Statius, Sylvae, V, 4 and Fiammetta's Prayer to Sleep.' *American Journal of Philology* 80 (1959): 390–5.

Crescini, Vincenzo. *Contributo agli studi sul Boccaccio con documenti inediti*. Turin: Ermanno Loescher, 1887.

Curtius, Ernst Robert. *European Literature and the Latin Middle Ages*. 1948. Trans. Willard R. Trask. New York: Bollingen, 1953.

Da Rif, Bianca Maria. 'La Miscellanea Laurenziana XXXIII, 31.' *Studi sul Boccaccio* 7 (1973): 59–124.

David, Michel. 'Boccaccio pornoscopo?' In *Medioevo e rinascimento veneto con altri studi in onore di Lino Lazzarini*. Vol. 1, ed. R. Avesani, G. Billanovich, and G. Pozzi. Padua: Antenore, 1979. 215–43.

Davis, Charles T. 'Topographical and Historical Propaganda in Early Florentine Chronicles and in Villani.' *Medioevo e Rinascimento* 2 (1988): 33–51.

De Michelis, Cesare. *Contraddizioni nel* Decameron. Milan: Guanda, 1983.

De Sanctis, Francesco. 'Il Decameron' (chap. 9). In *Storia della letteratura italiana*, ed. Niccolò Gallo, intro. by Natalino Sapegno. Turin: Einaudi, 1962.

Delcorno Branca, Daniela. *Boccaccio e le storie di re Artù*. Bologna: Il Mulino, 1991.

– '"Cognominato prencipe Galeotto," I sottotitolo illustrato del Paragino It. 482.' *Studi sul Boccaccio* 23 (1995): 79–88.

Delcorno, Carlo. 'Dante e l'"exemplum" medievale.' *Lettere Italiane* 35, 1 (Jan.–Mar. 1983): 3–28.

– 'Studi sugli "exempla" e il *Decameron*. II. Modelli esemplari in tre novelle (I 1, III 8, II 2).' *Studi sul Boccaccio* 15 (1985–6): 189–214.

Di Benedetto, Filippo. 'Leonzio, Omero e le "Pandette."' *Italia medioevale e umanistica* 12 (1969): 53–112.

Edmunds, Lowell. 'A Note on Boccaccio's Sources for the Story of Oedipus in *De casibus illustrium virorum* and in the *Genealogia*.' *Aevum* 56 (1982): 148–52.

Ferrante, Joan M. 'The Frame Characters of the *Decameron*: A Progression of Virtues,' *Romance Philology* 19 (1965): 212–26.

– 'Narrative Patterns in the *Decameron*.' *Romance Philology* 31 (1978): 585–604.

– *The Political Vision of the Divine Comedy.* Princeton: Princeton University Press, 1984.

Fido, Franco. *Il regime delle simmetrie imperfette.* Milan: Franco Angeli, 1988.

Filosa, Elsa. 'Il "mondo alla rovescia" nella "Valle delle donne": Eros muliebre e trasgressione sociale nel *Decameron.*' *Fusta: Journal of Italian Literature and Culture* 13 (fall 2004–spring 2005): 9–18.

Flasch, Kurt. *Giovanni Boccaccio, Poesie nach der Pest. Der Anfang des "Decameron."* Italian translation, *Poesia dopo la peste: Saggio su Boccaccio.* Trans. Rosa Taliani. Bari: Laterza, 1995.

Forni, Pier Massimo. *Adventures in Speech: Rhetoric and Narration in Boccaccio's* Decameron. Philadelphia: University of Pennsylvania Press, 1996.

Foscolo, Ugo. *Discorso storico sul testo del Decamerone.* 1825. Lugano: G. Ruggia e C., 1828.

Foster, Kenelm. *The Two Dantes and Other Studies.* Berkeley: University of California Press, 1977.

Foster, Kenelm, and Patrick Boyde. *Dante's Lyric Poetry.* Oxford: Oxford University Press, 1967.

Gasparini, Leone. *Echi e reminiscenze di vita e storia napoletana nel* Decamerone. Naples: Deperro, 1975.

Gasparotto, Giovanni. 'Lucrezio fonte diretta del Boccaccio?' *Memorie dell'Accademia Patavina di Scienze, Lettere, Arti.* Classe Scienze Morali 81 (1969): 5–34.

Getto, Giovanni. 'La peste del *Decameron* e il problema della fonte lucreziana.' *Giornale storico della letteratura italiana* 135 (1958): 507–23.

– *Vita di forme e forme di vita nel* Decameron. Turin: G.B. Petrini, 1972.

Giamatti, A. Bartlett. *The Earthly Paradise and the Renaissance Epic.* Princeton: Princeton University Press, 1966.

– 'Hippolytus among the Exiles: The Romance of Early Humanism.' In *Poetic Traditions of the English Renaissance.* New Haven: Yale University Press, 1982.

Gibaldi, Joseph. 'The *Decameron* Cornice and the Responses to the Disintegration of Civilization.' *Kentucky Romance Quarterly* 24 (1977): 349–57.

Gilbert, Creighton E. *Poets Seeing Artists' Work: Instances in the Italian Renaissance.* Florence: Olschki, 1991.

Gittes, Tobias Foster. '"O vendetta di Dio": The Motif of Rape and Retaliation in Dante's *Inferno.*' *Modern Language Notes* 120, 1, (Jan. 2005): 1–29.

Grabher, Carlo. 'Particolari influssi di Andrea Capellano sul Boccaccio.' *Annali della facoltà di lettere e filosofia dell'università di Perugia* 5 (1967–8): 309–32.

Graf, Arturo. *Miti, leggende e superstizioni del medio evo.* Rome: Plurima, 1989.

Gravdal, Kathryn. *Ravishing Maidens: Writing Rape in Medieval French Literature and Law.* Philadelphia: University of Pennsylvania Press, 1991.

Greene, Thomas M. 'Forms of Accommodation in the *Decameron*.' *Italica* 45 (1968): 297–313.

Grieve, Patricia. *Floire and Blancheflor and the European Romance*. Cambridge Studies in Medieval Literature 32. New York: Cambridge University Press, 1997.

Griffin, Robert. 'Boccaccio's Fiammetta: Pictures at an Exhibition.' *Italian Quarterly* 72 (1975): 75–94.

Hambuechen Potter, Joy. *Five Frames for the Decameron: Communication and Social Systems in the Cornice*. Princeton: Princeton University Press, 1982.

Hardin, Richard F. 'Milton's Nimrod.' *Milton Quarterly* 22 (1988): 38–44.

Hartwig, Otto. *Quellen und Forschungen zur ältesten Geschichte der Stadt Florenz*. Marburg: N.G. Elwert, 1875–80.

Hauvette, Henri. *Boccace: Étude biographique et littéraire*. Paris: Armand Colin, 1914.

Hemmerdinger, Bertrand. 'Le Boccaccianus perdu du Lucrèce.' *Belfagor* 23 (1968): 741.

Higginbotham, James. *Piscinae: Artificial Fishponds in Roman Italy*. Chapel Hill: University of North Carolina Press, 1997.

Hollander, Robert. *Boccaccio's Two Venuses*. New York: Columbia University Press, 1977.

– 'The Proem of the *Decameron*: Boccaccio between Ovid and Dante.' In *Miscellanea di studi danteschi in memoria di Silvio Pasquazi*. Naples: Federico & Ardia, 1993.

– '"Utilità" in Boccaccio's "Decameron."' *Studi sul Boccaccio* 15 (1985–6): 215–31.

Hollander, Robert, and Courtney Cahill. 'Day Ten of the *Decameron*: The Myth of Order.' *Studi sul Boccaccio* 23 (1995): 113–70.

Hortis, Attilio. *Accenni alle scienze naturali nelle opere di Giovanni Boccaccio*. Trieste: Tipografia del Lloyd Austro-Ungarico, 1877.

– *Cenni di Giovanni Boccaccio intorno a Tito Livio*. Trieste: Tipografia del Lloyd Austro-Ungarico, 1877.

– *Studi sulle opere latine del Boccaccio*. Trieste: Julius Dase, 1879; facsimile reprint, Rome: Adelmo Polla, Editore, 1988.

Hyde, J.K. 'Real and Imaginary Journeys in the Late Middle Ages.' *Bulletin of the John Rylands Library* 65 (1982–3): 125–47.

Hyde, Thomas. 'Boccaccio: The Genealogies of Myth.' *PMLA* 100, nos. 4–6 (1985): 737–45.

Jacquart, Danielle, and Claude Thomasset. *Sexuality and Medicine in the Middle Ages*. Princeton: Princeton University Press, 1988.

Janson, H.W. *Apes and Ape Lore in the Middle Ages and the Renaissance*. London: Warburg Institute, University of London, 1952.

Kallendorf, Craig. 'From Virgil to Vida: The Poeta Theologus in Italian Renaissance Commentary.' *Journal of the History of Ideas* 56 (1995): 41–62.

Katzenellenbogen, Adolf. *Allegories of the Virtues and Vices in Medieval Art from Early Christian Times to the Thirteenth Century.* Trans. Alan J.P. Crick. 1939. Reprinted Toronto: University of Toronto Press, 1989.

Kern, Edith. 'The Gardens of the *Decameron* Cornice.' *PMLA* 66 (1951): 505–23.

Kircher, Timothy. *The Poet's Wisdom: The Humanists, the Church, and the Formation of Philosophy in the Early Renaissance.* Leiden: Brill, 2006.

Kirkham, Victoria. *The Sign of Reason in Boccaccio's Fiction.* Florence: Olschki, 1993.

Kleinhenz, Christopher. 'Texts, Naked and Thinly Veiled: Erotic Elements in Medieval Italian Literature.' In *Sex in the Middle Ages: A Book of Essays*, ed. Joyce Salisbury. New York: Garland, 1991.

Kugel, James L. *The Bible As It Was.* Cambridge, MA: Harvard University Press, 1997.

Kuhn, Albert J. 'Shelley's Demogorgon and Eternal Necessity.' *Modern Language Notes* 74, 7 (Nov. 1959): 596–9.

Lansing, Richard, ed. *The Dante Encyclopedia.* New York: Garland, 2000.

Lanzoni, F. 'Il sogno presago della madre incinta nella letteratura medievale e antica.' *Analecta Bollandiana* 45 (1927): 225–61.

Levenstein, Jessica. 'Out of Bounds: Passion and the Plague in Boccaccio's *Decameron*.' *Italica* 73, 3 (autumn 1996): 313–35.

Levin, Harry. *The Myth of the Golden Age in the Renaissance.* Bloomington: Indiana University Press, 1969.

Lewis, C.S. *The Allegory of Love: A Study in Medieval Tradition.* London: Oxford University Press, 1936.

– *The Discarded Image: An Introduction to Medieval and Renaissance Literature.* Cambridge: Cambridge University Press, 1964.

Lippi, Emilio. 'Per l'edizione critica del volgarizzamento liviano.' *Studi sul Boccaccio* 11 (1980): 125–98.

– 'Una redazione particolare del volgarizzamento liviano.' *Studi sul Boccaccio* 10 (1978): 27–40.

Lovejoy, Arthur, and George Boas. *Primitivism and Related Ideas in Antiquity.* New York: Octagon, 1965.

Marchesi, Simone. *Stratigrafie decameroniane.* Florence: Olschki, 2004.

Marcus, Millicent. *An Allegory of Form: Literary Self-consciousness in the Decameron.* Saratoga, CA: Anma Libri, 1979.

– 'Faith's Fiction: A Gloss on the Tale of Melchisedech (*Dec.* I, 3).' *Canadian Journal of Italian Studies* 2 (1978–9): 40–55.

– 'The Sweet New Style Reconsidered: A Gloss on the Tale of Cimone (*Dec.* V, 1).' *Italian Quarterly* 81 (1980): 5–16.

Marino, Lucia. 'Prometheus, or the Mythographer's Self-Image.' *Studi sul Boccaccio* 12 (1980): 263–73.

Massaglia, Marina. 'Il giardino di Pomena.' *Studi sul Boccaccio* 15 (1985–6): 235–52.

Mazza, Antonia. 'L'inventario della "Parva Libreria" di Santo Spirito e la biblioteca del Boccaccio.' *Italia medioevale e umanistica* 9 (1966): 1–74.

Mazzacurati, Giancarlo. 'La regina e il buffone.' In *L'esperienza del tempo nel* Decameron. Turin: Terrenio, 1987. 7–12.

Mazzoni, Francesco. 'In una presunta fonte del Boccaccio.' *Studi danteschi* 29 (1950): 192–6.

Mazzotta, Giuseppe. *Dante, Poet of the Desert: History and Allegory in the* Divine Comedy. Princeton: Princeton University Press, 1979.

– *The World at Play in Boccaccio's* Decameron. Princeton: Princeton University Press, 1986.

McGregor, James H. *The Shades of Aeneas: The Imitation of Virgil and the History of Paganism in Boccaccio's* Filostrato, Filocolo, *and* Teseida. Athens: University of Georgia Press, 1991.

Migiel, Marilyn. *A Rhetoric of the Decameron.* Toronto: University of Toronto Press, 2003.

Morgan, Alison. *Dante and the Medieval Other World.* Cambridge: Cambridge University Press, 1990.

Nardi, Bruno. 'Intorno al sito del "Purgatorio" e al mito dantesco dell'Eden.' *Il giornale dantesco* 25, 4 (Oct.-Dec. 1922): 289–300.

Olobardi, Umberto. 'Lettura di una novella del Boccaccio.' *Leonardo* 21 (1943): 95–103.

Olson, Glending. *Literature as Recreation in the Middle Ages.* Ithaca, NY: Cornell University Press, 1982.

Osgood, Charles Grosvenor. 'Boccaccio's Knowledge of the *Life of Virgil.*' *Classical Philology* 25 (1930): 27–36.

– *Boccaccio on Poetry.* New York: Bobbs-Merrill, 1930.

Padoan, Giorgio. *Il Boccaccio, le muse, il Parnaso e l'Arno.* Florence: Olschki, 1978.

– 'Sulla genesi del *Decameron.*' In *Boccaccio: Secoli di vita. Atti del Congresso Internazionale Boccaccio,* ed. M.Cottino-Jones and Edward F. Tuttle. Ravenna: Longo, 1977. 144–8.

Panofsky, Erwin. *Meaning in the Visual Arts.* Chicago: University of Chicago Press, 1982.

– *Studies in Iconology: Humanistic Themes in the Art of the Renaissance.* 1939. Reprint, New York: Harper and Row, 1962.

Pastore Stocchi, Manlio. 'Altre annotazioni.7. Le galle di cane ("*Decameron*" VIII 6).' *Studi sul Boccaccio* 7 (1973): 200–8.

- 'Dioneo e l'orazione di Frate Cipolla.' *Studi sul Boccaccio* 10 (1977–8): 201–
  15.
- 'Il primo Omero del Boccaccio.' *Studi sul Boccaccio* 5 (1968): 99–122.

Pertusi, Agostino. *Leonzio Pilato fra Petrarca e Boccaccio.* Venice and Rome: Istituto
  per la collaborazione culturale, 1964.

- 'Venezia, la cultura greca e il Boccaccio.' *Studi sul Boccaccio* 10 (1977–8): 217–
  34.

Picone, Michelangelo. 'Il rendez-vous sotto il pino (*Dec.* VII, 7).' *Studi e problemi di
  critica testuale* 22 (1981): 71–85.

Pierrugues, P. *Glossarium eroticum linguae latinae.* Paris: Aug.-Fr. et Pr. Dondey-
  Dupré, Bibliopolas, 1826.

Piguet, Nicole. 'Variations autour d'un mythe ovidien dans l'oeuvre de Boccace.'
  Revue des études italiennes 31, 1–4 (1985): 25–35.

Poole, Gordon. 'Boccaccio's *Comedia delle ninfe fiorentine.*' *Annali dell'istituto uni-
  versitario orientale* 25, 2 (1983): 499–518.

Psaki, Regina. 'Boccaccio and Female Sexuality: Gendered and Eroticized Landscapes.' In *The Flight of Ulysses: Studies in Memory of Emmanuel Hatzantonis*, ed.
  Augustus A. Mastri. Chapel Hill, NC: Annali d'Italianistica, 1997.

Quaglio, Antonio Enzo. *Scienza e mito nel Boccaccio.* Padua: Liviana, 1967.

Rajna, Pio. 'L'Episodio delle questioni d'amore.' *Romania* 31 (1902): 28–81.

Rastelli, Dario. 'Il disinteresse narrativo nel *Decameron.*' *Siculorum gymnasium* 10
  (1957): 167–85.

Repetti, Emanuele. *Dizionario geografico, fiscio, storico della Toscana.* Florence:
  Presso l'autore e editore, 1833–46.

Reynolds, L.D., ed. *Texts and Transmission: A Survey of the Latin Classics.* Oxford:
  Clarendon Press, 1983.

Reynolds, L.D., and N.G. Wilson. *Scribes and Scholars: A Guide to the Transmission of
  Greek and Latin Literature.* 3rd ed. Oxford: Oxford University Press, 1991.

Ricci, Pier Giorgio. *Studi sulla vita e le opere del Boccaccio.* Milan: Riccardo Ricciardi,
  1985.

- 'Studi sulle opere latine e volgari del Boccaccio.' In *Rinascimento*, 2nd ser., 2.
  Florence: Sansoni, 1962.

Rossi, Aldo. 'Dante nella prospettiva del Boccaccio.' *Studi danteschi* 37 (1960):
  63–140.

Rossi, Luciano. 'Presenze ovidiane nel *Decameron.*' *Studi sul Boccaccio* 21 (1993):
  125–37.

Rykwert, Joseph. *On Adam's House in Paradise.* New York: Museum of Modern Art,
  1972.

Sabatini, Francesco. *Napoli angioina cultura e società.* Tirreni: Edizioni scientifiche
  italiane, 1975.

Sasso, Luigi. 'L'"interpretatio nominis" in Boccaccio.' *Studi sul Boccaccio* 12 (1980): 129–74.

Scaglione, Aldo D. *Nature and Love in the Late Middle Ages.* Westport, CT: Greenwood, 1976.

Serafini, Mario. 'Le tragedie di Seneca nella *Fiammetta* di Giovanni Boccaccio.' *Giornale storico della letteratura italiana* 126 (1949): 95–105.

Seznec, Jean. *The Survival of the Pagan Gods: The Mythological Tradition and Its Place in Renaissance Humanism and Art.* Princeton: Princeton University Press, 1972.

Simonelli, M.P. 'Prima diffusione e tradizione manoscritta del *Decameron.*' In *Boccaccio: Secoli di vita: Atti del Congresso Internazionale Boccaccio*, ed. M. Cottino-Jones and Edward F. Tuttle, 136–40. Ravenna: Longo, 1977.

Singleton, Charles S. 'On Meaning in the *Decameron.*' *Italica* 21, 3 (Sep. 1944): 117–24.

Smarr, Janet Levarie. *Boccaccio and Fiammetta: The Narrator as Lover.* Urbana: University of Illinois Press, 1986.

– 'Ovid and Boccaccio: A Note on Self-Defense.' *Medievalia* 13 (1987): 247–53.

Stierle, Karlheinz. 'Three Moments in the Crisis of Exemplarity: Boccaccio, Petrarch, Montaigne, and Cervantes.' *Journal of the History of Ideas* 59, 4 (Oct. 1998): 581–95.

Stillinger, Thomas. 'The Language of Gardens: Boccaccio's *Valle delle donne.*' *Traditio* 39 (1983): 310–21.

Stych, F.S. *Boccaccio in English: A Bibliography of Editions, Adaptations, and Criticism.* Westport, CT: Greenwood Press, 1995.

Swift, Louis J. 'Lactantius and the Golden Age.' *American Journal of Philology* 89, 2 (Apr. 1968): 129–56.

Tanzer, Helen H. *The Villas of Pliny the Younger.* New York: Columbia University Press, 1924.

Thomasset, Claude. 'De la nature féminine.' In *Histoire des femmes.* Vol. 2. *Le moyen âge*, ed. George Duby and Michèle Perrot. Paris: Plon, 1991.

Torraca, Francesco. *Per la biografia di Giovanni Boccaccio.* Milan: Società Editrice Dante Alighieri di Albrighi, Segati e C., 1912.

Usher, Jonathan. 'Apicius, Seneca, and Surfeit: Boccaccio's Sonnet 95.' *Modern Langage Notes* 118 (2003): 46–59.

– 'Frame and Novella Gardens in the *Decameron.*' *Medium Aevum* 58 (1989): 274–85.

– 'Global Warming in the Sonnet: The Phaethon Myth in Boccaccio and Petrarch.' *Studi sul Boccaccio* 28 (2000): 125–83.

– 'A Quotation from the *Culex* in Boccaccio's *De casibus.*' *Modern Language Review* 97, 2 (Apr. 2002): 312–23.

Van Acker, L. 'L'oeuvre Latin de Boccacce et Nicholas Trevet.' *L'antiquité classique* 33 (1964): 414–18.

Velli, Giuseppe. 'L'apoteosi di Arcita: Ideologia e coscienza storica nel *Teseida*.' *Studi e problemi di critica testuale* 5 (1972): 33–66. Reprinted in *Petrarca e Boccaccio: tradizione, memoria, scrittura*. Padua: Antenore, 1979. 122–55.

Watkins, Renee Neu. 'Petrarch and the Black Death: From Fear to Monuments.' *Studies in the Renaissance* 19 (1972): 196–223.

Weiss, Roberto. 'Notes on the Popularity of the Writings of N. Trevet.' *Dominican Studies* 1 (1948): 261–5.

– *The Renaissance Discovery of Classical Antiquity.* New York: Humanities Press, 1969.

Wilkins, Ernest Hatch. 'Calmeta.' *Modern Language Notes* 21, 7 (1906): 212–16.

– *The Trees of the* Genealogia deorum *of Boccaccio.* Chicago: Caxton Club, 1923.

Wilson, N.G. *From Byzantium to Italy: Greek Studies in the Italian Renaissance.* Baltimore: Johns Hopkins University Press, 1992.

Witt, Ronald G. 'Coluccio Salutati and the Conception of the *Poeta Theologus* in the Fourteenth Century.' *Renaissance Quarterly* 30, 4 (winter 1997): 538–63.

Wright, Herbert G. *Boccaccio in England from Chaucer to Tennyson.* Bristol: Athlon Press, 1957.

Zago, Esther. 'Women, Medicine, and the Law in Boccaccio's *Decameron*.' In *Women Healers and Physicians: Climbing a Long Hill*, ed. Lilian R. Furst. Lexington: University Press of Kentucky, 1997.

Index